# Genius:
## In Their Own Words

# Genius:
# In Their Own Words

## The Intellectual Journeys
## of Seven Great
## 20th-Century Thinkers

EDITED AND WITH AN INTRODUCTION BY
David Ramsay Steele

FOREWORD BY
Arthur C. Danto

OPEN COURT
Chicago and La Salle, Illinois

To order books from Open Court, call toll free 1-800-815-2280.

Library of Congress Cataloging-in-Publication Data

Genius—in their own words : the intellectual journeys of seven great 20th-century thinkers / edited and with an introduction by David Ramsay Steele; foreword by Arthur C. Danto.
       p.   cm.
    Includes bibliographical references and index.
    ISBN 0-8126-9504-6 (pbk. : alk. paper)
    1. Philosophers—Biography.   I. Steele, David Ramsay.

  B104.G46 2002
  190'.9'04—dc21                                                          2002066332

# Contents

# Foreword

## Philosophical Autobiography

In one of the innumerable digressions that make up the texture of Arthur Schopenhauer's masterpiece, *The World as Will and Idea,* he addresses the topic of geniuses almost *en passant.* "These appear singly and sparingly in the course of centuries," he writes, appealing to an image from Virgil that one can never again encounter without being reminded of the metaphoric use that Schopenhauer made of it: "Singly they appear, swimming by in the vast waste of the waves."

In Virgil's poem, this passage occurs as part of a famous set piece—a disaster at sea, where a vindictive goddess seeks to thwart an expedition of Trojans who have set out to establish a new homeland in Italy. It is a scene of terror and destruction, where masts break and ropes snap, and men are blown overboard to drown in the tempest-tost sea.

But Schopenhauer changes the optics of the scene, almost as if it were seen from a great distance, and turns it into a poetic representation of solitary figures tracing a path in the vast unknown. It is difficult not to believe that he has himself as a thinker in mind, alone and struggling—one of the sparse company of original philosophical minds, like Plato and Kant, who appear "singly and sparingly" down the ages. In Schopenhauer's century, for example, there were in all perhaps half a dozen such solitary swimmers, mostly German, as it happens: Fichte, Schelling, Hegel, and Nietzsche. In the previous century there was Kant, of course, as well as Berkeley and Hume, everyone else being relatively minor. But in no century have there been very many, and in most centuries none at all.

The lives of the philosophers has been a subject of natural curiosity, beginning in ancient times, and we have a magnificent example of a paradigmatic philosophical life in Plato's portrait of Socrates. Plato even gives

Socrates a spoken autobiography in the *Apology*. But philosophical autobiography is a singularly small corpus, even given the exiguity of philosophers themselves, and perhaps the best examples of it use autobiography as a form of philosophical writing, as in Saint Augustine's *Confessions*, or Descartes's *Meditations*.

Hume, who thought of himself as a man of letters, wrote an inspiring but brief autobiography, and Nietzsche, who thought of himself as a prophet, wrote the exclamatory *Ecce Homo* which it is difficult not to take as predictive of his breakdown. The form of philosophical writing of course often implies an involuntary self-portrait, in the sense that we feel we can tell from the text what sort of person the philosopher was. And no matter how impersonal the text, the personality of the author is often revealed in examples and casual observations. But this is a far cry from knowing what the life was like, which produced the texts we still ponder.

A life in any case is different from a career, and so an autobiography is different from a curriculum vitae. And this is true even when, with the professionalization of philosophy in the twentieth century, most philosophers became academics. Even in an era when the writings of philosophers have had to meet the standards of professional journals and academic committees, it remains the case that the philosophical creators appear "singly and sparingly," and their lives have a fascination because of the audacity and vastness of their ideas. Since so much of philosophical writing has the form of comments and criticisms, replies and reviews, there remains in philosophy the expectation of the kind of total vision that is implied in such sweeping titles as *Mysticism and Logic* (Russell), *Being and Nothingness* (Sartre), *Truth and Method* (Gadamer), *I and Thou* (Buber), or *Language, Truth, and Logic* (Ayer), whose autobiographies, among others, are printed here.

Part of what brings us to philosophy is the thirst for the widest possible vistas, and the story of how these intrepid explorers broke through to theirs, told in their own words, constitutes a rare genre in the literature of discovery and intellectual courage.

### Arthur C. Danto

Emeritus Johnsonian Professor of Philosophy
Columbia University

# Introduction

In the history of human thought, the past one hundred years have witnessed a vast and terrifying cataclysm, in which enormous ideological systems collided like galaxies and were thrown into disorder. Old certainties have been called into question, old hopes dashed, and old creeds pulverized.

The seven individual voices assembled here provide us with a richly contrasted mosaic capturing the intellectual turbulence of recent decades:

- Bertrand Russell (1872–1970), the radical English lord who combined withering skepticism with passionate militancy in the promotion of ethical ideals;

- Albert Einstein (1879–1955), who overthrew classical physics and prepared the way for quantum mechanics, though he could never accept its more radical implications;

- Martin Buber (1878–1965), who built a new edifice of existential humanism out of the most elementary human relationships;

- Sarvepalli Radhakrishnan (1888–1975), a key figure in explaining the applications of traditional Indian thought to the problems of the modern West;

- Hans-Georg Gadamer (1900–2002), a prophet of the 'hermeneutic revolution', who extended the method of interpretation of texts to all areas of human thought and practice;

- Jean-Paul Sartre (1905–1980), whose novels, plays, and philosophical works mercilessly analyze the plight of humans "condemned to be free";

- A.J. Ayer (1910–1989), who became a superstar of logical positivism, years after he had left logical positivism behind.

BERTRAND RUSSELL led a long life, crammed with accomplishment. He became steadily more notorious until his death at the age of 98. Russell was a controversial celebrity because of his anti-war activities and his views on sexual morality—once regarded as shocking but nowadays decidedly tame. Like many major thinkers who achieved fame in their lifetimes, Russell was best known for matters having little to do with his truly outstanding accomplishments.

Russell's *Principles of Mathematics* (1903) and the later three-volume *Principia Mathematica* (1910–1913), co-written with Alfred North Whitehead, are his most momentous works. These books set the direction for philosophy of mathematics over the next fifty years. They developed the position which came to be known as logicism: that the propositions of mathematics are reducible to logic, and therefore give us no descriptive information about the world.

Investigating the mathematics of classes, Russell at this time discovered the brain-teaser that has ever since been known as Russell's Paradox. Attempts to solve it have tested the limits of philosophical ingenuity. The paradox relates to *the class of all classes that are not members of themselves*: if this class is a member of itself, then it follows that it is not a member of itself, and if it is not a member of itself, then it follows that it is a member of itself. As Russell pointed out, this can be paralleled by the Paradox of the Barber: if the village barber shaves all the men in the village who don't shave themselves, does he shave himself? Whichever way we answer, we get a contradiction. Russell's own solution to the paradox was his Theory of Types, incorporated into *Principia Mathematica*, though still not universally accepted as adequate.

In 1905 Russell invented his Theory of Definite Descriptions, a breakthrough which showed how a whole swath of philosophical confusion could be cleared away by the sickle of precise language. It was a recurring problem of many venerable philosophical discussions that non-existent objects had to be accorded a kind of 'being', so that it became problematic to deny any reality to 'the golden mountain', 'the round square', or 'the creator of the universe'. The Theory of Definite Descriptions solved this problem by reformulation: statements about the round square are translated into statements about '$x$, where $x$ is round, and $x$ is square', which do not presuppose that any actual thing fulfills both descriptions.

Russell's *Our Knowledge of the External World* (Open Court, 1914) was the beginning of his novel approach to epistemology (the branch of philosophy concerned with how we can know things). Russell tried to reformulate empiricism (the view that the evidence of our senses is fundamental) through the medium of modern logic. The classic exposition of Russell's new philosophy was *The Theory of Logical Atomism* (1918), which first appeared in *The Monist*, under the editorship of Paul Carus.

During the First World War, while Russell was pouring out a stream of new philosophical thought, he was also engaged in militant opposition to the war, generally labelled 'pacifism', though Russell was never a pacifist in the strict sense of being opposed to the use of force under all circumstances. He was forbidden to leave Britain, then fined, then fired from his professorship at Cambridge, and finally imprisoned (for insulting the United States, a wartime ally). In prison he wrote his classic *Introduction to Mathematical Philosophy*.

Having given away nearly all his inheritance to needy friends, Russell had to live by his writing. In the 1920s he visited Russia and China, writing books about each of them, turned out tomes on popular science, and authored the scandalous *Marriage and Morals*, as well as a popular work on education, whose principles he put into practice by operating a 'progressive' school.

In the 1930s, like so many others, Russell at first looked ahead to the looming war with the presumption that it was just as insupportable as the previous one, but then switched to a pro-war position because of the unique menace of Hitlerism. He taught at the University of Chicago and UCLA, then accepted an appointment to teach philosophy at the City College of New York in 1940. This appointment led to a storm of virulent hostility from infuriated Christians, who succeeded in having it rescinded, on the ground that Russell was morally unfit to teach. Russell would frequently cite the incident as an excellent example of Christian love and forbearance.

After World War II, Russell saw Soviet Russia as the main enemy, and at one point even countenanced the pre-emptive nuclear bombing of Russia, at a time when the U.S. had the atomic bomb and the Soviet Union did not. But after Soviet Russia had acquired a thermonuclear capability, Russell moved by stages to a standpoint known as unilateralism. Though he never recommended unilateral disarmament by the United States, he favored unilateral disarmament and withdrawal from Nato by U.S. allies such as Britain and France.

Russell had always been a sharp critic of Marxist doctrine and an ardent democrat and anti-Communist, yet he increasingly came to see thermonuclear war as the chief threat to humankind, and the United States as the chief obstacle to nuclear disarmament. His appraisal of such developments as the

Cuban Missile Crisis and the Vietnam War was harshly anti-American, and he took the side of the conspiracy theorists in the question of the Kennedy assassination. During these later years Russell made no original contributions to philosophy, but did find time to write some diverting and best-selling popular fiction, *Nightmares of Eminent Persons* and *Satan in the Suburbs*.

ALBERT EINSTEIN is known to all as the greatest physicist of the twentieth century. His ideas of physical reality were always bound up with purely philosophical conceptions and with a religious sense of life.

In his youth Einstein was impressed by the influential views of Ernst Mach, often described as 'positivism'. Mach believed that scientific theories summarize, in condensed form, what has been observed and what is expected to be observed. They should say nothing about what cannot be observed.

In later life, Einstein discarded Mach's positivism as philosophically naive. Einstein came to hold that imagination, amounting almost to fantasy, rather than the accumulation of facts, is decisive for understanding the cosmos and our place in it, or as he would put it, for following the thoughts of the Almighty.

To Einstein, 'positivism' means the view that the facts are manifest and speak for themselves, and that science strives to adapt itself more and more closely to facts. In the positivist view, it is vital not to get too far ahead of the factual data and not to speculate wildly about what cannot be measured. Since facts are supposedly discovered by observation—by using the five senses, aided by scientific instruments—positivism therefore means extreme empiricism: knowledge comes from looking at the world, and theory merely systematizes this knowledge.

Einstein's mature philosophical outlook is a wholehearted rejection of positivism and empiricism. He believes in the free play of the human imagination, in the bold construction of theories. These theories can be distinguished from mere fantasy, according to Einstein, by one thing only: their connection with the world of experience. But this connection he sees as intuitive, not logical, and as relating the whole of a theory to the whole of experience, not confirming each bit of the theory by observation.

Einstein was acutely aware of the problems bequeathed to modern humankind by Hume and Kant. The Scotsman David Hume (1711–1776) had conclusively shown that even the most commonplace and necessary metaphysical concepts, like the notion of cause and effect, cannot be deduced logically from the facts of experience. Furthermore, even their likelihood or plausibility cannot be deduced in this way. This led Hume reluctantly to conclude that reason was unreasonable, as it could not support the validity of concepts which were practically indispensable in everyday life.

Immanuel Kant (1724–1804) agreed that the most essential metaphysical ideas—time, space, and causality—cannot be demonstrated. They therefore have to be accepted. But since there's no escape from them, they must, Kant supposed, be the creations of the human mind itself. The mind imposes these 'categories' on reality, because it cannot experience reality in any other way. According to Kant, it is pointless to try to prove or disprove such fundamental metaphysical categories: pure reason reaches its limits when it tries to depart from what is given in experience.

Einstein approached this philosophical problem in a completely different way. While agreeing with Hume and Kant that we need metaphysics to make sense of reality as we experience it, Einstein pointed out that, from the standpoint of logic, all propositions are assumptions, "freely chosen posits," and this applies to those propositions closest to the experience of our senses, just as much as to the more 'abstract' propositions.

Within a theoretical system, said Einstein, a correct proposition is one which can be derived by logic from that system. A theoretical system as a whole can be provisionally accepted as true according to how well it is co-ordinated with the totality of our experience.

Early in his career, Einstein had helped to found quantum theory, but he later became alarmed at the direction mainstream quantum mechanics was taking, under the influence of Niels Bohr and the 'Copenhagen Interpretation'. Einstein's famous remark that "God does not play dice with the Universe" expressed both his skepticism about the subjectivistic and indeterminist aspects of quantum physics, and his ever-present belief in an intelligence behind the cosmos.

MARTIN BUBER was the child of assimilated Viennese Jewish parents, though raised by his grandparents who were observant Jews. In his youth, Buber became immersed in general European culture and abandoned all Jewish observances. An interest in the philosopher Friedrich Nietzsche impelled Buber to become preoccupied with cultural and spiritual renewal, and therefore to become active in the Zionist movement.

In 1901 the great Zionist leader Theodor Herzl made Buber editor of the Zionist weekly *Die Welt* (The World), but he did not last the year in that position. Sharp differences quickly developed between Buber and Herzl. Buber favored immediate agricultural settlements in Palestine as a road to spiritual renewal, while Herzl concentrated on political diplomacy with a view to securing a legal basis for a Jewish homeland. From 1916 until 1924, Buber edited *Der Jude* (The Jew), the main forum for Zionist intellectuals. Buber, however, adopted a distinctly unpopular minority position by advocating Jewish co-operation with the majority inhabitants of Palestine, and the eventual formation of a binational Arab-Jewish state.

A committed socialist from an early age, Buber argued that Marx and Engels had prematurely dismissed the so-called 'Utopians'. Pointing to the failure of Marxism to advance its original goals, Buber's book *Paths in Utopia* argued most eloquently for a rebirth of utopian socialism with a spiritual foundation.

Following his marriage to the Zionist author Paula Winckler, Buber took up the study of Hasidism, the Eastern European form of grass-roots Jewish pietism, then scorned by cultivated intellectuals for its supposed backwardness and naivety. Buber came to see in Hasidism a healing power for the malaise of Judaism and of humankind. Buber held that the three vital human relationships—between man and God, man and man, and man and nature—could be restored to their proper place, as in Hasidism, only by meeting the other person who stands "over against" one, on the three levels of divine, human, and natural.

At first Buber was deeply impressed by the mystical aspect of Hasidism, with its focus on the ecstatic moments of worship. Partly under the influence of the Christian existentialist philosopher Søren Kierkegaard, Buber then became dissatisfied with mysticism, viewing its experience of union with the absolute as illusory, since separate selves always continue to exist. By the time he came to write his most remarkable and widely-read work, *I and Thou*, in 1923, Buber could be described as a Jewish existentialist rather than a mystic: he criticized the mystic's pursuit of unification, emphasizing instead the fundamental notion of relation. To seek unification with God or with the Universe is to seek immersion, annihilation of the self, and thereby of lived actuality. Furthermore, a preoccupation with mystic union condemns everyday life to be regarded as worthless or illusory, tearing religious experience out of day-to-day experience. Buber thus came to place a high value on the non-mystical aspect of Hasidic teaching, which hallows mundane affairs with the breath of eternity.

In 1934 Buber became director of the organization for Jewish adult education and retraining of Jewish teachers throughout Germany. He courageously resisted the National Socialist government's steadily worsening crackdown on Jews and their cultural activities, until he was barred from teaching, whereupon he emigrated, at the age of 60, to Palestine. He became professor of social philosophy at the Hebrew University of Jerusalem, and after the establishment of the State of Israel, helped to found and then headed the Teacher Training College for Adult Education, which trained educators for the new immigrants now pouring into Israel.

In Jerusalem, Buber was a controversial figure because of his persistent opposition to mainstream Zionist policy toward the Palestinian Arabs, especially as he did not hesitate to point out the affinities between the dominant Zionist line and German National Socialism. In 1939 he helped establish the League for Jewish-Arab Rapprochement and Co-operation and in 1942 the Jewish 'binationalist' political group called Ihud. Buber argued that, by insisting on the military imposition of a Jewish instead of a binational state, and the effective reduction of the Palestinians to second-class citizenship, Zionism would merely set up a fragile militaristic enclave of the West, isolated among the already-rooted peoples of the Middle East. After the establishment of the State of Israel, Buber abandoned his binational proposals, but continued to protest the injustice of the Jewish state's treatment of Palestinians.

From the 1920s, Buber had participated in the Jewish-Christian dialogue. His book, *Two Types of Faith*, written during the siege of Jerusalem and published in 1951, gave this dialogue a new turn. The book was at first bitterly controversial, especially among Christian theologians, some of whom denounced it while others accepted it as helpful and illuminating. Buber drew a contrast between the faith of the Hebrew prophets and of Jesus, with its essentially Jewish character, and the faith of Paul and John, which came to define the new religion. *Two Types of Faith* paid tribute to Christianity, while candidly insisting that Jews would never accept the divinity or the messiahship of Jesus.

In his last years Buber was honored as the most eminent Israeli scholar and philosopher, though out of sympathy with the mainstream politics of his country. He continued with his political activities, writing, teaching, and his translation of the Jewish Bible. Upon his death, Buber was mourned by many Palestinians as well as Jews, and a delegation of the Arab Students' Organization placed a wreath on his grave.

SARVEPALLI RADHAKRISHNAN is best known for his many erudite yet popular books, such as *Indian Philosophy* (1923–27), *An Idealist View of Life* (1929), *East and West in Religion* (1933), and *Eastern Religions and Western Thought* (1939). Radhakrishnan explained the West to the East and the East to the West. As he said, the British believed that because they had acquired control of India, they understood it, but Radhakrishnan showed that Western views of Hinduism were rife with misconceptions. At the same time, he maintained that India should learn from Christianity and from Western technology.

Radhakrishnan argued for positions that have since become commonplace: that all religions have a historical development and none is final or perfect, and that therefore all of the world's religions can learn from each other, and should work in harmony to tackle such issues as peace, the environment, and social justice. According to Radhakrishnan, the apparent decline of religion in the modern world is largely illusory. Religion can never disappear but merely takes new forms. The various substitute religions which have risen up in the twentieth century, such as humanism, evolutionism, or dialectical materialism, are inadequate.

Radhakrishnan fully accepts the reality of the material world and the findings of modern physical science, and rejects such doctrines as panpsychism, which holds that all reality is fundamentally conscious. But he argues that religious experience, particularly the mystical, is so similar in content across cultures that it has to be accorded the same objectivity as basic physical facts, though the interpretation of those facts, like the theories of science, is more tentative and questionable than the fundamental reality glimpsed in religious experience.

Radhakrishnan's metaphysics is a form of idealism, understood as the ultimate dependence of the universe, and of physical processes, upon transcendental forces. Mechanical cause-and-effect is one way to understand specific parts of the Universe, and where it is fruitful, it should be used, but the breakdown of classical physics shows that it does not capture the whole truth. If determinism and classical physics were the whole truth, then every possible arrangement of matter would already have occurred and would occur repeatedly over long stretches of time. Instead, the events of nature are "infinite and formless" and constantly give rise to genuine novelty. Radhakrishnan also maintains that mechanistic analysis could not capture the reality of organic holism, where, even in the simplest physical entities, "the plan of the whole controls the character of the subordinate parts which enter into them."

Radhakrishnan was an admirer of Gandhi and a spokesman for the rights of the Untouchables in India. His attitude to the caste system was measured: while agreeing that it would be unjust to perpetuate it in its existing form, he considered that it had incidental benefits which had often been overlooked.

From 1946 to 1952, Radhakrishnan led the Indian delegation to the United Nations Educational Scientific and Cultural Organization. In 1949 he was made Indian ambassador to the Soviet Union, and upon his return to India in 1952 he was elected President, succeeding Rajendra Prasad, the first president of India following independence. Radhakrishnan retired from politics in 1957.

HANS-GEORG GADAMER was the most prominent figure in one of the twentieth century's most influential intellectual movements, philosophical hermeneutics. The term 'hermeneutics' refers to the art and theory of interpretation. At one time it meant the interpretation by theologians of sacred texts; later it came to be extended to the interpretation of all texts, and finally to interpretation of the world in general.

The protestant theologian Friedrich Schleiermacher (1768–1834) drew attention to the famous 'hermeneutic circle', in which the interpretation of each part of a text depends on the interpretation of the whole, and therefore of every part. The philosopher Wilhelm Dilthey (1833–1911) argued that the approach of hermeneutics could be extended to every discipline where interpretation and understanding are required. In Dilthey's view, this applies to the human sciences, like history and sociology, but not to natural sciences like physics and biology.

In the 1920s and 1930s, Gadamer's slow development of philosophical hermeneutics did not attract much attention. His reputation soared, however, following the publication of his book *Truth and Method* in 1960. His numerous earlier writings had been mostly ponderous and unexciting articles mainly concerned with the detailed analyses of texts such as Plato's dialogues, whereas *Truth and Method* has surprising passages of clarity, wide applicability, and eloquent force.

Perhaps the most memorable passage is his swift demolition of the assumption that philosophers should begin by discarding all of their prejudices. Prejudices, says Gadamer, are "conditions of understanding." This does not mean that all prejudices have to be preserved: it does mean that there is reciprocity rather than opposition between tradition and reason.

Gadamer's defense of prejudice led to a dispute with the philosopher Jürgen Habermas who attacked Gadamer's thought for being too confined by the past.

Gadamer has had some influence on American philosophers, but like most recent thinkers in continental Europe, he has had more influence on American academics in disciplines other than philosophy, especially legal, political, and literary theory. Gadamer's view of interpretation is that the interpreter has a conversation with what is interpreted which if successful will result in "a fusion of horizons."

Gadamer's standpoint that there is no uniquely correct interpretation of a text was warmly welcomed by American literary theorists. In fact, Gadamer's view is more moderate than the anti-intentionalism which dominated American literary theory after World War II. Gadamer does not say that any interpretation of a work will do. He holds that most imaginable interpretations are eliminated by close attention to the text. Yet more than one interpretation is possible, analogous to the view of a physical object from various angles, the author's intention is not always decisive, and interpretation does require creativity

During the National Socialist period, Gadamer walked a narrow line between the possibility of political threats to his survival and the outward compromises needed to survive. By his own account, he did not leave Germany when this was possible, because he believed, like others at the time, that irrational excrescences such as antisemitism would quickly become inoperative. His academic career advanced, though slowly. As he explains in his contribution to the present volume, when he felt obliged to give the Hitler salute, he did so in a noticeably half-hearted fashion.

After the war, Gadamer continued to exercise his survival skills as he found himself in the Soviet-occupied zone of Germany, which became the German Democratic Republic. As one of the few surviving notable German professors to have held aloof from any official ties with the Nazi Party, he was made rector of Leipzig University. After five years in this job, he was about to leave to take up a position in West Germany, when he was arrested by the Russians and interrogated for three days, before being released. Gadamer's discretion under the Third Reich and then under German Communism has been criticized by some and defended by others. Since he must have carefully avoided any official link with the Nazi or Communist parties, there is no reason to doubt his later statements that he was privately unsympathetic to these horrible governments. To have been more outspoken would no doubt have led to his own disappearance into the cellars of the secret police, without accomplishing much of anything. Having lived for seventeen years under regimes where careless words spelled death, Gadamer was absolutely reticent about his personal life and his innermost feelings, and will be a tough nut for any biographer to crack.

JEAN-PAUL SARTRE enjoyed the heights of fame—as philosopher, novelist, playwright, and political agitator, and was even celebrated for his private life. In France and, to a lesser extent even in the swirling phantom-world outside France, his every pronouncement was felt to be historic. He first became a celebrity in 1938 with his novel, *Nausea*, probably the most outstanding work of fiction since Plato's dialogues to give expression to original philosophical ideas. His first major work of philosophy was *Sketch for a Theory of the Emotions*, which took the analysis of human passions in a new direction that can be seen as presaging recent explorations by Robert C. Solomon, Antonio R. Damasio, and Ralph D. Ellis.

Sartre's most important work, *Being and Nothingness*, appeared under the German occupation in 1943. Here he solved the mystery of consciousness by demonstrating that consciousness is—nothing. Or, as he sometimes put it, consciousness "is not what it is and is what it is not." Extending Husserl's emphasis on the fact that consciousness is always 'intentional'—always 'about' something—Sartre inferred that consciousness has no being, and used this finding to argue for an original conception of freedom, as something inescapable, outside the physical world, vertiginous, and unconditional.

'Existentialist' was a name first applied to Sartre and Simone de Beauvoir in 1944, then extended retrospectively to Heidegger, Jaspers, Kierkegaard, Nietzsche, and even Dostoyevsky. After the war's end, existentialism was all the rage in the cafés of Paris, and Sartre was its prophet. Although his involvement with the French resistance to German occupation had been tentative and peripheral, it was enough to certify him as the kind of intellectual who was in rather short supply: a French patriot and yet a progressive leftist.

Existentialism's catch-phrases, coined by Sartre, became clichés of the Left Bank (the café subculture of Paris intellectuals). 'Existence precedes essence', meaning that humans exist before they acquire a purpose or meaning. We are 'condemned to be free', meaning that the alibis for evading responsibility are useless (and, strictly speaking, that human choices are uncaused). 'Existence is futile' and 'Mankind is a useless passion' were other histrionic slogans of defiance originated by Sartre and taken up by his numerous imitators, as well as by his intermittent life partner Simone de Beauvoir and such acolytes as his cabaret disciple, the voluptuous singer Juliette Gréco, who even became marketable outside the Left Bank, following her nose job. His plays were successful and controversial, the most popular being *Huis clos* (a title impossible to translate in a few words, and now best known in English as *No Exit*), with its lugubrious line, "Hell is other people."

During the Cold War, Sartre favored the Soviet bloc, and in the early 1950s announced that he had become a Marxist, though he regarded the Communist Party as purveyors of a sadly mutilated version of Marxism. For the most part he was ambivalent anent the nature of the Soviet regime, neither denouncing it as an evil tyranny nor glorifying it in the manner of the Communists. He identified with the anti-Western movements of the Third World and, after the student riots of May 1968 had impressed upon him that the Communist Party was an anti-revolutionary force, he came to be identified by the media as a Maoist. Although his political perspective was close to that of various French Maoist groups, with whom he co-operated, Sartre scoffingly rejected the label.

Sartre was superhumanly prolific and often changed the emphases and nuances of his views, moving on to new concerns, and expressing annoyance with critics who would expect him to defend his earlier opinions. Notoriously, he failed to complete nearly all his projected large-scale undertakings. Among many examples, he never finished the final volume of his four-volume sequence of World War II novels, *Roads to Freedom*, though the three published volumes were best-sellers. He also failed to complete the final volume of his enormous biography of the novelist Gustave Flaubert, after the first three mammoth volumes had appeared, to generally rapturous praise.

In 1964 Sartre was awarded the Nobel Prize for Literature, but contemptuously declined this accolade from the bourgeois world. President de Gaulle forbade Sartre's incarceration for politically motivated criminal acts of civil disobedience, with the remark "You don't jail Voltaire." Sartre's virtual blindness in his last years explains why his contribution to this volume came to be the transcription of an interview rather than a written autobiography. His lifelong habit of driving himself to prodigious literary output with a balanced diet of nicotine and amphetamines probably hastened his death in 1980. Fifty thousand people followed his funeral procession through the streets of Paris

ALFRED JULES AYER burst upon the world with his early book *Language, Truth, and Logic*, which achieved a stunning commercial success, altogether amazing for a work of pure philosophy. Even in hindsight, its popular appeal is hard to explain and the reasons for it are still controversial. It continues to sell healthily every year. One thing is clear, however: the book was widely read by non-philosophers as the manifesto of something called 'logical positivism', a movement which philosophers themselves are more inclined to call 'logical empiricism'.

By the time the book became so hugely successful, virtually no philosophers, and certainly not Ayer, still adhered to logical positivism, whose heyday among professional philosophers was conclusively over before 1950. At this time, the rage among English-speaking philosophers was 'linguistic analysis', also known as 'ordinary language philosophy', a fad which Ayer (like Russell) always roundly condemned. But non-philosophers apparently loved the sound of the phrase 'logical positivism' and stubbornly refused to be told that it was not the reigning philosophy of the age.

These unwashed readers of Ayer's book, however, understood the gist of it: that numerous things people like to say, such as 'There is a God' or 'The universe is one' or 'The future is predetermined' are neither true nor false, but meaningless gibberish. They are metaphysical, and it has been shown—so the logical positivists maintained—that all metaphysics is strictly nonsense. The opposites of these statements: 'There is no God', 'The universe is many', and 'The future is open' are just as meaningless. Logical positivists, and following them linguistic analysts, would respond to such statements by asserting that they 'couldn't understand them', the implication being that the person uttering them was so egregiously muddleheaded as to fancy that they did mean something. It became a standing joke that there was a very advanced Oxford philosopher who had attained to the highest peak of being unable to understand any assertion whatsoever, but whoever this personage may have been, he was not Ayer.

As for statements like 'Cold-blooded killing of innocent people is wrong', the logical positivist response was that these are not true statements, but expressions of the feelings of the person uttering them. Although this has the form of a statement, it is equivalent to saying 'Cold-blooded killing of innocent people!' in a tone of horror. This theory of moral statements—or pseudo-statements—is also accepted by some philosophers who are not logical empiricists, and is known as the Emotive Theory of Ethics.

In the 1950s and 1960s many writers in the humanities revealed that they had been influenced by Ayer's book, in denouncing as 'metaphysical' views with which they disagreed. This approach could too easily be used in facile and mechanical fashion to dismiss any claims that were highly abstract or that went beyond what could be directly measured.

*Language, Truth, and Logic* appeared in 1936, and did not have huge sales at first, partly because the publisher did not believe that such a work could possibly sell. It was Ayer's account of philosophical views he had imbibed on his recent visit to Vienna. Sales of the book really picked up at the end of World War II, by which time Ayer had moved on from logical positivism. But its success helped to launch him as a public figure in Britain, where, as 'Freddy Ayer', later 'Sir Alfred Ayer', he became a household name for his liberal views on sexual conduct and his opposition to theistic religion. He was an effective campaigner for the legalization of homosexual behavior in Britain.

Throughout his life, Ayer continued to make first-rate contributions to philosophy. They are not revolutionary and did not create the popular splash of *Language, Truth, and Logic*, but they are careful and elegantly written contributions to epistemology and metaphysics, and Ayer was always prepared to change his mind on any issue where the weight of arguments against his earlier positions had accumulated. The most important are *The Problem of Knowledge* (1956), *Metaphysics and Common Sense* (1969), and *Probability and Evidence* (1972).

Ayer's life ended in a strangely public and equivocal way, appropriate to his multifaceted career as thinker, popular expositor, and media personality. In 1988 he died, in the sense that his heart stopped for four minutes, and before returning to normal consciousness had a mystical or hallucinatory 'near-death experience', if not an experience of actual death. The infamous atheist wrote an account of this adventure which appeared in the ineffably conservative *Sunday Telegraph* under the title (not Ayer's), 'What I Saw When I Was Dead . . .' Ayer concluded that the episode had "slightly weakened my conviction that my genuine death, which is due fairly soon, will be the end of me," an observation which aroused such a storm that he felt obliged to publish a correction. A few months later, Sir Freddy again departed from this vale of tears, this time without a return ticket. The entertaining episode appears in full at the end of Ayer's contribution to this volume.

# Genius:
## In Their Own Words

BERTRAND RUSSELL (1872–1970), the giant of twentieth-century philosophy, was also a political activist and journalist. He was imprisoned for his anti-war activities in the First World War, but supported the Second because of the peculiar evil of Hitler. From 1920 on, he outspokenly attacked the totalitarian system of Soviet Russia; beginning in the 1960s he saw nuclear war as all-important and the United States as the main obstacle to peace. His most brilliant work, in philosophy of mathematics, was done between 1903 and 1913, but he continued to pour out beautifully written books and articles on many subjects until late in life.

# Bertrand
# RUSSELL

## " *Not the starry heavens, but their effects on human percipients, have excellence.* "

MY MOTHER HAVING DIED WHEN I WAS two years old, and my father when I was three, I was brought up in the house of my grandfather, Lord John Russell, afterwards Earl Russell. Of my parents, Lord and Lady Amberley, I was told almost nothing—so little that I vaguely sensed a dark mystery. It was not until I was 21 that I came to know the main outlines of my parents' lives and opinions. I then found, with a sense of bewilderment, that I had gone through almost exactly the same mental and emotional development as my father had.

3

It was expected of my father that he should take to a political career, which was traditional in the Russell family. He was willing, and was for a short time in Parliament (1867–68); but he had not the temperament or the opinions that would have made political success possible. At the age of 21 he decided that he was not a Christian, and refused to go to Church on Christmas Day. He became a disciple, and afterwards a friend, of John Stuart Mill, who, as I discovered some years ago, was (so far as is possible in a non-religious sense) my godfather. My parents accepted Mill's opinions, not only such as were comparatively popular, but also those that still shocked public sentiment, such as women's suffrage and birth control. During the general election of 1868, at which my father was a candidate, it was discovered that, at a private meeting of a small society, he had said that birth control was a matter for the medical profession to consider. This let loose a campaign of vilification and slander. A Catholic bishop declared that he advocated infanticide; he was called in print a "filthy foulmouthed rake"; on election day, cartoons were exhibited accusing him of immorality, altering his name to "Vice-count Amberley," and accusing him of advocating "The French and American system."[1] By these means he was defeated. The student of comparative sociology may be interested in the similarities between rural England in 1868 and urban New York in 1940. The available documents are collected in *The Amberley Papers,* by my wife and myself. As the reader of this book will see, my father was shy, studious, and ultra-conscientious— perhaps a prig, but the very opposite of a rake.

My father did not give up hope of returning to politics, but never obtained another constituency,[2] and devoted himself to writing a big book, *Analysis of Religious Belief,* which was published after his death. He could not, in any case, have succeeded in politics, because of his very exceptional intellectual integrity; he was always willing to admit the weak points on his own side and the strong points on that of his opponents. Moreover his health was always bad, and he suffered from a consequent lack of physical vigor.

My mother shared my father's opinions, and shocked the 1860s by addressing meetings in favor of equality for women. She refused to use the phrase 'women's rights', because, as a good utilitarian, she rejected the doctrine of natural rights.

---

1. (Note by Russell) My parents, when in America, had studied such experiments as the Oneida community. They were therefore accused of attempting to corrupt the purity of English family life by introducing un-English transatlantic vices.

2. In the U.K., a 'constituency' is an electoral district at the national level.

My father wished my brother and me to be brought up as freethinkers, and appointed two freethinkers as our guardians. The Court of Chancery, however, at the request of my grandparents, set aside the will, and I enjoyed the benefits of a Christian upbringing.

In 1876, when after my father's death I was brought to the house of my grandparents, my grandfather was eighty-three and had become very feeble. I remember him sometimes being wheeled about out-of-doors in a bath-chair, sometimes in his room reading *Hansard* (the official report of debates in Parliament). He was invariably kind to me, and seemed never to object to childish noise. But he was too old to influence me directly. He died in 1878, and my knowledge of him came through his widow, my grandmother, who revered his memory. She was a more powerful influence upon my general outlook than anyone else, although, from adolescence onward, I disagreed with very many of her opinions.

My grandmother was a Scotch Presbyterian, of the border family of the Elliots. Her maternal grandfather suffered obloquy for declaring, on the basis of the thickness of the lava on the slopes of Etna, that the world must have been created before B.C. 4004. One of her great-grandfathers was Robertson, the historian of Charles V.

She was a Puritan, with the moral rigidity of the Covenanters, despising comfort, indifferent to food, hating wine, and regarding tobacco as sinful. Although she had lived her whole life in the great world until my grandfather's retirement in 1866, she was completely unworldly. She had that indifference to money which is only possible to those who have always had enough of it. She wished her children and grandchildren to live useful and virtuous lives, but had no desire that they should achieve what others would regard as success, or that they should marry 'well'. She had the Protestant belief in private judgment and the supremacy of the individual conscience. On my twelfth birthday she gave me a Bible (which I still possess), and wrote her favorite texts on the fly-leaf. One of them was "Thou shalt not follow a multitude to do evil;" another, "Be strong, and of a good courage; be not afraid, neither be Thou dismayed; for the Lord Thy God is with thee whithersoever thou goest." These texts have profoundly influenced my life, and still seemed to retain some meaning after I had ceased to believe in God.

At the age of 70, my grandmother became a Unitarian; at the same time, she supported Home Rule for Ireland, and made friends with Irish Members of Parliament, who were being publicly accused of complicity in murder. This shocked people more than now seems imaginable. She was passionately opposed to imperialism, and taught me to think ill of the Afghan and Zulu wars, which occurred when I was about seven. Concerning the occupation of Egypt, however, she said little, as it was due to Mr. Gladstone, whom she admired. I remember an argument I had with my German governess, who said that the English, having once gone into Egypt, would never come out, whatever they might promise, whereas I maintained, with much patriotic passion, that the English never broke promises. That was sixty years ago, and they are there still.[3]

My grandfather, seen through the eyes of his widow, made it seem imperative and natural to do something important for the good of mankind. I was told of his introducing the Reform Bill in 1832. Shortly before he died, a delegation of eminent nonconformists assembled to cheer him, and I was told that fifty years earlier he had been one of the leaders in removing their political disabilities. In his sitting-room there was a statue of Italy, presented to my grandfather by the Italian Government, with an inscription: "A Lord John Russell, L'Italia Riconoscente." I naturally wished to know what this meant, and learnt, in consequence, the whole saga of Garibaldi and Italian unity. Such things stimulated my ambition to live to some purpose.

My grandfather's library, which became my schoolroom, stimulated me in a different way. There were books of history, some of them very old; I remember in particular a sixteenth-century Guicciardini. There were three huge folio volumes called *L'Art de vérifier les dates.* They were too heavy for me to move, and I speculated as to their contents; I imagined something like the tables for finding Easter in the Prayer-Book. At last I became old enough to lift one of the volumes out of the shelf, and I found, to my disgust, that the only 'art' involved was that of looking up the date in the book. Then there were *The Annals of Ireland* by the Four Masters, in which I read about the men who went to Ireland before the Flood and were drowned in it; I wondered how the Four Masters knew about them, and read no further. There were also more ordinary books, such as Machiavelli and Gibbon and Swift, and a book in four volumes that I never opened: *The Works of Andrew Marvell Esq. M.P.* It was not till I grew up that I discovered Marvell was a poet rather than a politician. I was not supposed to read any of these books; otherwise I should probably not have read any of them. The net result of

---

3. This was written in 1943. The British-backed constitutional monarchy was ended by the coup of Gamal Abdel Nasser in 1952.

them was to stimulate my interest in history. No doubt my interest was increased by the fact that my family had been prominent in English history since the early sixteenth century. I was taught English history as the record of a struggle against the King for constitutional liberty. William Lord Russell, who was executed under Charles II, was held up for special admiration, and the inference was encouraged that rebellion is often praiseworthy.

A great event in my life, at the age of eleven, was the beginning of Euclid, which was still the accepted textbook of geometry. When I had got over my disappointment in finding that he began with axioms, which had to be accepted without proof, I found great delight in him. Throughout the rest of my boyhood, mathematics absorbed a very large part of my interest. This interest was complex: partly mere pleasure in discovering that I possessed a certain kind of skill, partly delight in the power of deductive reasoning, partly the restfulness of mathematical certainty; but more than any of these (while I was still a boy) the belief that nature operates according to mathematical laws, and that human actions, like planetary motions, could be calculated if we had sufficient skill. By the time I was fifteen, I had arrived at a theory very similar to that of the Cartesians. The movements of living bodies, I felt convinced, were wholly regulated by the laws of dynamics; therefore free will must be an illusion. But, since I accepted consciousness as an indubitable datum, I could not accept materialism, though I had a certain hankering after it on account of its intellectual simplicity and its rejection of 'nonsense'. I still believed in God, because the First Cause Argument seemed irrefutable.

# A Passionate Interest in Religion

Until I went to Cambridge at the age of 18, my life was a very solitary one. I was brought up at home, by German nurses, German and Swiss governesses, and finally by English tutors; I saw little of other children, and when I did they were not important to me. At 14 or 15 I became passionately interested in religion, and set to work to examine successively the arguments for free will, immortality, and God. For a few months I had an agnostic tutor with whom I could talk about these problems, but he was sent away, presumably because he was thought to be undermining my faith. Except during these months, I kept my thoughts to myself, writing them out in a journal in Greek letters to prevent others from reading them. I was suffering the unhappiness natural to lonely adolescence, and I attributed my unhappiness to loss of religious belief. For three years I thought about religion, with a determination not to let my thoughts be influenced by my desires. I discarded first free will, then immortality; I believed in God until I was just 18, when I found in Mill's *Autobiography* the sentence: "My father taught me that the question 'Who made me'? cannot be answered, since it immediately suggests the further question 'Who made God'?" In that moment I decided that the First Cause Argument is fallacious.

During these years I read widely, but as my reading was not directed, much of it was futile. I read much bad poetry, especially Tennyson and Byron; at last, at the age of 17, I came upon Shelley, whom no one had told me about. He remained for many years the man I loved most among great men of the past. I read a great deal of Carlyle, and admired *Past and Present*, but not *Sartor Resartus*. "The Everlasting Yea" seemed to me sentimental nonsense. The man with whom I most nearly agreed was Mill. His *Political Economy*, *Liberty*, and *Subjection of Women* influenced me profoundly. I made elaborate notes on the whole of his *Logic*, but could not accept his theory that mathematical propositions are empirical generalizations, though I did not know what else they could be.

All this was before I went to Cambridge. Except during the three months when I had the agnostic tutor mentioned above, I found no one to speak to about my thoughts. At home I concealed my religious doubts. Once I said that I was a utilitarian, but was met with such a blast of ridicule that I never again spoke of my opinions at home.

# A New World at Cambridge

Cambridge opened to me a new world of infinite delight. For the first time I found that, when I uttered my thoughts, they seemed to be accepted as worth considering. Whitehead, who had examined me for entrance scholarships, had mentioned me to various people a year or two senior to me, with the result that within a week I met a number who became my life-long friends. Whitehead, who was already a Fellow and Lecturer, was amazingly kind, but was too much my senior to be a close personal friend until some years later. I found a group of contemporaries, who were able, rather earnest, hard-working, but interested in many things outside their academic work—poetry, philosophy, politics, ethics, indeed the whole world of mental adventure. We used to stay up discussing till very late on Saturday nights, meet for a late breakfast on Sunday, and then go for an all-day walk. Able young men had not yet adopted the pose of cynical superiority which came in some years later, and was first made fashionable in Cambridge by Lytton Strachey. The world seemed hopeful and solid; we all felt convinced that nineteenth-century progress would continue, and that we ourselves should be able to contribute something of value. For those who have been young since 1914 it must be difficult to imagine the happiness of those days.

Among my friends at Cambridge were McTaggart, the Hegelian philosopher; Lowes Dickinson, whose gentle charm made him loved by all who knew him; Charles Sanger, a brilliant mathematician at College, afterwards a barrister, known in legal circles as the editor of *Jarman on Wills*; two brothers, Crompton and Theodore Llewelyn Davies, sons of a Broad Church clergyman most widely known as one of 'Davies and Vaughan', who translated Plato's *Republic*. These two brothers were the youngest and ablest of a family of seven, all remarkably able; they had also a quite unusual capacity for friendship, a deep desire to be of use to the world, and unrivalled wit. Theodore, the younger of the two, was still in the earlier stages of a brilliant career in the government service when he was drowned in a bathing accident. I have never known any two men so deeply loved by so many friends. Among those of whom I saw most were the three brothers Trevelyan, great-nephews of Macaulay. Of these the oldest became a Labour politician and resigned from the Labour Government because it was not sufficiently socialistic; the second became a poet and published, among other things, an admirable translation of Lucretius; the third, George, achieved fame as an historian. Somewhat junior to me was G.E. Moore, who later had a great influence upon my philosophy.

The set in which I lived was very much influenced by McTaggart, whose wit recommended his Hegelian philosophy. He taught me to consider British empiricism 'crude', and I was willing to believe that Hegel (and in a lesser degree Kant) had a profundity not to be found in Locke, Berkeley, and Hume, or in my former pope, Mill. My first three years at Cambridge, I was too busy with mathematics to read Kant or Hegel, but in my fourth year I concentrated on philosophy. My teachers were Henry Sidgwick, James Ward, and G.F. Stout. Sidgwick represented the British point of view, which I believed myself to have seen through; I therefore thought less of him at that time than I did later. Ward, for whom I had a very great personal affection, set forth a Kantian system, and introduced me to Lotze and Sigwart. Stout, at that time, thought very highly of Bradley; when *Appearance and*

*Reality* was published, he said it had done as much as is humanly possible in ontology. He and McTaggart between them caused me to become a Hegelian; I remember the precise moment, one day in 1894, as I was walking along Trinity Lane, when I saw in a flash (or thought I saw) that the Ontological Argument is valid.[4] I had gone out to buy a tin of tobacco; on my way back, I suddenly threw it up in the air, and exclaimed as I caught it: "Great Scott, the ontological argument is sound!" I read Bradley at this time with avidity, and admired him more than any other recent philosopher.

# Escape from Idealism

After leaving Cambridge in 1894, I spent a good deal of time in foreign countries. For some months in 1894, I was honorary attaché at the British Embassy in Paris, where I had to copy out long dispatches attempting to persuade the French Government that a lobster is not a fish, to which the French Government would reply that it was a fish in 1713, at the time of the Treaty of Utrecht. I had no desire for a diplomatic career, and left the Embassy in December, 1894. I then married, and spent most of 1895 in Berlin, studying economics and German Social Democracy. The Ambassador's wife being a cousin of mine, my wife and I were invited to dinner at the Embassy; but she mentioned that we had gone to a Socialist meeting, and after this the Embassy closed its doors to us. My wife was a Philadelphia Quaker, and in 1896 we spent three months in America. The first place we visited was Walt Whitman's house in Camden, New Jersey; she had known him well, and I greatly admired him. These travels were useful in curing me of a certain Cambridge provincialism; in particular, I came to know the work of Weierstrass, whom my Cambridge teachers had never mentioned. After these travels, we settled down in a workman's cottage in Sussex, to which we added a fairly large work-room. I had at that time enough money to live simply without earning, and I was therefore able to devote all my time to philosophy and mathematics, except the evenings, when we read history aloud.

---

4. The Ontological Argument for the existence of God was advanced by Anselm of Canterbury (1033–1109). In one of its versions, it proceeds from the fact that 'God' is defined as a being than which nothing greater could be imagined, and the fact that a God who exists is greater than a God who does not exist, to the conclusion that there must be a God.

In the years from 1894 to 1898, I believed in the possibility of proving by metaphysics various things about the universe that religious feeling made me think important. I decided that, if I had sufficient ability, I would devote my life to philosophy. My fellowship dissertation, on the foundations of geometry, was praised by Ward and Whitehead; if it had not been, I should have taken up economics, at which I had been working in Berlin. I remember a spring morning when I walked in the Tiergarten, and planned to write a series of books in the philosophy of the sciences, growing gradually more concrete as I passed from mathematics to biology; I thought I would also write a series of books on social and political questions, growing gradually more abstract. At last I would achieve a Hegelian synthesis in an encyclopaedic work dealing equally with theory and practice. The scheme was inspired by Hegel, and yet something of it survived the change in my philosophy. The moment had a certain importance: I can still, in memory, feel the squelching of melting snow beneath my feet, and smell the damp earth that promised the end of winter.

During 1898, various things caused me to abandon both Kant and Hegel. I read Hegel's *Greater Logic,* and thought, as I still do, that all he says about mathematics is muddle-headed nonsense. I came to disbelieve Bradley's arguments against relations,[5] and to distrust the logical bases of monism. I disliked the subjectivity of Kant's Transcendental Aesthetic. But these motives would have operated more slowly than they did, but for the influence of G.E. Moore. He also had had a Hegelian period, but it was briefer than mine. He took the lead in rebellion, and I followed, with a sense of emancipation. Bradley argued that everything common sense believes in is mere appearance; we reverted to the opposite extreme, and thought that *everything* is real that common sense, uninfluenced by philosophy or theology, supposes real. With a sense of escaping from prison, we allowed ourselves to think that grass is green, that the sun and stars would exist if no one was aware of them, and also that there is a pluralistic timeless world of Platonic ideas. The world, which had been thin and logical, suddenly became rich and varied and solid. Mathematics could be *quite* true, and not merely a stage in dialectic. Something of this point of view appeared in my

---

5. Francis Herbert Bradley (1846–1924) argued in Book 1 of his *Appearance and Reality* that all common-sense and most philosophical conceptions are self-contradictory since they involve relations, and the very notion of a relation is self-contradictory. Therefore Reality, or the Absolute, which is free of contradictions, must be radically different from Appearance.

*Philosophy of Leibniz.* This book owed its origin to chance. McTaggart, who would, in the normal course, have lectured on Leibniz at Cambridge in 1898, wished to visit his family in New Zealand, and I was asked to take his place for this course. For me, the accident was a fortunate one.

# A Honeymoon with Mathematical Philosophy

The most important year in my intellectual life was the year 1900, and the most important event in this year was my visit to the International Congress of Philosophy in Paris. Ever since I had begun Euclid at the age of eleven, I had been troubled about the foundations of mathematics; when, later, I came to read philosophy, I found Kant and the empiricists equally unsatisfactory. I did not like the synthetic a priori,[6] but yet arithmetic did not seem to consist of empirical generalizations. In Paris in 1900, I was impressed by the fact that, in all discussions, Peano and his pupils had a precision which was not possessed by others. I therefore asked him to give me his works, which he did. As soon as I had mastered his notation, I saw that it extended the region of mathematical precision backwards towards regions which had been given over to philosophical vagueness. Basing myself on him, I invented a notation for relations. Whitehead, fortunately, agreed as to the importance of the method, and in a very short time we worked out together such matters as the definitions of series, cardinals, and ordinals, and the reduction of arithmetic to logic. For nearly a year, we had a rapid series of quick successes. Much of the work had already been done by Frege, but at first we did not know this. The work that ultimately became my contribution to *Principia Mathematica* presented itself to me, at first, as a parenthesis in the refutation of Kant.

In June 1901, this period of honeymoon delight came to an end. Cantor had a proof that there is no greatest cardinal; in applying this proof to the

---

6. Many philosophers have held that those statements which are self-evidently true are 'analytic': they are logical truisms. Immanuel Kant (1724–1804) maintained that there are 'synthetic a priori' statements, which are both self-evidently true and descriptions of the world. Partly due to the influence of Russell, the vast majority of English-speaking philosophers in the twentieth century rejected the synthetic a priori.

universal class, I was led to the contradiction about classes that are not members of themselves. It soon became clear that this is only one of an infinite class of contradictions. I wrote to Frege, who replied with the utmost gravity that *"die Arithmetik ist ins Schwanken geraten."*[7] At first, I hoped the matter was trivial and could be easily cleared up; but early hopes were succeeded by something very near to despair. Throughout 1903 and 1904, I pursued will-o'-the wisps and made no progress. At last, in the spring of 1905, a different problem, which proved soluble, gave the first glimmer of hope. The problem was that of descriptions, and its solution suggested a new technique.

# Attempts to Solve the Contradictions

Scholastic realism was a metaphysical theory, but every metaphysical theory has a technical counterpart. I had been a realist in the scholastic or Platonic sense; I had thought that cardinal integers, for instance, have a timeless being. When integers were reduced to classes of classes, this being was transferred to classes. Meinong, whose work interested me, applied the arguments of realism to descriptive phrases. Everyone agrees that 'The golden mountain does not exist' is a true proposition. But it has, apparently, a subject, 'the golden mountain', and if this subject did not designate some object, the proposition would seem to be meaningless. Meinong inferred that there is a golden mountain, which is golden and a mountain, but does not exist. He even thought that the existent golden mountain is existent, but does not exist. This did not satisfy me, and the desire to avoid Meinong's unduly populous realm of being led me to the theory of descriptions. What was of importance in this theory was the discovery that, in analyzing a significant sentence, one must not assume that each separate word or phrase has significance on its own account. 'The golden mountain' can be part of a significant sentence, but is not significant in isolation. It soon appeared that class-symbols could be treated like descriptions, i.e., as non-significant parts of significant sentences. This made it possible to see, in a general way, how a solution of the contradictions might be possible. The particular solution offered in *Principia Mathematica* had various defects, but at any rate it showed that the logician is not presented with a complete *impasse*.

---

7. Arithmetic has been sent into a tailspin.

The theory of descriptions, and the attempt to solve the contradictions, had led me to pay attention to the problem of meaning and significance. The definition of 'meaning' as applied to words and 'significance' as applied to sentences is a complex problem, which I tried to deal with in *The Analysis of Mind* (1921) and *An Inquiry into Meaning and Truth* (1940). It is a problem that takes one into psychology and even physiology. The more I have thought about it, the less convinced I have become of the complete independence of logic. Seeing that logic is a much more advanced and exact science than psychology, it is clearly desirable, as far as possible, to delimit the problems that can be dealt with by logical methods. It is here that I have found Occam's Razor useful.

Occam's Razor, in its original form, was metaphysical: it was a principle of parsimony as regards 'entities'. I still thought of it in this way while *Principia Mathematica* was being written. In Plato, cardinal integers are timeless entities; they are equally so in Frege's *Basic Laws of Arithmetic*. The definition of cardinals as classes of classes, and the discovery that class-symbols could be 'incomplete symbols', persuaded me that cardinals as entities are unnecessary. But what had really been demonstrated was something quite independent of metaphysics, which is best stated in terms of 'minimum vocabularies'. I mean by a 'minimum vocabulary' one in which no word can be defined in terms of the others. All definitions are theoretically superfluous, and therefore the whole of any science can be expressed by means of a minimum vocabulary for that science. Peano reduced the special vocabulary of arithmetic to three terms; Frege and *Principia Mathematica* maintained that even these are unnecessary, and that a minimum vocabulary for mathematics is the same as for logic. This problem is a purely technical one, and is capable of a precise solution.

There is need, however, of great caution in drawing inferences from minimum vocabularies. In the first place, there are usually, if not always, a number of different minimum vocabularies for a given subject-matter; for example, in the theory of truth-functions we may take 'not-$p$ or not-$q$' or 'not-$p$ and not-$q$' as undefined, and there is no reason to prefer one choice to the other. Then again there is often a question as to whether what seems to be a definition is not really an empirical proposition. Suppose, for instance, I define 'red' as 'those visual sensations which are caused by wave-lengths of such and such a range of frequencies'. If we take this as what the word 'red' means, no proposition containing the word can have been known before the undulatory theory of light was known and wave-lengths could be measured; and yet the word 'red' was used before these discoveries had been made. This makes it clear that in all everyday statements containing the word 'red' this word does not have the meaning assigned to it in the above definition. Consider the question: 'Can everything that we know about colors be known to a blind man?' With the above definition, the answer is yes; with a definition derived from everyday experience, the answer is no. This problem shows how the new logic, like the Aristotelian, can lead to a narrow scholasticism.

# We Cannot Do Without Universals

Nevertheless, there is one kind of inference which, I think, can be drawn from the study of minimum vocabularies. Take, as one of the most important examples, the traditional problem of universals. It seems fairly certain that no vocabulary can dispense wholly with words that are more or less of the sort called 'universals'. These words, it is true, need never occur as nouns; they may occur only as adjectives or verbs. Probably we could be content with one such word, the word 'similar', and we should never need the word 'similarity'. But the fact that we need the word 'similar' indicates some fact about the world, and not only about language. What fact it indicates about the world, I do not know.

Another illustration of the uses of minimum vocabularies is as regards historical events. To express history, we must have a means of speaking of something which has only happened once, like the death of Caesar. An undue absorption in logic, which is not concerned with history, may cause this need to be over-looked. Spatiotemporal relativity has made it more difficult to satisfy this need than it was in a Newtonian universe, where points and instants supplied particularity.

Thus, broadly speaking, minimum vocabularies are more instructive when they show a certain kind of term to be indispensable than when they show the opposite.

In some respects, my published work, outside mathematical logic, does not at all completely represent my beliefs or my general outlook. Theory of knowledge, with which I have been largely concerned, has a certain essential subjectivity; it asks 'how do *I* know what I know?' and starts inevitably from personal experience. Its data are egocentric, and so are the earlier stages of its argumentation. I have not, so far, got beyond the earlier stages, and have therefore seemed more subjective in outlook than in fact I am. I am not a solipsist, nor an idealist; I believe (though without good grounds) in the world of physics as well as in the world of psychology. But it seems clear that whatever is not experienced must, if known, be known by inference. I find that the fear of solipsism[8] has prevented philosophers from facing this problem, and that either the necessary principles of inference have been left vague, or else the distinction between what is known by experience and what is known by inference has been denied. If I ever have the leisure to undertake another serious investigation of a philosophical problem, I shall attempt to analyse the inferences from experience to the world of physics, assuming them capable of validity, and seeking to discover what principles of inference, if true, would make them valid. Whether these principles, when discovered, are accepted as true, is a matter of temperament; what should not be a matter of temperament should be the proof that acceptance of them is necessary if solipsism is to be rejected.

# The Menace of War

I come now to what I have attempted to do in connection with social questions. I grew up in an atmosphere of politics, and was expected by my elders to take up a political career. Philosophy, however, interested me more than politics, and when it appeared that I had some aptitude for it, I decided to make it my main work. This pained my grandmother, who alluded to my investigation of the foundations of geometry as "the life you have been leading," and said in shocked tones: "O Bertie, I hear you are writing *another* book." My political interests, though secondary, nevertheless, remained very strong. In 1895, when in Berlin, I made a study of German Social Democracy, which I liked as being opposed to the Kaiser, and disliked as (at that time) embodying Marxist orthodoxy. For a time, under the influence of Sidney Webb, I became an imperialist, and even supported the Boer War. This point of view, however, I abandoned completely in 1901; from that time onwards, I felt an intense dislike of the use of force in human relations, though I always admitted that it is sometimes necessary. When Joseph Chamberlain, in 1903, turned against free trade, I wrote and spoke against

---

8. A solipsist would be someone who held that the entire universe, including all other persons, existed only in his mind, as a kind of highly intricate dream. Philosophers are not solipsists nor tempted by solipsism, but most philosophers hold that coming up with a good argument which rules out solipsism is a serious problem.

him, my objections to his proposals being those of an internationalist. I took an active part in the agitation for women's suffrage. In 1910, *Principia Mathematica* being practically finished, I wished to stand for Parliament, and should have done so if the Selection Committee had not been shocked to discover that I was a freethinker.

The First World War gave a new direction to my interests. The war, and the problem of preventing future wars, absorbed me, and the books that I wrote on this and cognate subjects caused me to become known to a wider public. During the war I had hoped that the peace would embody a rational determination to avoid future great wars; this hope was destroyed by the Versailles Treaty. Many of my friends saw hope in Soviet Russia, but when I went there in 1920 I found nothing that I could like or admire. I was then invited to China, where I spent nearly a year. I loved the Chinese, but it was obvious that the resistance to hostile militarisms must destroy much of what was best in their civilization. They seemed to have no alternative except to be conquered or to adopt many of the vices of their enemies. But China did one thing for me that the East is apt to do for Europeans who study it with sensitive sympathy: it taught me to think in long stretches of time, and not to be reduced to despair by the badness of the present. Throughout the increasing gloom of the past twenty years, this habit has helped to make the world less unendurable than it would otherwise have been.

In the years after my return from China, the birth of my two older children caused me to become interested in early education, to which, for some time, I devoted most of my energy. I have been supposed to be an advocate of complete liberty in schools, but this, like the view that I am an anarchist, is a mistake. I think a certain amount of force is indispensable, in education as in government; but I also think that methods can be found which will greatly diminish the necessary amount of force. This problem has both political and private aspects. As a rule, children or adults who are happy are likely to have fewer destructive passions, and therefore to need less restraint, than those who are unhappy. But I do not think that children can be made happy by being deprived of guidance, nor do I think that a sense of social obligation can be fostered if complete idleness is permitted. The question of discipline in childhood, like all other practical questions, is one of degree. Profound unhappiness and instinctive frustration is apt to produce a deep grudge against the world, issuing, sometimes by a very roundabout road, in cruelty and violence. The psychological and social problems involved first occupied my attention during the war of 1914–18. I was especially struck by the fact that, at first, most people seemed to enjoy the war. Clearly this was due to a variety of social ills, some of which were educational. But while individual parents can do much for their individual children, large-scale educational reform must depend upon the state, and therefore upon prior political and economic reforms. The world, however, was moving more and more in the direction of war and dictatorship, and I saw nothing useful that I could do in practical matters. I therefore increasingly reverted to philosophy, and to history in relation to ideas.

# No Emotional Consolation in Philosophy

History has always interested me more than anything else except philosophy and mathematics. I have never been able to accept any general schema of historical development, such as that of Hegel or that of Marx. Nevertheless, general trends can be studied, and the study is profitable in relation to the present. I found much help in understanding the nineteenth century from studying the effect of liberal ideas in the period from 1814 to 1914.[9] The two types of liberalism, the rational and the romantic, represented by Bentham and Rousseau respectively, have continued, ever since, their relations of alternate alliance and conflict.

The relation of philosophy to social conditions has usually been ignored by professional philosophers. Marxists are interested in philosophy as an *effect,* but do not recognize it as a *cause.* Yet plainly every important philosophy is both. Plato is in part an effect of the victory of Sparta in the Peloponnesian war, and is also in part among the causes of Christian theology. To treat him only in the former aspect is to make the growth of the medieval church inexplicable. I am at present writing a history of western philosophy from Thales to the present day, in which every important system is treated equally as an effect and as a cause of social conditions.

My intellectual journeys have been, in some respects, disappointing. When I was young I hoped to find religious satisfaction in philosophy; even after I had abandoned Hegel, the eternal Platonic world gave me something non-human to admire. I thought of mathematics with reverence, and suffered when Wittgenstein led me to regard it as nothing but tautologies. I have always ardently desired to find some justification for the emotions

---

9. See Russell's book, *Freedom and Organization, 1814–1914* (1934).

inspired by certain things that seemed to stand outside human life and to deserve feelings of awe. I am thinking in part of very obvious things, such as the starry heavens and a stormy sea on a rocky coast; in part of the vastness of the scientific universe, both in space and time, as compared to the life of mankind; in part of the edifice of impersonal truth, especially truth which, like that of mathematics, does not merely describe the world that happens to exist. Those who attempt to make a religion of humanism, which recognizes nothing greater than man, do not satisfy my emotions. And yet I am unable to believe that, in the world as known, there is anything that I can value outside human beings, and, to a much lesser extent, animals. Not the starry heavens, but their effects on human percipients, have excellence; to admire the universe for its size is slavish and absurd; impersonal non-human truth appears to be a delusion. And so my intellect goes with the humanists, though my emotions violently rebel. In this respect, the 'consolations of philosophy' are not for me.

In more purely intellectual ways, on the contrary, I have found as much satisfaction in philosophy as any one could reasonably have expected. Many matters which, when I was young, baffled me by the vagueness of all that had been said about them, are now amenable to an exact technique, which makes possible the kind of progress that is customary in science. Where definite knowledge is unattainable, it is sometimes possible to prove that it is unattainable, and it is usually possible to formulate a variety of exact hypotheses, all compatible with the existing evidence. Those philosophers who have adopted the methods derived from logical analysis can argue with each other, not in the old aimless way, but co-operatively, so that both sides can concur as to the outcome. All this is new during my lifetime; the pioneer was Frege, but he remained solitary until his old age. This extension of the sphere of reason to new provinces is something that I value very highly. Philosophic rationality may be choked in the shocks of war and the welter of new persecuting superstitions, but one may hope that it will not be lost utterly or for more than a few centuries. In this respect, my philosophic life has been a happy one.

*Bertrand Russell*

BRYN MAWR, PENNSYLVANIA
JULY, 1943

ALBERT EINSTEIN (1879–1955) is best known for being the creator of the Special and General Theories of Relativity, which revolutionized our view of the Universe, yet he made numerous other important contributions to science, most notably the discovery of the photon and the proof from Brownian motion that molecules exist. In philosophy and in physics, Einstein was greatly influenced by Hume and Mach, though he rejected Mach's view that scientific laws essentially summarize experimental results, and came to see the basic postulates of all laws as free creations of the human mind. Einstein's view of the Universe was fully deterministic, and he therefore rejected the way in which quantum theory was being taken by Niels Bohr. Subsequent developments in physics have vindicated Bohr and disappointed Einstein's expectations.

# Albert
# EINSTEIN

## " *All concepts are freely chosen posits.* "

HERE I SIT IN ORDER TO WRITE, AT THE age of sixty-seven, something like my own obituary. I am doing this not merely because Dr. Schilpp has persuaded me to do it, but because I do, in fact, believe that it is a good thing to show those who are striving alongside of us how our own striving and searching appears in retrospect. After some reflection, I came to feel how imperfect any such attempt is bound to be. For, however brief and limited one's working life may be, and however predominant may be the way of error, the exposition of that which is worthy of communication does nonetheless not come easy—today's person of sixty-seven is by no means the same as was the one of fifty, of thirty, or of twenty. Every reminiscence is colored by one's present state, hence by a deceptive point of view. This consideration could easily deter one.

Nevertheless much can be gathered out of one's own experience that is not open to another consciousness.

When I was a fairly precocious young man I became thoroughly impressed with the futility of the hopes and strivings that chase most men restlessly through life. Moreover, I soon discovered the cruelty of that chase, which in those years was much more carefully covered up by hypocrisy and glittering words than is the case today. By the mere existence of his stomach everyone was condemned to participate in that chase. The stomach might well be satisfied by such participation, but not man insofar as he is a thinking and feeling being. As the first way out there was religion, which is implanted into every child by way of the traditional education-machine. Thus I came—though the child of entirely irreligious (Jewish) parents—to a deep religiousness, which, however, reached an abrupt end at the age of twelve. Through the reading of popular scientific books I soon reached the conviction that much in the stories of the Bible could not be true. The consequence was an orgy of fanatical freethinking coupled with the impression that youth is intentionally being deceived by the state through lies; it was a crushing impression. Mistrust of every kind of authority grew out of this experience, a skeptical attitude toward the convictions that were alive in any specific social environment—an attitude that has never again left me, even though, later on, it has been tempered by a better insight into the causal connections.

It is quite clear to me that the religious paradise of youth, which was thus lost, was a first attempt to free myself from the chains of the merely personal, from an existence dominated by wishes, hopes, and primitive feelings. Out yonder there was this huge world, which exists independently of us human beings and which stands before us like a great, eternal riddle, at least partially accessible to our inspection and thinking. The contemplation of this world beckoned as a liberation, and I soon noticed that many a man whom I had learned to esteem and to admire had found inner freedom and security in its pursuit. The mental grasp of this extra-personal world within the frame of our capabilities presented itself to my mind, half consciously, half unconsciously, as a supreme goal. Similarly motivated men of the present and of the past, as well as the insights they had achieved, were the friends who could not be lost. The road to this paradise was not as comfortable and alluring as the road to the religious paradise; but it has shown itself reliable, and I have never regretted having chosen it.

What I have said here is true only in a certain sense, just as a drawing consisting of a few strokes can do justice to a complicated object, full of perplexing details, only in a very limited sense. If an individual enjoys well-ordered thoughts, it is quite possible that this side of his nature may grow more pronounced at the cost of other sides and thus may determine his mentality in increasing degree. In this case it may well be that such an individual sees in retrospect a uniformly systematic development, whereas the actual experience takes place in kaleidoscopic particular situations. The great variety of the external situations and the narrowness of the momentary content of consciousness bring about a sort of atomizing of the life of every human being. In a man of my type, the turning point of the development lies in the fact that gradually the major interest disengages itself to a far-reaching degree from the momentary and the merely personal and turns toward the striving for a conceptual grasp of things. Looked at from this point of view, the above schematic remarks contain as much truth as can be stated with such brevity.

# Thinking and Wondering

What, precisely, is 'thinking'? When, on the reception of sense impressions, memory pictures emerge, this is not yet thinking. And when such pictures form sequences, each member of which calls forth another, this too is not yet 'thinking'. When, however, a certain picture turns up in many such sequences, then—precisely by such return—it becomes an organizing element for such sequences, in that it connects sequences in themselves unrelated to each other. Such an element becomes a tool, a *concept*. I think that the transition from free association or 'dreaming' to thinking is characterized by the more or less pre-eminent role played by the concept. It is by no means necessary that a concept be tied to a sensorily cognizable and reproducible sign (word); but when this is the case, then thinking becomes thereby capable of being communicated.

With what right—the reader will ask—does this man operate so carelessly and primitively with ideas in such a problematic realm without making even the least effort to prove anything? My defense: all our thinking is of this nature of free play with concepts; the justification for this play lies in the degree of comprehension of our sensations that we are able to achieve with its aid. The concept of truth cannot yet be applied to such a structure; to my thinking this concept becomes applicable only when a far-reaching agreement or convention concerning the elements and rules of the game is already at hand.

I have no doubt but that our thinking goes on for the most part without the use of signs (words) and beyond that to a considerable degree unconsciously. For how, otherwise, should it happen that sometimes we 'wonder' quite spontaneously about some experience? This 'wondering' appears to occur when an experience comes into conflict with a world of concepts already sufficiently fixed within us. Whenever such a conflict is experienced sharply and intensively it reacts back upon our world of thought in a decisive way. The development of this world of thought is in a certain sense a continuous flight from 'wonder'.

A wonder of this kind I experienced as a child of four or five years when my father showed me a compass. That this needle behaved in such a determined way did not at all fit into the kind of occurrences that could find a place in the unconscious world of concepts (efficacy produced by direct 'touch'). I can still remember—or at least believe I can remember—that this experience made a deep and lasting impression upon me. Something deeply hidden had to be behind things. What man sees before him from infancy causes no reaction of this kind; he is not surprised by the falling of bodies, by wind and rain, nor by the moon, nor by the fact that the moon does not fall down, nor by the differences between living and nonliving matter.

At the age of twelve I experienced a second wonder of a totally different nature—in a little book dealing with Euclidean plane geometry, which came into my hands at the beginning of a school year. Here were assertions, as for example the intersection of the three altitudes of a triangle at one point, that—though by no means evident—could nevertheless be proved with such certainty that any doubt appeared to be out of the question. This lucidity and certainty made an indescribable impression upon me. That the axioms had to be accepted unproved did not disturb me. In any case it was quite sufficient for me if I could base proofs on propositions whose validity appeared to me beyond doubt. For example, I remember that an uncle told me about the Pythagorean theorem before the holy geometry booklet had come into my hands. After much effort I succeeded in proving this theorem on the basis of the similarity of triangles; in doing so it seemed to me evident that the relations of the sides of the right-angled triangles would have to be completely determined by one of the acute angles. Only whatever did not in similar fashion seem to be 'evident' appeared to me to be in need of any proof at all. Also, the objects with which geometry is concerned seemed to be of no different type from the objects of sensory perception, 'which can be seen and touched'. This primitive conception, which probably also lies at the bottom of the well-known Kantian inquiry concerning the possibility of 'synthetic judgments *a priori*', obviously rests upon the fact that the relation of geometrical concepts to objects of direct experience (rigid rod, finite interval, etc.) was unconsciously present.

# My Epistemological Credo

If it thus appeared that it was possible to achieve certain knowledge of the objects of experience by means of pure thinking, this wonder rested upon an error. Nevertheless, for anyone who experiences it for the first time, it is marvellous enough that man is capable at all of reaching such a degree of certainty and purity in pure thinking as the Greeks showed us for the first time to be possible in geometry.

Now that I have allowed myself to be carried away sufficiently to interrupt my barely started obituary, I shall not hesitate to state here in a few sentences my epistemological credo, although in what precedes something has already incidentally been said about this. This credo actually evolved only much later and very slowly and does not correspond to the point of view I held in younger years.

I see on the one side the totality of sense experiences and, on the other, the totality of the concepts and propositions that are laid down in books. The relations between the concepts and propositions among themselves are of a logical nature, and the business of logical thinking is strictly limited to the achievement of the connection between concepts and propositions among themselves according to firmly laid down rules, which are the concern of logic. The concepts and propositions get 'meaning', or 'content', only through their connection with sense experiences. The connection of the latter with the former is purely intuitive, not itself of a logical nature. The degree of certainty with which this connection, or intuitive linkage, can be undertaken, and nothing else, differentiates empty fantasy from scientific 'truth'. The system of concepts is a creation of man, together with the rules of syntax, which constitute the structure of the conceptual systems. Although the conceptual systems are logically entirely arbitrary, they are restricted by the aim of permitting the most nearly possible certain and complete co-ordination with the totality of sense experiences; secondly they aim at the greatest possible sparsity of their logically independent elements (basic concepts and axioms), i.e., their undefined concepts and underived, postulated propositions.

A proposition is correct if, within a logical system, it is deduced according to the accepted logical rules. A system has truth-content according to the certainty and completeness of its possibility of co-ordination with the totality of experience. A correct proposition borrows its 'truth' from the truth-content of the system to which it belongs.

A remark as to the historical development. Hume saw clearly that certain concepts, as for example that of causality, cannot be deduced from the material of experience by logical methods. Kant, thoroughly convinced of the indispensability of certain concepts, took them—just as they are selected—to be the necessary premises of any kind of thinking and distinguished them from concepts of empirical origin. I am convinced, however, that this distinction is erroneous or, at any rate, that it does not do justice to the problem in a natural way. All concepts, even those closest to experience, are from the point of view of logic freely chosen posits, just as is the concept of causality, which was the point of departure for this inquiry in the first place.

# My Early Education

And now back to the obituary. At the age of twelve through sixteen I familiarized myself with the elements of mathematics, including the principles of differential and integral calculus. In doing so I had the good fortune of encountering books that were not too particular regarding logical rigor, but that permitted the principal ideas to stand out clearly. This occupation was, on the whole, truly fascinating; there were peaks whose impression could easily compete with that of elementary geometry—the basic idea of analytical geometry, the infinite series, the concepts of derivative and integral. I also had the good fortune of getting to know the essential results and methods of the entire field of the natural sciences in an excellent popular exposition, which limited itself almost throughout to qualitative aspects (Bernstein's *Popular Books on Natural Science,* a work of five or six volumes), a work that I read with breathless attention. I had also already studied some theoretical physics when, at the age of seventeen, I entered the Polytechnic Institute of Zürich as a student of mathematics and physics.

There I had excellent teachers (for example, Hurwitz and Minkowski), so that I should have been able to obtain a mathematical training in depth. I worked most of the time in the physical laboratory, however, fascinated by the direct contact with experience. The balance of the time I used, in the main, in order to study at home the works of Kirchhoff, Helmholtz, Hertz, and so forth. The fact that I neglected mathematics to a certain extent had its cause not merely in my stronger interest in the natural sciences than in mathematics but also in the following peculiar experience. I saw that mathematics was split up into numerous specialties, each of which could easily absorb the short lifetime granted to us. Consequently, I saw myself in the position of Buridan's ass, which was unable to decide upon any particular bundle of hay. Presumably this was because my intuition was not strong enough in the field of mathematics to differentiate clearly the fundamentally important, that which is really basic, from the rest of the more or less dispensable erudition. Also, my interest in the study of nature was no doubt stronger; and it was not clear to me as a young student that access to a more profound knowledge of the basic principles of physics depends on the most intricate mathematical methods. This dawned upon me only gradually after years of independent scientific work.

True enough, physics also was divided into separate fields, each of which was capable of devouring a short lifetime of work without having satisfied the hunger for deeper knowledge. The mass of insufficiently connected experimental data was overwhelming here also. In this field, however, I soon learned to sniff out that which might lead to fundamentals and to turn aside from everything else, from the multitude of things that clutter up the mind and divert it from the essentials. The hitch in this was, of course, that one had to cram all this stuff into one's mind for the examinations, whether one liked it or not. This coercion had such a discouraging effect upon me that, after I had passed the final examination, I found the consideration of any scientific problems distasteful to me for an entire year. Yet I must say that in Switzerland we had to suffer far less under such coercion, which smothers every truly scientific impulse, than is the case in many another locality. There were altogether only two examinations; aside from these, one could just about do as one pleased. This was especially the case if one had a friend, as did I, who attended the lectures regularly and who worked over their content conscientiously. This gave one freedom in the choice of pursuits until a few months before the examination, a freedom I enjoyed to a great extent, and I have gladly taken into the bargain the resulting guilty conscience as by far the lesser evil. It is, in fact, nothing short of a miracle that the modern methods of instruction have not yet entirely strangled the holy curiosity of inquiry; for this delicate little plant, aside from stimulation, stands mainly in need of freedom; without this it goes to wrack and ruin without fail. It is a very grave mistake to think that the enjoyment of seeing and searching can be promoted by means of coercion and a sense of duty. To the contrary, I believe that it would be possible to rob even a healthy beast of prey of its voraciousness if it were possible, with the aid of a whip, to force the beast to take food continuously even when not hungry, especially if the food handed out under such coercion were to be selected accordingly.

# Physics as I Found It

Now to the field of physics as it presented itself at that time. In spite of great productivity in particulars, dogmatic rigidity prevailed in matters of principle: in the beginning (if there was such a thing), God created Newton's laws of motion together with the necessary masses and forces. This is all; everything beyond this follows from the development of appropriate mathematical methods by means of deduction. What the nineteenth century achieved on the strength of this, especially through the application of partial differential equations, was bound to arouse the admiration of every receptive person. Newton was probably the first to reveal, in his theory of the propagation of sound, the efficacy of partial differential equations. Euler had already created the foundation of hydrodynamics. But the more sophisticated development of the mechanics of discrete masses, as the basis of all physics, was the achievement of the nineteenth century. What made the greatest impression upon the student, however, was not so much the technical development of mechanics or the solution of complicated problems, as the achievements of mechanics in areas that apparently had nothing to do with mechanics: the mechanical theory of light, which conceived of light as the wave motion of a quasi-rigid elastic ether; and above all the kinetic theory of gases: the independence of the specific heat of monatomic gases from the atomic weight, the derivation of the equation of the state of a gas and its relation to the specific heat, the kinetic theory of the dissociation of gases, and above all the quantitative relationship between viscosity, heat conduction, and diffusion of gases, which also furnished the absolute magnitude of the atom. At the same time these results supported mechanics as the foundation of physics and of the atomic hypothesis, which latter was already firmly rooted in chemistry. In chemistry, however, only the ratios of the atomic masses played any role, not their absolute magnitudes, so that atomic theory could be viewed more as a visualizing symbol than as knowledge concerning the actual composition of matter. Apart from this it was also of profound interest that the statistical theory of classical mechanics was able to deduce the basic laws of thermodynamics, something in essence already accomplished by Boltzmann.

We must not be surprised, therefore, that, so to speak, all physicists of the previous century saw in classical mechanics a firm and definitive foundation for all physics, indeed for the whole of natural science, and that they never grew tired in their attempts to base Maxwell's theory of electromagnetism, which, in the meantime, was slowly beginning to win out, upon mechanics as well. Even Maxwell and H. Hertz, who in retrospect are properly recognized as those who shook the faith in mechanics as the final basis of all physical thinking, in their conscious thinking consistently held fast to mechanics as the confirmed foundation of physics. It was Ernst Mach who, in his *History of Mechanics,* upset this dogmatic faith; this book exercised a profound influence upon me in this regard while I was a student. I see Mach's greatness in his incorruptible skepticism and independence; in my younger years, however, Mach's epistemological position also influenced me very greatly, a position that today appears to me to be essentially untenable. For he did not place in the correct light the essentially constructive and speculative nature of all thinking and more especially of scientific thinking; in consequence, he condemned theory precisely at those points where its constructive-speculative character comes to light unmistakably, such as in the kinetic theory of atoms.

Before I enter upon a critique of mechanics as the foundation of physics, something general will have to be said first about the points of view from which physical theories may be analyzed critically at all. The first point of view is obvious: the theory must not contradict empirical facts. However evident this demand may in the first place appear, its application turns out to be quite delicate. For it is often, perhaps even always, possible to retain a general theoretical foundation by adapting it to the facts by means of artificial additional assumptions. In any case, however, this first point of view is concerned with the confirmation of the theoretical foundation by the available empirical facts.

The second point of view is not concerned with the relationship to the observations but with the premises of the theory itself, with what may briefly but vaguely be characterized as the naturalness or logical simplicity of the premises (the basic concepts and the relations between these). This point of view, whose exact formulation meets with great difficulties, has played an important role in the selection and evaluation of theories from time immemorial. The problem here is not simply one of a kind of enumeration of the logically independent premises (if anything like this were at all possible without ambiguity), but one of a kind of reciprocal weighing of incommensurable qualities. Furthermore, among theories with equally 'simple' foundations, that one is to be taken as superior which most sharply delimits the otherwise feasible qualities of systems (i.e., contains the most specific claims). Of the 'scope' of theories I need not speak here, inasmuch as we are confining ourselves to such theories as have for their object the *totality* of all physical phenomena. The second point of view may briefly be characterized as concerned with the 'inner perfection' of the theory, whereas the first point of view refers to the 'external confirmation'. The following I reckon as also belonging to the inner perfection of a theory: We prize a theory more highly if, from the logical standpoint, it does not involve an arbitrary choice among theories that are equivalent and possess analogous structures.

I shall not attempt to excuse the lack of precision of the assertions contained in the last two paragraphs on the grounds of insufficient space at my disposal; I must confess herewith that I cannot at this point, and perhaps not at all, replace these hints by more precise definitions. I believe, however, that a sharper formulation would be possible. In any case it turns out that among the oracles there usually is agreement in judging the 'inner perfection' of the theories and even more so concerning the degree of 'external confirmation'.

And now to the critique of mechanics as the basis of physics.

# The Attempt to Base All Physics on Mechanics

From the first point of view (confirmation by experiment) the incorporation of wave optics into the mechanical picture of the world was bound to arouse serious misgivings. If light was to be interpreted as undulatory motion in an elastic body (ether), this had to be a medium that permeates everything, because of the transversality of the light waves, in the main resembling a solid body, yet incompressible, so that longitudinal waves did not exist. This ether had to lead a ghostly existence alongside the rest of matter, inasmuch as it seemed to offer no resistance whatever to the motion of 'ponderable' bodies. In order to explain the indices of refraction of transparent bodies as well as the processes of emission and absorption of radiation, one would have had to assume complicated interactions between the two types of matter, something that was not even seriously tried, let alone achieved.

Furthermore, the electromagnetic forces necessitated the introduction of electric masses that, although they had no noticeable inertia, yet interacted with each other and whose interaction was, moreover, in contrast to the force of gravitation, of a polar type.

What eventually made the physicists, after hesitating a long time, abandon their faith in the possibility that all physics could be founded upon Newton's mechanics, was the electrodynamics of Faraday and Maxwell. For this theory and its confirmation by Hertz's experiments showed that there are electromagnetic phenomena that by their very nature are detached from all ponderable matter—namely the waves in empty space that consist of electromagnetic 'fields'. If mechanics was to be maintained as the foundation of physics, Maxwell's equations had to be interpreted mechanically. This was zealously but fruitlessly attempted, whereas the equations themselves turned out to be increasingly fruitful. One got used to operating with these fields as independent substances without finding it necessary to account for their mechanical nature; thus mechanics as the basis of physics was being abandoned, almost imperceptibly, because its adaptation to the facts presented itself finally as a hopeless task. Since then, there exist two types of conceptual elements: on the one hand, material points with forces at a distance between them and, on the other hand, the continuous field. We are at an intermediate state of physics without a uniform basis for the whole, a state that—although unsatisfactory—is far from having been overcome.

# Newton and Absolute Space

Now for a few remarks concerning the critique of mechanics as the foundation of physics from the second, the interior, point of view. In today's state of science, after the abandonment of the mechanical foundation, such a critique retains only a methodological relevance. But such a critique is well suited to show the type of argumentation that, in the selection of theories in the future, will have to play an ever greater role the more the basic concepts and axioms are removed from what is directly observable, so that the confrontation of the implications of theory by the facts becomes constantly more difficult and more drawn out. First in line to be mentioned is Mach's argument, which, incidentally, had already been clearly recognized by Newton (the bucket experiment). From the standpoint of purely geometrical description, all rigid co-ordinate systems are logically equivalent. The equations of mechanics (for example the law of inertia) claim validity only when referred to a specific class of such systems, that is, the 'inertial systems'. In this connection the co-ordinate system as a material object is without any significance. Hence to justify the need for this specific choice one must search for something that exists beyond the objects (masses, distances) with which the theory deals. For this reason, absolute space as originally determinative was quite explicitly introduced by Newton as the omnipresent active participant in all mechanical events; by 'absolute' he obviously means: uninfluenced by the masses and by their motion. What makes this state of affairs appear particularly ugly is the fact that there are supposed to be infinitely many inertial systems, relative to each other in uniform and irrotational translation, which are supposed to be distinguished among all other rigid systems.

Mach conjectures that in a truly reasonable theory inertia would have to depend upon the interaction of the masses, precisely as was true for Newton's other forces, a conception that for a long time I considered in principle the correct one. It presupposes implicitly, however, that the basic theory should be of the general type of Newton's mechanics: masses and their interaction as the original concepts. Such an attempt at a resolution does not fit into a consistent field theory, as will be immediately recognized.

How essentially sound Mach's critique is, however, can be seen particularly clearly from the following analogy. Let us imagine people who construct a mechanics, who know only a very small part of the Earth's surface and who also cannot see any stars. They will be inclined to ascribe special physical attributes to the vertical dimension of space (direction of the acceleration of falling bodies) and, on the ground of such a conceptual basis, will offer reasons that the Earth is in most places horizontal. They might not let themselves be influenced by the argument that in its geometrical properties space is isotropic and that it is therefore unsatisfactory to postulate basic physical laws according to which there is to be a preferential direction; they will probably be inclined (analogously to Newton) to assert the absoluteness of the vertical, as proved by experience, as something with which one simply would have to come to terms. The preference given to the vertical over all other spatial directions is precisely analogous to the preference given to inertial systems over other rigid co-ordinate systems.

# Action at a Distance

Now to consider other arguments that also concern themselves with the inner simplicity, or naturalness, of mechanics. If one accepts the concepts of space (including geometry) and time without critical doubts, then there exists no reason to object to the idea of action at a distance, even though such a concept is unsuited to the ideas one forms on the basis of the raw experience of daily life. However, there is another consideration that makes mechanics, taken as the basis of physics, appear primitive. Essentially there are two laws:

(1) the law of motion

(2) the expression for the force or the potential energy.

The law of motion is precise, although empty as long as the expression for the forces is not given. For postulating the latter, however, there is an enormous degree of arbitrariness, especially if one drops the requirement, which is not very natural in any case, that the forces depend only on the co-ordinates (and not, for example, on their derivatives with respect to time). Within the framework of that theory alone it is entirely arbitrary that the forces of gravitation (and electricity), which come from one point, are governed by the potential function $(1/r)$. Additional remark: it has long been known that this function is the spherically symmetric solution of the simplest (rotation-invariant) differential equation $\Delta^2 \phi = 0$; it would therefore not have been far-fetched to regard this as a clue that this function was to be considered as resulting from a spatial law, an approach that would have eliminated the arbitrariness in the force law. This is really the first insight that suggests a turning away from the theory of action at a distance, a development that—prepared by Faraday, Maxwell, and Hertz—really begins only later in response to the external pressure of experimental data.

I would also like to mention, as one internal asymmetry of this theory, that the inertial mass that occurs in the law of motion also appears in the law of the gravitational force, but not in the expressions for the other forces. Finally I would like to point to the fact that the division of energy into two essentially different parts, kinetic and potential energy, must be felt to be unnatural; H. Hertz felt this to be so disturbing that, in his very last work, he attempted to free mechanics from the concept of potential energy (that is, from the concept of force).

# Lorentz's Audacious Step

Enough of this. Newton, forgive me; you found just about the only way possible in your age for a man of the highest reasoning and creative power. The concepts that you created are even today still guiding our thinking in physics, although we now know that they will have to be replaced by others farther removed from the sphere of immediate experience, if we aim at a profounder understanding of relationships.

'Is this supposed to be an obituary?' the astonished reader will likely ask. I would like to reply: essentially, yes. For the essential in the being of a man of my type lies precisely in *what* he thinks and *how* he thinks, not in what he does or suffers. Consequently, the obituary can limit itself in the main to the communicating of thoughts that have played a considerable role in my endeavors. A theory is the more impressive the greater the simplicity of its premises, the more different kinds of things it relates, and the more extended its area of applicability. Hence the deep impression that classical thermodynamics made upon me. It is the only physical theory of universal content concerning which I am convinced that, within the framework of the applicability of its basic concepts, it will never be overthrown (for the special attention of those who are skeptics on principle).

The most fascinating subject at the time that I was a student was Maxwell's theory. What made this theory appear revolutionary was the transition from action at a distance to fields as the fundamental variables. The incorporation of optics into the theory of electromagnetism, with its relation of the speed of light to the electric and magnetic absolute system of units as well as the relation of the index of refraction to the dielectric constant, the qualitative relation between the reflection coefficient of a body and its metallic conductivity—it was like a revelation. Aside from the transition to field theory, i.e., the expression of the elementary laws through differential equations, Maxwell needed only one single hypothetical step—the introduction of the electrical displacement current in the vacuum and in the dielectrica and its magnetic effect, an innovation that was almost preordained by the formal properties of the differential equations. In this connection I cannot suppress the remark that the pair Faraday-Maxwell has a most remarkable inner similarity with the pair Galileo-Newton—the former of each pair grasping the relations intuitively, and the second one formulating those relations exactly and applying them quantitatively.

What rendered the insight into the essence of electromagnetic theory so much more difficult at that time was the following peculiar situation. Electric or magnetic 'field intensities' and 'displacements' were treated as equally elementary variables, empty space as a special instance of a dielectric body. *Matter* appeared as the bearer of the field, not *space*. By this it was implied that the carrier of the field should have velocity, and this was naturally to apply to the 'vacuum' (ether) also. Hertz's electrodynamics of moving bodies rests entirely upon this fundamental attitude.

It was the great merit of H.A. Lorentz that he brought about a change here in a convincing fashion. In principle a field exists, according to him, only in empty space. Matter—considered to consist of atoms—is the only seat of electric charges; between the material particles there is empty space, the seat of the electromagnetic field, which is produced by the position and velocity of the point charges located on the material particles. Dielectric behavior, conductivity, and so on, are determined exclusively by the type of mechanical bindings between the particles that constitute the bodies. The particle charges create the field, which, on the other hand, exerts forces upon the charges of the particles, thus determining the motion of the latter according to Newton's law of motion. If one compares this with Newton's system, the change consists in this: action at a distance is replaced by the field, which also describes the radiation. Gravitation is usually not taken into account because of its relative smallness; its inclusion, however, was always possible by enriching the structure of the field, that is to say, by expanding Maxwell's field laws. The physicist of the present generation regards the point of view achieved by Lorentz as the only possible one; at that time, however, it was a surprising and audacious step, without which the later development would not have been possible.

If one views this phase of the development of theory critically, one is struck by the dualism that lies in the fact that the material point in Newton's sense and the field as continuum are used as elementary concepts side by side. Kinetic energy and field energy appear as essentially different things. This appears all the more unsatisfactory as, according to Maxwell's theory, the magnetic field of a moving electric charge represents inertia. Why not then the *whole* of inertia? Then only field energy would be left, and the particle would be merely a domain containing an especially high density of field energy. In that case one could hope to deduce the concept of the mass point together with the equations of motion of the particles from the field equations—the disturbing dualism would have been removed.

H.A. Lorentz knew this very well. However, Maxwell's equations did not permit the derivation of the equilibrium of the electricity that constitutes a particle. Only different, nonlinear field equations could possibly accomplish such a thing. But no method existed for discovering such field equations without deteriorating into adventurous arbitrariness. In any case, one could believe that it would be possible by and by to find a new and secure foundation for all of physics upon the path so successfully initiated by Faraday and Maxwell.

# The Discovery of Quanta

Accordingly, the revolution begun by the introduction of the field was by no means finished. Then it happened that, around the turn of the century, independently of what we have just been discussing, a second fundamental crisis set in, the seriousness of which was suddenly recognized owing to Max Planck's investigations into heat radiation (1900). The history of this event is all the more remarkable because, at least in its first phase, it was not in any way influenced by any surprising discoveries of an experimental nature.

On thermodynamic grounds Kirchhoff had concluded that the energy density and the spectral composition of radiation in a cavity enclosed by impervious walls of the temperature $T$ must be independent of the nature of the walls. That is to say, the monochromatic density of radiation $\rho$ is a universal function of the frequency $v$ and of the absolute temperature $T$. Thus arose the interesting problem of determing this function $\rho(v,T)$. What could theoretically be ascertained about this function? According to Maxwell's theory the radiation had to exert a pressure on the walls, determined by the total energy density. From this Boltzmann concluded, by means of pure thermodynamics, that the entire energy density of the radiation $(\int \rho dv)$ is proportional to $T^4$. In this way he found a theoretical justification of a law that had previously been discovered empirically by Stefan—he connected this empirical law with the basis of Maxwell's theory. Thereafter, by way of an ingenious thermodynamic consideration, which also made use of Maxwell's theory, W. Wien found that the universal function p of the two variables V and T would have to be of the form

$$\rho \approx v^3 f\left(\tfrac{v}{T}\right),$$

whereby $f(v/T)$ is a universal function of the one variable $v/T$. It was clear that the theoretical determination of this universal function $f$ was of fundamental importance—this was precisely the task that confronted Planck. Careful measurements had led to a rather precise empirical determination of the function $f$. Relying on those empirical measurements, he succeeded in the first place in finding a statement that rendered the measurements very well indeed:

$$\rho = \frac{8\pi h v^3}{c^3} \frac{1}{exp(hv/kT) - 1}$$

whereby $h$ and $k$ are two universal constants, the first of which led to quantum theory. Because of the denominator; this formula looks a bit queer. Was it possible to derive it theoretically? Planck actually did find a derivation, the imperfections of which remained at first hidden, which latter fact was most fortunate for the development of physics. If this formula was correct, it permitted, with the aid of Maxwell's theory, the calculation of the average energy $E$ of a quasi-monochromatic oscillator within the field of radiation:

$$E = \frac{h\nu}{exp\,(h\nu/kT) - 1}$$

Planck preferred to attempt calculating this latter magnitude theoretically. In this effort, thermodynamics, for the time being, no longer proved helpful, and neither did Maxwell's theory. This expression had one aspect that was most encouraging. For high temperatures (with $\nu$ fixed) it yielded the expression

$$E = kT$$

This is the same expression obtained in the kinetic theory of gases for the average energy of a mass point capable of oscillating elastically in one dimension. For in kinetic gas theory one gets

$$E = (R/N)T,$$

where $R$ denotes the gas constant, and $N$ the number of molecules per mole, from which constant one can compute the absolute size of the atom. Equating these two expressions one gets

$$N = R/k.$$

The one constant of Planck's formula consequently furnishes exactly the correct size of the atom. The numerical value agreed satisfactorily with the determinations of $N$ by means of kinetic gas theory, though the latter were not very accurate.

This was a great success, which Planck clearly recognized. But the matter has a serious drawback, which Planck fortunately overlooked at first. For the same considerations demand in fact that the relation $E = kT$ would also have to be valid for low temperatures. In that case, however; it would be all over with Planck's formula and with the constant $h$. From the existing theory, therefore, the correct conclusion would have been: the average kinetic energy of the oscillator is either given incorrectly by the theory of gases, which would imply a refutation of [statistical] mechanics; or else the average energy of the oscillator follows incorrectly from Maxwell's theory, which would imply a refutation of the latter. Under such circumstances it is most probable that both theories are correct only in the limit, but are otherwise false; this is indeed the situation, as we shall see in what follows. If Planck had drawn this conclusion, he probably would not have made his great discovery, because pure deductive reasoning would have been left without a foundation.

Now back to Planck's reasoning. On the basis of the kinetic theory of gases Boltzmann had discovered that, aside from a constant factor, entropy was equal to the logarithm of the 'probability' of the state under consideration. Through this insight he recognized the nature of processes that, within the meaning of thermodynamics, are 'irreversible'. Seen from the molecular-mechanical point of view, however, all processes are reversible. If one calls a state defined in terms of the molecular theory a microscopically described one, or; more briefly, a micro-state, and a state described in terms of thermodynamics a macro-state, then an immensely large number $(Z)$ of states belong to a macroscopic condition. $Z$ then is a measure of the probability of a chosen macro-state. This idea appears to be of outstanding importance also because its applicability is not limited to a microscopic description on the basis of mechanics. Planck recognized this and applied Boltzmann's principle to a system consisting of very many resonators of the same frequency $v$. The macroscopic state is given by the total energy of the oscillation of all resonators, a micro-state by the fixation of the (instantaneous) energy of each individual resonator. In order to be able to express the number of micro-states belonging to a macro-state by means of a finite number, Planck divided the total energy into a large but finite number of identical energy elements $\xi$ and asked: in how many ways can these energy elements be divided among the resonators? The logarithm of this number; then, furnishes the entropy and thus (via thermodynamics) the temperature of the system. Planck got his radiation formula if he chose his energy elements $\xi$ to have the magnitude $\xi = hv$. The decisive element in this procedure is that the result depends on taking for $\xi$ a definite finite value, i.e., on not going to the limit $\xi = 0$. This form of reasoning does not make obvious the fact that it contradicts the mechanical and electrodynamic basis upon which the derivation otherwise depends. Actually, however, the derivation presupposes implicitly that energy can be absorbed and emitted by the individual resonator only in 'quanta' of magnitude $hv$, that is, that the energy of a mechanical structure capable of oscillations as well as the energy of radiation can be transferred only in such quanta—in contradiction to the laws of mechanics and electrodynamics. The contradiction with dynamics was here fundamental; whereas the contradiction with electrodynamics might be less fundamental. For the expression for the density of radiation energy, though *compatible* with Maxwell's equations, is not a necessary consequence of these equations. That this expression furnishes important mean values is shown by the fact that the Stefan-Boltzmann law and Wien's law, which are based on it, are in agreement with experience.

All of this was quite clear to me shortly after the publication of Planck's fundamental work; so that, without having a substitute for classical mechanics, I could nevertheless see to what kind of consequences this law of temperature radiation leads for the photoelectric effect and for other related phenomena of the transformation of radiation energy, as well as for the specific heat of (especially) solid bodies. All my attempts, however, to adapt the theoretical foundation of physics to this new type of knowledge failed completely. It was as if the ground had been pulled out from under one, with no firm foundation to be seen anywhere upon which one could have built. That this insecure and contradictory foundation was sufficient to enable a man of Bohr's unique instinct and sensitivity to discover the principal laws of the spectral lines and of the electron shells of the atoms, together with their significance for chemistry, appeared to me as a miracle—and appears to me a miracle even today. This is the highest form of musicality in the sphere of thought.

# Brownian Motion and the Reality of Atoms

My own interest in those years was less concerned with the detailed consequences of Planck's results, however important these might be. My main question was: what general conclusions can be drawn from the radiation formula concerning the structure of radiation and even more generally concerning the electromagnetic foundation of physics? Before I take this up, I must briefly mention a number of investigations that relate to the Brownian motion and related objects (fluctuation phenomena) and that in essence rest upon classical molecular mechanics. Not acquainted with the investigations of Boltzmann and Gibbs, which had appeared earlier and actually exhausted the subject, I developed the statistical mechanics and the molecular-kinetic theory of thermodynamics based upon it. My principal aim in this was to find facts that would guarantee as much as possible the existence of atoms of definite finite size. In the midst of this I discovered that, according to atomic theory, there would have to be a movement of suspended microscopic particles capable of being observed, without knowing that observations concerning the Brownian motion were already long familiar. The simplest derivation rested upon the following consideration. If the molecular-kinetic theory is essentially correct, a suspension of visible particles must possess the same kind of osmotic pressure satisfying the gas laws as a solution of molecules. This osmotic pressure depends upon the actual magnitude of the molecules, that is, upon the number of molecules in a gram-equivalent. If the density of the suspension is not homogeneous, the osmotic pressure is inhomogeneous, too, and gives rise to a compensating diffusion, which can be calculated from the known mobility of the particles. This diffusion can, on the other hand, also be considered the result of the random displacement—originally of unknown magnitude—of the suspended particles owing to thermal agitation. By comparing the amounts obtained for the diffusion current from both types of reasoning, one obtains quantitatively the statistical law for those displacements, in other words the law of Brownian motion. The agreement of these considerations with experience together with Planck's determination of the true molecular size from the law of radiation (for high temperatures) convinced the skeptics, who were quite numerous at that time (Ostwald and Mach among them), of the reality of atoms. The hostility of these scholars toward atomic theory can undoubtedly be traced back to their positivistic philosophical attitude. This is an interesting example of the fact that even scholars of audacious spirit and fine instinct can be hindered in the interpretation of facts by philosophical prejudices. The prejudice—which has by no means disappeared—consists in the belief that facts by themselves can and should yield scientific knowledge without free conceptual construction. Such a misconception is possible only because one does not easily become aware of the free choice of such concepts, which, through success and long usage, appear to be immediately connected with the empirical material.

The success of the theory of Brownian motion again showed conclusively that classical mechanics always led to trustworthy results whenever it was applied to motions in which the higher time derivatives of the velocity are negligible. Upon this recognition a relatively direct method can be based that permits us to learn something concerning the constitution of radiation from Planck's formula. One may argue that in a space filled with radiation a freely moving (vertically to its plane), quasi-monochromatically reflecting mirror would have to go through a kind of Brownian movement, the mean kinetic energy of which equals *1/2 (R/N) T* (*R* = gas constant for one gram-molecule, *N* = the number of molecules per mole, *T* = absolute temperature). If radiation were not subject to local fluctuations, the mirror would gradually come to rest because, owing to its motion, it reflects more radiation on its front than on its reverse side. The mirror, however, must experience certain random fluctuations of the pressure exerted upon it because of the fact that the wave packets, constituting the radiation, interfere with one another. These can be computed from Maxwell's theory. This calculation, then, shows that these pressure variations (especially in the case of small radiation densities) are by no means sufficient to impart to the mirror the average kinetic energy *1/2 (R/N) T* In order to get this result one has to assume rather that there exists a second type of pressure variations, not derivable from Maxwell's theory, corresponding to the assumption that radiation energy consists of indivisible point-like localized quanta of energy *hv* [and of momentum *hv/c*; (*c* = velocity of light)], which are reflected undivided. This way of looking at the problem showed in a drastic and direct way that a type of immediate reality has to be ascribed to Planck's quanta, that radiation must, therefore, possess a kind of molecular structure as far as its energy is concerned, which of course contradicts Maxwell's theory. Considerations about radiation based directly on Boltzmann's entropy probability relation (probability taken to equal statistical temporal frequency) also lead to the same result. This dual nature of radiation (and of material corpuscles) is a major property of reality, which has been interpreted by quantum mechanics in an ingenious and amazingly successful fashion. This interpretation, which is looked upon as essentially definitive by almost all contemporary physicists, appears to me to be only a temporary expedient; I will make a few remarks on this point later.

# Rejecting Absolute Simultaneity

Reflections of this type made it clear to me as long ago as shortly after 1900, that is, shortly after Planck's trailblazing work, that neither mechanics nor electrodynamics could (except in limiting cases) claim exact validity. Gradually I despaired of the possibility of discovering the true laws by means of constructive efforts based on known facts. The longer and the more desperately I tried, the more I came to the conviction that only the discovery of a universal formal principle could lead us to assured results. The example I saw before me was thermodynamics. The general principle was there given in the theorem: the laws of nature are such that it is impossible to construct a perpetual motion machine, a *perpetuum mobile* (of the first and second kind). How, then, could such a universal principle be found? After I had reflected on this for ten years, I was able to find such a principle, which resulted from a paradox I had come across much earlier, at the age of sixteen: if I pursue a beam of light with the velocity $c$ (velocity of light in a vacuum), I should observe such a beam of light as an electromagnetic field at rest though spatially oscillating. There seems to be no such thing, however; neither on the basis of experience nor according to Maxwell's equations. From the very beginning it appeared to me intuitively clear that, judged from the standpoint of such an observer, everything would have to happen according to the same laws as for an observer who, relative to the Earth, was at rest. For how should the first observer know, or be able to determine, that he is in a state of fast uniform motion?

One sees that in this paradox the germ of the special relativity theory is already contained. Today everyone knows, of course, that all attempts to clarify this paradox satisfactorily were condemned to failure as long as the axiom of the absolute character of time, or of simultaneity, was rooted unrecognized in the unconscious. To recognize clearly this axiom and its arbitrary character already implies the essentials of the solution of the problem. The type of critical reasoning required for the discovery of this central point was decisively furthered, in my case, especially by the reading of David Hume's and Ernst Mach's philosophical writings.

One had to understand clearly what the spatial co-ordinates and the time fixation of an event signified in physics. The physical interpretation of the spatial co-ordinates presupposed a rigid body of reference, which, moreover; had to be in a more or less definite state of motion (inertial system). In a given inertial system the co-ordinates denoted the results of certain measurements with rigid (stationary) rods. (One should always be aware that the presupposition of the existence in principle of rigid rods is a presupposition suggested by approximate experience but is, in principle, arbitrary.) With such an interpretation of the spatial co-ordinates the question of the validity of Euclidean geometry becomes a problem of physics.

If, then, one tries to interpret the time of an event analogously, one needs a means for the measurement of the difference in time (a periodic process, internally determined, and realized by a system of sufficiently small spatial extension). A clock at rest relative to the system of inertia defines a local time. The local times of all space points taken together are the 'time', which belongs to the selected system of inertia, if a means is given to 'set' these clocks relative to each other. One sees that *a priori* it is not at all necessary that the 'times' thus defined in different inertial systems agree with one another. One would have noticed this long ago if, for the practical experience of everyday life, light did not present (because of the large value of $c$) the means for fixing an absolute simultaneity.

The presuppositions of the existence (in principle) of (ideal, or perfect) measuring rods and clocks are not independent of each other; a light signal that is reflected back and forth between the ends of a rigid rod constitutes an ideal clock, provided that the postulate of the constancy of the light velocity in vacuum does not lead to contradictions.

# The Insight of Special Relativity

The above paradox may then be formulated as follows. According to the rules of connection, used in classical physics, between the spatial co-ordinates and the time of events in the transition from one inertial system to another; the two assumptions of

(1) the constancy of the light velocity

(2) the independence of the laws (thus especially also of the law of the constancy of the light velocity) from the choice of inertial system (principle of special relativity)

are mutually incompatible (despite the fact that both taken separately are based on experience).

The fundamental insight of the special theory of relativity is this: assumptions (1) and (2) are compatible if relations of a new type ('Lorentz transformation') are postulated for the conversion of co-ordinates and times of events. With the given physical interpretation of co-ordinates and time, this is by no means merely a conventional step but implies certain hypotheses concerning the actual behavior of moving measuring rods and clocks, which can be experimentally confirmed or disproved.

The universal principle of the special theory of relativity is contained in the postulate: the laws of physics are invariant with respect to Lorentz transformations (for the transition from one inertial system to any other arbitrarily chosen inertial system). This is a restricting principle for natural laws, comparable to the restricting principle of the nonexistence of the *perpetuum mobile* that underlies thermodynamics.

First a remark concerning the relation of the theory to 'four-dimensional space'. It is a widespread error that the special theory of relativity is supposed to have, to a certain extent, first discovered or; at any rate, newly introduced, the four-dimensionality of the physical continuum. This, of course, is not the case. Classical mechanics, too, is based on the four-dimensional continuum of space and time. But in the four-dimensional continuum of classical physics the subspaces with constant time value have an absolute reality, independent of the choice of the frame of reference. Because of this, the four-dimensional continuum breaks down naturally into a three-dimensional and a one-dimensional (time), so that the four-dimensional point of view does not force itself upon one as *necessary*. The special theory of relativity, on the other hand, creates a formal dependence between the way in which the space co-ordinates on the one hand, and the time co-ordinates on the other; must enter into the natural laws.

Minkowski's important contribution to the theory lies in the following: before Minkowski's investigation it was necessary to carry out a Lorentz transformation on a law in order to test its invariance under such transformations; but he succeeded in introducing a formalism so that the mathematical form of the law itself guarantees its invariance under Lorentz transformations. By creating a four-dimensional tensor calculus, he achieved the same thing for the four-dimensional space that the ordinary vector calculus achieves for the three spatial dimensions. He also showed that the Lorentz transformation (apart from a different algebraic sign due to the special character of time) is nothing but a rotation of the co-ordinate system in the four-dimensional space.

First, a critical remark concerning the theory as it is characterized above. It is striking that the theory (except for the four-dimensional space) introduces two kinds of physical things, i.e., (1) measuring rods and clocks, (2) all other things, for example the electromagnetic field, the material point, etc. This, in a certain sense, is inconsistent; strictly speaking, measuring rods and clocks should emerge as solutions of the basic equations (objects consisting of moving atomic configurations), not, as it were, as theoretically self- sufficient entities. The procedure justifies itself, however, because it was clear from the very beginning that the postulates of the theory are not strong enough to deduce from them equations for physical events sufficiently complete and sufficiently free from arbitrariness in order to base upon such a foundation a theory of measuring rods and clocks. If one did not wish to forego a physical interpretation of the co-ordinates in general (something that, in itself, would be possible), it was better to permit such inconsistency— with the obligation, however, of eliminating it at a later stage of the theory. But one must not legitimize the sin just described so as to imagine that distances are physical entities of a special type, intrinsically different from other physical variables ('reducing physics to geometry', etc.).

We shall now inquire into the definitive insights that physics owes to the special theory of relativity.

(1) There is no such thing as simultaneity of distant events; consequently, there is also no such thing as immediate action at a distance in the sense of Newtonian mechanics. Although the introduction of actions at a distance, which propagate at the speed of light, remains feasible according to this theory, it appears unnatural; for in such a theory there could be no reasonable expression for the principle of conservation of energy. It therefore appears unavoidable that physical reality must be described in terms of continuous functions in space. The material point, therefore, can hardly be retained as a basic concept of the theory.

(2) The principles of the conservation of linear momentum and of energy are fused into one single principle. The inert mass of an isolated system is identical with its energy, thus eliminating mass as an independent concept.

The speed of light $c$ is one of the quantities that occurs in physical equations as a 'universal constant'. If, however, one introduces as the unit of time, instead of the second, the time in which light travels 1 cm, $c$ no longer occurs in the equations. In this sense one could say that the constant $c$ is only an *apparent* universal constant.

It is obvious and generally accepted that one could eliminate two more universal constants from physics by introducing, instead of the gram and the centimeter; properly chosen 'natural' units (for example, mass and radius of the electron).

If one considers this done, then only 'dimensionless' constants could occur in the basic equations of physics. Concerning such, I would like to state a proposition that at present cannot be based upon anything more than upon a faith in the simplicity, in other words the intelligibility, of nature: there are no *arbitrary* constants of this kind; that is to say, nature is so constituted that it is possible logically to lay down such strongly determined laws that within these laws only rationally completely determined constants occur (not constants, therefore, whose numerical value could be changed without destroying the theory).

# Special Relativity and Beyond

The special theory of relativity owes its origin to Maxwell's equations of the electromagnetic field. Conversely, the latter can be grasped formally in satisfactory fashion only by way of the special theory of relativity. Maxwell's equations are the simplest Lorentz-invariant field equations that can be postulated for an antisymmetric tensor derived from a vector field. This in itself would be satisfactory, if we did not know from quantum phenomena that Maxwell's theory does not do justice to the energetic properties of radiation. But as to how Maxwell's theory would have to be modified in a natural fashion, for this even the special theory of relativity offers no adequate foothold. Also, to Mach's question, 'How does it come about that inertial systems are physically distinguished above all other coordinate systems?' this theory offers no answer.

That the special theory of relativity is merely the first step of a necessary development only became completely clear to me in my efforts to represent gravitation in the framework of this theory. In classical mechanics, interpreted in terms of the field, the potential of gravitation appears as a *scalar* field (the simplest theoretical possibility of a field with a single component). Such a scalar theory of the gravitational field can easily be made invariant under the group of Lorentz transformations. The following program appears natural, therefore: The total physical field consists of a scalar field (gravitation) and a vector field (electromagnetic field); later insights may eventually make necessary the introduction of still more complicated types of fields; but to begin with one did not need to bother about this.

The possibility of realization of this program was, however, in doubt from the very first, because the theory had to combine the following things:

(1)  From the general considerations of special relativity theory it was clear that the inertial mass of a physical system increases with the total energy (therefore, for example, with the kinetic energy).

(2)  From very accurate experiments (especially from the torsion balance experiments of Eötvös) it was empirically known with very high accuracy that the gravitational mass of a body is exactly equal to its inertial mass.

It followed from (1) and (2) that the *weight* of a system depends in a precisely known manner on its total energy. If the theory did not accomplish this or could not do it naturally, it was to be rejected. The condition is most naturally expressed as follows: the acceleration of a system falling freely in a given gravitational field is independent of the nature of the falling system (especially therefore also of its energy content).

It turned out that, within the framework of the program sketched, this simple state of affairs could not at all, or at any rate not in any natural fashion, be represented in a satisfactory way. This convinced me that within the structure of the special theory of relativity there is no niche for a satisfactory theory of gravitation.

Now it came to me: the fact of the equality of inertial and gravitational mass, that is, the fact of the independence of the gravitational acceleration from the nature of the falling substance, may be expressed as follows: in a gravitational field (of small spatial extension) things behave as they do in a space free of gravitation, if one introduces into it, in place of an 'inertial system', a frame of reference accelerated relative to the former.

If one then interprets the behavior of a body with respect to the latter frame of reference as caused by a 'real' (not merely apparent) gravitational field, it is possible to regard this frame as an 'inertial system' with as much justification as the original reference system.

So, if one considers pervasive gravitational fields, not *a priori* restricted by spatial boundary conditions, physically possible, then the concept of 'inertial system' becomes completely empty. The concept of 'acceleration relative to space' then loses all meaning and with it the principle of inertia along with the paradox of Mach.

# How I Arrived at General Relativity

The fact of the equality of inertial and gravitational mass thus leads quite naturally to the recognition that the basic postulate of the special theory of relativity (invariance of the laws under Lorentz transformations) is too narrow, or in other words that an invariance of the laws must be postulated also relative to *nonlinear* transformations of the co-ordinates in the four-dimensional continuum.

This happened in 1908. Why were another seven years required for the construction of the general theory of relativity? The main reason lies in the fact that it is not so easy to free oneself from the idea that co-ordinates must have a direct metric significance. The transformation took place in approximately the following fashion.

We start with an empty, field-free space, as it occurs—related to an inertial system—within the meaning of the special theory of relativity, as the simplest of all imaginable physical situations. If we now think of a noninertial system introduced by assuming that the new system is uniformly accelerated against the inertial system (in a three-dimensional description) in one direction (conveniently defined), then there exists with reference to this system a static parallel gravitational field. The reference system may be chosen to be rigid, Euclidean in its three-dimensional metric properties. But the time in which the field appears as static is *not* measured by *equally constituted* stationary clocks. From this special example one can already recognize that the immediate metric significance of the co-ordinates is lost once one admits nonlinear transformations of the co-ordinates. To do the latter is, however, *obligatory* if one wants to do justice to the equality of gravitational and inertial mass through the foundations of the theory, and if one wants to overcome Mach's paradox regarding the inertial systems.

If, then, one must give up the notion of assigning to the co-ordinates an immediate metric meaning (differences of co-ordinates = measurable lengths, or times), one cannot but treat as equivalent all co-ordinate systems that can be created by the continuous transformations of the co-ordinates.

The general theory of relativity, accordingly, proceeds from the following principle: natural laws are to be expressed by equations that are covariant under the group of continuous co-ordinate transformations. This group replaces the group of the Lorentz transformations of the special theory of relativity, which forms a subgroup of the former.

This postulate by itself is of course not sufficient to serve as point of departure for the derivation of the basic equations of physics. One might even deny, to begin with, that the postulate by itself involves a real restriction for the physical laws; for it will always be possible to reformulate a law, conjectured at first only for certain co-ordinate systems, so that the new formulation becomes formally generally covariant. Further; it is evident right away that an infinitely large number of field laws can be formulated that have this property of covariance. The eminent heuristic significance of the general principle of relativity is that it leads us to the search for those systems of equations that are *in their general covariant* formulation the simplest *ones possible;* among these we shall have to look for the field equations of physical space. Fields that can be transformed into each other by such transformations describe the same real situation.

The major question for anyone searching in this field is this: of which mathematical type are the variables (functions of the co-ordinates) that permit the expression of the physical properties of space ('structure')? Only after that: which equations are satisfied by those variables?

The answer to these questions is today by no means certain. The path chosen by the first formulation of the general theory of relativity can be characterized as follows. Even though we do not know by what kind of field variables (structure) physical space is to be characterized, we do know with certainty a special case: that of the 'field-free' space in the special theory of relativity. Such a space is characterized by the fact that for a properly chosen co-ordinate system the expression

$$ds^2 = dx_1^2 + dx_2^2 + dx_3^2 - dx_4^2 \tag{1}$$

belonging to two neighboring points, represents a measurable quantity (square of distance), and thus has a real physical meaning. Referred to an arbitrary system this quantity is expressed as follows:

$$ds^2 = g_{ik}dx_i dx_k \tag{2}$$

whereby the indices run from 1 to 4. The $g_{ik}$ form a (real) symmetrical tensor. If, after carrying out a transformation on field (1), the first derivatives of the $g_{ik}$ with respect to the co-ordinates do not vanish, there exists a gravitational field with reference to this system of co-ordinates in the sense of the above consideration, but of a very special type. Thanks to Riemann's investigation of $n$-dimensional metric spaces, this special field can be characterized invariantly:

(1) Riemann's curvature-tensor $R_{iklm}$, formed from the coefficients of the metric (2), vanishes.

(2) The trajectory of a mass-point in reference to the inertial system, relative to which (1) is valid, is a straight line, hence an extremal (geodesic).

This last statement, however; is already a characterization of the law of motion based on (2). The *universal law* of physical space must be a generalization of the law just characterized. I now assumed that there are two steps of generalization:

(a) the pure gravitational field

(b) the general field (which is also to include quantities that somehow correspond to the electromagnetic field).

The case (a) was characterized by the fact that the field can still be represented by a Riemann metric (2), i.e., by a symmetric tensor, but without a representation of the form (1) (save on an infinitesimal scale). This means that in the case (a) the Riemann tensor does not vanish. It is clear, however; that in this case a field law must hold that is some generalization (loosening) of this law. If this generalized law also is to be of the second order of differentiation and linear in the second derivatives, then only the equation obtained by a single contraction

$$0 = R_{kl} = g^{im}R_{iklm}$$

was a prospective field law in the case (a). It appears natural, moreover, to assume that also in the case (a) the geodesic line is still to represent the law of motion of the material point.

It seemed hopeless to me at that time to venture the attempt of representing the total field (b) and to ascertain field laws for it. I preferred, therefore, to set up a preliminary formal frame for the representation of the entire physical reality; this was necessary in order to be able to investigate, at least preliminarily, the effectiveness of the basic idea of general relativity. This was done as follows.

In Newton's theory one can write the field law of gravitation thus:

$$\Delta\phi = 0$$

($\phi$ = gravitation potential), valid wherever the density of matter, $\rho$, vanishes. In general one has (Poisson's equation)

$$\Delta\phi = 4\pi k\rho \ (\rho = \text{mass density}).$$

In the relativistic theory of the gravitational field, *Rik* takes the place of $\Delta\phi$. On the right-hand side we shall then have to replace $\rho$ also by a tensor. Since we know from the special theory of relativity that the (inertial) mass equals the energy, we shall have to put on the right-hand side the tensor of energy density—more precisely, of the entire energy density that does not belong to the pure gravitational field. In this way one arrives at the field equation

$$R_{ik} - \frac{1}{2}\, g_{ik}\, R = -\, kT_{ik}.$$

The second member on the left-hand side is added because of formal considerations; for the left-hand side is written in such a way that its divergence, in the sense of the absolute differential calculus, vanishes identically. The right-hand side is a formal condensation of all things whose comprehension in the sense of a field theory is still problematic. Not for a moment, of course, did I doubt that this formulation was merely a makeshift in order to give the general principle of relativity a preliminary closed-form expression. For it was essentially *no more* than a theory of the gravitational field, which was isolated somewhat artificially from a total field of as yet unknown structure.

If anything in the theory as sketched—apart from the postulate of invariance of the equations under the group of continuous co-ordinate transformations—can possibly be claimed to be definitive, then it is the theory of the limiting case of a pure gravitational field and its relation to the metric structure of space. For this reason, in what immediately follows we shall speak only of the equations of the pure gravitational field.

The peculiarity of these equations lies, on the one hand, in their complicated structure, especially their nonlinear character with respect to the field variables and their derivatives, and, on the other hand, in the almost compelling necessity with which the transformation group determines this complicated field law. If one had stopped with the special theory of relativity, that is, with the invariance under the Lorentz group, then the field law $R_{ik} = 0$ would remain invariant also within the frame of this narrower group. But, from the point of view of the narrower group, there would be no off-hand grounds for representing gravitation by a structure as involved as the symmetric tensor $g_{ik}$. If, nonetheless, one would find sufficient reasons for it, there would then arise an immense number of field laws out of quantities $g_{ik}$, all of which are covariant under Lorentz transformations (not, however, under the general group). Even if, however, of all the conceivable Lorentz-invariant laws, one had accidentally guessed precisely the law belonging to the wider group, one would still not have achieved the level of understanding corresponding to the general principle of relativity. For, from the standpoint of the Lorentz group, two solutions would incorrectly have to be viewed as physically different if they can be transformed into each other by a nonlinear transformation of co-ordinates, that is, if from the point of view of the wider group they are merely different representations of the same field.

One more general remark concerning structure and group. It is clear that in general one will judge a theory to be the more nearly perfect the simpler a 'structure' it postulates and the broader the group concerning which the field equations are invariant. One sees now that these two desiderata get in each other's way. For example:[1] according to the special theory of relativity (Lorentz group) one can set up a covariant law for the simplest structure imaginable (a scalar field), whereas in the general theory of relativity (wider group of the continuous transformations of co-ordinates) there is an invariant field law only for the more complicated structure of the symmetric tensor. We have already given *physical* reasons for the fact that in physics invariance under the wider group has to be required: from a purely mathematical standpoint I can see no necessity for sacrificing the simpler structure to the generality of the group.

The group of general relativity is the first one requiring that the simplest invariant law be no longer linear and homogeneous in the field variables and their derivatives. This is of fundamental importance for the following

---

1. (Note by Einstein) To remain with the narrower group and at the same time to base the relativity theory of gravitation upon the more complicated (tensor-) structure implies a naive inconsequence. Sin remains sin, even if it is committed by otherwise ever so respectable men.

reason. If the field law is linear (and homogeneous), then the sum of two solutions is again a solution; so it is, for example, in Maxwell's field equations for the vacuum. In such a theory it is impossible to deduce from the field equations alone an interaction between structures that separately represent solutions of the system. That is why all theories up to now required, in addition to the field equations, special equations for the motion of material bodies under the influence of the fields. In the relativistic theory of gravitation, it is true, the law of motion (geodesic line) was originally postulated independently in addition to the field law. Subsequently, though, it turned Out that the law of motion need not (and must not) be assumed independently, but that it is already implicitly contained within the law of the gravitational field.

The essence of this truly involved situation can be visualized as follows: a single material point at rest will be represented by a gravitational field that is everywhere finite and regular, except where the material point is located: there the field has a singularity. If, however, one computes the field belonging to two material points at rest by integrating the field equations, then this field has in addition to the singularities at the positions of the material points a curve of singular points connecting the two points. It is possible, however, to stipulate a motion of the material points so that the gravitational field determined by them does not become singular anywhere except at the material points. These are precisely those motions described in first approximation by Newton's laws. One may say, therefore: the masses move in such fashion that the solution of the field equations is nowhere singular except at the mass points. This property of the gravitational equations is intimately connected with their nonlinearity, and this, in turn, results from the wider group of transformations.

Now it would of course be possible to object: if singularities are permitted at the locations of the material points, what justification is there for forbidding the occurrence of singularities elsewhere? This objection would be justified if the equations of gravitation were to be considered as equations of the total field. Since this is not the case, however, one will have to say that the field of a material particle will differ the more from a *pure gravitational field* the closer one comes to the location of the particle. If one had the field equations of the total field, one would be compelled to demand that the particles themselves could be represented as solutions of the complete field equations that are free of irregularities everywhere. Only then would the general theory of relativity be a *complete* theory.

# The Future of Quantum Theory

Before I enter upon the question of the completion of the general theory of relativity, I must take a stand with reference to the most successful physical theory of our period, namely the statistical quantum theory, which assumed a consistent logical form about twenty-five years ago, with Schrödinger, Heisenberg, Dirac, and Born. At present this is the only theory that permits a unitary grasp of experiences concerning the quantum character of micro-mechanical events. This theory, on the one hand, and the theory of relativity on the other, are both considered correct in a certain sense, although all efforts to fuse them into a single whole so far have not met with success. This is probably why among contemporary theoretical physicists there exist entirely differing opinions as to what the theoretical foundation of the physics of the future will look like. Will it be a field theory? Will it be in essence a statistical theory? I shall briefly indicate my own thoughts on this point.

Physics is an attempt conceptually to grasp reality as something that is considered to be independent of its being observed. In this sense one speaks of 'physical reality'. In pre-quantum physics there was no doubt as to how this was to be understood. In Newton's theory reality was determined by a material point in space and time, in Maxwell's theory by the field in space and time. In quantum mechanics the situation is less transparent. If one asks: does a $\Psi$-function of the quantum theory represent a real fact in the same sense as a material system of points or an electromagnetic field? One hesitates to reply with a simple yes or no. Why? What the $\Psi$-function (at a definite time) states, is this: what is the probability of finding a definite physical quantity $q$ (or $p$) in a definite given interval if I measure it at time $t$? The probability is here to be viewed as an empirically determinable, and therefore certainly a 'real' quantity, which I may determine if I create the same $\Psi$-function very often and each time perform a $q$-measurement. But what about the single measured value of $q$? Did the respective individual system have this $q$-value even before the measurement? To this question there is no definite answer within the framework of the existing theory, since the measurement is a process that implies a finite disturbance of the system from the outside; it would therefore be conceivable that the system obtains a definite numerical value for $q$ (or $p$), the measured numerical value, only through the measurement itself. For the further discussion I shall assume two physicists, $A$ and $B$, who represent different conceptions concerning the real situation as described by the $\Psi$-function.

A. The individual system (before the measurement) has a definite value of $q$ (or $p$) for all variables of the system, specifically *that* value which is determined by a measurement of this variable. Proceeding from this conception, he will state: the $\Psi$-function is not a complete description of the exact state of the system, but only an incomplete representation; it expresses only what we know about the system because of previous measurements.

B. The individual system (before the measurement) has no definite value of $q$ (or $p$). The measured value is produced by the act of measurement itself consistent with the probability appropriate to the $\Psi$-function. Proceeding from this conception, he will (or; at least, he may) state: The $\Psi$-function is an exhaustive description of the real situation of the system.

Now we present to these two physicists the following case. There is to be a system that at the time $t$ of our observation consists of two component systems $S_1$ and $S_2$, which at this time are spatially separated and (in the sense of the classical physics) interact with each other but slightly. The total system is to be described completely in terms of quantum mechanics by a known $\Psi$-function, say $\Psi_{12}$. All quantum theoreticians now agree upon the following. If I make a complete measurement of $S_1$, I obtain from the results of the measurement and from $\Psi_{12}$ an entirely definite $\Psi$-function $\Psi_2$ of the system $S_2$. The character of $\Psi_2$ then depends upon *what kind* of measurement I perform on $S_1$.

Now it appears to me that one may speak of the real state of the partial system $S_2$. To begin with, before performing the measurement on $S_1$, we know even less of this real state than we know of a system described by the $\Psi$-function. But on one assumption we should, in my opinion, insist without qualification: the real state of the system $S_2$ is independent of any manipulation of the system $S_1$, which is spatially separated from the former. According to the type of measurement I perform on $S_1$, I get, however, a very different $\Psi_2$ for the second partial system ($\Psi_2$, $\Psi_2$1, ...). Now, however, the real state of $S_2$ must be independent of what happens to $S_1$. For the same real state of $S_2$ it is possible therefore to find (depending on one's choice of the measurement performed on $S_1$) different types of $\Psi$-function. One can escape from this conclusion only by either assuming that the measurement of $S_1$ (telepathically) changes the real state of $S_2$ or by denying altogether that spatially separated entities possess independent real states. Both alternatives appear to me entirely unacceptable.

If now the physicists A and B accept this reasoning as valid, then B will have to give up his position that the $\Psi$-function constitutes a complete description of a real state. For in this case it would be impossible that two different types of $\Psi$-functions could be assigned to the identical state of $S_2$.

The statistical character of the present theory would then follow necessarily from the incompleteness of the description of the systems in quantum mechanics, and there would no longer exist any ground for the assumption that a future foundation of physics must be based upon statistics.

# Where I Disagree with Other Physicists

It is my opinion that the contemporary quantum theory represents an optimal formulation of the relationships, given certain fixed basic concepts, which by and large have been taken from classical mechanics. I believe, however, that this theory offers no useful point of departure for future development. This is the point at which my expectation deviates most widely from that of contemporary physicists. They are convinced that it is impossible to account for the essential aspects of quantum phenomena (apparently discontinuous and temporally undetermined changes of the state of a system; simultaneously corpuscular and undulatory qualities of the elementary carriers of energy) by means of a theory that describes the real state of things (objects) by continuous functions of space for which differential equations are valid. They are also of the opinion that in this way one cannot understand the atomic structure of matter and of radiation. They rather expect that systems of differential equations, which might be considered for such a theory, in any case would have no solutions that would be regular (free from singularities) everywhere in four-dimensional space. Above everything else, however, they believe that the apparently discontinuous character of elementary processes can be described only by means of an essentially statistical theory, in which the discontinuous changes of the systems are accounted for by continuous changes of the probabilities of the possible states.

All of these remarks seem to me to be quite impressive. But the crux of the matter appears to me to be this question: what can be attempted with some hope of success in view of the present situation of physical theory? Here it is the experiences with the theory of gravitation that determine my expectations. In my opinion, these equations are more likely to tell us something *precise* than all other equations of physics. Take, for instance,

Maxwell's equations of empty space by way of comparison. These are formulations corresponding to our experiences with infinitely weak electromagnetic fields. This empirical origin already determines their linear form; it has, however, already been emphasized above that the true laws cannot be linear. Such linear laws fulfill the superposition principle for their solutions; hence they contain no assertions concerning the interaction of elementary bodies. The true laws cannot be linear, nor can they be derived from such. I have learned something else from the theory of gravitation: no collection of empirical facts however comprehensive can ever lead to the setting up of such complicated equations. A theory can be tested by experience, but there is no way from experience to the construction of a theory. Equations of such complexity as are the equations of the gravitational field can be found only through the discovery of a logically simple mathematical condition that determines the equations completely or almost completely. Once one has obtained those sufficiently strong formal conditions, one requires only little knowledge of facts for the construction of the theory; in the case of the equations of gravitation it is the four-dimensionality and the symmetric tensor as expression for the structure of space that, together with the invariance with respect to the continuous transformation group, determine the equations all but completely.

Our task is that of finding the field equations for the total field. The desired structure must be a generalization of the symmetric tensor. The group must not be any narrower than that of the continuous transformations of co-ordinates. If one introduces a richer structure, then the group will no longer determine the equations as strongly as in the case of the symmetrical tensor as structure. Therefore it would be most beautiful if one were to succeed in expanding the group once more in analogy to the step that led from special relativity to general relativity. More specifically, I have attempted to draw upon the group of the complex transformations of the co-ordinates. All such endeavors were unsuccessful. I also gave up an open or concealed increase in the number of dimensions of space, an endeavor originally undertaken by Kaluza that, with its projective variant, even today has its adherents. We shall limit ourselves to the four-dimensional space and to the group of the continuous real transformations of co-ordinates. After many years of fruitless searching, I consider the solution sketched in what follows the one that is logically most satisfying.

In place of the symmetric $g_{ik}$ ($g_{ik} = g_{ki}$), the nonsymmetric tensor $g_{ik}$ is introduced. This quantity is composed of a symmetric part $s_{ik}$ and of a real or purely imaginary antisymmetric $a_{ik}$, thus:

$$g_{ik} = s_{ik} + a_{ik}.$$

Viewed from the standpoint of the group, the combination of $s$ and $a$ is arbitrary, because the tensors $s$ and $a$ individually have tensor character. It turns out, however, that these $g_{ik}$ (viewed as a whole) play a quite analogous role in the construction of the new theory to the symmetric $g_{ik}$ in the theory of the pure gravitational field.

This generalization of the space structure seems natural also from the standpoint of our physical knowledge, because we know that the electromagnetic field involves an antisymmetric tensor.

For the theory of gravitation it is furthermore essential that from the symmetric $g_{ik}$ it is possible to form the scalar density $\sqrt{|g_{ik}|}$ as well as the contravariant tensor $g_{ik}$ according to the definition

$$g_{ik}g^{il} = \delta_k{}^l \ (\delta_k{}^l = \text{Kronecker tensor}).$$

These structures can be defined in precise correspondence for the nonsymmetric $g_{ik}$, including tensor densities.

In the theory of gravitation it is further essential that, for a given symmetric $g_{ik}$-field, a field $\Gamma_{ik}{}^l$ can be defined, which is symmetric in the subscripts and which, considered geometrically, governs the parallel displacement of a vector. Analogously for the nonsymmetric $g_{ik}$ a nonsymmetric $\Gamma_{ik}{}^l$ can be defined, according to the formula

$$g_{ik,l} - g_{sk}\Gamma_{il}{}^s - g_{is}\Gamma_{lk}{}^s = 0, \tag{A}$$

which accords with the corresponding relation of the symmetric $g$, only that, of course, one must pay attention here to the position of the lower indices in the $g$ and $\Gamma$. Just as in the theory with symmetric $g_{ik}$, it is possible to form a curvature $R_{klm}{}^i$ out of the $\Gamma$, and from it a contracted curvature $R_{kl}$. Finally, by employing a variational principle together with (A), it is possible to find compatible field equations:

$$g^{\underline{is}}{}_{,s} = 0 \ \left(g^{\underline{ik}} = \tfrac{1}{2}\,(g^{ik} - g^{ki})\,\sqrt{-|g_{ik}|}\right) \tag{$B_1$}$$

$$\Gamma_{i\underline{s}}{}^s = 0 \ \left(\Gamma_{i\underline{s}}{}^s = \tfrac{1}{2}\,(\Gamma_{is}{}^s - \Gamma_{si}{}^s)\right) \tag{$B_2$}$$

$$R_{\underline{ik}} = 0 \tag{$C_1$}$$

$$R_{\underline{kl},m} + R_{\underline{lm},k} + R_{\underline{mk},l} = 0 \tag{$C_2$}$$

Each of the two equations $(B_1)$, $(B_2)$ is a consequence of the other if (A) is satisfied. $R_{\underline{kl}}$ denotes the symmetric, $R_{\underset{\smile}{kl}}$ the antisymmetric part of $R_{kl}$.

If the antisymmetric part of $g_{ik}$ vanishes, these formulas reduce to (A) and $(C_1)$—the case of the pure gravitational field.

I believe that these equations constitute the most natural generalization of the equations of gravitation.[2] The proof of their physical usefulness is a tremendously difficult task, inasmuch as mere approximations will not suffice. The question is: What solutions do these equations have that are regular everywhere?

This exposition has fulfilled its purpose if it shows the reader how the efforts of a life hang together and why they have led to expectations of a certain kind.

*A. Einstein.*

INSTITUTE FOR ADVANCED STUDY
PRINCETON, NEW JERSEY
[CA. 1946]

---

2. (Note by Einstein) The theory here proposed, according to my view, has a fair probability of being found valid, if the way to an exhaustive description of physical reality on the basis of the continuum turns out to be at all feasible.

MARTIN BUBER (1878–1965) was a truly outstanding religious philosopher, mystic, interpreter of Jewish scriptures, German prose stylist, and Zionist activist. Persecuted by the Nazis, he moved to Palestine in 1938. Within Zionism, he fought courageously and unsuccessfully, first for the institution of a bi-national Jewish-Palestinian state, then for a more just treatment of the Palestinians. By far his best known book is *I and Thou* (1922). Other great works include *Paths in Utopia* (1949) and *Two Types of Faith* (1950). The best biography is by Maurice Friedman: *Martin Buber's Life and Works* (1981–84).

# Martin BUBER

## " *The human means the taking place of that meeting which is latent in the being of the world.* "

### My Mother

IT CANNOT BE A QUESTION HERE OF recounting my personal life (I do not possess the kind of memory necessary for grasping great temporal continuities as such), but solely of rendering an account of some moments that my backward glance lets rise to the surface, moments that have exercised a decisive influence on the nature and direction of my thinking.

The earliest memory which has this character for me stems out of my fourth year of life. About a year before that the separation of my parents broke up the home of my childhood in Vienna (still today I see with closed eyes the Danube canal under the house, the sight of which I used to enjoy with a feeling of certainty that nothing could happen to me). At that time I had been brought to my grandparents on my father's side near Lvov,[1] then the capital city of the Austrian 'crownland' Galicia. They were both people of high rank, noble persons in the exact sense of the term and, in a special manner, suited to and supplementing each other. They were both disinclined to talk over the affairs of their own existence. Of what had taken place between my parents, nothing, of course, was spoken in my presence; but I suspect that it was also hardly ever a subject of discussion between them, except in a practical and unavoidable connection. The child itself expected to see his mother again soon; but no question passed his lips. Then there took place at one time what I have to tell here.

The house in which my grandparents lived had a great rectangular inner courtyard surrounded by a wooden balcony extending to the roof on which one could walk around the building at each floor. Here I stood once in my fourth year with a girl several years older, the daughter of a neighbor, to whose care my grandmother had entrusted me. We both leaned on the railing. I cannot remember that I spoke of my mother to my older comrade. But I hear still how the big girl said to me: "No, she will never come back." I know that I remained silent, but also that I cherished no doubt of the truth of the spoken words.

It remained fixed in me; from year to year it cleaved ever more to my heart, but after more than ten years I had begun to perceive it as something that concerned not only me, but all men. Later I once made up the word 'Vergegnung'—'mismeeting', or 'miscounter'—to designate the failure of a real meeting between men. When after another twenty years I again saw my mother, who had come from a distance to visit me, my wife, and my children, I could not gaze into her still astonishingly beautiful eyes without hearing from somewhere the word '*Vergegnung*' as a word spoken to me. I

---

1. The Polish city of Lvov, part of the Austro-Hungarian empire, was also known by its Austrian name, Lemberg. It is now Lviv, Ukraine.

suspect that all that I have learned about genuine meeting in the course of my life had its first origin in that hour on the balcony.

# My Grandmother

My grandmother Adele was one of those Jewesses of a certain period who, in order to create freedom and leisure for their husbands to study the Torah, managed the business with circumspect zeal. For my grandfather 'study of the teaching' had a special significance. Although an autodidact, he was a genuine philologist who is to be thanked for the first, and today still the authoritative, critical edition of a special class of Hebrew literature: the *Midrashim*—a unique mixture of interpretation of the Bible, wise sayings, and rich saga. In his civil occupation he was a great landowner, in addition a corn-merchant and the owner of phosphorite mines on the Austrian-Russian border. Beyond this he belonged to the number of the leading men of the Jewish community and to those of the town's chamber of commerce, experienced men with a judgment of their own. He never neglected these honorary offices; his own business, however, he left in general to his wife who conducted it all in a splendid and circumspect manner, but made no decision without consulting her spouse.

Among the Jews in the small Galician town where my grandmother grew up the reading of 'alien' literature was proscribed, but for the girls all readings, with the exception of edifying popular books, were held unseemly. As a fifteen-year-old she had set up for herself in the storehouse a hiding place in which stood volumes of Schiller's periodical *Die Horen*, Jean Paul's book on education, *Levana*, and many other German books which had been secretly and thoroughly read by her. When she was seventeen years old, she took them and the custom of concentrated reading with her into her marriage, and she reared her two sons in the respect for the authentic word that cannot be paraphrased. The same influence she later exercised on me. I learned even before I was fourteen (at that time I moved into the house of my father and my stepmother) what it means really to express something. I was affected in a special manner by the way that this woman handled the large-size, similarly bound copy-books in which every day she recorded income and expenditures: in between these entries she registered, after she had spoken them half aloud to herself, the passages which had become important to her out of her readings. Now and then she set down her own comments as well, which in no way imitated the style of the classic but from time to time stated something that she had to reply in intercourse with the great spirits. The same was true of her oral utterances: even when she obviously communicated the conclusion of a reflection, it had the appearance of something perceived. That undoubtedly came from the fact that with her, experiencing and reflecting on experience were not two stages but, as it were, two sides of the same process: when she looked at the street, she had at times the profile of someone meditating on a problem, and when I found her all alone in meditation, it seemed to me at times as if she listened. To the glance of the child, however, it was already unmistakable that when she at times addressed someone, she really addressed him.

My grandfather was a true philologist, a 'lover of the word', but my grandmother's love for the genuine word affected me even more strongly than his: because this love was so direct and so devoted.

# Languages

I went to school for the first time when I was ten years old. Up till then I received private tutoring, chiefly in languages, both because of my own inclination and talents and because for my grandmother a language-centered humanism was the royal road to education.

The multiplicity of human languages, their wonderful variety in which the white light of human speech at once fragmented and preserved itself, was already at the time of my boyhood a problem that instructed me ever anew. In instructing me it also again and again disquieted me. I followed time after time an individual word or even structure of words from one language to another, found it there again and yet had time after time to give up something there as lost that apparently only existed in a single one of all the languages. That was not merely 'nuances of meaning': I devised for myself two-language conversations between a German and a Frenchman, later between a Hebrew and an ancient Roman and came ever again, half in play and yet at times with beating heart, to feel the tension between what was heard by the one and what was heard by the other, from his thinking in another language. That had a deep influence on me and has issued in a long life into ever clearer insight.

My knowledge of languages as a boy also made it possible for me at times to provide my grandfather, whom I went to visit daily from my father's house, with a little help at his work. Thus it happened, for instance, that in reading 'Rashi' (Rabbi Shlomo Yizhaki), the great Bible and Talmud exegete of the eleventh century, my grandfather found a text explained through a reference to a French turn of speech and asked me how this was to be understood. I had at times to deduce from the Hebrew transcription the old French wording and now to make this understandable first to myself, then to my grandfather. Later, however, when I sat alone in my room in my father's house, I was oppressed by the question: what does it mean and how does it come about that one 'explains' something that was written in one language through something that one is accustomed to say in another language? The world of the Logos and of the Logoi opened itself to me, darkened, brightened, darkened again.

# My Father

From about the ninth year on I spent each summer on the estate of my father, and at fourteen I moved from my grandfather's house to my father's townhouse.

The influence of my father on my intellectual development was of a different kind from that of my grandparents. It did not derive at all from the mind.

In his youth my father had had strong intellectual interests; he had occupied himself seriously with the questions that had been raised in books such as Darwin's *Origin of Species* and Renan's *Life of Jesus.* But already early he dedicated himself to agriculture and devoted ever more of himself to it. Soon he was an exemplary phenomenon in the East Galician landed property.

When I was still a child, he brought with him from the Paris International Exhibition a great packing of breeding eggs of a type of hen still unknown in the east; he held it on his knees the whole long journey in order that no harm might come to it. Thirty-six years he worked with all kinds of implements whose specific effects he carefully tested in order to heighten the productivity of his soils.

He had mastered the technique of his age in his domain. But I noticed what really concerned him when I stood with him in the midst of the splendid herd of horses and observed him as he greeted one animal after the other, not merely in a friendly fashion but positively individually, or when I drove with him through the ripening fields and looked at him as he had the wagon halt, descended and bent over the ears again and again, in order finally to break one and carefully taste the kernels. This wholly unsentimental and wholly unromantic man was concerned about genuine human contact with nature, an active and responsible contact. Accompanying him thus on his way at times, the growing boy learned something that he had not learned from any of the many authors that he read.

In a special way the relationship of my father to nature was connected with his relationship to the realm that one customarily designates as the social. How he took part in the life of all the people who in one or another manner were dependent on him: the laborers attached to the estate, in their little houses that surrounded the estate buildings, houses built according to his design, the little peasants who performed service for him under conditions worked out with exact justice, the tenants; how he troubled about the family relationships, about the upbringing of children and schooling, about the sickness and aging of all the people—all that was not derived from any principles. It was solicitude not in the ordinary, but in the personal sense, in the sense of active responsible contact that could rise here to full reciprocity. In the town too my father did not act otherwise. To sightless charity he was fiercely averse; he understood no other help than that from person to persons, and he practiced it. Even in his old age he let himself be elected to the 'bread commission' of the Jewish community of Lemberg and wandered tirelessly around the houses in order to discover the people's real wants and necessities; how else could that take place except through true contact!

One thing I must still mention. My father was an elemental story teller. At times in conversation, just as its way led him, he told of people whom he had known. What he reported of them there was always the simple occurrence without any embroidery, nothing further than the existence of human creatures and what took place between them.

# The School

My school was called 'Franz Joseph's Gymnasium'. The language of instruction and of social intercourse was Polish, but the atmosphere was that, now appearing almost unhistorical to us, which prevailed or seemed to prevail among the peoples of the Austro-Hungarian empire: mutual tolerance without mutual understanding. The pupils were for the largest part Poles, in addition to which there was a small Jewish minority (the Ruthenians had their own schools). Personally the pupils got on well with one another, but the two groups as such knew almost nothing about each other.

Before 8 o'clock in the morning all the pupils had to be assembled. At 8 o'clock the signal bell sounded. One of the teachers entered and mounted the professor's lecturing desk, above which on the wall rose a large crucifix. At the same moment all the pupils stood up in their benches. The teacher and the Polish students crossed themselves; he spoke the Trinity formula, and they prayed aloud together. Until one might sit down again, we Jews stood silent and unmoving, our eyes glued to the floor.

I have already indicated that in our school there was no perceptible hatred of the Jews; I can hardly remember a teacher who was not tolerant or did not wish to pass as tolerant. But the obligatory daily standing in the room resounding with the strange service affected me worse than an act of intolerance could have affected me. Compulsory guests, having to participate as a thing in a sacral event in which no dram of my person could or would take part, and this for eight long years, morning after morning: that stamped itself upon the life-substance of the boy.

No attempt was ever made to convert any of us Jewish pupils; yet my antipathy to all missionary activity is rooted in that time. Not merely against the Christian mission to the Jews, but against all missionarizing among men who have a faith with roots of its own. In vain did Franz Rosenzweig try to win me for the idea of a Jewish mission among the non-Jews.

# The Two Boys

The classroom included five rows with six benches apiece. At each bench two pupils sat.

The furthest bench to the left, at the window, through which one saw nothing else than the almost empty square for play and sports, belonged to me and my best friend. For eight years we sat at this same bench, he to the left, I to the right.

The recesses in the teaching lasted a full quarter of an hour as a rule. When the weather was in some measure favorable, the whole school band used to storm out to the square and stay there in zealous activity until the signal bell. When the weather was all too adverse, we remained together in the classroom, but only on special occasions did a larger group form. Ordinarily the structure was only loose; a few youths stood telling things or discussing together, and the composition of these small groups changed according to the different themes that emerged from one time to the next.

Once, however, in a fall utterly spoiled by rain (in the winter before I was twelve) a special change took place that continued for some weeks.

In the third bench of the middle row sat two boys who until then had in no wise struck me, and probably also had not struck most of the others, as unusual. Now, however, they drew all glances to themselves. Day after day they conducted for us, without leaving the bench, mimic games with clown-like agility. They made no sound, and their faces remained unalterably severe. After some time the game took on an ever more penetratingly sexual character. Now the faces of the two looked as I imagined souls in the pains of hell, about which some of my fellow pupils knew to report to me in the tone of experts. All movements were cruelly forced. We stared at the two as long as the spectacle lasted. Shortly before the end of the recess they broke off. In our conversations the occurrence was never mentioned.

A few weeks after the spectacles had taken on this character, I was called to the school director. He received me with the gentle friendliness that we knew in him as something unalterable and asked me at once what I knew of the activities of the two. "I know nothing!" I screamed. He spoke again, just as gently as before. "We know you well," he said to me; "you are a good child, you will help us." "Help? Help whom?" I wanted—so it seems to me—to reply; but I remained silent, I stared silently at the director. Of what else happened almost nothing has penetrated into my memory, only that a great weeping as never before overcame me, and I was led away almost unconscious. A few hours later, however, when I tried at home to remember the last look of the director, it was not a gentle, but a frightened look that met me.

I was kept home for a few days, then I returned to school. The third bench of the middle row was empty and remained so until the end of the school year.

The long series of experiences that taught me to understand the problematic relationship between maxim and situation and thereby disclosed to me the nature of the true norm that commands not our obedience but ourselves, had begun with this convulsion of my childhood.

# The Horse

When I was eleven years of age, spending the summer on my grandparents' estate, I used, as often as I could do it unobserved, to steal into the stable and gently stroke the neck of my darling, a broad dapple-gray horse. It was not a casual delight but a great, certainly friendly, but also deeply stirring happening. If I am to explain it now, beginning from the still very fresh memory of my hand, I must say that what I experienced in touch with the animal was the Other, the immense otherness of the Other, which, however, did not remain strange like the otherness of the ox and the ram, but rather let me draw near and touch it. When I stroked the mighty mane, sometimes marvellously smooth-combed, at other times just as astonishingly wild, and felt the life beneath my hand, it was as though the element of vitality itself bordered on my skin, something that was not I, was certainly not akin to me, palpably the other, not just another, really the Other itself; and yet it let me approach, confided itself to me, placed itself elementally in the relation of *Thou* and *Thou* with me. The horse, even when I had not begun by pouring oats for him into the manger, very gently raised his massive head, ears flicking, then snorted quietly, as a conspirator gives a signal meant to be recognizable only by his fellow-conspirator; and I was approved. But once—I do not know what came over the child, at any rate it was childlike enough—it struck me about the stroking, what fun it gave me, and suddenly I became conscious of my hand. The game went on as before, but something had changed, it was no longer the same thing. And the next day, after giving him a rich feed, when I stroked my friend's head he did not raise his head. A few years later, when I thought back to the incident, I no longer supposed that the animal had noticed my defection. But at the time I considered myself judged.

# Philosophers

In that early period of my life, philosophy twice, in the form of two books, entrenched directly upon my existence—in my fifteenth and in my seventeenth year.

The two events do not allow themselves to be inserted into the process of appropriating a philosophical education, which was established in particular on a thorough reading of Plato (Greek was my favorite language). They were events which broke through the continuity—the presupposition of all genuine educational work—catastrophic events. In the first of them the philosophy confronted the catastrophic situation, delivering and helping. In the second the philosopher not only stirred me up but transported me into a sublime intoxication. Only after a long time was I able to escape this intoxication completely and attain to a certainty of the real.

Of the first of these two events I have told elsewhere, but it is of importance to me to interpret still more clearly something of what was reported there.

It says in that passage:

A necessity I could not understand swept over me: I had to try again and again to imagine the edge of space, or its edgelessness, time with a beginning and an end or a time without beginning or end, and both were equally impossible, equally hopeless—yet there seemed to be only the choice between the one or the other absurdity. (*Between Man and Man*, p. 136.)

Here it must be added above all that at that time the question about time had oppressed me in a far more tormenting fashion than that about space. I was irresistibly driven to want to grasp the total world process as actual, and that meant to understand it, 'time', either as beginning and ending or as without beginning and end. At each attempt to accept them as reality, both proved equally absurd. If I wanted to take the matter seriously (and I was ever again compelled to want just this), I had to transpose myself either to the beginning of time or to the end of time. Thus I came to feel the former like a blow in the neck or the latter like a rap against the forehead—no, there is no beginning and no end! *Or* I had to let myself be thrown into this or that bottomless abyss, into infinity, and now everything whirled. It happened thus time after time. Mathematical or physical formulas could not help me; what was at stake was the reality of the world in which one had to live and which had taken on the face of the absurd and the uncanny.

Then a book came into my hand, Kant's *Prolegomena*. In it was taught that space and time are 'nothing more than formal conditions of our sensory faculty', are 'not real properties that adhere to the things in themselves' but 'mere forms of our sensory perception'.

This philosophy exercised a great quieting effect on me. Now I needed no longer, tormented, to inquire of time a final time. Time was not a sentence hanging over me; it was mine, for it was 'ours'. The question was explained as unanswerable by its nature, but at the same time I was liberated from it, from having to ask it. Kant's present to me at that time was philosophical freedom.

About two years after that the other book took possession of me, a book that was, to be sure, the work of a philosopher but was not a philosophical book: Nietzsche's *Thus Spake Zarathustra*. I say "took possession of me," for here a teaching did not simply and calmly confront me, but willed and able—splendidly willed and splendidly able—utterance stormed up to and over me. This book, characterized by its author (in the book *Ecce Homo*) as the greatest present that had ever been made to mankind up till then, worked on me not in the manner of a gift but in the manner of an invasion which deprived me of my freedom, and it was a long time until I could liberate myself from it.

Nietzsche himself wished 'the basic conception' of this book to be understood as an interpretation of *time:* its interpretation as 'eternal return of the same', that is, as an infinite sequence of finite periods of time, which are like one another in all things so that the end phase of the period goes over into its own beginning. This conception, evaluated by its proclaimer as the most abysmal teaching, is no teaching at all but the utterance of an ecstatically lived-through possibility of thought played over with ever new variations. The 'Dionysian' pathos has by no means been transformed here into a philosophical one, as Nietzsche already early had in mind. It has remained Dionysian, as its modern variant, produced by the enthusiasm of the Dionysian man over his own heights and depths.

Kant had not undertaken to solve the sense-confusing riddle that is set us by the being of time; he completed the philosophical limitation of it in that he made it into a problem of we ourselves being referred to the form of time. Nietzsche, who wanted to have nothing to do with philosophical self-moderations, set in the place of one of the primal mysteries of time—the manifest mystery of the uniqueness of all happening—the pseudo-mystery of the 'eternal return of the same'.

Although the boy of seventeen did not and could not accept this conception, there still took place in his spirit a, so to speak, negative seduction. As he appears to me in my memory, after so many years—through Kant, who understood time as the form of 'our' perception, the way could not open to him to ask the question: 'But if time is only a form in which we perceive, where are 'we'? Are we not in the timeless? Are we not in eternity?' By that, of course, a wholly other eternity is meant than the circular one which Zarathustra loves as 'fatum'. What is meant is what is incomprehensible in itself, that which sends forth time out of itself and sets is in that relationship to it that we call existence. To him who recognizes this, the reality of the world no longer shows an absurd and uncanny face: because eternity is. That the entrance to this way long remained closed to me is to be traced to a certain, not insignificant, extent to that fascination by *Zarathustra*.[2]

---

2. (Note by Buber) I was at that time so taken by the book that I decided to translate it into Polish and had even translated the first part. I had just gone to the second part when I received the letter of a known Polish author who likewise had translated several sections of the book and proposed to me to do the work in common. I preferred renouncing in his favor.

# Vienna

I spent my first year of university studies in Vienna, the city of my birth and my earliest childhood. The detached, flat memory images appear out of the great corporal context like slides of a magic lantern, but also many districts that I could not have seen address me as acquaintances. This original home of mine, now foreign, taught me daily, although still in unclear language, that I had to accept the world and let myself be accepted by it; it was indeed ready to be accepted. Something was established at that time that in later years could not become recast through any of the problematics of the age.

The lectures of those two semesters, even the significant scholarly ones, did not have a decisive effect on me. Only some seminars into which I had prematurely flung myself, rather than the seminar as such, immediately exerted a strong influence: the regulated and yet free intercourse between teacher and students, the common interpretations of texts, in which the master at times took part with a rare humility, as if he too were learning something new, and the liberated exchange of question and answer in the midst of all scholastic fluency—all this disclosed to me, more intimately than anything that I read in a book, the true actuality of the spirit, as a 'between'.

What affected me most strongly, however, was the Burgtheater into which at times, day after day, I rushed up three flights after several hours of 'posting myself' in order to capture a place in the highest gallery. When far below in front of me the curtain went up and I might then look at the events of the dramatic *agon* as, even if in play, taking place here and now, it was the word, the 'rightly' spoken human word that I received into myself, in the most real sense. Speech here first, in this world of fiction as fiction, won its adequacy; certainly it appeared heightened, but heightened to itself. It was only a matter of time, however, until—as always happened—someone fell for a while into recitation, a 'noble' recitation. Then, along with the genuine spokenness of speech, dialogical speech or even monological (in so far as the monologue was just an addressing of one's own person as a fellow man and no recitation), this whole world, mysteriously built out of surprise and law, was shattered for me—until after some moments it arose anew with the return of the over-against.

Since then it has sometimes come to pass, in the midst of the casualness of the everyday, that, while I was sitting in the garden of an inn in the countryside of Vienna, a conversation penetrated to me from a neighboring table, (perhaps an argument over falling prices by two market wives taking a rest) in which I perceived the spokenness of speech, sound becoming 'Each-Other'.

# A Lecture

My third semester, during which I completed my twentieth year of life, I spent in Leipzig.

What had the strongest effect on me there was undoubtedly hearing Bach's music, and in truth Bach's music so sung and played—of that I was certain at that time and have remained certain—as Bach himself wished that it be sung and played. But it would be fruitless for me to undertake to say, indeed, I cannot even make clear to myself—in what way Bach has influenced my thinking. The ground-tone of my life was obviously modified in some manner and through that my thinking as well. In general I am not at all in the position, in these autobiographical fragments, to report on such great and mysterious things. In its stead I shall tell here of a small incident that took place then and, as it later proved, was not unimportant.

I had for some time occupied myself with the talks and writings of Ferdinand Lassalle and with his biography too. I admired his spiritual passion and his readiness, in personal as in public life, to stake his existence. What was manifestly problematic in his nature went unnoticed; it did not even concern me. When a socialist club whose meetings I had attended a few times invited me to deliver a lecture, I decided to speak about Lassalle and did so. The lecture that I delivered was the image of a hero after the model of Carlyle. I pointed to a destiny that was intended for tragedy from the beginning. This tragedy was manifested in the path of his work—the failure of his undertaking to lay the foundation of a new society—but also in that of his life up till his absurd and yet symbolically significant death.[3]

When I had finished, the applause was great. Then an old man came up to me. He was, as he at once communicated to me, a tailor by trade and had in his youth belonged to Lassalle's most intimate circle. He seized my hand and held it fast for a long time. Then he looked at me enthusiastically and said: "Yes! Thus, thus he was!"

---

3. Ferdinand Lassalle (1825–1864) was the outstanding leader of the German socialist movement. Frequently imprisoned, he collaborated with Bismarck in the hope of creating a welfare state. He was killed in a foolish duel.

An almost tender feeling came over me: 'How good it is to be confirmed thus!' But even at that moment a fright suddenly fell upon me and pierced through my thoughtless joy: 'No, it is I who have been the confirmer, the lying confirmer of an idol!'

The true, hidden, cast aside, issue of my Lassalle studies revealed itself in a flash: the knowledge of the unmanageable contradiction that had burned in a bold and vain heart and out of it had been hurled into the human world. I stammered a salutation to the friendly tailor and fled.

In the following weeks I sought, with the most inadequate means and with the lack of success that was its due, to substitute for the smashed hero's bust a kind of analytical representation: this proved to be an only seemingly legitimate simplification. Slowly, waveringly, grew the insight into the problematic reality of human existence and into the fragile possibility of doing justice to it. Bach helped me.

# The Cause and the Person

It was at the Sixth Zionist Congress, 1902. Herzl had just launched the thunder of his denunciation against the opposition; he had answered the criticism of Davis Trietsch, less with factual arguments than with personal counter-criticism in which he dealt with Trietsch's own colonizing activities. The chief thrust was a record that had been taken down from a 'victim' of this activity.

(It must be mentioned here that in the days after this incident I was a member of what was virtually a board of arbitration appointed by the Congress. That board decided, by a vote of three to two—I was one of the minority—to issue no detailed statement on the result of its investigations, but some details may be made public today.)

Apart from the fact that this thrust was directed against the person rather than against his cause, it was not executed with a correct sword; the 'victim' was no victim, and the record—well, it was a record. . . . Herzl swung his weapon in good faith; no doubt existed about that. But he had not examined it closely enough beforehand.

After his speech Herzl retired into his conference room. Berthold Feiwel and I soon followed him there to point out, as friends of Trietsch, the untenable nature of his accusations, and to demand the appointment of a committee to make an inquiry into them. As we walked the short distance to the conference room, I was profoundly perturbed. I had already, indeed, since the previous Congress, stood in decisive opposition to Herzl, but this opposition had been wholly objective, and I had not ceased for a moment to have faith in the man. Now, for the first time, my soul revolted—so violently that I still have a physical recollection of it. When I entered the room, however, my agitation was in an instant transformed by the sight that met me, and the heart that had just been pounding grew numb.

Only Herzl and his mother were in the room. Frau Jeannette sat in an armchair, silent and unmoving, but her face and eyes shining with the most lively sympathetic participation—splendid in sympathy as I had known once in my grandmother. Herzl was pacing up and down the room with long strides, exactly like a caged lion. His vest was unbuttoned, his breast rose and fell; I had never dreamed that he, whose gestures were always mastered and masterly, could breathe so wildly. It was only later that I noticed his pallor, so strongly did his eyes flash and burn.

It became at once compellingly clear to me that here it was impossible to remain inwardly the representative of one side. Outside, in the hall, was a man, my friend and ally, who had been hurt, who had suffered a public injustice. But here was the author of the injustice, whose blow had dealt the wound—a man who, though misled, was still my leader, sick with zeal; a man consumed with zeal for his faith: his faith in his cause and in himself, the two inextricably bound together.

I was twenty-four years of age and this was perhaps the first time that I set foot on the soil of tragedy where there is no longer such a thing as being in the right. There was only one thing to learn that was greater still: how out of the grave of being in the right the right is resurrected. But this is something I only learned many years later.

Our task had become inwardly impracticable: for speaking to this man opposite, one could only essentially appeal from 'his cause,' which he so lived, to the—truth of his cause, and who could do that? But, of course, we carried out our task: we pointed out, demanded what we were authorized and obliged to point out and demand.

Herzl continued to pace up and down the room, giving no sign that he was listening. Occasionally I glanced at his mother—her face had darkened; there was something there that terrified me, I did not know what it was, but it was there.

Suddenly, however, Herzl stopped before us, and spoke to us. His tone was by no means what we might have expected—it was a passionate but smiling tone, although there was no smile on his lips. "I would have taken him to task in a wholly different way!" he exclaimed. "Wholly differently! But there before the platform, directly opposite me, a girl—his fiancée, I have heard—placed herself; there she stood, her eyes flashing at me. A wonderful person, I tell you! I could not do it!"

And now his mouth, too, smiled, as though liberated. And who could have refrained from smiling with him? The charmer 'Told' smiled in his romantic way; I, undoubtedly, smiled too, like a school-boy who has discovered that Horace meant real friends and real sweethearts, and even on the once more brightened face of the old—no, not old at all—gentlewoman in the armchair there was a smile, such as I have only observed in the Jewish women of that generation. The secret of that smile has been lost.

It was no longer possible to reply. In the light of the non-objectivity of his confession concerning the reason for his forbearance, the nonobjectivity of his attack naturally seemed even more grave. And yet . . . ! We discharged our task, everything now going off smoothly, impersonally, without difficulties of any sort and we took our leave. This was the last time that I saw Herzl at such close quarters.

Then I did not want to recollect that image, but since then—after the angel had done his work,[4] the angel whose nameless presence had at that time frightened Herzl's mother and me—I have often thought over that occasion.

What, indeed, was Theodor Herzl's attitude toward the cause and the person? And how is it in general with these two, 'cause' and 'person'?

That to Herzl his cause was indissolubly bound up with his person—this fact manifested itself clearly enough in his fight against Ahad Ha'am[5] when he summoned us young men, who in that situation stood on the side of his opponent, to 'find our way back to *the movement*'. Probably this is the case with most of the men who act in history. His fundamental view was certainly that there was little sense in discussing principles and methods, since, in the final analysis, everything depends not upon them, but upon the person to whom their realization and application is entrusted, in other words: upon the individual who uses them, and by means of them serves. Serves whom? Just the cause that is indissolubly bound up with the person? We appear to be reasoning in a circle.

---

4. Theodor Herzl, the great leader of Zionism, died of a heart attack in 1904.

5. 'Ahad Ha'am', meaning 'one of the people', was the adopted name of Asher Ginsberg, who in opposition to Herzl's political Zionism represented an essentially cultural Zionism.

But let us regard the problem from the other side, from the side of the people. Let us consider, for example, the concept of Max Weber, according to whom genuine democracy means to appoint a leader whom one trusts and to follow him as long as he accomplishes his task, but if he fails, to call him to account, to judge him, to depose him, even 'To the gallows with him!'[6] The cause, therefore, is bound up with the person as long as his power of leadership, his 'charisma', to use Weber's term, proves effective. From this point of view we can understand Herzl's attitude toward his critics; it is charismatic. This is why he does not say: 'You are wrong, for matters stand thus and so', but rather: 'You are wrong, for you are not the man to do this properly—you lack the *charisma*'.

But is this concept right or wrong? It cannot be set aside by a cheap ideology composed of a mediocre policy and a mediocre morality. The 'history of the world' so far attests to it. Only our hope for a different leadership and a different following, for a truly dialogical relationship between the two, contests it. In any case, the categories of the objective and the subjective, with which we are so familiar, do not in truth hold for the problem that has opened up to us.

But the fiancée with the flashing eyes! Is this not certainly a dreadful lack of objectivity? I do not know. Perhaps through the impression that his opponent had one, even if only one human being who would take his part thus, Herzl had been gripped by the question whether there might not be yet another reality, different from that of obvious world history—a reality hidden and powerless because it has not come into power; whether there might not be, therefore, men with a mission who have not been called to power and yet are, in essence, men who have been summoned; whether excessive significance has not perhaps been ascribed to the circumstances that separate the one class of men from the other; whether success is the only criterion; whether the unsuccessful man is not destined at times to gain a belated, perhaps posthumous, perhaps even anonymous victory which even history refuses to record: whether, indeed, when even this does not happen, a blessing is not spoken, nonetheless, to these abandoned ones, a word that confirms them; whether there does not exist a 'dark' charisma. The man who acts in history does not allow himself to be overwhelmed by such questions, for if he did so, he would have to despair, and to withdraw. But the moments in which they touch him are the truly religious moments of his life.

---

6. This refers to the well-known account of a discussion between Max Weber and General Erich Ludendorff, given in Marianne Weber's book *Max Weber*.

# The Zaddik

In my childhood I spent every summer on an estate in Bukovina. There my father took me with him at times to a nearby village of Sadagora. Sadagora is the seat of a dynasty of 'zaddikim' (zaddik means righteous, proven), that is, of Hasidic rabbis. There no longer lives in the present-day community that high faith of the first Hasidim, that fervent devotion which honored in the zaddik the perfected man in whom the immortal finds its mortal fulfillment. Rather the present-day Hasidim turn to the *zaddik* above all as the mediator through whose intercession they hope to attain the satisfaction of their needs. Even in these degenerate Hasidim there still continues to glow, in the unknown ground of their souls, the word of Rabbi Eliezar that the world was created for the sake of the perfected man (the zaddik), even though there should be only one.

This I realized at that time, as a child, in the dirty village of Sadagora from the 'dark' Hasidic crowd that I watched—as a child realizes such things, not as thought, but as image and feeling—that the world needs the perfected man and that the perfected man is none other than the true helper. Certainly, the power entrusted to him has been misinterpreted by the faithful, had been misused by himself. But is it not at base a legitimate, the legitimate power, this power of the helping soul over the needy? Does there not lie in it the seed of future social orders?

At any rate, in a childish fashion, these questions already dawned on me at that time. And I could compare on the one side with the head man of the province whose power rested on nothing but habitual compulsion; on the other with the rabbi, who was an honest and God-fearing man, but an employee of the 'directorship of the cult'. Here, however, was another, an incomparable; here was, debased yet uninjured, the living double kernel of humanity: genuine *community* and genuine *leadership*.

The palace of the *rebbe*, in its showy splendor, repelled me. The prayer house of the Hasidim with its enraptured worshippers seemed strange to me. But when I saw the *rebbe* striding through the rows of the waiting, I felt, 'leader', and when I saw the Hasidim dance with the Torah, I felt 'community'. At that time there rose in me a presentiment of the fact that common reverence and common joy of soul are the foundations of genuine human community.

In 1910 or 1911, in Bukovina, not far from Sadagora, after a lecture that I had delivered, I went, with some members of the association that had arranged the evening, into a coffee house. I like to follow the speech before many, whose form allows no reply, with a conversation with a few in which person acts on person and my view is set forth directly through going into objection and question.

We were just discussing a theme of moral philosophy when a well-built middle-aged Jew of simple appearance came up to the table and greeted me. To my no doubt somewhat distant return greeting, he replied with words not lacking a slight reproof: "Doctor! Do you not recognize me?" When I had to answer in the negative, he introduced himself as M., the brother of a former steward of my father's. I invited him to sit with us, inquired about his circumstances of life and then took up again the conversation with the young people. M. listened to the discussion, which had just taken a turn toward somewhat abstract formulations, with eager attentiveness. It was obvious that he did not understand a single word; the devotion with which he received every word resembled that of the believers who do not need to know the content of a litany since the arrangement of sounds alone gives them all that they need, and more than any content could.

After a while, nonetheless, I asked him whether he had perhaps something to say to me; I should gladly go to one side with him and talk over his concern. He vigorously declined. The conversation began again and with it M.'s listening. When another half hour had passed, I asked him again whether he did not perhaps have a wish that I might fulfill for him; he could count on me. No, no, he had no wish, he assured me. It had grown late; but, as happens to one in such hours of lively interchange, I did not feel weary; I felt fresher, in fact, than before, and decided to go for a walk with the young people. At this moment M. approached me with an unspeakably timid air. "Doctor," he said, "I should like to ask you a question." I bid the students wait and sat down with him at a table. He was silent. "Just ask, Mr. M.," I encouraged him; "I shall gladly give you information as best I can." "Doctor," he said, "I have a daughter." He paused; then he continued, "And I also have a young man for my daughter." Again a pause. "He is a student of law. He passed the examinations with distinction." He paused again, this time somewhat longer. I looked at him encouragingly; I supposed that he would entreat me to use my influence in some way on behalf of the presumptive son-in-law. "Doctor," he asked, "is he a steady man?" I was surprised, but felt that I might not refuse him an answer. "Now, Mr. M.," I explained, "after what you have said, it can certainly be taken for granted that he is industrious and able." Still he questioned further. "But Doctor," he said, "does he also have a good head?"— "That is even more difficult to answer," I replied; "but at any rate he has not succeeded with industry alone, he must also have something in his head." Once again M. paused; then he asked, clearly as a final question, "Doctor, should he now become a judge or a lawyer?"—"About that I can give you no information," I answered. "I do not know the young man, indeed, and even if I did know him, I should hardly be able to advise in this matter." But then M. regarded me with a glance of almost melancholy renunciation, half-complaining, half-understanding, and spoke in an indescribable tone, composed in equal part of sorrow and humility: "Doctor, you do not *want* to say—now, I thank you for what you have said to me."

As a child, I had received an image of the *zaddik* and through the sullied reality had glimpsed the pure idea, the idea of the genuine leader of a genuine community. Between youth and manhood this idea had arisen in me through knowledge of Hasidic teaching as that of the perfected man who realizes God in the world. But now in the light of this droll event, I caught sight in my inner experience of the *zaddik*'s function as a leader. I who am truly no *zaddik*, no one assured in God, rather a man endangered before God, a man wrestling ever anew for God's light, ever anew engulfed in God's abysses, nonetheless, when asked a trivial question and replying with a trivial answer, then experienced from within for the first time the true *zaddik*, questioned about revelations and replying in revelations. I experienced him in the fundamental relation of his soul to the world: in his responsibility.

# The Walking Stick and the Tree

After a descent during which I had to utilize without a halt the late light of a dying day, I stood on the edge of a meadow, now sure of the safe way, and let the twilight come down upon me. Not needing a support and yet willing to afford my lingering a fixed point, I pressed my walking stick against a trunk of an oak tree. Then I felt in twofold fashion my contact with being: here, where I held the stick, and there, where it touched the bark. Apparently only where I was, I nonetheless found myself there too where I found the tree.

At that time dialogue appeared to me. For the speech of man is like that stick wherever it is genuine speech, and that means: truly directed address. Here, where I am, where ganglia and organs of speech help me to form and to send forth the word, here I 'mean' him to whom I send it, I intend him, this one unexchangeable man. But also there, where he is, something of me is delegated, something that is not at all substantial in nature like that being here, rather pure vibration and incomprehensible; that remains there, with him, the man meant by me, and takes part in the receiving of my word. I encompass him to whom I turn.

# Question and Answer

It was in May of the year 1914 (my wife and I and our two children, now had already lived some eight years in a suburb of Berlin) when Reverend Hechler, whom I had not seen for a long time, called me. He was just in Berlin and would like to visit me. Soon afterward he came.

I had become acquainted with Hechler in the autumn of 1899 in a railroad carriage. The much older man began a conversation with me in which we soon learned that we shared the same views. Through a real eschatological belief in the living Christ, he stood close to the Zionist movement to which I then had belonged for a short time. The return of the Jewish people to their homeland was to him the promised presupposition of the return of Christ. He journeyed just then to the Grand Duke of Baden to whom he had a short time before introduced Herzl. He had been an educator of princes and was highly esteemed in many European courts.

In the course of the conversation I handed to Hechler the manuscript of a 'hymn' to the awakening Jewish people which I had written shortly before. This hymn filled him with such enthusiasm (entirely without basis) that he declared that he must read it to the Grand Duke. Soon afterward he had not merely done this but had published the questionable little opus without my knowledge. When I opened the door of my Berlin dwelling to Hechler, I was struck by how aged, but also by how upright he was. After the warm mutual greeting, he drew forth from one of the gigantic pockets of his havelock a bundle of papers wrapped in a blue-white cloth. Out of it, first of all, he pulled forth the manuscript together with the proofs of that poem of 1899, but then a large sheet that he slowly unfolded. It was a graphic representation of the prophecy of Daniel on which he indicated to me, as if on a map of a historical period, the exact point in which we just now found ourselves. Then he spoke somewhat as follows: "Dear friend. I come from Athens (he had earlier been the teacher of the Greek princes, among others). I have stood on the spot where Paul spoke to the Athenians of the unknown God. And now I come to you to say to you that in this year the world war will break out."

The certainty which was expressed in this sentence stemmed, as I have only later understood, out of a peculiar fusion of spheres: the believing interpretation of Daniel had been mixed and concretized with material flowing to it from the courts of Europe, without an awareness of what took place thus in the depths of the soul having penetrated into that consciousness. But what struck me most forcibly in the sentence that he spoke was the word 'world war' which I heard then for the first time. What kind of a 'war' was that—so I asked myself although still by no means clearly enough—which embraced the 'world'? Clearly something essentially different at any rate from what one had formerly called 'war'! From that hour dates the presentiment that has from then on grown in me, that the historical time of 'wars' was over and something different, only seemingly of that same nature, but becoming ever more different and ever more monstrous, was getting ready to swallow history and with it men.

Hechler stayed a few hours with us. Then I accompanied him to the railway station. In order to get there, one first had to go to the end of the small street of the 'colony', in which we lived and then on a narrow path covered with coal-dust, the so-called 'black path' along the railroad tracks. When we had reached the corner where the colony street met this path, Hechler stood still, placed his hand on my shoulder and said: "Dear friend! We live in a great time. Tell me: Do you believe in God?" It was a while before I answered, then I reassured the old man as best I could: he need have no concern about me in this matter. Upon this I brought him to the railway station and installed him in his train.

When I now returned home, however, and again came to that corner where the black path issued into our street, I stood still. I had to ponder to the depths of the matter. Had I said the truth? Did I 'believe' in the God whom Hechler meant? What was the case with me? I stood a long time on the corner determined not to go further before I had found the right answer.

Suddenly in my spirit, there where speech again and again forms itself, there arose without having been formulated by me, word for word distinct:

'If to believe in God means to be able to talk about him in the third person, then I do not believe in God. If to believe in him means to be able to talk to him, then I believe in God.' And after a while, further: 'The God who gives Daniel such foreknowledge of this hour of human history, this hour before the "world war," that its fixed place in the march of the ages can be

foredetermined, is not my God and not God. The God to whom Daniel
prays in his suffering is my God and the God of all.'

I remained standing for a long while on the corner of the black path and
gave myself up to the clarity, now beyond speech, that had begun.

# A Conversion

In my earlier years the 'religious' was for me the exception. There were hours
that were taken out of the course of things. From somewhere or other the
firm crust of everyday was pierced. Then the reliable permanence of appearances broke down; the attack which took place burst its law asunder.
'Religious experience' was the experience of an otherness which did not fit
into the context of life. It could begin with something customary, with consideration of some familiar object, but which then became unexpectedly
mysterious and uncanny, finally lighting a way into the lightning-pierced
darkness of the mystery itself. But also, without any intermediate stage, time
could be torn apart—first the firm world's structure then the still firmer
self-assurance flew apart and you were delivered to fulness. The 'religious'
lifted you out. Over there now lay the accustomed existence with its affairs,
but here illumination and ecstasy and rapture held without time or
sequence. Thus your own being encompassed a life here and a life beyond,
and there was no bond but the actual moment of the transition.

The illegitimacy of such a division of the temporal life, which is stream-
ing to death and eternity and which only in fulfilling its temporality can be
fulfilled in face of these, was brought home to me by an everyday event, an
event of judgment, judging with that sentence from closed lips and an
unmoved glance such as the ongoing course of things loves to pronounce.

What happened was no more than that one forenoon, after a morning of
'religious' enthusiasm, I had a visit from an unknown young man, without
being there in spirit. I certainly did not fail to let the meeting be friendly, I
did not treat him any more remissly than all his contemporaries who were
in the habit of seeking me out about this time of day as an oracle that is
ready to listen to reason. I conversed attentively and openly with him—only
I omitted to guess the questions which he did not put. Later, not long after,
I learned from one of his friends—he himself was no longer alive—the
essential content of these questions; I learned that he had come to me not
casually, but borne by destiny, not for a chat but for a decision. He had come

to me, he had come in this hour. What do we expect when we are in despair and yet go to a man? Surely a presence by means of which we are told that nevertheless there is meaning.

Since then I have given up the 'religious' which is nothing but the exception, extraction, exaltation, ecstasy; or it has given me up. I possess nothing but the everyday out of which I am never taken. The mystery is no longer disclosed, it has escaped or it has made its dwelling here where everything happens as it happens. I know no fulness but each mortal hour's fulness of claim and responsibility. Though far from being equal to it, yet I know that in the claim I am claimed and may respond in responsibility, and know who speaks and demand a response.

I do not know much more. If that is religion then it is just everything, simply all that is lived in its possibility of dialogue. Here is space also for religion's highest forms. As when you pray you do not thereby remove yourself from this life of yours but in your praying refer your thought to it, even though it may be in order to yield it; so too in the unprecedented and surprising, when you are called upon from above, required, chosen, empowered, sent, you with this your mortal bit of life are meant. This moment is not extracted from it, it rests on what has been and beckons to the remainder which has still to be lived. You are not swallowed up in a fulness without obligation, you are willed for the life of communion.

# Report on Two Talks

I shall tell about two talks. One apparently came to a conclusion, as only occasionally a talk can come, and yet in reality remained unconcluded; the other was apparently broken off and yet found a completion such as rarely falls to the lot of discussions.

Both times it was a dispute about God, about the concept and the name of God, but each time of a very different nature.

On three successive evenings I spoke at the adult folk-school of a German industrial city on the subject 'Religion as Reality.' What I meant by that was the simple thesis that 'faith' is not a feeling in the soul of man but an entrance into reality, an entrance into the *whole* reality without reduction and curtailment. This thesis is simple but it contradicts the usual way of thinking. And so three evenings were necessary to make it clear, and not merely three lectures but also three discussions which followed the lectures. At these discussions I was struck by something which bothered me. A large part of the audience was evidently made up of workers but none of them spoke up. Those who spoke and raised questions, doubts, and reflections were for the most part students (for the city had a famous old university). But all kinds of other circles were also represented; the workers alone remained silent. Only at the conclusion of the third evening was this silence, which had by now become painful for me, explained. A young worker, came up to me and said: "Do you know, we can't speak in there, but if you would meet with us to-morrow, we could talk together the whole time." Of course I agreed.

The next day was a Sunday. After dinner I came to the agreed place and now we talked together well into the evening. Among the workers was one, a man no longer young, whom I was drawn to look at again and again because he listened as one who really wished to hear. Real listening has become rare in our time. It is found most often among workers, who are not indeed concerned about the person speaking, as is so often the case with the *bourgeois* public, but about what he has to say. This man had a curious face. In an old Flemish altar picture representing the adoration of the shepherds one of them, who stretches out his arms toward the manger, has such a face. The man in front of me did not look as if he might have any desire to do the same; moreover, his face was not open like that in the picture. What was notable about him was that he heard and pondered, in a manner as slow as it was impressive. Finally, he opened his lips as well. "I have had the experience," he explained slowly and impressively, repeating a saying which the astronomer Laplace is supposed to have used in conversation with Napoleon, "that I do not need this hypothesis 'God' in order to be quite at home in the world." He pronounced the word 'hypothesis' as if he attended the lectures of the distinguished natural scientist who had taught in that industrial and university city and had died shortly before. Although he did not reject the designation 'God' for his idea of nature, that naturalist spoke in a similar manner whether he pursued zoology or *Weltanschauung*.

The brief speech of the man struck me; I felt myself more deeply challenged than by the others. Up till then we had certainly debated very seriously, but in a somewhat relaxed way; now everything had suddenly become severe and hard. How should I reply to the man? I pondered awhile in the now severe atmosphere. It came to me that I must shatter the security of his *Weltanschauung*, through which he thought of a 'world' in which one 'felt at home'. What sort of a world was it? What we were accustomed to call world was the world of the senses, the world in which there exists vermilion and grass green, C major and B minor, the taste of apple and of wormwood. Was this world anything other than the meeting of our own senses with those unapproachable events about whose essential definition physics always troubles itself in vain? The red that we saw was neither there in the 'things', nor here in the 'soul'. It at times flamed up and glowed just so long as a red-perceiving eye and a red-engendering 'oscillation' found themselves over against each other. Where then was the world and its security? The unknown 'objects' there, the apparently so well-known and yet not graspable 'subjects' here, and the actual and still so evanescent meeting of both, the 'phenomena'—was that not already three worlds which could no longer be comprehended from one alone? How could we in our thinking place together these worlds so divorced from one another? What was the being that gave this 'world', which had become so questionable, its foundation?

When I was through a stern silence ruled in the now twilit room. Then the man with the shepherd's face raised his heavy lids, which had been lowered the whole time, and said slowly and impressively, "You are right."

I sat in front of him dismayed. What had I done? I had led the man to the threshold beyond which there sat enthroned the majestic image which the great physicist, the great man of faith, Pascal, called the God of the Philosophers. Had I wished for that? Had I not rather wished to lead him to the other, Him whom Pascal called the God of Abraham, Isaac, and Jacob, Him to whom one can say Thou?

It grew dusk, it was late. On the next day I had to depart. I could not remain, as I now ought to do; I could not enter into the factory where the man worked, become his comrade, live with him, win his trust through real life-relationship, help him to walk with me the way of the creature who *accepts* the creation. I could only return his gaze.

Some time later I was the guest of a noble old thinker. I had once made his acquaintance at a conference where he gave a lecture on elementary folk-schools and I gave one on adult folk-schools. That brought us together, for we were united by the fact that the work 'folk' has to be understood in both cases in the same all-embracing sense. At that time I was happily surprised at how the man with the steel-gray locks asked us at the beginning of his talk to forget all that we believed we knew about his philosophy from his books. In the last years, which had been war years, reality had been brought so close to him that he saw everything with new eyes and had to think in a new way. To be old is a glorious thing when one has not unlearned what it means to *begin;* this old man had even perhaps first learned it thoroughly in old age. He was not at all young, but he was old in a young way, knowing how to begin.

He lived in another university city situated in the west. When the theology students of that university invited me to speak about prophecy, I stayed with the old man. There was a good spirit in his house, the spirit that wills to enter life and does not prescribe to life where it shall let it in.

One morning I got up early in order to read proofs. The evening before I had received galley proofs of the preface of a book of mine, and since this preface was a statement of faith,[7] I wished to read it once again quite carefully before it was printed. Now I took it into the study below that had been offered to me in case I should need it. But here the old man already sat at his writing-desk. Directly after greeting me he asked me what I had in my hand, and when I told him, be asked whether I would not read it aloud to him. I did so gladly. He listened in a friendly manner but clearly astonished, indeed with growing amazement. When I was through, he spoke hesitatingly, then, carried away by the importance of his subject, ever more passionately. "How can you bring yourself to say 'God' time after time? How can you expect that your readers will take the word in the sense in which you wish it to be taken? What you mean by the name of God is something above all human grasp and comprehension, but in speaking about it you have lowered it to human conceptualization. What word of human speech is so misused, so defiled, so desecrated as this! All the innocent blood that has been shed for it has robbed it of its radiance. All the injustice that it has been used to cover has effaced its features. When I hear the highest called 'God,' it sometimes seems almost blasphemous."

The kindly eyes flamed. The voice itself flared. Then we sat silent for awhile facing each other. The room lay in the flowing brightness of early morning. It seemed to me as if a power from the light entered into me. What I now answered, I cannot today reproduce but only indicate.

"Yes," I said, "it is the most heavy-laden of all human words. None has become so soiled, so mutilated. Just for this reason I may not abandon it. Generations of men have laid the burden of their anxious lives upon this word and weighed it to the ground; it lies in the dust and bears their whole burden. The races of man with their religious factions have torn the word to pieces; they have killed for it and died for it, and it bears their finger-marks and their blood. Where might I find a word like it to describe the highest! If I took the purest, most sparkling concept from the inner

---

7. It was the Foreword to the collected edition of Buber's *Talks on Judaism* (1923).

treasure-chamber of the philosophers, I could only capture thereby an unbinding product of thought. I could not capture the presence of Him whom the generations of men have honored and degraded with their awesome living and dying. I do indeed mean Him whom the hell-tormented and heaven-storming generations of men mean. Certainly, they draw caricatures and write 'God' underneath; they murder one another and say 'in God's name'. But when all madness and delusion fall to dust, when they stand over against Him in the loneliest darkness and no longer say 'He, He' but rather sigh 'Thou', shout 'Thou', all of them the one word, and when they then add 'God', is it not the real God whom they all implore, the One Living God, the God of the children of man? Is it not He who *hears* them? And just for this reason is not the word 'God' the word of appeal, the word which has become a *name,* consecrated in all human tongues for all times? We must esteem those who interdict it because they rebel against the injustice and wrong which are so readily referred to 'God' for authorization. But we may not give it up. How understandable it is that some suggest we should remain silent about the 'last things' for a time in order that the misused words may be redeemed! But they are not to be redeemed *thus.* We cannot cleanse the word 'God' and we cannot make it whole; but, defiled and mutilated as it is, we can raise it from the ground and set it over an hour of great care."

It had become very light in the room. It was no longer dawning, it was light. The old man stood up, came over to me, laid his hand on my shoulder and spoke: "Let us be friends." The conversation was completed. For where two or three are truly together, they are together in the name of God.

# Samuel and Agag

I once met on a journey a man whom I already knew through an earlier meeting. He was an observant Jew who followed the religious tradition in all the details of his life-pattern. But what was for me essential (as had already become unmistakably clear to me at that first meeting) was that this relationship to tradition had its origin and its constantly renewed confirmation in the relationship of the man to God.

When I now saw him again, it turned out that we fell into a discussion of biblical questions, and indeed not of peripheral questions but central ones, central questions of faith. I do not know exactly any longer in what connection we came to speak of that section of the Book of Samuel in which it is told how Samuel delivered to King Saul the message that his dynastic rule would be taken from him because he had spared the life of the conquered prince of the Amalekites. I reported to my partner in dialogue how dreadful it had already been to me when I was a boy to read this as the message of God (and my heart compelled me to read it over again or at least to think about the fact that this stood written in the Bible). I told him how already at that time it horrified me to read or to remember how the heathen king went up to the prophet with the words on his lips, "Surely the bitterness of death is past," and was hewn to pieces by him. I said to my partner: "I have never been able to believe that this is a message of God. I do not believe it."

With wrinkled forehead and contracted brows, the man sat opposite me and his glance flamed into my eyes. He remained silent, began to speak, became silent again. "So?" he broke forth at last, "So? You do not believe it?" "No," I answered, "I do not believe it." "So? so?" he repeated almost threateningly. "You do not believe it?" And I once again: "No." "What . . . what . . ."—he thrust the words before him one after the other—"what do you believe then?" "I believe," I replied without reflecting, "that Samuel has misunderstood God." And he, again slowly, but more softly than before: "So? You believe that?" And I: "Yes." Then we were both silent. But now something happened the like of which I have rarely seen before or since in this my long life. The angry countenance opposite me became transformed, as if a hand had passed over it soothing it. It lightened, cleared, was now turned toward me bright and clear. "Well," said the man with a positively gentle tender clarity, "I think so too." And again we became silent, for a good while.

There is in the end nothing astonishing in the fact that an observant Jew of this nature, when he has to choose between God and the Bible, chooses God: the God in whom he believes, Him in whom he can believe. And yet, it seemed to me at that time significant and still seems so to me today. The man later came to the land of Israel and here I met him once again, some time before his death. Naturally I regarded him then as the speaker of that word of one time; but in our talk the problem of biblical belief was not touched on. It was, indeed, no longer necessary.

For me, however, in all the time since that early conversation the question has again and again arisen whether at that time I expressed in the right manner what I meant. And again and again I answered the question in the same way: Yes and No. Yes in so far as it concerns what had been spoken of in that conversation; for there it was right to answer my partner in his language and within the limits of his language in order that the dialogue might not come to naught and that the common insight into one truth at times afforded to two men might fulfill itself, in no matter how limited a way. In so far as it concerns that, Yes. But No when it concerns both recognizing oneself and making known that man and the human race are inclined to misunderstand God. Man is so created that he can understand, but does not have to understand, what God says to him. God does not abandon the created man to his needs and anxieties; He provides him with the assistance of His word; He speaks to him, He comforts him with His word. But man does not listen with faithful ears to what is spoken to him. Already in hearing he blends together command of heaven and statute of earth, revelation to the existing being and the orientations that he arranges himself. Even the holy scriptures of man are not excluded, not even the Bible. What is involved here is not ultimately the fact that this or that form of biblical historical narrative has misunderstood God; what is involved is the fact that in the work of throats and pens out of which the text of the Old Testament has arisen, misunderstanding has again and again attached itself to understanding, the manufactured has been mixed with the received. We have no objective criterion for the distinction; we have only faith—when we have it. Nothing can make me believe in a God who punishes Saul because he has not murdered his enemy. And yet even today I still cannot read the passage that tells this otherwise than with fear and trembling. But not it alone. Always when I have to translate or to interpret a biblical text, I do so with fear and trembling, in an inescapable tension between the word of God and the words of man.

# Beginnings

The question of the possibility and reality of a dialogical relationship between man and God, thus of a free partnership of man in a conversation between heaven and earth whose speech in address and answer is the happening itself, the happening from above and the happening from below, had already accosted me in my youth. In particular since the Hasidic tradition had grown for me into the supporting ground of my own thinking, hence since about 1905, that had become an innermost question for me. In the language of the writings on the dialogical principle that arose many years later, it appears emphatically for the first time in the autumn of 1907 in the introduction to my book, *The Legend of the Baal-Shem*. This introduction was concerned with the radical distinction between myth in the narrower sense (the myth of the mythologists) and legend. It said:

The legend is the myth of the calling. In pure myth there is no difference of being . . . Even the hero only stands on another rung than the god, not over against him; they are not the I and the Thou . . . The god of pure myth does not call, he begets; he sends forth the begotten, the hero. The god of the legend calls, he calls the son of man: the prophets, the saints . . . The legend is the myth of I and Thou, of caller and called, of the finite that enters into the infinite and of the infinite that needs the finite.

Here the dialogical relationship is thus exemplified in its highest peak: because even on this height the essential difference between the partners persists unweakened, while even in such nearness the independence of man continues to be preserved.

From this event of the exception, of the extraction, however, my thought now led me, ever more earnestly, to the common that can be experienced by all. The clarification took place first of all here too in connection with my interpretation of Hasidism: in the Preface, written in September 1919 to my book, *Der Grosse Maggid und seine Nachfolge* (1921), the Jewish teaching was described as "wholly based on the two-directional relation of human I and divine Thou, on reciprocity, on the *meeting*." Soon after, in the autumn of 1919, followed the first, still unwieldy draft of *I and Thou*.

There now followed two years in which I could do almost no work except on Hasidic material, but also—with the exception of Descartes's *Discourse on the Method* which I again took up—read no *philosophica* (therefore the works connected with the subject of dialogue by Cohen, Rosenzweig, and Ebner [8] I read only later, too late to affect my own thought). This was part of a procedure that I understood at that time as a spiritual askesis. Then I was able to begin the final writing of *I and Thou*, which was completed in the spring of 1922. As I wrote the third and last part, I broke the reading-askesis and began with Ebner's fragments. His book showed me, as no other since then, here and there in an almost uncanny nearness, that in this our time men of different kinds and traditions had devoted themselves to the search for the buried treasure. Soon I also had similar experiences from other directions.

---

8. (Note by Buber) Herrmann Cohen, *Religion der Vernunft aus den Quellen des Judentums* (1919); Franz Rosenzweig. *Der Stern der Erlösung* (1919); Ferdinand Ebner, *Das Wart und die geistigen Realitäten* (1921). Therefore Rosenzweig states in one of his letters *(Briefe,* p. 462) that in December 1921 I did not yet know his book.

Of the initiators I had already as a student known Feuerbach and Kierkegaard. Yes and No to them had become a part of my existence. Now there surrounded me in spirit a growing circle of men of the present generations who were concerned, even if in unequal measure, about the one thing that had become for me an ever more vital matter. The basic view of the twofold nature of the human attitude is expressed in the beginning of *I and Thou*. But I had already prepared the way for this view in the distinction presented in my book *Daniel* (1913) between an 'orienting', objectifying basic attitude and a 'realizing', making-present one. This is a distinction that coincides in its core with that carried through in *I and Thou* between the I-It relation and the I-Thou relation, only the latter is no longer grounded in the sphere of subjectivity but in that between the beings. But this is the decisive transformation that took place in a series of spirits in the time of the first World War. It announced itself in very manifold meanings and spheres, but the fundamental connection between them, stemming out of the disclosed transformation of the human situation, is unmistakable.

# A Tentative Answer

Asked about a tentative answer which might then be the chief conclusion expressible in conceptual language of my experiences and observations, I can give no other reply than confess to the knowledge comprehending the questioner and myself: to be man means to be *the* being that is over-against. The insight into this simple fact has grown in the course of my life. It has been expressed in divers other theses of like subject and similar construction, and I certainly hold many of them to be not incorrect; my knowing leads to just this, however, that it is this over-againstness which matters.

In this thesis the definite article is fully accentuated. All beings in nature are indeed placed in a being-with-others, and in each living being this enters as perception of others and action toward others in work. But what is peculiar to man is that one can ever and again become aware of the other as this being existing over-against him, over against whom he himself exists. He becomes aware of the other as one who relates to him out of his selfhood and to whom he relates out of his selfhood. By virtue of this characteristic reserved to him, man has not simply entered into being as one species among other species—only just so much more manifoldly endowed—but as a special sphere. For here, and within what we call world only here, does the meeting of the one with the other take place in full reality. Certainly there is nowhere in all world-immanence a self-enclosed unity—this is as such transcendence—but each individual is directed and referred to the other. Only in man, however, does this interrelatedness transform itself and issue into the reality of meeting in which the one exists over against the other as his other, as one able in common presence at once to withstand him and confirm him. Where this self-being turned toward the partner over against one is not lived, the sphere of man is still unrealized. The human means the taking place from one time to another of that meeting which is latent in the being of the world.

The insight that I have intimated here encounters ever again an impressive argument—only rarely, to be sure, in an outspoken manner, mostly as the wordless self-emphasis of 'spiritual' persons. It is argued through a reference, mostly only just presented, to the alleged essential nature of mental work. This takes place not in a living over-against, ready for give and take, but in a fundamentally impermeable being-in-oneself that is alone accessible to the 'spirit', that is, to ideas and images that emerge out of the all-encompassing depths of the self. The thinking of the thinker is said to bear the most unmistakable witness that this is so.

My experiences and observations have taught me to see it otherwise. Out of all the ages of man about whose spiritual work I know, I have become acquainted not merely with no great configuration, but also with no great thought whose origin was not to be gathered from the self-involving contact with existing being over against one. The evolved substance which the spirit brings as a work into the ages has come to it out of the unreserved meetings of its personal bearers with otherness. For as in other respects there is in the world-immanence no self-enclosed unity, so also there is in it no self-enclosed unity of the spirit. Only through opening out, through entering into openness, does the spirit that has descended into the human realm win that coherence in work that has not already passed away in becoming. The fortress into which the self-possessed spirituality retreats before the exacting demand of answering life over against one is a gloriously painted coulisse.

It is the spirit that, having entered into the being of man, enables and fits him to live over-against in distance and relation; the spirit has thereby empowered man to be a special sphere of being. From this primal process has come forth the highest work-treasure of man, speech, the manifest proclamation of existing reciprocity between the one and the other. But the gifts of the spirit have also brought with them the great danger, becoming ever greater, that threatens mankind. It has belonged to the constitution of the human person as the bearer of the spirit that the basic situation of existing over-against also carries over here into the inwardness of the person. Thus there could develop a relationship of the individual to himself foreign to the non-human world, although here there naturally belonged to the situation of 'being over-against' nothing of the structural difference and the independence of answer of being over-against in actual dialogue—unless it was in the cases of a sickness that splits the personal coherence. But now at the same time the possibility opened that the dialogic of the soul cut itself off from all real communicating with the otherness outside it and degenerated into a self-enjoying of individual meaning, indeed to a hybris of an All-Self that arrogates to itself the self-enclosed unity of the Godhead existing before all creations and emanations. What was to be found as existing outside of the self was no longer the partner of a genuine reciprocity, but ultimately only the objective knots within a psyche that might certainly have been conceived in theory as more or less universal, but was lived as exclusively individual. By means of the universalizing philosophical positions, this individual self could be identified in practice simply with the Self and was no longer exposed to the claim of otherness.

My experience and observations have taught me to recognize in this degeneration the opponent of mankind, steadily increasing in might during the epochs of history, but especially in our time. It is none other than the spirit itself, cut off, that commits the sin against the holy spirit.

# Books and Men

If I had been asked in my early youth whether I preferred to have dealings only with men or only with books, my answer would certainly have been in favor of books. In later years this has become less and less the case. Not that I have had so much better experiences with men than with books; on the contrary, purely delightful books even now come my way more often than purely delightful men. But the many bad experiences with men have nourished the meadow of my life as the noblest book could not do, and the good experiences have made the Earth into a garden for me. On the other hand, no book does more than remove me into a paradise of great spirits, where my innermost heart never forgets I cannot dwell long, nor even wish that I could do so. For (I must say this straight out in order to be understood) my innermost heart loves the world more than it loves the spirit. I have not, indeed, cleaved to life in the world as I might have; in my relations with it I fail it again and again; again and again I remain guilty towards it for falling short of what it expects of me, and this is partly, to be sure, because I am so indebted to the spirit. I am indebted to the spirit as I am to myself, but I do not, strictly speaking, love it, even as I do not, strictly speaking, love myself. I do not in reality love him who has seized me with his heavenly clutch and holds me fast; rather I love her, the 'world', who comes again and again to meet me and extends to me a pair of fingers.

Both have gifts to share. The former showers on me his manna of books; the latter extends to me the brown bread on whose crust I break my teeth, a bread of which I can never have enough: men. Aye, these tousle-heads and good-for-nothings, how I love them! I revere books—those that I really read—too much to be able to love them. But in the most venerable of living men I always find more to love than to revere: I find in him something of this world, that is simply there as the spirit never can be there. The spirit hovers above me powerfully and pours out his exalted gift of speech, books; how glorious, how weird! But she, the human world, needs only to cast a wordless smile, and I cannot live without her. She is mute; all the prattle of men yields no word such as sounds forth constantly out of books. And I listen to it all in order to receive the silence that penetrates to me through it, the silence of the creature. But just the human creature! That creature means a mixture. Books are pure, men are mixed; books are spirit and word, pure spirit and purified word; men are made up of prattle and silence, and their silence is not that of animals but of men. Out of the human silence behind the prattle the spirit whispers to you, the spirit as *soul*. She, she is the beloved.

Here is an infallible test. Imagine yourself in a situation where you are alone, wholly alone on Earth, and you are offered one of the two, books or men. I often hear men prizing their solitude but that is only because there are still men somewhere on Earth even though in the far distance. I knew nothing of books when I came forth from the womb of my mother, and I shall die without books, with another human hand in my own. I do, indeed, close my door at times and surrender myself to a book, but only because I can open the door again and see a human being looking at me.

SARVEPALLI RADHAKRISHNAN (1888–1975) was an influential interpreter of Hindu spirituality to the modern world, and a profound religious philosopher in his own right. He combined a distinguished teaching career with a life in politics, and was elected the second President of India in 1962. His best-known works are *An Idealist View of Life* (1932) and *Eastern Religions and Western Thought* (1939). He wrote the following statement in the Indian Embassy in Moscow, where he was at the time Indian Ambassador to the Soviet Union.

# Sarvepalli
# RADHAKRISHNAN

## " *No man, however enlightened and holy he may be, can ever really be saved until all the others are saved.* "

NO MAN'S STORY OF HIS OWN LIFE CAN fail to be of interest to others, if it is written in sincerity. Even if the stage be small and the role of the participant a minor one, the interactions of chance and circumstance with human desires and ideals that shape the destinies of any individual are of some interest to his fellows. But of all writing, autobiographical writing is the most delicate. We do not wish to confess our deeds and misdeeds in public. We are inclined to show to the world more of our successes than of our setbacks, more of our gains than of our losses. Robert Browning tells us that the meanest of mankind has two sides to his life, one to face the world with and the other to show the woman he loves. We have two sides, one in ordinary life and the other when we write about ourselves for the public. We want to live an imaginary life in other people's ideas of us. We then direct our efforts to seeming what we are not. Besides, any sensitive man who takes life seriously is somewhat inaccessible to the public. If he happens to be a writer, he does not generally reveal himself except through his writings, where he recreates his personal experiences by clothing them with general significance. Through his writings, which constitute his main life work, he tries to communicate the vital ideas which have shaped his life. My writings are no more than fragments of a confession.

There are some who make up their mind early what they are going to be and plan carefully from their early years to reach their goal. They find out what they wish to do and try to do it with all their might. I cannot say that I came to the study of philosophy as one dedicated from childhood to the service of the altar. I am not a philosopher because I could not help being one. "Life," says Dilthey, "is a mysterious fabric, woven of chance, fate and character." That philosophy became the subject of my special study—was it a part of my destiny, was it the result of my character, or was it mere chance?

When I was a young student of seventeen in the Madras Christian College, and was vacillating about the choice of a subject from out of the five options of mathematics, physics, biology, philosophy, and history, a cousin of mine, who took his degree that year, passed on his textbooks in philosophy to me, G.F. Stout's *Manual of Psychology;* J. Welton's *Logic* (two volumes), and J. S. Mackenzie's *Manual of Ethics;* and that decided my future interest. To all appearance this is a mere accident. But when I look at the series of accidents that have shaped my life, I am persuaded that there is more in this life than meets the eye. Life is not a mere chain of physical causes and effects. Chance seems to form the surface of reality, but deep down other forces are at work. If the universe is a living one, if it is spiritually alive, nothing in it is merely accidental. "The Moving Finger writes; and, having writ,/moves on."

When, however, the study of philosophy became my life's work, I entered a domain which has sustained me both intellectually and spiritually all these years. My conception of a philosopher was in some ways similar to that of

Marx, who proclaimed in his famous *Theses on Feuerbach* that philosophy had hitherto been concerned with *interpreting* life, but that the time had come for it to *change* life. Philosophy is committed to a creative task. Although in one sense philosophy is a lonely pilgrimage of the spirit, in another sense it is a function of life.

# I Chose Wisdom

I spent the first eight years of my life in a small town in South India, Tirutani, which is even today a great center of religious pilgrimage. My parents were religious in the traditional sense of the term. I studied in Christian missionary institutions for twelve years, Lutheran Mission High School, Tirupati (1896–1900), Voorhees College, Vellore (1900–1904), and the Madras Christian College (1904–1908). Thus I grew up in an atmosphere where the unseen was a living reality. My approach to the problems of philosophy from the angle of religion as distinct from that of science or of history was determined by my early training. I was not able to confine philosophy to logic and epistemology.

There are tasks and responsibilities open to an Indian student of philosophic thought, living in this profoundly meaningful period of history. The prominent feature of our time is not so much the wars and the dictatorships which have disfigured it, but the impact of different cultures on one another, their interaction, and the emergence of a new civilization based on the truths of spirit and the unity of mankind. The tragedies and catastrophes which occupy so much of the foreground of our consciousness are symbolic of the breakdown of the separatist tendencies and the movement towards the integration of national societies in a single world whole. In the confusions of the contemporary scene, this fallible, long-suffering and apparently helpless generation should not overlook the great movement towards integration in which it is participating.

Through her connection with Great Britain, India is once again brought into relationship with the Western world. The interpenetration of the two great currents of human effort at such a crisis in the history of the human race is not without meaning for the future. With its profound sense of spiritual reality brooding over the world of our ordinary experience, with its lofty insights and immortal aspirations, Indian thought may perhaps wean us moderns from a too exclusive preoccupation with secular life or with the temporary formulations in which logical thought has too often sought to imprison spiritual aspiration. We do not seem to be mentally or spiritually prepared for the increasing intimacy into which remote peoples are drawn by the force of physical and economic circumstances. The world which has found itself as a single body is feeling for its soul. May we not prepare for the truth of the world's yet unborn soul by a free interchange of ideas and the development of a philosophy which will combine the best of European humanism and Asiatic religion, a philosophy profounder and more living than either, endowed with greater spiritual and ethical force, which will conquer the hearts of men and compel peoples to acknowledge its sway? Such a view of the function of philosophy in modern life is born out of a necessity of thought and an Indian student may perhaps make a little contribution to the development of a world perspective in philosophy.

The danger of all human occupation is present also in philosophy, the danger of accepting standard solutions and performing mechanically, through sheer laziness and inertia, the established modes of thinking. If we teach ready-made doctrines and see in any system of thought perfection and completeness, we miss the true spirit of enquiry. There cannot be an authentic philosophical situation unless there is uneasiness about prevalent opinions. If we lose the capacity to doubt we cannot get into the mood of philosophic thought. Whitehead's observation that "life is an offensive against the repetitive mechanism of the universe" is true of the philosophic life also.

If we take any philosopher as a *guru,* if we treat his works as gospel, if we make of his teaching a religion complete with dogma and exegesis, we may become members of the congregation of the faithful, but will not possess the openness of mind essential for a critical understanding of the master's views. The true teachers help us to think for ourselves in the new situations which arise. We would be unworthy disciples if we did not question and criticize them. They try to widen our knowledge and help us to see clearly. The true teacher is like Kṛṣṇa in the *Bhagavadgītā,* who advises Arjuna to think for himself and do as he chooses, *yathā icchasi tathā kuru* (*Bhagavadgītā,* xviii, 63).

There is, however, a longing in the human mind for eternal truths embodied in fixed formulas which we need not discuss, modify or correct. We do crave a constant rule of life, a sure guide to heaven. Devotion to a master who lays down the law gives us rest, confidence, and security. To minds wearied and worried by doubt, authoritarian religions give a sense of release and purpose. We cannot, however, expect rational criticism from those who have too much reverence for authority.

Again, tradition in human life takes the place of instinct in animals. It makes a man think, feel, and desire in forms that have prevailed in the human environment for centuries and about whose validity he feels no misgivings whatsoever. We are all born to our traditions. In regard to them there is a certain degree of inevitability. We are as little free in choosing our cultural ancestors as we are in choosing our physical ancestors. Insofar as a person lives according to tradition and obeys it instinctively, he leads a life of faith, of a believer. The need for philosophy arises when faith in tradition is shaken.

In the matter of tradition the Americans are in a fortunate position because they have no ancestors and no classic soil. Goethe, in a little poem, *Amerika, du hast es besser* (America, You Have It Better), writes "Your fate is happier than that of our old continent. You have no ruined chateaux . . . you are not troubled by vain memories and useless quarrels." India, however, has had a long tradition and I grew up in it. I started therefore with a prejudice in its favor.

# The Undermining of Tradition

My teachers in Christian missionary institutions cured me of this faith and restored for me the primordial situation in which all philosophy is born. They were teachers of philosophy, commentators, interpreters, apologists for the Christian way of thought and life, but were not, in the strict sense of the term, seekers of truth. By their criticism of Indian thought they disturbed my faith and shook the traditional props on which I leaned.

While the undogmatic apprehensions and the discipline of mind which Hinduism provides as the essential means for the discovery of truth are established in a rigorously logical manner, while the great insights, fundamental motives and patterns of thought of Hindu religion have meaning for us even today, it has taken on in its long history many arbitrary and fanciful theories and is full of shackles which constrict the free life of the spirit. Besides, we live in a time when we have become the inheritors of the world's thought. We have accumulated much historical knowledge about religions and philosophies. We find that innumerable people before us have raised these questions about the nature of the universe, the principle of being and have given answers which they treated as final and absolute. The very multiplicity of these absolutisms makes it difficult for us to assume, if we are honest, that our absolutism is the true one and all others false. Faced by these conflicting and competing absolutisms, we become either traditionalists or sceptics. A critical study of the Hindu religion was thus forced on me.

I started my professional life as a teacher of philosophy in the Madras Presidency College in April 1909, where I worked for the next seven years. During that period I studied the classics of Hinduism, the *Upaniṣads*, the *Bhagavadgītā* and the commentaries on the *Brahma Sūtra* by the chief ācāryas, Śaṁkara, Rāmānuja, Madhva, Nimbārka and others, the Dialogues of the Buddha as well as the scholastic works of Hinduism, Buddhism, and Jainism.

Among the Western thinkers, the writings of Plato, Plotinus, and Kant, and those of Bradley and Bergson influenced me a great deal. My relations with my great Indian contemporaries, Tagore and Gandhi, were most friendly for nearly thirty years, and I realize the tremendous significance they had for me.

Although I admire the great masters of thought, ancient and modern, Eastern and Western, I cannot say that I am a follower of any, accepting his teaching in its entirety. I do not suggest that I refused to learn from others or that I was not influenced by them. While I was greatly stimulated by the minds of all those whom I have studied, my thought does not comply with any fixed traditional pattern. For my thinking had another source and proceeded from my own experience, which is not quite the same as what is acquired by mere study and reading. It is born of spiritual experience rather than deduced from logically ascertained premises. Philosophy is produced more by our encounter with reality than by the historical study of such encounters. In my writings I have tried to communicate my insight into the meaning of life. I am not sure, however, that I have succeeded in conveying my inmost ideas. I tried to show that my general position provides a valid interpretation of the world, which seems to me to be consistent with itself, to accord with the facts as we know them, and to foster the life of spirit.

# Continuity with the Past

Human minds do not throw up sudden stray thoughts without precedents or ancestors. History is continuity and advance. There is no such thing as utterly spontaneous generation. Philosophic experiments of the past have entered into the living mind of the present. Tradition links generations one with another and all progress is animated by ideas which it seems to supersede. The debt we owe to our spiritual ancestors is to study them. Traditional continuity is not mechanical reproduction; it is creative transformation, an increasing approximation to the ideal of truth. Life goes on not by repudiating the past but by accepting it and weaving it into the future in which the past undergoes a rebirth. The main thing is to remember and create anew. Confucius said: "He who by reanimating the Old can gain knowledge of the New is fit to be a teacher" (*Analects.* II.10. Waley's translation).

Indian people have concentrated for centuries on the problems of divine reality, human life and destiny. Philosophic wisdom has been the drive and inspiration of their culture. We today think with our past and from the level to which the past has taken us. Indian wisdom has also contributed effectively to the cultural developments of the regions of South-East Asia, which till yesterday were called Further India. The characteristic features of Indian culture can still be discerned "from Ayuthia and Angkor to Borobudur and Bali." India's historic influence spread through the arts of peace and not the weapons of war, through moral leadership and not political domination. Her influence could be discerned in the development of European thought from the time of the Orphic mysteries. Today Indian wisdom is essential not only for the revival of the Indian nation but also for the re-education of the human race.

When that noble and generous thinker, Professor J.H. Muirhead, invited me in 1917 to write an account of Indian Philosophy for his Library of Philosophy, I accepted his call, though not without considerable doubt. To outline the history of Indian philosophic thought, which has had a long span of development of over three thousand years on a cautious estimate, is indeed a prodigious task and I was aware that it was beyond the capacity of any single person. It might be done by a band of scholars in a co-operative undertaking, spread over a number of years, with the assistance of many research workers. The result of such an undertaking would not be a book but an encyclopedia. No scholar, however learned, can know everything in so vast a field. There will be gaps and mistakes. Besides, history is not only seeing but also thinking. Thinking is always constructive, if not creative. Historical writing is a creative activity. It is different from historical research. By the latter we acquire a knowledge of the facts in their proper succession, the raw material. It is the task of historical writing to understand these facts and give us a feel of the past, communicate to us the vibration of life. This requires knowledge as well as sensibility. The writer may at times allow his personal bias to determine his presentation. His sense of proportion and relevance may not be shared by others. His work at best will be a personal interpretation and not an impersonal survey.

There is also the danger that we are inclined to interpret ancient systems in a manner acceptable to modern minds. Such efforts sometimes overstep the mark and make ancient thinkers look very much like contemporaries of ours. Often a sense of hero-worship exalts the classical thinkers above the level of history. Instead of trying to understand them, as they are, as human beings, however great in mind and spirit they may be, we give to them imaginary perfections and treat their writings as sacred texts which contain solutions for our present problems.

I was aware of the dangers and difficulties involved in an adequate historical interpretation of Indian thought as well as of my own limitations, philosophical and linguistic. I therefore assumed a modest task: to produce an introduction to a vast, varied, and complex process of development, a book which will arouse the interest of readers in the insights and inspirations of the Indian genius. I tried to unroll a great panorama in which every element has some charm or interest. I tried not to overstate any case or indulge in personal dislike for its own sake.

History of philosophy should not be reduced to a mere statement of doctrines in chronological order. These doctrines are propositions, sentences with a meaning. Meanings are not absolute. They have no sense apart from when and by whom and for whom they were meant. The formulators of philosophical systems are not abstract thinkers or anonymous beings without birthdate or dwelling place. The date of a thinker and the place of the origin and growth of his thought are not external labels tacked on to systems, merely for placing them in their proper chronological order. Like all thought, philosophical thought belongs to the context of life. Its exponents belong to their age with its living beliefs and traditions, its scientific notions and myths. If we are to gain insight from the study of past writers, we must remove them from us, emphasize their distance in time and realize how different in many ways they are from us. To understand their thought we must learn to feel and understand their world even as they felt and understood it, never approaching them with condescension or contempt. Only in that way can we understand their living effective communication with us.

There have been historians of Indian philosophy who looked upon India's philosophic thought as a continuity in which it progressed rationally from one conception to another, where systems succeeded each other in intelligible order until it culminated in their own thought. All that was past was a progression towards their own present thinking. Mādhava's *Sarvadar-śanasaṁgraha* is a well-known instance of the treatment of the history of thought as a continuous progress to *Advaita Vedānta*. In the West, Hegel related the past history of thought as a collection of errors over against which stood out his own idealism as the truth. Intellectual unselfishness or humility is the mother of all writing, even though that writing may relate to the history of philosophy.

Though we cannot say that systems succeed each other in an ordered progression, there is no arbitrariness. Changes of life have brought about changes in thought and *vice versa*. The past philosophical development in East and in West has an integral reality. It is not a bewildering maze of clashing opinions, utterly irrational. We can discern an order in the dynamic interplay of ideas.

In all philosophical interpretation, the right method is to interpret thinkers at their best, in the light of what they say in the moments of their clearest insight. There is no reason why philosophical writers should not be judged as other creative artists are, at least in the main, on the basis of their finest inspirations.

Ancient Indians do not belong to a different species from ourselves. An actual study of their views shows that they ask questions and find answers analogous in their diversity to some of the more important currents in modern thought. The systems of Nāgārjuna and Śaṁkara, for example, are marvels of precision and penetration, comparable to the very best of Western thought.

# Bringing East and West Together

In rethinking the systems of the past, I sometimes employ terms with which the Western readers are familiar. I am aware of the limitations of the comparative method which can be either a bane or a blessing. We cannot overlook the different emphases, not only between East and West, but in the different systems of the East as well as in those of the West. These differences, when valid, are complementary, not contradictory. In many detailed investigations there is agreement between the thinkers of the East and the West.

The comparative method is relevant in the present context, when the stage is set, if not for the development of a world philosophy, at least for that of a world outlook. The different parts of the world cannot anymore develop separately and in independence of each other. Even as our political problem is to bring East and West together in a common brotherhood which transcends racial differences, so in the world of philosophy we have to bring about a cross-fertilization of ideas. If systems of philosophy are themselves determined by historical circumstances, there is no reason why the methods adopted in historical interpretation should not take into account the needs and conditions of the age. Each interpreter appeals to his own generation. He is wise to let the generation that succeeds him choose its own exponents. It will do so whether he likes it or not. His work is fulfilled if he keeps the thought alive in his generation, helps his successors to some extent, and attempts to answer, so far as he can, the desire of his age.

Though I have not had a sense of vocation, a sense that I was born to do what I am now carrying out, my travels and engagements in different parts of the world for over a generation gave me a purpose in life. My one supreme interest has been to try to restore a sense of spiritual values to the millions of religiously displaced persons, who have been struggling to find precarious refuges in the emergency camps of Art and Science, of Fascism and Naziism, of Humanism and Communism. The first step to recovery is to understand the nature of the confusion of thought which absorbs the allegiance of millions of men. Among the major influences which foster a spirit of skepticism in regard to religious truth are the growth of the scientific spirit, the development of a technological civilization, a formal or artificial religion which finds itself in conflict with an awakened social conscience, and a comparative study of religions.

# The Achievements of Science

The victories of science have been so dazzling and its progress so rapid that our minds are filled with scientific conceptions and habits of life. From the time Copernicus removed the Earth from the center of the Universe, the primacy of man in the universe has disappeared. Till Galileo founded modern mathematical physics, the mathematically exact movements of the heavenly bodies were traced to psychic forces, supernatural agents, a vast hierarchy of angelic beings who inhabit the stars and control our destiny. The two centuries after Newton witnessed wide developments in astronomy, physics, and chemistry, especially in increasing knowledge of the dimensions of the universe and of the nature and workings of matter. Sir James Jeans writes:

The last hundred years have seen more change than a thousand years of the Roman Empire, more than a hundred thousand years of the Stone Age. This change has resulted in large part from the applications of physical science, which, through the use of steam, electricity and petrol, and by way of the various industrial arts, now affects almost every moment of our existences. Its use in medicine and surgery may save our lives; its use in warfare may involve us in utter ruination. In its more abstract aspects it has exerted a powerful influence on our philosophies, our religions and our general outlook of life. (*The Growth of Physical Science* [1947])

Scientists seek to explain organic life in accordance with clearly perceptible natural laws. Man himself is no exception to the general laws which govern organic processes. He should see himself as a part of an irrefragable web of cause and effect, of inviolable law. He is not a free being, capable of choice, able to decide whether he shall write classics of wisdom or advertisements for cosmetics. Heracleitus said long ago, "Man's character is his fate" (*Fragment*, 121).

In the view of modern psychology, man is not master of himself even in his conscious ego. The conscious life of the soul is governed by animal instincts hidden and embedded in the unconscious. According to Freud:

> Humanity has in the course of time had to endure from the hands of science two great outrages upon its naive self-love. The first was when it realised that our Earth was not the centre of the universe, but only a tiny speck in the world-system. . . . That is associated in our minds with the name of Copernicus. . . . The second was when biological research robbed man of his peculiar privilege of having been specially created, and relegated him to a descent from the animal world, implying an ineradicable animal nature in him; this transvaluation has been accomplished in our time upon the instigation of Charles Darwin, Wallace and their predecessors. . . . But man's craving for grandiosity is now suffering the third and most bitter blow from present day psychological research, which is endeavouring to prove to the 'ego' of each one of us that he is not even master in his own house but that he must remain content with the veriest scraps of information about what is going on unconsciously in his own mind. (*Introductory Lectures on Psychoanalysis*. English translation by G.I. Riviere, p. 240)

Freedom of the will is an egotistic delusion. Descartes said, "I regard the human body as a machine so built and put together that, still, although it had no mind, it would not fail to move in all the same ways as at present, since it does not move by the direction of its will." Sir Charles Sherrington writes:

Descartes's conception of the doings of man still finds its echo in official Russia. The citizen there taken *en gros,* seems to be viewed as a system of reflexes. The State can 'condition' and use these systems of reflexes. 'Reflexology,' as it is there called, becomes a science of Man on which the State leans. In 'reflexology' Descartes would find Ivan Pavlov of Petrograd his greatest successor; and the successor was an experimentalist as Descartes was not. (*The Integrative Action of the Nervous System*)

Human personality is determined by the external environment by which it is surrounded. It has no principle in it by which it can resist the environment. Such a view makes short work of miracles, of effective prayer and reduces man, dressed in a little brief rationality, to the level of circles and stones. What we call the soul of man is but an empty word. A highly developed cerebral animal, that is what man is.

# Ethics, History, and Metaphysics

Human values are determined by the chance situation in which man finds himself and to which he has to adjust his way of living. Professor John Dewey writes: "Life is a process of experimented adjustment in a precarious world. Problems are solved when they arise, namely in action, in the adjustment of behaviour" (*Influence of Darwin on Philosophy*, p. 44). From such a view it follows that moral standards are subject to change. Professor Dewey says, "Values are as unstable as the forms of clouds. The things that possess them are exposed to all the contingencies of existence, and they are indifferent to our likings and tastes." Compare this with Jean-Paul Sartre: "My freedom is the unique foundation of values. And since I am the being by virtue of whom values exist, nothing, absolutely nothing can justify me in adopting this or that value or scale of values. As the unique basis of the existence of values, I am totally unjustifiable. And my freedom is in anguish at finding that it is the baseless basis of values" (Quoted in Marcel's *The Philosophy of Existence*, p. 63).

Philosophers claim to establish history as a realm in which the freedom of man may be demonstrated as against the autocracy of nature. Professor Collingwood argues that historical thought is the discovery of individuality, which is freedom. Modern historical investigation, however, has discovered in increasing measure the predominance of geographical, economic, social, and other causes even in the most outstanding of human achievements. It is argued that man and his civilization are merely the products of natural and material forces. This view is not peculiar to Marx.

It is the contention of the Logical Positivists that nothing that is not evident to the senses or to the extension of the senses provided by scientific instruments has any claim to truth. Metaphysics which discusses problems of God and soul are idle speculation. Religion is an emotional reaction. Religion and metaphysics are no doubt facts of human life, like poetry and fiction. They are an outlet for the gratification of our emotions, but do not satisfy the desire for knowledge. Only those statements are true which admit of empirical verification by an appeal to sense data or the data of introspection. But propositions dealing with religion, relating to God's existence, attributes and activities, like all judgments of value, fall outside these limits. They cannot be empirically verified. They are merely the expression of emotions, admitting neither of truth nor of falsehood.

The fear of metaphysics is unreal. But the metaphysical nature of man will not remain vacant. It will have a content. Metaphysical emptiness does not exist, for it is itself a metaphysics, a skeptical metaphysics. To refuse to philosophize is in itself a kind of philosophy. The "malady of contemporary empiricistic philosophizing," as Einstein calls it, will not last long.

# The Doom of the Universe

To crown it all, science presents a gloomy picture of the future of the universe. The inorganic irreversible evolution imposed by Carnot-Clausius's law, also called the second law of thermodynamics, corresponds to an evolution toward more and more 'probable' states, characterized by an ever-increasing symmetry, a levelling of energy. The universe tends towards an equilibrium where all the dissymmetries will be flattened out, where all motion will have stopped, where absolute cold will reign.

All that remains for man to do is to be born, to grow up, to earn and to spend, to mate, to produce offspring, to grow old, and at last to sleep forever, safe in the belief that there is no purpose to be served in life except the fulfilment of the needs of man set in a vast and impersonal framework of mechanical processes. The Earth turns, the stars blaze and die, and man need not waste his thought on seeking a different destiny.

The most remarkable feature of the scientific culture is its universality. It is one, though its achievements may be in different places and by different persons. There are no competing scientific cultures as there are competing religions or competing codes of law. In the geographical sense also it is universal, in that it has penetrated all parts of the world. Nature is one, and therefore science is one. A universal human community is the social aspiration of science.

The barriers which restrict the free flow of scientific information for reasons of security are against our conceptions of the universality of science. They increase distrust and anxiety and hamper international co-operation. Nations, instead of co-operating with one another for improving the material conditions of human life, are competing with one another over the possession of the means for annihilating vast populations and even making parts of the earth temporarily uninhabitable. Many famous scientists who are still animated by the true spirit of science call for an open exchange of information about all aspects of science, atomic science included. If it is done under international auspices and with proper safeguards, it will relieve tension, restore confidence, and result in a radical readjustment in international relationships.

A scientific frame of mind has become a part of the mental outfit of even ordinary men and women. The respect hitherto given to poets, priests and philosophers is now transferred to scientists and technicians. The more they lay bare the hidden springs of the universe, the more they master the secrets of the atom, the less significant do we become and the more dwarfed by power.

A scientific view of the world has shaken the foundations of many of the ancient creeds. Their authoritarian formulas do not carry conviction to the inquiring mind. Myths of creation are repudiated by geology. Conceptions of mind and soul are revolutionized by biology and psychology. Supernatural events on which religions are based are explained in a naturalistic way by anthropology and history. Though belief in miracles occurs in certain circumstances and in certain epochs, they never happened in fact; for the world is bound by invariable laws working through nature and history in an unbroken chain of cause and effect. Once upon a time, perhaps, religion helped men to liberate themselves from primitive superstitions and crude beliefs. This very process of emancipation demands the supersession of religion, its myths and legends, its obsolete theories and antiquated muddles. No religion which tolerates these superstitions can be accepted by mankind today. As we are now advancing to a new stage of civilization, it is argued, we have to discard religion as an outworn instrument of a dead past. "When we become men we put away childish things," said St. Paul. We are no longer young; we have outgrown our toys. The exploitation of human infantilism should now disappear.

The whole spirit of science is opposed to that of religion as ordinarily understood. Its attitude is frankly empirical, whereas the religious temper tends to be dogmatic. While scientific hypotheses are provisional, religious creeds profess finality. The former induce an attitude of humility and tolerance, the latter breed intolerance and fanaticism. The authoritarian attitude of religions and the incredible beliefs accepted by them have made it difficult for honest men to accept religious creeds. We cannot say with Dostoyevsky "If any one could prove to me that Christ is outside the truth, I would prefer to stay with Christ and not with truth." For us nothing can be true by faith if it is not true by reason. The temper of science combines skepticism with openness to new facts. If life is languishing from religion, it is due to dogmatic religion as much as to mechanistic science.

# Technological Civilization

Technology is the manipulation of the environment in the interests of human life. It has been with us from the beginning of our history. The creation and use of artificial tools has distinguished human life from that of the animals. The epochs of human history are distinguished by the character of their technology: stone age, bronze age, iron age. If man does not use artificial techniques, he will remain completely at the mercy of nature and its hazards. By the invention of technical appliances he emancipates himself to some extent from his bondage to nature. He defies the weather by building huts and houses and living in them. He becomes independent of fig leaves and animal skins by the use of the spinning wheel and the loom. He produces what he wants by agriculture. From that dim and distant date when the human creature struck out the first flint instrument, through all the ages until now, when man belts the globe with radio and annihilates whole cities with atom bombs from the sky, the course of human life has been a career of material conquest and mechanical achievement. The pen, the brush, the spade, the lever, the pulley, the locomotive and the internal combustion engine form a continuous ascent. Yet we never considered the previous civilizations to be technological in character. Man, not the machine, was still the master. Today the machine has become the dominating factor of civilization.

The first great triumph of the machine was the industrial revolution, a product of science, of the spirit of invention, and of the large-scale organization of labor. The steam engine, electric power, and the development of chemistry helped the technological revolution. The application of machines to agriculture and industry has revolutionized the conditions of life. If we have the will, it is possible for us to eliminate from the world, hunger, want, poverty, disease, ignorance. We are capable of nourishing, clothing and housing every inhabitant of the Earth. The techniques of medicine and surgery, hygiene and sanitation, are sufficient to produce everywhere conditions of life which would guarantee to a high degree long life and healthy development for all. The cinema and the radio allow an almost unlimited spread of fundamental education. We have at our disposal means which would safeguard a high standard of life, material and cultural, for all mankind.

If hunger and disease, poverty and ignorance, which are no more inevitable, are still to be found in large parts of the Earth, it is because we are abusing the technical possibilities in the interests of wrong social, political, and international power relations. What is wrong is not technology but the social and cultural life of man, its purely industrial and utilitarian view of life, its cult of power and comfort.

# Effects of Industrial Technology on Human Relations

Technology has changed not only man's relations to nature but man's relations to man. So long as the technical appliances were controlled by human elements, so long as society was able to assimilate them, the social equilibrium was maintained; but, unfortunately for us, the greatest advances in technology happened in an age of ethical confusion and social chaos. A society spiritually and ethically enfeebled allowed the development of great industries without proper safeguards. The natural community of life was broken up. Cottage industries, where the craftsmen owned the means of production, have been displaced by large concerns, where the means of production are owned by men of wealth.

As a result all the evils of class distinctions of rich and poor, advanced and backward nations, have sprung up. There is concentration of productive power and wealth in a few hands or their monopolization by a state bureaucracy. The means have become more important than the ends. Men are being used for the production of material goods at the expense of their mental and physical health. The machine invented by man now controls his will. The farmers and craftsmen have become technicians; and cultures have become standardized with the result that we have the same films, the same magazines, and the same dance-tunes all over the world. In previous ages we also had tools for destructive purposes. We had weapons of war; but these weapons have today become dangerous. The war industries are controlled by the State, and in this way modern totalitarian States developed. The new developments have produced instability and confusion, political strains and economic stresses. We cannot overlook the obvious fact that human society is changed as much by a revolution in the methods of production as by a revolution in the forms of government.

In the highly industrialized countries we have colossal systems of power dealing with huge numbers of men and women and vast masses of material. Men and women in large numbers are taken out of their natural context, cut adrift from their moorings and brought under a different system of life. They have ceased to be persons, subjects with inner life and personal choice, and have become objects, things, instruments. Men need to be rooted in place, custom, and habit. These children of the machine are uprooted, displaced persons, immigrants. An organic society, through large-scale industrialization, has become an amorphous inorganic mass. There is a complete distortion of the basic conditions of normal human life. Man is handed over to the organization where efficiency is treated as the supreme end. Inefficiency is punished by unemployment in democratic societies or by the more severe penalties of slavery or liquidation in non-democratic ones.

In an industrial civilization we strive for the kind of success which is measured by bank balances. This ambition leads to aggressiveness which takes many forms: envy, rivalry, conflict. Competition for success creates tensions and makes human beings unbalanced and neurotic. As our enslavement to the economic machine is rising, human values are declining. We are at war with others because we are at war with ourselves.

The uprooted individual, mindless, traditionless, believes in nothing or anything. Skepticism and superstition hold the field. As he has no inward being, his surface nature is moulded by widespread and insistent propaganda. Any self-constituted savior of society, who promises to provide food and shelter at the price of subjection to his leadership, wins a following. The omnipotent State rushes into the void caused by the disappearance of traditional values, and lays claim to the overriding loyalty of all that come within its orbit. The establishment of dictatorships and the increasing supremacy of the State even in democracies are characteristic features of our time. With its ever-growing reliance on objective criteria of thought and ever deepening ignorance of the real nature of human life, contemporary technological civilization has become a social disease. We see on all sides the apotheosis of power and the withering of man who has been cut off from the sources of self-renewal. Having lost his sense of responsibility he is capable of almost limitless self-deception. New superstitions have sprung up which inspire millions of men and women with the fervour, the sanctions and the inhibitions of great religions. We seem to be caught up in a momentum of evil which is dragging us down to disaster. Mr. George Orwell thought that we shall all be living under totalitarian tyrannies by 1984.

# Practical Atheism and the Frailty of Religion

The two world wars have revealed, apart from the destruction, human and material, unparalled in recorded history, the enormous capacity for cruelty and evil of which human nature is capable. The fact that it has been possible for us to fall so easily into barbarism shows how frail our religious culture has been. Macaulay's words to the Wilberforces, that there were not two hundred men in London who believed in the Bible, may be a gross exaggeration; but they indicate that many of the leading men were unbelievers.

Almost all of us are atheists in practice, though we may profess belief in God. We may visit temples, attend services, repeat prayers; but we do all this with a kind of reverent inattention, or sacred negligence. We deny God's existence in everything that we do. We bow down before the world, flesh and power. Fénelon writes in his *Letters:* "There is practically nothing that men do not prefer to God. A tiresome detail of business, an occupation utterly pernicious to health, the employment of time in ways one does not dare to mention. Anything rather than God." If we are religious, we must live our religion. If our actions are opposed to those which are demanded by our religion, we cannot say that we are religious. We are really unbelievers, because we not only fail to carry out the demands of our religion but do not even think that these demands are to be carried out. If anyone tells us that we should adopt the precepts of Jesus in our daily life, we laugh at him and advise him to substitute for them some inventions of our own.

For a few earnest spirits, religion has been escapism. The Psalmist cries: "Man walketh in a vain shadow and disquieteth himself in vain." "Oh, that I had wings like a dove, for then would I flee away and be at rest." We divide the world into God and creation, absolute unity and purity on one side, and a realm of discord and hostility on the other. We strive to escape from the unbearable sadness of the actual into an ideal world where we satisfy our lonely self in the silent spaces of speculation.

If we do not interpret religion as a way of escape, we make it a defense of the established order. It comes to terms with the civilization in which it is placed, by justifying its judgments. The Erastian view of Christianity believes that the Church exists for enforcing obedience to social laws by means of supernatural sanctions which control those details of personal conduct that are beyond the reach of state laws. There does not seem to be any essential difference between a religious man and a nonreligious one, in regard to individual and social life. They both live by the law of the world. Jesus rejected the temptation of the kingdom of this world; but his followers adopt a compromising conformist attitude to the state, to the kingdom of Caesar, by employing the distinction between Caesar's things and God's things. Even the founders of religions accept the sufferings of the majority of human beings as part of their necessary lot in life, if not as a penance for some heavy guilt which they had incurred in their previous lives. They treat existing institutions as part of an eternal divine order. Poverty, disease, slavery, and war have all been justified and sanctioned by religion. Future happiness is promised as a recompense for present suffering.

Even those who do not themselves take religion seriously adopt it as a device to reconcile suffering men to their condition. That realistic if not devout psychologist, Napoleon, made the well-known comment:

> What is it that makes the poor man think it quite natural that there are fires in my parlour while he is dying of cold? That I have ten coats in my wardrobe while he goes naked? That at each of my meals enough is served to feed his family for a week? It is simply religion which tells him that in another life I shall be only his equal and that he actually has more chances of being happy there than I. Yes, we must see to it that the floors of the churches are open to all, and that it does not cost the poor man much to have prayers said on his tomb.

Social idealists with their love of equality and hatred of sham, who burn with a passion to create tolerable conditions of good life for the weltering mass of men, find religion to be worthless at its best and vicious at less than best. "Heaven help us, said the old religion; the new one from the very lack of that faith will teach us all the more to help one another" (George Eliot). Militant atheism, then, is the answer to dishonest religion.

Religions cannot claim to be the great civilizing agencies of the world. Although it is true that they, to some extent, inspired spiritual life, encouraged the arts, disciplined the mind and fostered the virtues of charity and peace, they have also filled the world with wars and tortured the souls and burnt the bodies of men. When we note the magnificent achievements of religion we should not fail to note the incredible corruption and degradation in its record. It has given its sanction to many forms of exploitation and violence. On the supreme issue which faces mankind today, peace or war, religions have been hesitant and complacent, if not militant and reactionary.

Since 1500 mankind has been steadily marching towards the formation of a single society. The two wars have led to a shrinkage of space and contraction of the world. The physical unity of the world requires to sustain it a psychological oneness. The barriers of dogmatic religions are sterilizing men's efforts to co-ordinate their forces to shape the future. Each religion is a rival to others. There are some things which are more important than our particularist allegiances: truth and humanity and that universal religious consciousness which is the common possession of all human beings by virtue of their spiritual endowment. So long as our group loyalties are strong and overriding we cannot belong to the general human society.

Religion, as it has been functioning, is unscientific and unsocial. On account of these features of traditional religion large sections of humanity are the victims of unwilling disbelief. It is an age of incoherence in thought and indecision in action. Our values are blurred, our thought is confused, our aims are wavering, and our future is uncertain. There are bits of knowledge here and there but no visible pattern. In his 1933 poem, *The Second Coming*, W.B. Yeats refers to our condition in memorable words which we may well ponder:

> Things fall apart; the centre cannot hold.
> Mere anarchy is loosed upon the world.
> The blood-dimmed tide is loosed, and everywhere
> The ceremony of innocence is drowned;
> The best lack all conviction, while the worst are full of passionate
>    intensity.

If we are to overcome the dangers that threaten us, we must confront them fearlessly and take the measure of their power to injure us. The issue for religion in our day is not in regard to doctrinal differences or ritual disagreements, but it concerns the very existence of religion. The state of coldness or indifference which ignores religion is more deadly than open rejection. Even Marx looks upon religion not as insignificant but as pernicious. Our modern intellectuals sum up the situation thus: some think God exists, some think not, it is impossible to tell, but it does not matter.

The mind of the world requires to be pulled together and the present aimless stare of dementia replaced by a collective rational purpose. We need a philosophy, a direction and a hope, if the present state of indecision is not to lead us to despair. Belief may be difficult, but the need for believing is inescapable. We are in search of a spiritual religion that is universally valid, vital, clear-cut, one that has an understanding of the fresh sense of truth and the awakened social passion which are the prominent characteristics of the religious situation today. The severe intellectual honesty and the burning passion for social justice are not to be slighted. They are expressions of spiritual sincerity. Our religion must give us an energy of thought which does not try to use evasions with itself, which dares to be sincere, an energy of will which gives us the strength to say what we believe and do what we say. If the world is today passing through a mood of atheism, it is because a higher religion is in process of emergence. Doubt and denial of God have often proved dialectical moments in the history of religions, ways by which mankind has increased its knowledge of God and emancipated itself from imperfect conceptions of religion.

# The Birth of a New Religion

The opposite of religion is not irreligion but a counter-religion. "Men think they can do without religion," writes Amiel. "They do not know that religion is indestructible, and that the question simply is, which will you have?" When the Buddha denied the Vedic gods, he did so in the name of a higher religion. When Socrates was put to death on the charge of atheism, his offence was the repudiation of an imperfect religion. When Christians were brought into the Roman amphitheater to undergo martyrdom for their convictions, the pagan mob shouted "The atheists to the lions." Atheism has often been the expression of the vitality of religion, its quest for reality in religion. The fact that man is unable or unwilling to acknowledge God means only that he cannot accept the ideas and beliefs about God framed by men, the false gods which obscure the living and ineffable God. Today the world is very sick, for it is passing through a crisis of the birth of a new religion.

Whereas the scientific mind is satisfied with secondary causes, the philosophic mind demands final causes. Philosophy is an attempt to explain the world to which we belong. It is experience come to an understanding with itself. Experience relates to the world of objects, of things, of nature studied by the natural sciences; the world of individual subjects, their thoughts and feelings, their desires and decisions, studied by the social sciences, like psychology and history; the world of values, studied by literature, philosophy and religion. We must weave into a consistent pattern the different sides of our experience. There can be no bifurcation between them. We must endeavor to frame a coherent system of general ideas in terms of which the different types of experience can be interpreted. Even if we may not be able to reach a final and adequate answer, it is useful to make the attempt. After all, the wisest of us, like Socrates, are ignorant men thinking aloud, faced by the infinitude and complexity of the world.

A spiritual interpretation of the universe is based on a number of arguments, which may not be separately infallible, but they do strengthen one another. We may indicate them by looking at the question from the three different angles of the object, the subject, and the spirit.

# Cosmic Evolution

The Indian thinkers, Hindu and Buddhist, viewed the world as a stream of happenings, a perpetual flow of events. Change is the essence of existence. The ultimate units of the concrete flow of experience are neither points of space nor instants of time nor particles of matter. They are events which have a three-dimensional character, a concrete content occupying a point of space at an instant of time. Śivāditya (eleventh century) in his *Saptapadārthi* observes that the concrete filling, space and time are in reality one only (*ākā sāditrayaṁ tu vastuta ekam eva,* 27). Space, time, matter, or life are abstractions from a happening with a qualitative character and a spatio-temporal setting. This world or saṁsāra is a process consisting of events, to use Whitehead's expressions.

The world process is not an incessant fluctuation comparable to a surging sea. It is a movement with a direction and a goal. Aristotle said that, if nothing depended on time for its realization, everything would already have happened. If time is a necessary element in the structure of the cosmic process then nature is a creative advance. The idea of evolution is not unknown to Indian thinkers, though they conceived it as a metaphysical hypothesis rather than as an empirically verified theory.

If the cosmos is a process, what is it that proceeds, and what is its destination? In the ancient Upaniṣad, the *Taittirīya* (eighth century B.C.), cosmic evolution is represented by the five stages of matter (*anna*), life (*prāṇa*) perceptual-instinctive consciousness (*manas*), reflective consciousness (*vijñāna*), and spiritual or creative consciousness (*ānanda*). In the cosmic process we have the successive emergence of the material, the organic, the animal, the human, and the spiritual orders of existence.

# The Emergence of Matter, Life, and Mind

Materiality is the first manifested form of cosmic existence. From unmanifested being we get the material manifestation. If matter grows into life, is there anything in matter compelling it to grow into life? Can the emergence of life be traced to the working of the principle of matter? It is assumed that it is the work of life itself energizing in and on the conditions of matter and applying to it its own laws and principles. Life exhibits characteristics which go beyond the general laws of inorganic processes. Living organisms respond to situations in a way that they preserve and perpetuate themselves. Their nutritive, reparatory and reproductive functions are 'intelligent', though not guided by intelligence. They are full of 'prospective adaptations'. Their actions tend to produce results which are beneficial to the individual and the species. Such actions, on the part of human individuals, are due to foresight. We need not postulate any mysterious vital force; but we must recognize that life is a unique kind of activity for which the formulas of matter and energy are not adequate.

Similarly when mind emerges out of life, it is due to the principle of mind working with its own impulses and necessities in life. Mind is not a kind of ghost introduced into the living organism. The principles of life and mind are not to be treated as working on independent lines in the conscious being. The unity of the living whole is preserved when the quality of mind arises.

Animals are conscious; men are self-conscious, and so have greater dignity than stones, or plants, or animals. By overlooking the distinction between men and animals, Hitler, for example, argued that the individual is nothing, it is the group that counts. Nature, he argued in his *Mein Kampf*, is ruthless in regard to individual lives and considerate only for the development of the species. He thought of man as merely the highest of the animals. "It is not necessary that any of us should live," he said. "It is only necessary that Germany should live." Even John Dewey argues in a similar vein:

> Within the flickering inconsequential acts of separate selves dwells a sense of the whole which claims and dignifies them. In its presence we put off mortality and live in the universal. The life of the community in which we live and have our being is the fit symbol of this relationship. The acts in which we express the perception of ties which bind us to others are its only rites and ceremonies. (*Human Nature and Conduct*, p. 332)

History is not a branch of biology. The drama of human personalities is distinct from life in the animal kingdom. Social sciences which deal with the story of man in society are a separate category from natural sciences.

Men have a restless reaching out for ideals. The human individual has to work his evolution consciously and deliberately. His growth is not effected fortuitously or automatically. He has to act responsibly and co-operate willingly with the purpose of evolution. If he falls into the external sphere, if he does not recognize his own dignity, the law of Karma rules. If he withdraws from the external, he can participate creatively in the cosmic development.

Looking back on the millions of years of the steady climb of life on the path of evolution, it seems presumptuous for us to imagine that with thinking man evolution has come to an end. The Upaniṣad affirms that there is a further step to be taken. Animal cunning has become human foresight; human self-consciousness must grow into comprehensive vision, into illumined consciousness (Compare *Jalālu'd Dīn Rūmī:* "First came he from the realm of the inorganic, long years dwelt he in the vegetable state, passed into the animal condition, thence towards humanity; whence again, there is another migration to be made." *Mathnawī* 4.3637f).

We must pass beyond the dualities and discords of intellect and possess truth as our inherent right. Ānanda, or joy, which is, according to St. Paul, one of the fruits of the spirit, is the stage we have to reach. The new spiritual man differs from the present intellectual man as much as the latter differs from the animal and the animal from the plant. Every human individual is a historical becoming. What we are here and now is the result of what we were, what we thought, what we felt and willed, what we did during earlier periods of our personal history. We cannot understand a human individual except as a process in time. There is no such thing as an I-substance. When we speak of the essence of the human individual, we refer not to his existence or the series of changes through which he passes, but to the plan or pattern of behaviour which he is attempting to realize. Human life presses forward through blood and tears to realize its form. As progress at the human level is willed, not determined, we are participants in history, not mere spectators of it. We can do much to determine our own future. If we follow false lights and seek for finite and relative progress, which is often precarious and disappointing, we do not further our own evolution. If, on the other hand, we overcome the narrowness of our ego, open out to others, overflow and communicate love and joy, we foster our growth. By our freely chosen activities we may retard or further the march of the world to its consummation. We are living our lives in the process of a great gestation. The slowness of the process, the occasional backslidings in any historical period do not disprove the possibility of development. History is neither a chapter of accidents, nor a determined drift. It is a pattern of absolute significance.

There is as much discontinuity between the human and the spiritual as there is between the human and the animal. Spiritual life is not only the negation but the fulfilment of the human life. We sometimes stress the continuity, sometimes the newness of it. "Behold, I make all things new."

# The Goal of the Cosmic Process

The meaning of history is to make all men prophets, to establish a kingdom of free spirits. The infinitely rich and spiritually impregnated future, this drama of the gradual transmutation of intellect into spirit, of the son of man into the son of God, is the goal of history. When death is overcome, when time is conquered, the kingdom of the eternal spirit is established.

Ānanda, spirit, which is the goal of evolution, comprises all the rest. It is not unrelated to the others which it has superseded and resolved into itself. All of them are activities of the Spirit. Each of them in its operation in the whole presupposes the others. Since all are necessary to the whole, no one can claim a primacy which belongs to the whole or the Spirit itself. We cannot unify the categories by annihilating them. Matter and life are different. The different levels of existence are not to be treated as inferior or degraded. In its place everything has value. The world is of one piece, though it has different stages which cannot be partitioned.

In cosmic evolution, the different stages are not opposed as good and evil. It is an evolution from one stage to another and the different stages are distinguishable only within a unity. The one Spirit is manifesting itself in its various activities which are all partial and therefore inadequate. Wholeness belongs to the Spirit itself.

It follows that we should not assume that body is the lower element out of which evil arises. The whole man, body, mind and spirit, is one. Spirit is not to be delivered out of entanglement with the body. In the Rabbinical phrase the body is the "scabbard of the soul." It is "the temple of the Holy Spirit" (I *Corinthians*. III: 6, 18). It is, according to Hindu thought, the instrument of ethical life, *dharma-sādhanam*. Even the lowest form of manifestation is an expression of the Divine, *annaṁ brahmeti vyajānāt.*

# Philosophy as the Criticism of Categories

There is a tendency to apply categories, which have proved helpful and even necessary in certain areas, to other areas, by the sheer impetus of the search for a comprehensive theory of being. In the eighteenth century Laplace conceived a theory of world mechanics. In the nineteenth century the Darwinian principle of natural selection was extended to all phenomena, living, minded, and purposive. We can explain the lower by the higher, not *vice versa*. There is not a single type of law to which all existence conforms.

The Upaniṣads believe that the principle of Spirit is at work at all levels of existence, molding the lower forms into expressions of the higher. The splendor of Spirit, which in Greek philosophy was identified with the transcendental and timeless world of Ideas, or in Christian thought is reserved for the divine supernatural sphere, is making use of natural forces in the historical world. The highest product of cosmic evolution, *ānanda* or spiritual freedom, must also be the hidden principle at work, slowly disclosing itself. Spirit creates the world and controls its history by a process of perpetual incarnation. Spirit is working in matter that matter may serve the Spirit.

To account for the world of change, which is a progressive manifestation of the values of spirit, we assume not only the principle of spirit but also the principle of non-being which is being gradually overcome. We struggle with chaos, we mold crude primordial being into forms expressive of spirit. Spirit represents all that is positive in becoming. The things of the world are struggling to reach the spirit by overcoming their inner void, the interval between what they are and what they aim to be. This negative principle measures the distance between being and becoming. The world process can only be conceived as a struggle between two antagonistic but indispensable principles of being and non-being. What is called non-being is the limiting concept on the object side, the name for the unknown, the hypothetical cause of the object world. This non-being is an abstraction, that which remains when we abstract from the world all that gives it existence, form, and meaning. It is the unmanifested, imperceptible, all but nothing, capable of receiving, though not without resistance, existence, form, and meaning. It is a demand of thought more than a fact of existence, the limit of the downward movement, the lowest form which is all but nonexistent. It is the absence of form, though there is nothing in the actual world which is completely devoid of form. In Indian thought it is called *prakṛti*, the *avyakta*, the unmanifested, the formless substrate of things. It is potentially all things. The two, spirit and nature, *puruṣa* and *prakṛti*, are not two ultimate principles. They are parts of one World-Spirit, which divided into two, *dvedhā apātayat*, for the sake of cosmic development (*Bṛhad-āraṇyaka Upaniṣad.* I.4.3). The two are opposite, yet complementary poles of all existence. They are not altogether independent of each other. The principle of non-being is dependent on being. It is that without which no effort would be possible or necessary. It is essential for the unfolding of the divine possibility. It is the material through which ideals are actualized. Proclus says that matter is a "child of God." So it is able to reveal spirit.

*Prakṛti* is not absolute non-being. It is unformed non-being which is powerless to form itself into being without the guidance of *puruṣa*, or the self. The existential development is not out of utter nothing or the absolute absence of all being. Nothing is the conceptual opposite of what truly and authentically is. If God creates out of nothing, he must be able to relate himself to nothing. But he cannot know nothing, for Pure Being excludes from itself all nullity. There is an inconscient world of being from out of which different worlds form themselves under the guidance of spirit. The dualism of *puruṣa* and *prakṛti* cannot be ultimate. The World-Spirit confronted by chaos or the waters over which the Spirit broods are both the expressions of the Supreme Being.

# The Inadequacy of Naturalistic Theories

The theory of the Upaniṣads seems to receive confirmation in the attempts made by scientific metaphysicians to account for the nature of the cosmic process. Naturalist philosophers attempt to explain the cosmic process on strictly mechanical principles. They confuse a descriptive method for the creative cause. They argue that neither man nor animal was created by divine power within a period of a week, but that they both developed over millions of years by exceedingly slow processes of organic change. No intelligence operates as a cause in material or organic events. The expressions of intelligence we have in the world are themselves effects or results of physical activity, produced by the causes of matter and motion, known or unknown.

If, however, we are obliged to assume a controlling or directing intelligence at any part of the cosmic process, naturalism is repudiated. The central issue is, whether we can account for the whole range of natural phenomena in terms of the composition of forces, whether we can, for example, account for life on principles which govern inorganic phenomena or for mind on principles which govern inorganic and organic processes. When naturalist metaphysicians speak of evolution as self-sufficient and self-explanatory, they confuse a descriptive statement with a metaphysical explanation. They speak of forms of change, and not of origins and causes. They attribute all changes to external influences and fail to recognize the need for creative acts.

Greek naturalism regarded natural causation as a sufficient principle of explanation, but the representative Greek thinkers did not look upon the world as intelligible in and of itself. They attempted to explain the temporal world by relation to the world of eternal forms. *Nous* or *Logos* forms chaos into order and gives the unformed matter or *Hyle* its form. The question of the origin of the stuff which is shaped by *Nous* is not clearly answered.

# Dialectical Materialism

Dialectical materialism admits self-movement within matter and uses the word 'matter' in a vague and wavering sense, by attributing to it qualities of spirit, creative activity, and intelligence. Material forces in a given correlation act uniformly as regards their results. If there is a change in the direction of the forces there will be a change in the results. We are not told how the changes in the forces and their direction are brought about. The way in which matter behaves is 'objective dialectic' and its reflection in consciousness is 'subjective dialectic'. Marx identifies the two without offering any proofs for it. Dialectic may be an account of development in nature and social reality; but it is not its explanation. It is a method of interpretation, not a philosophy of history.

Engels observes that our mastery of nature is due to our knowledge of it:

> At every step we are reminded that we by no means rule over nature like a conqueror over a foreign people, like something standing outside nature. Our mastery of it consists in the fact that we have the advantage over all other beings of being able to know and correctly apply its laws. (*Dialectics of Nature*)

This knowledge gives us our superiority to material nature which is unconscious of its possibilities. It also illustrates the kinship between man and nature which implies a source of unity. The dualism between the two cannot be abolished by making nature a form of spirit as in Hegel or spirit a form of nature as in Marx.

In his notes on Hegel's *Logic*, Lenin abandoned the grosser elements of Marx's materialism and emphasized the reality of the perceived world rather than its materiality. He did not, however, develop the implications of the realist doctrine.

# Bergson's Creative Evolution

Bergson is definite that even organic developments cannot be explained on principles of natural selection, adaptation to environment, and variations. He argues that evolution would have stopped long ago if perfect adaptation to environment were its goal. He postulates an *élan vital* which governs the life-movement, urging it onwards to the creation of new species. With a wealth of detail Bergson shows up the insufficiency of the mechanistic theory. For Bergson, "duration means the invention and creation of forms, the continual elaboration of the absolutely new" (*Creative Evolution*. English translation 1911, p. 11). Only he assumes that this creative adventure is without a preconceived end or plan. Bergson exalts duration to the position of God. Duration is the clue to the mystery of existence. What is the origin of creative evolution? Bergson speaks of an interruption in the forward progress of the spiritual principle, a falling away in the opposite direction which is matter. There is no satisfactory account in Bergson of the rise of matter, of the accident of interruption. In the organic world the vital impulse makes use of matter and molds it for its own purposes. For Bergson, reality is spirit and matter is the lapse from it.

# Lloyd Morgan, Alexander, and Whitehead

Lloyd Morgan makes a distinction between resultants and emergents. The former are continuations of the old while the latter refer to the new and unpredictable developments which take place at critical stages in the process of nature. Life is not a resultant of matter; nor is mind a resultant of life. Neither could have been anticipated before the event, even with a complete knowledge of the conditions preceding their emergence. They are absolutely new. Lloyd Morgan gives us a description of the processes of nature, but does not offer any explanation of them. He gives a phenomenological account and not a metaphysical theory. What gives to events their initial impetus, their structural pattern? Lloyd Morgan accounts for the complex process of evolution with its continuities and advances, resultants and emergents by an operative divine principle and activity. The creative activity of God is the only explanation for the cosmic evolution. Lloyd Morgan does not give an adequate account of the relation of the timeless divine purpose and the temporal unfolding.

Samuel Alexander, in his *Space, Time, and Deity*, holds that the Universe has evolved out of the matrix of space-time. The characteristic of the world as movement is stressed by the adoption of time as basic to reality. Change is the universal characteristic of all things that have sprung out of the primal matrix. Reality is, for Alexander, a continuance of point-instants. From out of the matrix of space-time, different stages of being endowed with special characteristics develop, motion, matter, life, mind and its values, and deity. "The higher quality emerges from the lower plane of existence and has its roots in it, yet it raises itself above it and no longer belongs to it; it arranges its possessor in a new order of being." Life rises out of materiality and gives rise to mind. Values emerge next on the scale of evolution and the highest being to emerge out of the space-time matrix is God.

> Deity is the next higher empirical quality to mind which the Universe is engaged in bringing to birth. Deity is the quality which attends upon or more strictly, is equivalent to, previous or lower existences of the order of mind, which itself rests upon a lower basis of qualities and emerges when certain complexities and refinements and arrangements have been reached. (*Space, Time, and Deity*, II, p. 347)

God is not behind us. He is the supreme goal toward which the cosmic process tends in time. For Alexander, God is not the creator of the world, but, like matter and mind, a creature in the space-time universe. God is not a finished being but an eternal becoming. "He can never realize the idea of Himself, but finds Himself continually on the way towards this idea." In other words, cosmic existences are striving for ever more perfect forms of life. Man is evolving towards godhead. The universe seems to be a god-making one. Alexander cannot reduce new stages of being into special groupings of the old processes. There is the creativity of evolution which we have to accept with "natural piety." "The continual change and movement of things through the divine *nisus* moves ever upwards, towards ever higher, richer and more perfect forms." This *nisus* is the driving force of the whole process.

We cannot account for cosmic evolution by space-time and motion. To say that the future emerges from the past is a statement of fact. It is not an explanation. Does it emerge from the past because it is already present in a more or less latent form in the past? Unless we posit an Absolute, perfect and changeless and outside time and so outside the evolutionary process, we cannot be sure of the direction of the evolution or the accomplishment of its purpose. If what Alexander says is true that God is the end of the evolutionary process, He is also the beginning. God cannot be the end if He were not also the beginning. God the consequent is also God the antecedent. There is, however, some point in Alexander's contention that God is a quality which in its completeness has yet to be achieved.

In Whitehead's philosophy the space-time of Alexander is replaced by space-time-matter. Space-time by itself is abstract and formal. The most elementary concrete unit is the *event* which has the formal characteristics of space-time and a material content or filling. When we wish to specify the character of events, we refer to objects. Objects are not events or complexes of events but qualify or are situated in events. "The structure of events provides the framework of the externality of nature within which objects are located" (*Principles of Natural Knowledge,* p. 80). Whitehead rejects the dualisms and bifurcations and emphasizes the pervasive characters of organism, self-enjoyment and creativeness. To the question, why do some material forms become living ones, Whitehead's answer is: "All such connections are formed by the creative process which is the world itself." Nature is organic as a whole and in its parts. An electron has this organic structure even as a human being. The organic character of events is derived from their filling by organized objects. There is an ingression of eternal objects into nature. The two together are "intrinsically inherent in the total metaphysical situation" (*Science and the Modern World*, p. 228). Whitehead warns us against viewing the eternal objects and the passage as abstractions from the real. "Actual occasions," he says, "are only selections from the realm of possibilities" (p. 255). The possible is eternal in which nothing can happen or pass and the actual is of the nature of passage and it is difficult to know how the actual passage can be contained in the eternal possible. The actual is external to the possible. There is nothing in the world of the possible answering to the passage of the actual. What is the status of eternal objects? If they are real, we have a bifurcation: if unreal, they have no metaphysical significance. The possible, which is the ultimate reality, contains the actual *eminenter,* says Whitehead. The actual event is divisible, whereas the object is organic and indivisible. While the world of events is characterized by change and diversity, the world of objects is characterized by unity and permanence. When objects become ingredient to the framework of events, they impose unity and permanence and thus distort the nature of the framework.

Being organic, nature has scope for development, for the production of the new. The flow of events is a process in which all the past is gathered up and borne along by the current into the present and the future. The creative advance into novelty is explained by the divine creative thrust which informs and drives forward the becoming of the world. What is before all creation is the Absolute. God is with all creation. God is not an exception to the nature of the empirical world but is its central illustration. The primordial God of Whitehead is "the unlimited conceptual realization of the absolute wealth of potentiality" (*Process and Reality*, p. 486), but he is deficient in actuality. "The consequent nature of God . . . is the realization of the actual world in the unity of his nature and through the transformation of his wisdom. The primordial nature is conceptual, the consequent nature is the weaving of God's physical feelings upon his primordial concepts" (p. 488).

The concretization of the conceptual plan requires a fullness of existence, an objectification in the medium of potential matter. The actual world presupposes both the ideal plan and the concrete setting: "In God's nature permanence is primordial and flux is derivative from the world; in the world's nature, flux is primordial and permanence is derivative from God." While God is seeking existence, the world is seeking unity and perfection. The end of the world is reached when the ultimate unity of the multiplicity of actual fact with the primordial conceptual fact is realised. For

Whitehead, the world process has its origin in God, is sustained by him and returns into him. God is not merely a future possibility but the creative source and final goal of the universal. "He is the beginning and the end, the alpha and the omega." For Whitehead, God and the world are both expressions of the original creativity which is the Absolute. They are essential to and interact with each other in subordination to the original creativity which manifests itself in both. We seem to be near the concept of the spirit of God brooding over the waters.

These various interpretations of the cosmic process, dominated by the scientific spirit, are agreed in thinking that the temporal process gives meaning to our existence. They also feel that it is not easy to account for the complex world of perpetual change on strictly scientific principles. If there is the emergence of what is genuinely new in the cosmic process, then the cosmic series is not self-explanatory. Our search for the reality of the world, for the structure of the cosmos, reveals the presence of something invisible and eternal which is working within the visible and temporal world. An element of mystery which refuses to reduce the meaning of the process to rational intelligibility is assumed by the scientific metaphysicians. Within the temporal process itself, science offers explanations for particular events, but it cannot deal with the why of the temporal process as a whole. It does not contain its origin or meaning within itself. It is not self-explanatory. The meaning of the mystery, the origin and the end of the world, cannot be scientifically apprehended. They require to be investigated metaphysically.

# The Primacy of Being

Philosophy is a quest of truth which underlies existence. The very name *metaphysics* characterizes the type of inquiry which goes beyond what is given to us. Whereas science deals with existent objects, philosophy tries to envisage the hidden structure, discover and analyze the guiding concepts of ontological reality. Why is there something rather than nothing? Why is there this world rather than another?

The very existence of this world implies the existence of Being from which the world derives. Being is the foundation of all existence, though it is not itself anything existent. It is not something like a stone or a plant, an animal or a human individual. Whenever we say that anything is, we make use of the concept of Being. It is therefore the most universal and the most comprehensive concept. We unfold the nature of Being by the study of existences, though we cannot prove it. It is self-evident. If Being were not, nothing could possibly exist. Being is in all that exists. We live in the world of existence, we think of some kind of existence or other, but in metaphysics we get beyond the sphere of daily life, the objects of science, and rise to the transcendent conception of Being itself. Being posits everything but is not itself posited. It is not an object of thought, it is not the result of production. It forms an absolute contrast to and is fundamentally different from all that is. If anything exists, then Being is. As this world exists, Being is. *Aseitas* means the power of Being to exist absolutely in virtue of itself, requiring no cause, no other justification for its existence except that its very nature is to be. There can be only one such Being and that is the Divine Spirit. To say that God exists *a se*, of and by reason of Himself, is to say that God is Being itself.

This is the concept of Brahman as it is formulated in the Upaniṣads. It is the *I am that I am* of the Christian Scripture. It is also the central doctrine of Catholic Christianity. St. Thomas Aquinas describes God as *Esse* or Being, pure and simple. In Him there is no distinction whatever. Even the distinction between the knowing subject and the known object is lost. God knows Himself, not through representations of Himself, but without mediation, through His own being. God is absolute as distinct from dependent or conditioned being. As the ground of an ordered multiplicity He is one and not multiple. That which is to make all conditions possible cannot itself be subject to conditions.

Why has evolution taken this direction and not another? Why has the world this character and not any other? In other words, why is the world what it is and not another? Being which is the ultimate basis of all existence, which is independent and has nothing outside it to control it, has freely willed to realise this world, to actualize this possibility. Absolute Being is also absolute freedom. To the question, why should such an order exist at all, the only answer is because the Absolute is both Being and Freedom. He is *actus purus*, unconditional activity. All the worlds would collapse into nothingness if He were not active. His will prevents Being from being the abyss of nothingness. The 'given' fact of the world in which we are all involved is a mystery. The genesis of the universe with its specific character is traced to Being-Activity. As to why this possibility and not another is selected, is intelligible solely as mystery which we have only to acknowledge. It is the will of God.

There are two sides of the Supreme, Essential Transcendent Being which we call Brahman: free activity which we call *Īśvara*: the timeless, spaceless reality and the conscious active delight creatively pouring out its powers and qualities, the timeless calm and peace and the timeful joy of activity freely, infinitely expressing itself without any lapse into unrest or bondage. When we refer to the free choice of this specific possibility, we deal with the Īśvara side of the Absolute. Pure Being without any expression or variation moves out of its primal poise so that worlds may spring into existence. Pure Being is not locked up in its own transcendence. *Īśvara* is the Absolute in action as Lord and Creator. (Compare this with Origen's account of the co-eternity of the Son with the Father: "There never can have been a time when He was not. For when was the Divine Light destitute of its effulgence?" *De Principiis,* IV: 28.)

The created world is contingent because it depends on the free will of the Supreme. Possible realities have potential being in the Absolute, existent realities have actual being though they are contingent. The Supreme has necessary being or, more accurately, it is its own being (*svayambhu*) and it is infinite because it possesses infinite possibilities. The mystery of the world abides in freedom. Freedom is the primordial source and condition of all existence. It precedes all determination.

# Infinite Possibility and the Actual World

This world, we have seen, is not a machine. It is an act of worship. It is in love with God, as Aristotle said, and is working towards Him. Its possibility, the eternal idea which it is accomplishing, is conceived by the Greeks as an abstract principle, the timeless *Logos*. The words of the Prologue to St. John's Gospel make out that it is a personal being who is the moving dynamism of history. "In the beginning was the *Logos*, and the *Logos* was with God and the *Logos* was God. The same was in the beginning with God. All things were made by Him. . . . In Him was life; and the life was the light of men." It is a definite manifestation of that which in the end of time brings with it the victory of the divine will over the powers that threaten the meaning of life. It perfects the historical revelation and completes the meaning of earthly existence. It is the Divine Logos which permeates the world and forms it into a cosmos. According to Hindu thought, the God who is shaping the universe is not the Absolute, free from all relativity, but the active personal being who shares in the life of his finite creatures. He bears in them and with them the whole burden of their finitude. The Spirit has entered into the world of non-spirit to realize one of the infinite possibilities that exist potentially in Spirit. Unconditioned Being becomes conditioned by the assumption of the creation of a specific possibility. A further definition of the Supreme Being's relation to the world is given by stating that the World Spirit creates, sustains and ultimately resolves the universe. These three aspects are brought out by the names, Brahmā, Viṣṇu, and Śiva.

They represent the three sides of God's activity in regard to the world. These three represent different functions of the one Supreme and are not, except figuratively, to be regarded as different persons. God the conceptual is logically prior to God the cosmic, who is logically prior to God the consequent or the final perfection. The Ideas of Brahma are seeking concrete expression and Viṣṇu is assisting the world's striving for perfection. During the process all his qualities of wisdom, love and patience find expression and help the fluent world to reach its end, God is spiritual Reality, unconditioned freedom, and absolute love.

In the Upaniṣads, a fourfold distinction of the Supreme Being is set forth. 1. Brahman, the Absolute Being; 2. Īśvara, the unconditioned free activity; 3. Hiraṇya-garbha, Prajă-pati, Brahmā, the World-Spirit in its subtle form; and 4. Virāj, the World-Spirit in its gross form. (*See Indian Philosophy* I, pp. 169–173. *Māṇḍūkya Upaniṣad* gives us a two-fold dialectic, relating not only to Reality but also to the being who apprehends it.)

These bring out different aspects of the Supreme. There is a tendency to regard the Supreme as Īśvara or God as subordinate to the Supreme as Brahman or Godhead. For Eckhart God is secondary, not primary, for it assumes the distinction of subject and object while Godhead transcends this distinction. A being is different from what he does. I feel that these disclose great depths in the Supreme Being and only logically can we distinguish them. They are all united in the Supreme.

# The Reality of the World

This world is not an illusion; it is not nothingness, for it is willed by God and therefore is real. Its reality is radically different from the being of Absolute-God. The Absolute alone has non-created divine reality; all else is dependent, created reality. This is the significance of the doctrine of *māyā*. It does not mean that the temporal process is a tragedy or an aberration. The reality of the world is not in itself but it is in the thought and being of the Creator. It is what God thought and willed it to be before it was.

There is a beginning to time as well as an end. When we say that time is infinite, all that we mean is that its future is indefinite or incalculable. Between these two points, the beginning and the end, between the start and the finish, what happens is real and significant, not only for us but for the World-Spirit. God is so intensely concerned with this history that He not only looks on the human life as an interested spectator but He actively intervenes in it. It is not correct to say that this intervention took place only once. Every moment in the temporal process is a moment of decision. It is charged with an extreme tension. History is not a cyclic movement. It is full of new things, because God works in it and reveals Himself in it. The end of the time process is the triumph of the World-Spirit, or to use the phrases of Greek classical thought, the triumph of *Nous* over chaos.

There are laws of nature, physical, biological, and psychological. These laws are comprehensively designated *Karma*. The Creator does not use the forces of nature to reward virtue or punish sin. Jesus said: "Think you that the eighteen upon whom the Tower in Siloam fell were sinners above all that dwelt in Jerusalem? I tell you nay. He maketh his sun to rise on the evil and on the good and sendeth rain on the just and on the unjust" (*Matthew* V, 45). In this world there are no rewards or punishments but only consequences. There is no arbitrariness in the world. The laws of nature are the expression of the divine mind. The *Śvetāśvatara Upaniṣad* states that God is the ordainer or overlord of Karma, *karmādhyakṣaḥ*. Karma is not ultimate or absolute. It is the expression of God's will and purpose. It has an important and indispensable function in the divine economy. It belongs to the created world. If God is bound up to the order of nature, if He is responsible for the world without the power of redeeming it, if His will is inflexible that no prayer can reach, if He sanctions all the evil as well as the good in the world, if He treats the tears of the children and the agony of the innocents as just ingredients in a world of sacred necessity, the world becomes meaningless. The Supreme is love and knowledge, goodness and power. He is related to everything and every one in the universe. He responds to everything and to everything's response to Him.

# Human Freedom

God is not fate, nor an impersonal, abstract determining power. We are not puppets moved hither and thither by the blind impersonal necessity of omnipotent matter or the sovereignty of divine providence. We cannot say that everything is finished before it starts and the last day of reckoning will read what the first day of creation wrote. In that case nothing new can happen and there is no room for contingency. The future has yet to be made. Our present choices give a new form even to the past so that what it means depends on what we do now.

The freedom of will possessed by self-conscious individuals makes possible sin and discord. They are not willed by the Divine, though they fall within His purpose. When we are self-willed we surrender to the restraint exercised by the play of mechanical forces. We are then the victims of Karma. We are free to do differently. We can turn our eyes towards the Light in prayer, make an effort of genuine attention to empty our mind of selfish desires and let the thought of the Eternal fill it. We will then bear within us the very power to which necessity or Karma is in subjection. It is our community with the Eternal that endows us with creative quality. It helps us to remake our environment and realize new types of achievement which will enrich the experience of the human race. Keats spoke of the world as the "vale of soul-making" and declared in the same letter 39 that "as various as the lives of men are—so various become their souls and thus does God make individual beings, Souls, Identical Souls, of the sparks of his own essence" (28th April, 1819. Colvin's edn., p. 256).

An individual is free when he attains universality of spirit, but his liberated self retains its individuality as a center of action so long as the cosmic process lasts. For complete liberation implies not only harmony within the self but also harmony with the environment. Complete freedom is therefore impossible in an imperfect world. Those who have attained to the consciousness of the Eternal work within the world to set other men forward in their journey toward the goal. In a true sense the ideal individual and the perfect society arise together.

The redemption of the world is not to be treated completely *sub specie historiae*. It is an eternal operation. There is a steady advance in our apprehension of the ideal which belongs to the eternal world. Nicolas of Cusa says:

> To be able to know ever more and more without end, this is our likeness to the eternal wisdom. Man always desires to know better what he knows and to love more what he loves; and the whole world is not sufficient for him because it does not satisfy his craving for knowledge.

Our ultimate aim is to live in the knowledge and enjoyment of the absolute values. When this aim is reached, the mortal becomes the immortal and time is taken over into eternity. Temporal life is treated as contingent, transient, perishable, non-eternal, as its end is to be transfigured. Human life on this planet is a brief episode and its eternal value is however preserved in the abode of all eternal values, the Absolute-God. The actual fabric of the world with its loves and hates, with its jealousies and competitions, with its unasked helpfulness, sustained intellectual effort and intense moral struggle, is no more than existences dancing on the stillness of Pure Being. These things are not final and fundamental. They are not by any means illusory, an evil dream from which we have to wake up as soon as possible. It is wrong to think that the universe exists for us only to escape from it. Existence, rather, is here to be redeemed. If the Supreme is one and many, if He is Being and Activity, if He is transcendent and immanent, then the Spirit lives in the world, Being is in existence. The aim of the cosmic evolution is to reveal the Spirit.

# God and the World

In his book on *God and the Astronomers* (1933) Dr. W.R. Inge refers to my view and points out that, if God is bound up with and immanent in the evolving Universe, He must share the fate of the Universe. If the second law of thermodynamics is true, that the Universe is running down like a clock and a time will come when there will be no life or consciousness, the universe will reach a state of static eventlessness which is another name for extinction. If God is the soul of the Universe, He is the soul of a doomed universe. If the world is as necessary to God as God is to the world, a time will come when God will be no more. A god under the sentence of death is no god at all.

This objection is not fatal to the view I have indicated. This world is the accomplishment of a specific possibility from the infinite possibilities whose ideal home is the Absolute. From the primary reality of Absolute-God, the derived reality of the world ensues. This world is creaturely being. It exists because and so long as God wills it to be.

While God is distinct from the world He is not separate from it. The world exists by the sustaining presence and activity of God. Without this presence and activity, it would collapse into nothingness. In this world one possibility of the divine is being accomplished in space and time. There is the operation of the divine in it. From this it does not follow that the world is organic to God. If anything, it is organic to this specific divine possibility which is in process of accomplishment. This possibility is regarded as the soul or the entelechy of the world; we may call it the World-Spirit. The soul of this particular world is a manifestation of the Absolute-God. When this possibility is realised, when the plan of the universe is fulfilled, there is an end to this world. Its disappearance is consistent with its created character.

# Kant's Antinomy

The whole question of the status of time was raised by Kant in his Antinomies of Pure Reason. *"Thesis:* The world has a beginning in time and is confined within the limits of space. *Antithesis:* The world has neither beginning in time nor bounds in space but is infinite, *as* in space so also in time." This antinomy cannot be solved, for, according to Kant, reason finds itself in the power of transcendental appearance. Within the limits of the phenomenal world, the contradiction cannot be overcome. We cannot think that time will come to an end in time or that it will go on endlessly. How can the end of time occur within time?

When the end of the cosmic history is reached, we have passed beyond the limits of history. We have transcended time. It is not a question of an end in time but an end of time.

So long as there is the struggle, the process of becoming, the overcoming of non-being by being, we have the time process. But when all individuals have escaped from their alienation, from their slavery to the world, when all externality is overcome, there is the awakening of the Spirit in them all. When the Kingdom of Spirit is established on Earth as it is in Heaven above, God the antecedent becomes God the consequent. There is a coincidence of the beginning and the end. If it is held that the end will never be accomplished, that there will be perpetual singing and no completion in a song, that it is always a journeying without any journey's end, then the cosmic process will have no meaning at all. "Thy kingdom come" is the meaning of history, and the coming of the kingdom is the triumph of meaning. The truth about the Earth is the *brahmaloka,* the transfiguration of the cosmos, the revolutionary change in men's consciousness, a new relationship among them, an assimilation to God. It is the attainment of wholeness, the overcoming of disruption, the surmounting of all false antinomies, the transcending of time in eternity, which we objectify as *brahmaloka.*

The attainment of spiritual freedom by all, universal salvation or *sarvamukti* is not inconsistent with the law of entropy. When we are all liberated, time is transcended, *saṁsāra* becomes *mokṣa* or *nirvāṇa*. According to Mahāyāna Buddhism, universal redemption is the aim of the Buddha. St. Paul extends his hope of "redemption into the glorious liberty of the children of God" to the "whole creation." This cosmic deliverance, which is the close of the world, cannot be accurately described as a terrestrial future for it is a supramundane present.

When everyone achieves his fulfilment, the cosmic purpose is fulfilled. Pure undistorted truth of eternity burns up the world. The end of the process is in continuity with the beginning and when the two coincide, cosmic existence lapses into Absolute Being.

# The End of the World

The possibility of the passing away of the present order of things is not only admitted but demanded by the view here set forth. When humanity, still captive in its germ, reaches its full stature of which we can not now imagine the greatness and the majesty, it unites with its source in the past. The World-Spirit, called Brahmā, Hiraṇya-garbha, is admitted to be finite, mortal, though he creates beings who gain immortality (atha yan martyaḥ sann amṛtān asṛjata. *Bṛhad-āraṇyaka Upaniṣad*. Again, hiraṇyagarbhaṁ paśyata jāyamānam. Behold the World-Spirit, as he is being born. *Śvetāśvatara Upaniṣad* IV, 12).

He is said to be the first-born, the first embodied being (*Śiva Purāṇa*. V.1.8.22; "Death is his body." *yasya mṛtyuś śarīram. Subāla Upaniṣad.*) He strives to express his spirit through the body of non-being, the principle of objectivity. He is *tamaś śarīraka paramātmā*.

The meaning of time is beyond the confines of time. Time has meaning because it comes to an end. If it is unending, it is meaningless. Time process can be understood only in the light of the end it aims at; the victory over time, the victory over this disrupted, fallen condition, victory over alienation, estrangement, enslavement by the objective. We conceive the end itself as taking place in historical time, though it is illogical to relate to history in simply historical terms what is beyond history. Though it may not be possible for us to think of the end of time except in terms of time, yet the end is not a term in the time series. It belongs to another order of existence, inasmuch as it marks the end of time itself. It is victory over time. It is life eternal.

Though the present order of things must pass away, there will be other world orders in an endless series; for God is infinite possibility. We do not equate God with this evolutionary process. The dissolution of the world does not in any way affect the Absolute-God; for its knowledge of all possibilities is free from relativity. God is not merely the past, the present, and the future of this world: he is the transcendental principle of this and all possible worlds, whether they are to be realized or not. Even from the strictly scientific point of view, the process of gradual degradation of energy must have had a beginning. If the whole universe is running down like a clock, it must have been wound up at the beginning. If it was wound up once, what prevents it from being wound up again, if another possibility requiring this type of structure is to be started?

# The Human Condition and the Quest for Being

The religious implications of the terraced view of nature given in the *Taittirīya Upaniṣad* are confirmed by an analysis of human nature and its concrete manifestations. For the modern mind, philosophy is not speculative idealism; it is positive knowledge of actuality. Actuality is not only cosmic but individual. *ātmānaṁ viddhi.* Know thyself, has been the direction to the seeker from very early times.

The study of the nature of the human individual started in that crucial period of human history, 800 to 200 B.C. The spiritual leaders of all subsequent history emerged in it, Lao-Tse, Confucius, the writers of the Upaniṣads, and Gautama the Buddha, Zoroaster and the Prophets of Israel, Socrates and the Greek philosophers.

The novelty of the existentialist approach is greatly exaggerated. In the Upaniṣads we find frequent psychological analyses of the human individual, which have a certain resemblance to the existentialist approach. For the Indian thinkers including the Buddha, human life is a transitional stage from which we have to advance to a new conception of reality. The human being is a *saṁsārin*, a perpetual wanderer, a tramp on the road. His life is incessant metamorphosis. The wheel of life *saṁsāra-cakra* turns ceaselessly. This change will continue until man reaches his fulfilment. Indian thinkers will not view with sympathy the tendency which we find among a few existentialists to accept the human predicament of distress and crisis as final and even find satisfaction in it. The delight of some existentialists in anguish, their acceptance of anarchy as destiny, their contented contemplation of man's disaster and nothingness, their preoccupation with the morbid and the perverse, their rejection of absolute and universal values—will not find much support in the writings of the ancient Indian thinkers or for that matter of the modern existentialists who are religiously inclined like Karl Jaspers and Gabriel Marcel. The problem of religion is bound up with man's intellectual nature, his distinctive way of knowing himself and the world in which he lives.

Hindu thought looks upon man as the victim of ignorance, *avidyā*, which gives rise to selfish desire, *kāma*. The Upaniṣads speak to us of the agony of finite creatures living in time, the world of karma, the agony of feeling that we are at the mercy of time. This feeling of distress is universal. But they affirm the reality of another life, where we are liberated from the rule of time, from the bonds of karma. The reality of *mokṣa* or liberation inspires us with hope that we can triumph over time, It is a hope and a faith until the transcension of time occurs.

Legend or history tells us that the Buddha had everything he wanted materially and culturally and was yet haunted by vague dissatisfactions. From wanderings in the city he learnt that disease and death were regarded as inescapable evils. His discovery of the fact of human suffering led him to a psychological investigation of the causes of pain. He started out by trying all the methods for reaching knowledge currently accepted. He consulted hermits, practised austerities, went without food. It seemed silly to weaken and torture the body. He was not getting any the wiser. He withdrew into solitary meditation and tried to think things out. He declared that all suffering is due to ignorance of the impermanent nature of things and selfish craving. When we are the victims of ignorance, we absolutize our own ego, oppose it to society and miss our moral vocation. Ignorance is not something outside of man. He lives in it, for it is that in which historical man is involved. So long as he lives his unregenerate life in time, the life of craving and aversion, suffering will be his lot. A sense of blankness overtakes the seeking spirit, which makes the world a waste and life a vain show. But he can free himself from suffering, by the awareness of eternity, by the enlightenment that liberates the ego and transfigures its temporal experience.

The symbolism of the second chapter of *Genesis* expresses the same truth. We have tasted the fruit of the tree of knowledge and the fall of man is the result. This intellectual knowledge is a leap forward in man's awareness. It is said to be a fall because it produces a fissure or a cleavage in man's life, a break in the natural order of things. Animals do no evil for they do not know the distinction between good and evil. Even if man is an animal, he is the only animal that knows that he is an animal. The development of self-consciousness is, according to Hegel, the development of unhappy consciousness, for all divided consciousness is unhappy consciousness. Adam and Eve were smitten with fear the moment they became aware of the new relationship with reality into which they entered by eating of the fruit of the "tree of knowledge of good and evil." They are smitten with fear because of their anxiety that they may not rise equal to the sense of obligation which that awareness conveys. Adam in his temptation and fall is not an individual at the beginning of history but is man at every stage in that history. The fall is a logical way of representing the need for getting out of the fallen condition. The withdrawal of integration with the environment is not purposeless; for it opens out an immense vista of self-development until we recover integration at a higher level. This view is indicated in the Orphic myth concerning the origin of the human soul, which speaks of a fall of man's spirit from a higher to a lower world.

Existentialists are firm in their view that man is not a mere biological urge or an embodied social function. He is not to be treated on the pattern of an object, which is non-existential. There is a certain degree of unintelligibility in regard to existential facts. They are not completely thinkable. They are resistant to thought. Existence in this sense is experienced but not explained. The human self is not an object of scientific knowledge. It is immersed in being; it participates in the creative intention of the cosmos. Man is essentially the possessor of freedom, not a mere thing which is a product of physical processes or an unreal appearance of the Absolute. Existentialism is a protest against the tendency to reduce the reality of the individual to forms of thought or universal relations. Man has an incommunicable uniqueness about him. He is not the Platonic universal differentiated by the presence of accidental forms. Individuals differ from each other not only in their accidental properties but in their essential natures, in the forms or patterns which they are attempting to realize.

Being self-conscious, man is essentially free. In the interests of human freedom the existentialists even deny the reality of the transcendent. Marx says: "Man is free only if he owes his existence to himself." Nicolai Hartmann adopts the theory of postulatory atheism. We postulate the non-existence of God for the sake of human independence. Nietzsche's Zarathustra exclaims: "If there were gods, who could bear not to be a god? Therefore there are no gods." In different ways the two characteristics of the human being are brought out, his self-consciousness and moral freedom.

Unsophisticated minds may take life as they find it and may not vex themselves about its limitations. But even they cannot for all time be immune to the questionings of fate, The events of the world seem to be essentially unstable and fleeting, energizing and vanishing never to return. There is nothing that we can grasp, nothing that we can keep. The day of life sinks inevitably into the night of death, *maraṇāntaṁ hi jīvitam*. The dread of something impending, the uncanny apprehension of something evil that is to happen, makes the thinking man feel that there is nothing to live for. The sense of the impermanence of things is a recurring theme in all religious literature. Akbar carved a beautiful saying over the gate of the city which he deserted as soon as it was built. "Said Jesus, may his name be blessed, 'This world is a bridge, pass over it, but build no house upon it'."

For Heidegger, all existence is infected with the character of time, of historicity. Nothing can escape the fate of history. All existence is threatened with two dreadful convictions, that of death and transitoriness and the dread of death. Man, Heidegger says, is aware of the intense actuality of life at the moment life is ebbing away. That drawing of the lonely Nietzsche with deep eyes and musical fingertips following the sinking sun on his deathbed sums up the meaning of life. Is it possible, asks Heidegger, that time, despite its ontological nature and despite all the consequences that follow from it, offers us a ground for our existence and a certainty that will permit us to gain a fundamental tranquility of soul? "Temporality discloses itself as the meaning of real dread (*Sorge*)." In the exciting moments of fear, in the devastating experience of being thrown into the world of space and time, man finds that he stands on the obscure ground of a mysterious nothing, which is not a mere mathematical zero but something more positive than that. When man experiences this 'nothingness' in all its existential weight he suffers from a feeling of profound unrest and care, a 'radical insecurity of being'. This sense of nothingness is not so much a metaphysical concept as a psychological state, an inner condition which provokes the sense of dread and starts the religious quest.

# The Sense of Dread

Unless man is free to disobey the commands, he will not have the opportunity to conform to them freely and deliberately. Man's creative will is the source of selfish ambition as well as disinterested love. Although the true law of man's being is love, a harmonious relation among all living things, he rebels against this law when he imagines himself, not a single individual in the whole but the whole itself. A defiant self-affirmation which leads to enslavement, a false freedom which destroys itself, overtakes him. There is a complete sundering of that sense of compassion which is the intuitive sense of kinship and union with life, which was found in the earlier stages at an instinctive level. The possibility of the misuse of freedom becomes an actuality. Freedom passes into wilfulness and wilfulness gives rise to evil. The fact of moral freedom produces sin, though sin is not a necessary consequence of it. The abuse of freedom results in sins. To be good is to be capable of all evil and yet commit none. Sin is the refusal to grow, to evolve. It is to defy the cosmic destiny.

Jesus asks us to be delivered, not from temptation but, from evil. He knows that temptations come. Even the greatest of us are not free from them. We have to face them, though we need not go out of our way to find them. At no stage on Earth can we be sure that we can be free from temptations. St. Paul says: "Let him that thinketh he standeth take heed lest he fall" (I. *Corinthians* X). Temptations are as inescapable as the air we breathe; but it is no less human to withstand them than it is to be tempted. When we are tempted we need not assume that the battle is lost. We can hold our ground as long as life lasts. The purpose of the trials and temptations is not that we may fall but that we may rise.

Kierkegaard, to whom the existentialist philosophers trace their descent, asserts that man is not an object to be known but a subject with a self to acquire. Man exists because he has freedom. It is freedom that helps him to reintegrate his personality. So far as man is human he must do either good or evil. If he drifts, he is forfeiting his humanity. It is better to do evil than surrender to automatism; for then we exist at least.

The fact of freedom, according to Kierkegaard, produces anxiety, the fear that we may abuse our freedom. He says, "Anxiety is the psychological condition which precedes sin. It is so near, so fearfully near to sin, and yet it is not the explanation for sin" (*Der Begriff der Angst,* p. 89). Anxiety is the precondition of sin, the fear that we may sin. It is a basic constituent of human freedom. Sin is not a psychological problem, but dread or anxiety-neurosis is. It is a redeeming quality that we are anxious, for under the stress of passion or fear, starvation, or religious frenzy, we are likely to do the most terrific deeds.

Kierkegaard defines self as spirit, "a relationship which relates itself to itself." It does not create itself but is created by another power and is therefore a "derived, constituted relationship," a relationship which relates itself to its own self and in doing so relates itself to this power. In this cycle of relationships there is in man's very nature dis-relationship leading to despair, to sickness unto death of which Christ spoke, according to Kierkegaard, when he raised Lazarus from the dead (John XI:4). "This sickness is not unto death, but for the glory of God, that the son of God might be glorified thereby." This despair is integral to man's existential inwardness, to his relationship to the eternal.

When man looks at himself, the disorders of the flesh, the unendurable error of the senses, the fearful perversions of the heart, the debased instincts of nature, he stands aghast. His self-respect as a human being is hurt, and he feels himself degraded. He detects and beholds sin as an incomprehensible necessity, something older and deeper than his will for good. The fact of sin is an empirical discovery, not a theological dogma. Man is afraid of the unintelligible forces that control him. To gain security he strives all the time to enslave nature, enslave man. Man is a paradox. He desires things which are seemingly incompatible. He is the rival of his fellows and yet seeks peace and unity with them. He is in love with life and yet on occasions is prepared for death. In moments of self-analysis he examines his past, feels unsure of himself, pulled this way and that, feels distressed in spirit and sick unto death. Unhappiness is essentially a state of disruption and division. Man is haunted by doubts, What am I? From what causes do I derive my being? To what conditions shall I return?

The tension in human nature is what makes man interesting. Without it he would not become aware of his utter nothingness, his forlornness, his insufficiency, his dependence, his weakness, his emptiness. His anguish and suffering have a dialectical necessity. The roots of religion are in this inner torment which has to be resolved. He must strive after unity with nature, with man, with himself. Only when he is victorious in his struggle does he attain human dignity. We are seekers, pilgrims on the march for the city that is to be, for we have no abiding city on Earth. We must reach out beyond the frontiers of our dual, divided consciousness. We cannot remain content within an impermeable solitude of our own anguished desires. We cannot remain for ever in a state of unfulfilment. Even the lowest forms of life strive after adjustment.

The ancestors of man played an important part in this great drama of cosmic evolution, though they did not understand either the play or their part in it. Man has also to play his part, but with a knowledge of the structure and meaning of the play. By his intelligence he must comprehend the cosmic plan and by his will further it. Human progress does not depend on the slow action of physical or biological laws. It can be speeded up by our effort, if we liberate ourselves from bondage, if we escape from the life that is in part and enter into the life which is whole. The prayer of the Upaniṣads, "Lead me from the unreal to the real, lead me from darkness to light, lead me from death to immortality" (*asato mā sad gamaya tamaso mā mṛtyur gamaya mṛtyor mā amṛtaṁ gamaya. Bṛhad-āranyaka Upaniṣad* I.3.28) assumes that we live in a world of fear, of care, of abandonment, of death, of nothingness, and we seek a world of being, of fearlessness, of freedom, of spirit, of eternity. We seek to transcend the finitude of human existence and gain life eternal.

Sometimes we are tempted to go back, become unthinking and unreflective, sink into the simplicity of biological existence, submerge in the elemental animal. This would be a deliberate sacrifice of our wholeness, an abandonment of the attempt to achieve integrity. We cannot reverse the process and throw away our heritage. Self-conscious man cannot become the instinctive animal. Even if he refuses to employ his intellectual consciousness he cannot get back the original integration with the environment. Memory and expectancy will interfere. Job seeks his asylum in sleep but does not succeed. "When I say, my bed shall comfort me, my couch shall ease my complaint, then thou scarest me with dreams and terrifiest me through visions" (*Job* VII:13–14). We cannot shake off our rationality. We cannot get away from the strains of our self-consciousness. The cure for our unrest is not a relapse into the womb of the unconscious, but a rise into creative consciousness. What we aim at is the enlightenment of the sage and not the inexperience of the new-born babe.

We cannot cure the affliction caused by intellect, the loneliness, the insecurity and the anguish by drugs, by the myths of religion or the dogmas of politics. These plans of escape from the prison of our life may help a few for a little time. If we take opium we may find a few moments beautiful and calm in contrast to the jarring world outside; but they will not last. The unscientific dogmas, the crude superstitions tell us more about the mind of man than about the structure of reality, and cannot save man from skepticism.

If the lonely individual clings to something outside of him, he may gain security, but he does so at the expense of his integrity as an individual. We may renounce freedom of inquiry and bind our eyes from further seeking with the bandage of a final creed. We may thus be saved from making decisions or assuming responsibility for the future. But we will be disturbed and dissatisfied at the root, for the emergence of the individual self cannot be stifled. Happiness is in freedom, and freedom is in greatness of spirit.

It is argued that scientific progress will destroy the feeling of loneliness with which we regard the alien world and terminate the inability of men to determine their own destiny.

We may grant that we can anticipate the course of natural phenomena and even to some extent control it. But nature can never be tamed to do man's will. Her blind caprices, her storms and tempests, her cyclones and earthquakes will continue to shatter his work and dash his dreams. Man cannot alter the limits of his life or his body. "Thou fool, this night shall thy soul be required of thee." Increasing knowledge of science without a corresponding growth of religious wisdom only increases our fear of death. Our scientific culture is unparalleled in human history. We have dominated the forces of nature, controlled the seas and conquered the air. We have increased production, combatted disease, organized commerce, and made man master of his environment; and yet the lord of the Earth cannot live in safety. He has to hide under the earth, wear gas masks. He is haunted by the fears of wars and lives in the company of uncertainties. This war-haunted, machine-driven civilization cannot be the last word of human striving. Unless we are blind idiots or self-satisfied morons, we will know that scientific organization is not the fulfilment of the spirit of man. Science can do little in that region in which human disorder has been most striking, the sphere of human relationships.

# Social Progress

The fear which is the expression of man's rationality cannot be removed by any change in outer circumstances. We may abolish the horrors of the industrial age, clean up the slums and diminish drunkenness, yet the spirit of man cannot by these measures alone gain anything in security. In the most prosperous circumstances, our heart will still suffer from the torment of the infinite, from the anguish of beatitude. There are sufferings which can be overcome by changes in the social order, and it is our duty to achieve a social revolution and remove these social wrongs of hunger, cold, illiteracy, sickness, unemployment. But we have to recognize that there are certain evils which are organic to the spiritual condition of man and so cannot be removed by social changes. Dr. Johnson wrote two centuries ago:

How small of all that human hearts endure
That part which Kings or laws can cause or cure?

While we should liberate the spirit of man from the distorting influences of social slavery and cruelty, we must admit that the slavery of the mind and the cruelty of the heart can be removed only by another discipline.

Intellectual consciousness has inflicted the wounds, has brought about the fall. Full, free, creative consciousness must heal the wounds and secure redemption. If we remain at the level of intellectual consciousness, if we are satisfied with ourselves and the world, we are once-born. Our lives would be facile, unintentional, and unpurposive. The twice-born are those whose complex and ardent personalities are broken on the wheel of doubt and spiritual crisis and then reassembled, reanimated, and reintegrated.

Through the exercise of the intellectual consciousness man is able to discriminate between subject and object. Man, a product of nature, subject to its necessities, compelled by its laws, driven by its impulses, is yet a non-nature, a spirit who stands outside of nature, outside of his 'given' nature. He has the capacity for self-transcendence, the ability to make himself an object. Man therefore has affinities with a world of nature and with a world outside of nature. The Buddha, for example, distinguishes between karma and nirvāṇa. Karma is the principle which governs the world of objects, of cause and effect, nirvāṇa is the principle of subject which transcends the object, the center of being.

In *Being and Time* Heidegger draws a distinction between being and existence. The important fact about man is not that he exists but that he knows that he exists; he has the power to perceive the meaning of existence. Sub-human entities like stones, plants, and animals exist and pass on without a consciousness of their existence. They are incapable of either doubt or illumination. Man's existence includes the power, the determination to stand out of existence and in the truth of being. If man fails to transcend his existential limits, he too would be condemned to death and nothingness. He must first experience the void, the nothingness, the śūnya of the Mādhyamaka Buddhist, not for its own sake but for transcending it, for getting beyond the world of *saṁsāra* to the other shore of being. The experience of dread is the experience of the problem whether man shall attain to being or shall not, whether he shall annihilate nothingness and get beyond it or whether nothingness shall annihilate him. The self in man enables him to overcome the void, experience it, and then transcend it. We become conscious of reality through the disappointment with existence. Man's uneasiness and bewilderment arise from the fact of the absence of reality in the things of the world. We must get beyond the things of the world. "If any man come to me and hate not his father and mother and wife and children, and brethren and sisters yea and his own life also, he cannot be my disciple" (*Luke* XIV:26). To stand out of existence there must come upon the individual a sense of crucifixion, a sense of the agonizing annihilation, a sense of the utter nothingness of all this empirical existence which is subject to the law of change, death. Only through loneliness can nearness to reality be achieved. We must endure the terrible awakening summed up in Jesus's words, "My God, my God, why hast thou forsaken me?" When the individual withdraws from the empirical, when he penetrates to the center, when the objective world falls away, he affirms the reality of spirit, which is not an object, which is not a temporal existent, which, though in time, is not of it. He then realizes that time is not all, that death is not all, that it is possible to circumvent the time process and say with the Buddha or the Christ, "I have overcome the world." Faith in such a non-object principle is the defeat of death, and the renewal of life. When the spirit is affirmed, dread is annulled. Existentialist philosophers emphasise this essential phase of spiritual life, what the mystics call "the dark night of the soul."

If anguish were the permanent condition of human life, there would be no escape from the apotheosis of nihilism, which would deny any purpose in the world and reduce it to futility, negation, death. The one and only meaning of reality would be nothingness. The teaching of the Buddha has been misinterpreted as a nihilism, forgetting that the Buddha's emphasis is on man's power to overcome the void and attain nirvāṇa (See my *Introduction to the Dhammapada* [1950]). If existence were all, if the objective time series were all, if *saṁsāra* were all, there would be no escape from fear. If we are to avert the common doom of death, we must take the aid of everlasting hope that death is not all, that all-devouring time is not all. When the Indian thinkers affirm that the world is *māyā*, that it is not real, though existent, that we can escape from it, that it is possible for us to circumvent the time process, they affirm the reality of spirit which is not objective, which is not merely existent. When we attempt to modify the world in accordance with our hearts' desires we affirm the existence of our own spiritual center which is transcendent to the world of time. There is a reality which is different from existence, there is a subject which is non-object, there is a time-transcending element. Faith in such a non-object spirit means the defeat of death, and the renewal of life. Man's awareness of his finiteness and temporality means his consciousness of eternity. It is the consciousness of infinitude that produces in us the consciousness of the finitude. In the uncertainty of life we feel a distant certainty through which alone this uncertainty is made possible. Being as such contains the possibility of God and of man's dignity. If there were no Being, there would be no God, all would be perishing existence. If man's existence is not a mere void or pure nothingness, there is Being in existence. We can attain illumination of Being by facing bitterly the ultimate meaning of nothingness.

The act by which we become conscious of our existence, by which we affirm that things exist and individuals exist, transcends concepts and ideas. It is a mystery for the intellect, but we do have an intuition of it. The subject matter of this intuition is Being itself. This Being is not a Platonic essence or a pale abstraction but Being as the very structure of reality in which the act of existence is immersed. It is Being at its supreme plenitude informing the entire dynamism of existence. In perceiving Being we perceive the divine reality. The created realm is not outside Being. We confront Being in the world of existence, otherwise we will not be able to say that things exist, individuals exist. The order of existence implies an absolute irrefragable Being completely free from nothingness and death. An individual existence liable to death belongs to the totality of nature, the universal whole, the order of time of which we are all parts. Being with existence or nothingness implies Being without nothingness. This absolute Being is involved in our primordial intuition of existence. The universal whole whose part I am, this cosmic order is Being with nothingness from the very fact that we are all parts of it. Since the universal whole does not exist by itself there is another Being, transcendent and self-sufficient and unknown in itself, actuating all existents. This is Being without nothingness, Being by itself, Being which transcends the time order, the totality of nature. Existence is in Being. *Saṁsāra* is in nirvāṇa. Eternity is centered in time. That art thou. St. Paul asks: "Know you not that you are the temple of God and the Spirit of God dwelleth in you?" (I *Corinthians* III:18). When the Quakers tell us that the Christ Light shines in the hearts of men, and if we would but heed the light, we would come to experience His life and power within us, they are referring to this element of non-nature or spirit in us.

# The Moral Struggle

Whereas Heidegger takes us to being from existence from the logical side, Kierkegaard approaches the same problem from the moral side. According to the *Bhagavadgītā*, on the battleground of the human soul is waged the most desperate of all conflicts, that between the forces of good and of evil. The moral struggle is one between self and self, the locked and desperate encounter between the spirit and the flesh, between what the Christians call, the spirit of Christ and the flesh of Adam. When we have the torment of the struggle in moral life, the self feels itself divided against itself. The struggle itself is not possible unless we look upon the longing for the good and the rebellion against it as belonging to the same individual. The felt contradiction is possible only through the reality which is above the discord. The awareness of the antithesis between what we are and what we wish to be is implicitly the work of the unity which dwells in every creature. We strive to give spirit existence, make the spiritual actual and thus harmonize our whole nature. The perfection of man, the capacity to reach his fulfilment through freedom is contained in the state of care or anxiety. This feeling indicates man's subjection to an alien world, his contingency. The possibility of the misuse of freedom which is the cause of anxiety, according to Kierkegaard shows the dis-relationship of the self to its own self. The anxiety can be allayed only by reintegration, by "relating itself to its own self," and by willing to be itself. The self then becomes grounded in its own real being. It is then that we are truly free. The creative act of freedom is possible only on the part of one who has broken through the necessity of the natural world. The law of Karma—of necessity—reigns in the object world. Man with his creative acts can mold the closed circle of nature and disclose its possibilities. Man can continue the creative process in it by the exercise of freedom. By endowing man with self-consciousness, by making him in the image of God, the task is set to him, to continue the creation of the world. The human self incorporates in itself existence and value and is therefore capable of salvation.

In this quest for Being every man is alone. It begins in man himself, for inwards leads the mysterious path. It starts with a certain anguish of mind, the anguish which consists in a knowledge that a man can neither escape his own destiny nor the approach of death and the bewilderment of finding himself alone in the midst of an unfathomable universe.

The whole plan of evolution suggests that man has another destiny. It is the pressure of Reality which provokes the quest and the discontent. Unhappiness, consequent on *avidyā* or ignorance, is a metaphysical necessity which prepares for the restoration, for the attainment of *vidyā* or wisdom. The sense of the Beyond gives us soaring power. The ontological argument may not prove the existence of God, but it does prove the human predicament and its need for an Absolute.

Thus, through an analysis of the finite and contingent character of human existence, through logic and morality, we apprehend the reality of a Being which is not existence, of a Self which is not object, of a Spirit which is not actual. This Being, Subject, Spirit is not an object presented to thought. It is the basis and source of thought. The self-knowledge is not a psychological awareness of phenomena, a collection of images and memories. It is not an awareness of the ego. It is the intuition of Being, knowledge of the ontological self, the living depth of human existence. Existentialism is a stage in man's pilgrimage through life. It has to transcend itself; for an analysis of the human predicament reveals the fact of God as Being and God as Perfection.

# The Religion of the Spirit

When rational thought is applied to the empirical data of the world and of the human self, the conclusion of a Supreme who is Pure Being and Free Activity is reached; but it may be argued that it is only a necessity of thought, a hypothesis, however valid it may be. There is also an ancient and widespread tradition that we can apprehend the Eternal Being with directness and immediacy. When the Upaniṣads speak of *jñāna* or gnosis, when the Buddha speaks of *bodhi* or enlightenment, when Jesus speaks of the truth that will make us free, they refer to the mode of direct spiritual apprehension of the Supreme, in which the gap between truth and Being is closed. Their religion rests on the testimony of the Holy Spirit, on personal experience, on mysticism as defined by Thomas Aquinas, *cognitio dei experimentalis.* From the affirmations of spiritual experience, we find that it is possible to reconcile the conclusions of logical understanding with the apprehensions of integral insight.

There are different types of knowledge: perceptual, conceptual, and intuitive, and they are suited to different kinds of objects. Plotinus tells us that sense perceptions are below us, logical reasonings are with us, and spiritual apprehensions are above us.

The last type of knowledge may be called integral insight, for it brings into activity not merely a portion of our conscious being, sense or reason, but the whole. It also reveals to us not abstractions but the reality in its integrity. Existentialists dispute the priority of essence to existence. Whereas the possible is prior to the actual insofar as the genesis of the universe is concerned, in the world itself thought works on and in existence and abstracts from it. Thought reaches its end of knowledge in so far as it returns to being. Thought is essentially self-transcendent. It deals with an other than thought and so is only symbolic of it. Thinking deals with essences, and existences are unattainable to it. Existence is one way of being, though it is not the only way. Knowledge is reflection on the experience of existence. It is within being. The inadequacy of knowledge to being is stressed by Bradley in his distinction between *what* and *that*, between a logical category and actual being. In integral insight we have knowledge by identity. Although logical knowledge is mediate and symbolic, it is not false. Its construction is not an imaginative synthesis. It falls short of complete knowledge, because it gives the structure of being, not being itself. In integral insight we are put in touch with actual being. This highest knowledge transcends the distinction of subject and object. Even logical knowledge is possible because this highest knowledge is ever present. It can only be accepted as foundational. Being is Truth. *Sat* is *cit.*

We use the direct mode of apprehension, which is deeper than logical understanding, when we contemplate a work of art, when we enjoy great music, when we acquire an understanding of another human being in the supreme achievement of love. In this kind of knowledge the subject is not opposed to the object but is intimately united with it. By calling this kind of knowledge integral insight, we bring out that it does not contradict logical reason, though the insight exceeds the reason. Intellect cannot repudiate instinct any more than intuition can deny logical reason. Intellectual preparation is an instrument for attaining to the truth of the spirit, but the inward realization of the truth of spirit transcends all intellectual verification, since it exists in an immediacy beyond all conceivable mediation.

The Supreme is not an object but the absolute subject, and we cannot apprehend it by either sense-perception or logical inference. Kant was right in denying that being is a predicate. We are immersed in being. When the Upaniṣads ask us to grow from intellectual to spiritual consciousness, they ask us to effect an enlargement of our awareness by which the difficulties of insecurity, isolation, and death are overcome. We are called upon to grow from division and conflict into freedom and love, from ignorance to wisdom. Such wisdom cannot come except to those who are pure not only in heart but also in the intellect, which has to rid itself of all preconceptions. Unmediated apprehension of the primordial Spirit is the knowledge of God. It is achieved by a change of consciousness, the experience of a new birth. It means an illumined mind, a changed heart, and a transformed will. Wisdom composes the various elements of our mental life, modifies our being, restores our community with nature and society, and makes living significant. Wisdom is freedom from fear, for fear is the result of a lack of correspondence between the nature of the individual and his environment, the clash of the ego and the non-ego which is alien and indifferent to it. The struggle against the alien is the source of suffering. Man is a being who is straining towards infinity, in quest of eternity; but the condition of his existence, finite and limited, temporal and mortal, causes the suffering. When he attains 'integrality', there is harmony in his life and its expression is joy.

Through wisdom we grow into likeness with the Spirit. St. Thomas Aquinas observes: "By this light the blessed are made deiform, that is like God, according to the scriptural saying 'When he shall appear, we shall be like him and we shall see him as he is' " (I John III:2, quoted in *Summa Theologica* 1 q, 12, a, 5, C).

There is a tradition of direct apprehension of the Supreme in all lands, in all ages and in all creeds.[1] The seers describe their experiences with an impressive unanimity. They are "near to one another on mountains farthest apart." They certify, in words which ring both true and clear, of a world of spirit alive and waiting for us to penetrate. Indian religions take their stand on spiritual experience, on divine-human encounter, *kṛṣṇārjunasaṁvāda*, and so do the prophets and saints of other religions. Augustine writes: "I entered and beheld with the eye of my soul above the same eye of my soul, above my mind, the Light unchangeable" (*Confessions* VII:16). St. Bernard wrote that happy and blessed was he "who once or twice—or even once only—in this mortal life for the space of a moment has lost himself in God." St. John of the Cross speaks of that steady and established certitude of essential creative union which alone he considers worthy to be called the "spiritual marriage" of the soul:

---

1. (Note by Radhakrishnan) "The close agreement which we find in these records [of mystic life], written in different countries, in different ages, and even by adherents of different creeds (for Asia has here its own important contribution to make) can only be accounted for, if we hold that the mystical experience is a genuine part of human nature, which may be developed, like the arts, by concentrated attention and assiduous labour, and which assumes the same general forms whenever and wherever it is earnestly sought." W. R. Inge: *The Philosophy of Plotinus* (1918), I, p. 2. Rudolf Otto, in the Introduction to his book on *Mysticism: East and West,* observes: "We maintain that, in mysticism, there are wide and strong primal impulses working in the human soul which as such are completely unaffected by differences of climate, of geographical position or of race. These show, in their similarity, an inner relationship of types of human experience and spiritual life which is truly astonishing" (English translation, 1932, p. xvi).

What God communicates to the soul in this intimate union is utterly ineffable, beyond the reach of all possible words . . . in this state God and the soul are united as the window is with the light or the coal with the fire . . . this communication of God diffuses itself substantially in the whole soul or rather the soul is transformed in God. In this transformation the soul drinks of God in its very substance and its spiritual powers.

Spiritual experience, as distinct from religious feeling of dependence or worship or awe, engages our whole person. It is a state of ecstasy or complete absorption of our being. When the flash of absolute reality breaks through the normal barriers of the conscious mind it leaves a trail of illumination in its wake. The excitement of illumination is distinct from the serene radiance of enlightenment. The experience is not of a subjective psychic condition. The contemplative insight into the source of all life is not an escape into the subjective. The human individual can strip himself one after the other of the outer sheaths of consciousness, penetrate to the nerve and quick of his life until all else fades away into illimitable darkness, until he is alone in the white radiance of a central and unique ecstasy. This is the fulfilment of man. This is to be with God. This is to be of God. During our hurried passage through life there may come to us a few moments of transcendent joy, when we seem to stand literally outside our narrow selves and attain a higher state of being and understanding. All religions call upon us to renew those great moments and make the experience of spirit the center of our lives.

When the vision fades, the habitual awareness of this world returns. The so-called proofs of the existence of God are the results of critical reflection on the spiritual intuitions of the ultimate Fact of Spirit. These intuitions inspire the acts of reflection, which only confirm what has been apprehended in another way. The reflections are pure and true to the extent that they refer to the intuited facts. There is a perpetual disquiet because ultimate Being is not an object. Reflective accounts are thus only approximations.

Being as such is uncharacterizable and our descriptions and translations are in forms of objects which are less than Being and consequently are inadequate. Abstract ideals and intellectualizations do not deal justly with Being which is given to us as Absolute Presence in adoration and worship. It is through religious contemplation that we realize the Holy. It is not simple apprehension. It is the surrender of the self, its opening to the Supreme.

The experience of a pure and unitary consciousness in a world divided gives rise to the twofold conception of the Absolute as Pure Transcendent

Being lifted above all relativities, and the Free Active God functioning in the world. Some emphasise the transcendent aspect, the fulness of being, the sublime presence, the sovereignly subsistent 'other,' above all names and thought; others the immanent aspect, the fulness of life, the living personal God of love who made the world, gave us freedom, and wishes us to participate in the riches of life. St. John of the Cross says:

> Beyond all sensual images, and all conceptual determination, God offers Himself as the absolute act of being in its pure actuality. Our concept of God, a mere feeble analogue of a reality which overflows it in every direction, can be made explicit only in the judgment: Being is Being, an absolute positing of that which, lying beyond every object, contains in itself the sufficient reason of objects. And that is why we can rightly say that the very excess of positivity which hides the divine being from our eyes is nevertheless the light which lights up all the rest: *ipsa caligo summa est mentis illuminatio.*

We have here the two aspects of supracosmic transcendence and cosmic universality, the divine mystery which is inexpressible, Eckhart's Godhead, and the mystery which is directed towards the world, Eckhart's God. The God who reveals Himself to the world and to man is not the Absolute which is inexpressible, relationless mystery.

Attempts to rationalize the mystery, to translate into the language of concepts that which is inexpressible in concepts, have resulted in different versions. We may use the trinitarian conception to unfold the nature of the Supreme Being; the Brahman, the Absolute, is the first person, the second is Īśvara, and the third is the World-Spirit. The three persons are different sides of the one Supreme. They are not three different persons but are the one God who hides himself ("Verily Thou art a God that hidest Thyself." *Psalm* 103) and reveals himself in various degrees. In communicating their experiences the seers use words and symbols current in their world.

# Free Spirits

The liberated souls have overcome the power of time, the force of Karma. There is something in common between the wisdom of the sage and the simplicity of the child, serene trust and innocent delight in existence. The happy state of childhood is almost the lost paradise of the human mind. The free spirits are the rays of light that shine from the future, attracting us all who still dwell in darkness. They do not separate themselves from the world but accept the responsibility for perfecting all life. There is no such thing as individual salvation, for it presupposes the salvation of others, universal salvation, the transfiguration of the world.

No man, however enlightened and holy he may be, can ever really be saved until all the others are saved. Those individuals who have realized their true being are the integrated ones who have attained personal integrity. Their reason is turned into light, their heart into love, and their will into service. Their demeanor is disciplined and their singleness of spirit is established. Selfish action is not possible for them. Ignorance and craving have lost their hold. They are dead to pride, envy, and uncharitableness. The world in which they live is no more alien to them. It is hospitable, not harsh. It becomes alive, quakes, and sends forth its greetings. Human society becomes charged with the grace and grandeur of the eternal. These free spirits reach out their hands towards the warmth in all things. They have that rarest quality in the world, simple goodness, beside which all the intellectual gifts seem a little trivial. They are meek, patient, long-suffering. They do not judge others because they do not pretend to understand them. Because of their eager selfless love they have the power to soothe the troubled heart. To those in pain their presence is like the cool soft hand of someone they love, when their head is hot with fever. The released individuals are artists in creative living. With an awareness of the Eternal, they participate in the work of the world. Even as the Supreme has two sides of pure being and free activity, these liberated souls, who are the vehicles of divine life ("Grace makes us participants of the divine nature." II. Peter I:4), have also two sides: the contemplative and the active.

Their life is socially minded. We are members of a whole, parts of *brahmāṇḍa* (the cosmic egg), which is one, which is perpetually in transition until its final purpose is achieved. "No man liveth unto himself and no man dieth unto himself" (St. Paul). Their attitude is not one of lofty condescension or patronizing pity to lift a debased creature out of mire. But it is a conviction of the solidarity of the world *loka-saṁgraha* and a recognition that the low and the high are bound together in one spirit. Vicarious suffering, not vicarious punishment, is a law of spiritual life. The free spirits bend to the very level of the enslaved to emancipate their minds and hearts. They inspire, revive and strengthen the life of their generation.

From the time I was a student, I have heard criticisms made against Indian religions that they are world-negating and that the attitude of our religious men is one of withdrawal from the world. Though the supreme quest is for the freedom of the spirit, for the vision of God, there is also the realization of the ever-present need of the world for the light and guidance of free spirits. A life of service and sacrifice is the natural and inevitable expression and the proof of the validity of spiritual experience. After years of solitary contemplation the Buddha attained Enlightenment. The rest of his life was devoted to intense social and cultural work. According to Mahāyāna Buddhism, the released spirits retain their compassion for suffering humanity. Even those whose activities are limited to the instruction of their disciples participate in social leadership in so far as they aim at refashioning human society. Gandhi, well known as a religious man, did not strive to escape from the human scene to forge a solitary destiny. He said: "I am striving for the kingdom of salvation which is spiritual deliverance. For me the road to salvation is through incessant toil in the service of my country and of humanity. I want to identify myself with everything that lives. I want to live at peace with both friend and foe." He reckoned social reform and political action among his religious duties. He founded not a monastic order but a revolutionary party. Gandhi brought home to us the lessons of the saints of old, that no one who believes in spiritual values can abandon to their fate the millions of people whom misery and impossible conditions of life have condemned to a Hell on Earth. Active service is a part of spiritual life.

Although the unitive knowledge of God here and now is the final end of man, it remains true that some forms of social and cultural life put more obstacles in the way of individual development than others. It is our duty to create and maintain forms of social organization which offer the fewest possible impediments to the development of the truly human life. By improving the conditions of social life we remove powerful temptations to ignorance and irresponsibility and encourage individual enlightenment. Every man, whatever may be his racial or social origin, is potentially a son of God, made in his image. Human personality is sacred. The human person has a claim to be treated as an end in himself and is therefore entitled to the rights to life, freedom, and security. Freedom to be himself is the right of personality. These rights involve duties. Our legal and political systems must help the realization of our rights and the acceptance of our obligations. Our civilization has failed to the extent to which these ideals are denied or betrayed. We must work for the achievement of these ideals in accordance with the principles of freedom, truth, and justice. This is not to reduce religion to a sublimated social engineering.

There is a tendency in all religions, Eastern or Western, to neglect the practical side. Any one who approaches the New Testament will find that the emphasis is on other-worldliness. Jesus's teaching about the Kingdom of God and its righteousness, of its coming and of the conditions of our partaking in it, does not betray any interest in the structures of our temporal life. The letters of the Apostles are concerned with the preaching of salvation, the proclamation of Resurrection, of the divine judgment, of the restoration and perfection of all things beyond their historical existence. The few brief comments on the state, on marriage and family life, on the relations between masters and slaves, do not take away the essentially otherworldly character of the teaching of Jesus and his disciples. In the last century his teaching has been interpreted in a manner that shows its kinship with our social and cultural problems.

Religion is not a particular way of life but is the way of all life. Jesus said: "I am the Way, the Truth and the Life." Religious life is neither ascetic nor legalistic. It condemns mere externalism and does not insist on obedience to laws and ordinances. "Where the spirit of the Lord is, there is liberty." Liberty is freedom from all taboos and restrictions. We are not called upon to hate the world because it is the creation of a hostile demiurge. To look upon the world as undivine is a speculative aberration. God is not jealous of his own works. The world is an abyss of nothingness, if we take away its roots in the Divine. What the Indian thinkers aim at is action without attachment. It is action of an individual who is no more a victim of selfishness, who has identified himself with the divine center which is in him and in all things. Since he is not emotionally involved in the 'fruits of action', he is able to act effectively. True religion has elements in it of withdrawal from the world and of return to it. Its aim is the control of life by the power of spirit.

Our social conscience has been anaesthetized by a formal religion and it has now to be roused. In recent times, it is the atheists and not the saints that have taken the lead in the work of social enlightenment and justice. In the history of religions, however, the role of the religious leader has been important. Though dedicated to a life of contemplation he is led to act like a ferment of renewal in the structure of society. That great tradition of which Gandhi is the latest example, requires to be renewed.

The integrated individuals are the rare privileged beings who are in advance of their time. They are the forerunners of the future race,[2] who set before us the path we have to take, to rise from fallen to transfigured nature.

---

2. (Note by Radhakrishnan) Christ, said St. Paul, was to be the first born of a great brotherhood. *Romans* VIII:29.

They are not, however, to be regarded as unique and absolute manifestations of the Absolute. There cannot be a complete manifestation of the Absolute in the world of relativity. Each limited manifestation may be perfect in its own way, but is not the Absolute which is within all and above all. The life of a Buddha or a Jesus tells us how we can achieve the same unity with the Absolute to which they had attained and how we can live at peace in the world of manifested being. The light that lighteth everyone that cometh into the world shone in those liberated spir its with great radiance and intensity. The Kingdom of God is the Kingdom of persons who are spiritually free, who have overcome fear and loneliness. Every one has in him the possibil- ity of this spiritual freedom, the essence of enlightenment, is a *bodhisattva*. The divine sonship of Christ is at the same time the divine sonship of every man. The end of the cosmic process is the achievement of universal resur- rection, redemption of all persons who continue to live as individuals till the end of history.

The function of the discipline of religion is to further the evolution of man into his divine stature, develop increased awareness and intensity of understanding. It is to bring about a better, deeper and more enduring adjustment in life. All belief and practice, song and prayer, meditation and contemplation, are means to this development of direct experience, an inner frame of mind, a sense of freedom and fearlessness, strength and security. Religion is the way in which the individual organises his inward being and responds to what is envisaged by him as the ultimate Reality. It is essentially intensification of experience, the displacement of triviality by intensity.

# The Three Stages of Religious Life

Each individual is a member of a community where he shares work with others; but he is also an individual with his senses and emotions, desires and affections, interests and ideals. There is a solitary side to his being as distinct from the social, where he cherishes thoughts unspoken, dreams unshared, reticences unbroken. It is there that he shelters the questionings of fate, the yearning for peace, the voice of hope and the cry of anguish. When the Indian thinkers ask us to possess our souls, to be *ātmavantam*, not to get lost in the collective currents, not to get merged in the crowd of those who have emptied and crucified their souls, *ātmahano janāh*, who have got their souls bleached in the terrible unmercy of things, they are asking us to open out our inward being to the call of the transcendent. Religion is not a movement stretching out to grasp something, external, tangible and good, and to possess it. It is a form of being, not having, a mode of life. Spiritual life is not a problem to be solved but a reality to be experienced. It is new birth into enlightenment.

The Upaniṣads speak to us of three stages of religious life, *śravaṇa*, hearing, *manana*, reflection, *nididhyāsana* or disciplined meditation. We rise from one stage to another. Joachim of Floris in the twelfth century sees the story of man in three stages. The first is of the 'Father' of the Letter, of the Law, where we have to listen and obey. The second is of the 'Son'; here we have argument and criticism. Tradition is explained, authority is explicated. The third stage is of the Spirit, where we have 'prayer and song', meditation and inspiration (See Gerald Heard, *The Eternal Gospel* [1948], p. 6). Through these, the tradition becomes a vital and transforming experience. The life of Jesus, the witness of St. Paul, of the three apostles on the Mount of Transfiguration, of Ezekiel, and of scores of others are an impressive testimony to the fact of religion as experience. Muhammed is said to have received his messages in ecstatic states. St. Thomas, in the beginning of the Fourth Book of his *Summa Contra Gentiles*, speaks of three kinds of human knowledge of divine things. "The first of these is the knowledge that comes by the natural light of reason," when the reason ascends by means of creatures to God. The second "descends to us by way of revelation." The third is possible only to the human mind "elevated to the perfect intuition of the things that are revealed." Dante symbolized the first by Virgil, the second by Beatrice, the third by St. Bernard.

# Religion as Self-Knowledge

Though God is everywhere, he is found more easily in the soul. The inward light is never darkened and it enlightens with understanding the minds of those who turn to it. Our self is a holy temple of the Spirit into which we may not enter without a sense of awe and reverence.

> Behold Thou wert within and I abroad, and there I searched for Thee. Thou wert with me but I was not with Thee. Thou calledst and shoutedst, burstedst my deafness. Thou flashedst, shonedst, and scatteredst my blindness. Thou breathedst odours, and I drew in breath, and pant for Thee. I tasted and hunger

and thirst. Thou touchedst me, and I was on fire for Thy peace. (Augustine, *Confessions* X:38)

Thou wert more inward to me than my most inward part, and higher than my highest. (*Confessions* III:11)

Bishop Ullathorne says:

Let it be plainly understood that we cannot return to God unless we enter first into ourselves. God is everywhere, but not everywhere to us. There is but one point in the universe where God communicates with us, and that is the center of our own soul. There He waits for us; there He meets us; there He speaks to us. To seek Him, therefore, we must enter into our own interior. (*Groundwork of Christian Virtues*, p. 74)

When Kierkegaard tells us that truth is identical with subjectivity, he means that if it is objectified, it becomes relative. He does not mean that the truth is peculiar to and private to the individual. He makes out that we must go deep down into the subject to attain the experience of Universal Spirit. Whitehead says that "religion is what the individual does with his solitariness" (*Religion in the Making* [1926], p. 16). Each individual must unfold his own awareness of life, witness his own relation to the source or sources of his being and, in the light of his experience, resolve the tragedies and contradictions of his inward life. "If you are never solitary, then you are never religious" (*Ibid.*). It is in solitude that we prepare the human candle for the divine flame. This does not mean a facile commensurability between God and man. It means that man can transcend himself, can exceed his limits. To get at the transcendent within oneself, one must break through one's normal self. The revelation of the divine in man is of the character of an interruption of our routine self. We must impose silence on our familiar self, if the spirit of God is to become manifest in us. The divine is more deeply in us than we are ourselves. We attain to spirit by passing beyond the frontiers of the familiar self. If we do not mechanize the doctrine of Incarnation, of 'God manifest in the flesh,' we make out that man has access to the inmost being of the divine, in these moments of highest spiritual insight. The highest human life is life in God. In the words of Eckhart, "God in the fulness of his Godhead dwells eternally in His Image, the soul."

Religions prescribe certain conditions to which we have to submit if we are to gain religious illumination. Discipline of the intellect, emotions and will is a prerequisite for spiritual perception. Religious spirits use the catastrophes of the world as opportunities for creative work. The world is the field for moral striving. The purpose of life is not the enjoyment of the world but the education of the soul.

In the middle of January 1946 there was published the Report of the Commission appointed by the Archbishop of Canterbury "to survey the whole problem of modern evangelism with special reference to the spiritual needs and the prevailing intellectual outlook of the non-worshipping members of the community and to report on the organization and methods by which the needs can most effectively be met." This Report, entitled *The Conversion of England,* points out that religion has become a waning influence in the national life of the country and calls for a strengthening and quickening of spiritual life. Religion, it urges, is a conversion, a mental and spiritual revolution, a change from a self-centered to a God-centered life. It is a call to a new vision and understanding of life. The Report asks for the assertion of the primacy of spirit over the long dominant external forms of religion, submission to authority, subscription to a formula. The discipline of religion consists in turning inwards, deepening our awareness and developing a more meaningful attitude to life which frees us from bondage and hardening of the spirit. "Except ye be converted and become as little children, ye shall not enter into the kingdom of heaven."

There are different ways prescribed by religions to achieve this inward change. *Yoga* is used in Indian religions for the methods of drawing near to the Supreme. *Yoga* is a path, a praxis, and training by which the individual man, bleeding from the split caused by intelligence, becomes whole. Intellectual concentration *jñāna,* emotional detachment, *bhakti,* ethical dedication, *karma,* are all types of *Yoga.* In Patañjali's *Yoga Sūtra* we have a development of what Plato calls recollection, the way by which we steadily withdraw from externality, from our functions which are at the mercy of life and enter into our essential being, which is not the individual ego but the Universal Spirit. It is the act of recollection by which the recollecting self distinguishes its primal being from all that is confused with it, its material, vital, psychological and logical expressions. By recollection the self is assured of its participation in ultimate being, the principle of all positivity, the ontological mystery. We have power over the outer expressions. We may submit ourselves to despair, deny physical being by resorting to suicide, surpass all expressions and discover that deep down there is something other than these empirical manifestations. Even the thinking subject is only in relation to an object, but the spirit in us is not the subject of epistemology. It is primordial being.

When we are anchored in the mystery which is the foundation of our very being, our activities express "Thy will and not mine." When we are in Being we are beyond the moral world of freedom. Our deeds flow out of the heart of reality and our desires are swallowed up in love. Spiritual freedom is different from moral autonomy. The inward hold we get makes us the masters of life. Religion then is experience turning inwards towards the realization of itself.

# Religion and Religions

The Report on the *Conversion of England* deplores the unhappy divisions, the lack of charity among particular congregations, which obscure the fellowship of the Christian Church and calls upon the different Christian sects to continue and co-operate in the task of the conversion of England. It asks us to adopt the principle of unity in variety, which is not only a profound spiritual truth but the most obvious common sense.

If we seriously accept this principle we cannot stop at the frontiers of Christianity. We must move along a path which shall pass beyond all the differences of the historical past and eventually be shared in common by all mankind. Belief in exclusive claims and monopolies of religious truth has been a frequent source of pride, fanaticism and strife. The vehemence with which religions were preached and the savagery with which they were enforced are some of the disgraces of human history. Secularism and paganism point to the rivalries of religions for a proof of the futility of religion. A little less missionary ardor, a little more enlightened skepticism will do good to us all. Our attitude to other religions should be defined in the spirit of that great saying in a play of Sophocles, where Antigone says, "I was not born to share men's hatred, but their love." We must learn the basic principles of the great world religions as the essential means of promoting international understanding.

Besides, Whitehead observes that "the decay of Christianity and Buddhism as determinative influences in modern thought is partly due to the fact that each religion has unduly sheltered itself from the other. They have remained self-satisfied and unfertilised" (Quoted in Inge, *Mysticism and Religion* [1947], p. 40). A study of other living religions helps and enhances the appreciation of our own faith. If we adopt a wider historical view we obtain a more comprehensive vision and understanding of spiritual truth. Christian thinkers like St. Thomas Aquinas were willing to find confirmation of the truths of Christianity in the works of pagan philosophers. We live in a world which is neither Eastern nor Western, where every one of us is the heir to all civilization. The past of China, Japan, and India is as much our past as is that of Israel, Greece, and Rome. It is our duty and privilege to enlarge our faculties of curiosity, of understanding, and realize the spaciousness of our common ground. No way of life is uninteresting so long as it is natural and satisfying to those who live it. We may measure true spiritual culture by the comprehension and veneration we are able to give to all forms of thought and feeling which have influenced masses of mankind. We must understand the experience of people whose thought eludes our categories. We must widen our religious perspective and obtain a world wisdom worthy of our time and place.

Religious provincialism stands in the way of a unitary world culture which is the only enduring basis for a world community. "Shall two walk together except they be agreed?" To neglect the spiritual unity of the world and underline the religious diversity would be philosophically unjustifiable, morally indefensible, and socially dangerous.

The arrogant dislike of other religions has today given place to respectful incomprehension. it is time that we accustom ourselves to fresh ways of thinking and feeling. The interpenetration of obstinate cultural traditions is taking place before our eyes. If we have a sense of history we will find that human societies are by nature unstable. They are ever on the move giving place to new ones. Mankind is still in the making. The new world society requires a new world outlook based on respect for and understanding of other cultural traditions.

The procedure suggested here provides us with a basis for inter-religious understanding and co-operation. It involves an abandonment of missionary enterprises such as they are now. The "compassing of sea and land to make one proselyte"[3] is not possible when our ignorance of other peoples' faiths is removed. The main purpose of religious education is not to train others in our way of thinking and living, not to substitute one form of belief for another, but to find out what others have been doing and help them to do it better. We are all alike in need of humility and charity, of

---

3. (Note by Radhakrishnan) *Matthew* XXIII:15. C.S. Lewis writes: "Democrats by birth and education, we should prefer to think that all nations and individuals start level in the search for God, or even that all religions are equally true. It must be admitted at once that Christianity makes no concessions to this point of view."! *Miracles* (1947), p. 140.

repentance and conversion, of a change of mind, of a turning round. The missionary motives are derived from the conviction of the absolute superiority of our own religion and of supreme contempt for other religions. They are akin to the political motives of imperialist countries to impose their culture and civilization on the rest of the world. If missionary activities, such as they are now, are persisted in, they will become a prime factor in the spiritual impoverishment of the world. They are treason against Him who "never left himself without a witness." St. Justin said: "God is the word of whom the whole human race are partakers, and those who lived according to Reason are Christians even though accounted atheists . . . Socrates and Heracleitus, and of the barbarians, Abraham and many others." St. Ambrose's well-known gloss on I Corinthians XII:3, "all that is true, by whomsoever it has been said, is from the Holy Ghost," is ln conformity with the ancient tradition of India on this matter. "As men approach me, so I do accept them, men on all sides follow my path" says the *Bhagavadgītā.* "If the follower of any particular religion understood the saying of Junayd, 'The color of the water is the color of the vessel containing it', he would not interfere with the beliefs of others, but would perceive God in every form and in every belief," says ibn-ul-'Arabi.[4] Our aim should be not to make converts, Christians into Buddhists or Buddhists into Christians, but enable both Buddhists and Christians to rediscover the basic principles of their own religions and live up to them.

Every religion is attempting to reformulate its faith in accordance with modern thought and criticism. Stagnant and stereotyped religions are at variance with the psychology of modern life. If, in the name of religion, we insist on teaching much that modern knowledge has proved to be untrue, large numbers will refuse to accept devitalized doctrines. Aware of this danger, religions are emphasising the essential principles and ideals rather than the dogmatic schemes. For example, the moral and spiritual truths of Christianity, faith in the Divine Being, in the manifestation of the spiritual and moral nature of the Divine in the personality of Jesus, one of the eldest of many brothers, faith that we can receive strength and guidance by com-

---

4. (Note by Radhakrishnan) R.A. Nicholson, *Studies in Islamic Mysticism* (1921), p. 159. Compare this with Faridu'd Din Attar in *Maṇṭiqu't Tayr:* "Since then there are different ways of making the journey, no two (soul) birds will fly alike. Each finds a way of his own, on this road of mystic knowledge, one by means of the Mihrab and another through the Idol." See also Ananda K. Coomaraswamy, *The Bugbear of Literacy* (1947), Chapter 3.

munion with the Divine, are regarded as more important than beliefs in the miraculous birth, resurrection, ascension and the return of Jesus as the judge of mankind at the end of human history. The *Report of the Commission on Christian Doctrine* (1938), appointed by the Archbishops of Canterbury and York, made it permissible for English Churchmen to hold and to teach the Christian faith in accordance with the verified results of modern scientific, historical, and literary criticism. Other religions are also attempting to cast off the inessentials and return to the basic truths. Whereas the principles of religions are eternal, their expressions require continual development. The living faiths of mankind carry not only the inspiration of centuries but also the encrustations of error. Religion is a "treasure in earthen vessels" (St. Paul). These vessels are capable of infinite refashioning and the treasure itself of renewed application in each succeeding age of human history. The profound intuitions of religions require to be presented in fresh terms more relevant to our own experience, to our own predicament. If religion is to recover its power, if we are to help those who are feeling their way and are longing to believe, a restatement is essential. It is a necessity of the time. "I have many things to say unto you, but ye cannot bear them now; when he, the Spirit of Truth, is come, he will guide you into all the truth" (*John* XVI, 12f). Every religion is growing under the inspiration of the Divine Spirit of Truth in order to meet the moral and spiritual ordeal of the modern mind. This process of growth is securing for our civilization a synthesis on the highest level of the forces of religion and culture and enabling their followers to co-operate as members of one great fellowship.

# A World Fellowship of Religions

The world is seeking not so much a fusion of religions as a fellowship of religions, based on the realization of the foundational character of man's religious experience. William Blake says: "As all men are alike (though infinitely various), so all Religions, as all similars, have one source." The different religions may retain their individualities, their distinctive doctrines and characteristic pieties, so long as they do not impair the sense of spiritual fellowship. The light of eternity would blind us if it came full in the face. It is broken into colors so that our eyes can make something of it. The different religious traditions clothe the one Reality in various images and their visions could embrace and fertilize each other so as to give mankind a many-sided perfection, the spiritual radiance of Hinduism, the faithful obedience of Judaism, the life of beauty of Greek Paganism, the noble compassion of Buddhism, the vision of divine love of Christianity, and the spirit of resignation to the sovereign lord of Islam. All these represent different aspects of the inward spiritual life, projections on the intellectual plane of the ineffable experiences of the human spirit.

If religion is the awareness of our real nature in God, it makes for a union of all mankind based on communion with the Eternal. It sees in all the same vast universal need it has felt in itself. The different religions take their source in the aspiration of man towards an unseen world, though the forms in which this aspiration is couched are determined by the environment and climate of thought. The unity of religions is to be found in that which is divine or universal in them and not in what is temporary and local. Where there is the spirit of truth there is unity. As in other matters, so in the sphere of religion there is room for diversity and no need for discord. To claim that any one religious tradition bears unique witness to the truth and reveals the presence of the true God is inconsistent with belief in a living God who has spoken to men "by diverse portions and in diverse manners." God is essentially self-communicative (*Bhagavadgītā,* IV, 3), and is of ungrudging goodness, as Plato taught (*Timaeus,* 29B). There is no such thing as a faith once for all delivered to the saints. Revelation is divine-human. As God does not reveal His Being to a stone or a tree, but only to men, His revelation is attuned to the state of the human mind. The Creative Spirit is ever ready to reveal Himself to the seeking soul provided the search is genuine and the effort intense. The authority for revelation is not an Infallible book or an Infallible Church but the witness of the inner light. What is needed is not submission to an external authority but inward illumination which, of course, is tested by tradition and logic. If we reflect on the matter deeply we will perceive the unity of spiritual aspiration and endeavour underlying the varied upward paths indicated in the different world faiths. The diversity in the traditional formulations tends to diminish as we climb up the scale of spiritual perfection. All the paths of ascent lead to the mountain top. This convergent tendency and the remarkable degree of agreement in the witness of those who reach the mountain top are the strongest proof of the truth of religion.

Religious life belongs to the realm of inward spiritual revelation; when exteriorised it loses its authentic character. It is misleading to speak of different religions. We have different religious traditions which can be used for correction and enrichment. The traditions do not create the truth but clothe it in language and symbol for the help of those who do not see it themselves. They symbolize the mystery of the spirit and urge us to move from external significations, which reflect the imperfect state of our consciousness and social environment, to the thing signified. The symbolic character of tradition is not to be mistaken for reality. These are second-hand notions which fortify and console us so long as we do not have direct experience. Our different traditions are versions in a series, part of the historical and relative world in which we live and move. It we cling to these historically conditioned forms as absolute they will not rescue us from slavery to the momentary and the contingent. They leave us completely immersed in the relative. It does not mean that there is nothing central or absolute in religion. The unchanging substance of religion is the evolution of man's consciousness. The traditions help to take us to the truth above all traditions and of which the traditions are imperfect, halting expressions. If we love truth as such and not our opinions, if we desire nothing except what is true and acceptable to God, the present religious snobbery and unfriendliness will disappear. If we open ourselves up unreservedly to the inspirations of our age, we will get to the experience of the one Spirit which takes us beyond the historical formulations. Averroes, the Arab philosopher, distinguished between philosophic truth *(secundum rationem;* tattvam) and religious views *(secundum fidem;* matam). No single religion possesses truth compared with philosophic knowledge, though each religious view may claim to possess a fragment of the truth. "Yet every priest values his own creed as the fool his cap and bells." Our quarrels will cease if we know that the one truth is darkened and diversified in the different religions. If we are to remove the present disordered, divided state of the world, we have to adopt what William Law called a catholic spirit, a communion of saints in the love of God and all goodness, which no one can learn from that which is called orthodoxy in particular churches, but is only to be had by a total dying to all worldly views, by a pure love of God and by such an unction from above as delivers the mind from all selfishness and makes it love truth and goodness with an equality of affection in every man, whether he is Christian, Jew, or Gentile.

William Law says also:

> The chief hurt of a sect is this, that it takes itself to be necessary to the truth, whereas the truth is only then found when it is known to be of no sect but as free and universal as the goodness of God and as common to all names and nations as the air and light of this world.

*Maitrī Upaniṣad* says:

Some contemplate one name and some another. Which of these is the best? All are eminent clues to the transcendent, immortal, unembodied Brahman; these names are to be contemplated, lauded and at last denied. For by them one rises higher and higher in these worlds; but where all comes to its end, there he attains to the unity of the Person.

In the midst of the travail in which we are living we discern the emergence of the religion of the Spirit, which will be the crown of the different religions, devoted to the perfecting of humanity in the life of the spirit, that is, in the life of God in the soul. When God is our teacher, we come to think alike.

# Freedom from Dogma

The thought of the Upaniṣads, the humanism of Confucius, the teaching of the Buddha are marked by the comparative absence of dogma, and their followers are, therefore, relatively free from the evils of obscurantism and casuistry. This is due to the fact that there is greater emphasis in them on the experience of Spirit. Those whose experience is deepest do not speak of it because they feel that it is inexpressible. They feel that they are breaking, dividing, and betraying the experience by giving utterance to it. By their attitude of silence they affirm the primacy of Being over knowledge with the latter's distinction of subject and object. In the deepest spiritual experience we are not self-conscious. When we describe it, it is by way of second reflection, in which we turn the inward presence into an object of thought. We take care to observe that the truth goes beyond the traditional forms. Ruysbroeck says about the reality known by the seer: "We can speak no more of Father, Son and Holy Spirit, nor of any creature, but only of one Being, which is the very substance of the Divine Persons. There were we all one before our creation, for this is our super-essence. There the Godhead is in simple essence without activity." A devout Catholic of the Counter-Reformation period, J.J. Olier, observes: "The holy light of faith is so pure, that compared with it, particular lights are but impurities: and even ideas of the saints, of the Blessed Virgin and the sight of Jesus Christ in his humanity are impediments in the way of the sight of God in His purity." When the seers try to communicate their vision in greater detail they use the tools put into their hands by their cultural milieu. Jesus interprets his experience in terms of notions current in contemporary Jewish thought. We perhaps owe the doctrine of the world's imminent dissolution to the

Jewish circle of ideas. So long as we are on Earth we cannot shake off the historical altogether.

# The Mystery of Spiritual Life

Sometimes we exteriorize the mystery of spiritual life. Religions which believe in the reality of spiritual life interpret the dogmas with reference to it. Religious views are not so much attempts to solve the riddle of the universe as efforts to describe the experience of sages. The concepts are verbalizations of intense emotional experience. They are lifted out of their true empiricism and made historical rather than experimental, objective instead of profound inward realization. Christ is born in the depths of spirit. We say that he passes through life, dies on the Cross and rises again. These are not so much historical events which occurred once upon a time as universal processes of spiritual life, which are being continually accomplished in the souls of men. Those who are familiar with the way in which the Kṛṣṇa story is interpreted will feel inclined to regard Christhood as an attainment of the soul; a state of inward glorious illumination in which the divine wisdom has become the heritage of the soul. The annunciation is a beautiful experience of the soul. It relates to the birth of Christhood in the soul, "the holy thing begotten within." The human soul from the Holy Breath, *Devakī* or *daivī prakṛti,* divine nature is said to be the mother of Kṛṣṇa. Mary, the mother of the Christ child, is the soul in her innermost divine nature. Whatever is conceived in the womb of the human soul is always of the Holy Spirit.

The mandate of religion is that man must make the change in his own nature in order to let the divine in him manifest itself. It speaks of the death of man as we know him with all his worldly desires and the emergence of the new man. This is the teaching not only of the Upaniṣads and Buddhism but also of the Greek mysteries and Platonism, of the Gospels and the schools of Gnosticism. This is the wisdom to which Plotinus refers, when he says: "This doctrine is not new; it was professed from the most ancient times though without being developed explicitly; we wish only to be interpreters of the ancient sages, and to show by the evidence of Plato himself that they had the same opinions as ourselves" (*Enneads* V, I:8). This is the religion which Augustine mentions in his well-known statement: "That which is called the Christian Religion existed among the Ancients, and never did not exist, from the beginning of the human race until Christ came in the flesh, at which time the true religion, which already existed, began to be called Christianity"

(*Librum de vera religione*, Chapter 10). This truth speaks to us in varying dialects across far continents and over centuries of history. Those who overlook this perennial wisdom, the eternal religion behind all religions, this *sanātana dharma*, this timeless tradition, "wisdom uncreate, the same now that it ever was, and the same to be forevermore" (St Augustine), and cling to the outward forms and quarrel among themselves, are responsible for the civilized chaos in which we live. It is our duty to get back to this central core of religion, this fundamental wisdom which has been obscured and distorted in the course of history by dogmatic and sectarian developments.

At the level of body and mind, physique and temperament, talents and tastes, we are profoundly unlike one another; but at the deepest level of all, that of the spirit which is the true ground of our being, we are like one another. If religion is to become an effective force in human affairs, if it is to serve as the basis for the new world order, it must become more inward and more universal, a flame which cleanses our inward being and so cleanses the world. For such a religion the historical expressions of spiritual truth and the psychological idioms employed by religions to convey the universal truth cease to be rocks of offence. The barriers dividing men will break down and the reunion and integration of all, what the Russians call *sobornost*, an altogetherness in which we walk together creatively and to which we all contribute, a universal church will be established. Then will the cry of St. Joan in Bernard Shaw's epilogue to that play be fulfilled: "O God that madest this beautiful Earth, when will it be ready to receive thy saints?" Then will come a time when the world will be inhabited by a race of men, with no flaw of flesh or error of mind, freed from the yoke not only of disease and privation but of lying words and of love turned into hate. When human beings grow into completeness, into that invisible world which is the kingdom of heaven, then will they manifest in the outer world the Kingdom which is within them. That day we shall cease to set forth God dogmatically or dispute about his nature but leave each man to worship God in the sanctuary of his heart, to feel after him and to possess him.

While I never felt attracted to travelling for its own sake, I have travelled a great deal and lived in places far from home, in England and France, America and Russia. For some years, I have spent long periods in England and the qualities of the English people such as their love of justice, their hatred of doctrinairism, their sympathy for the underdog, made an impression on me. All Souls College, which has provided a second home for me all these years, has given me an insight into English intellectual life with its caution and stability, confidence and adventure. Whatever one may feel about the character of the Russian Government, the people there are kindly and human and their lives are filled as anywhere else with jokes and jealousies, loves and hates. Though I have not been able to take root in any of these foreign countries, I have met many, high and low, and learned to feel the human in them. There are no fundamental differences among the peoples of the world. They have all the deep human feelings, the craving for justice above all class interests, horror of bloodshed and violence. They are working for a religion which teaches the possibility and the necessity of man's union with himself, with nature, with his fellowmen, and with the Eternal Spirit of which the visible universe is but a manifestation and upholds the emergence of a complete consciousness as the destiny of man. Our historical religions will have to transform themselves into the universal faith or they will fade away. This prospect may appear strange and unwelcome to some, but it has a truth and beauty of its own. It is working in the minds of men and will soon be a realized fact. Human unity depends not on past origins but on future goal and direction, on what we are becoming and whither we are tending. Compared with the civilization that is now spreading over the Earth's surface, thanks to science and technology, the previous civilizations were restricted in scope and resources. Scientists claim that organic life originated on this planet some 1,200 million years ago, but man has come into existence on Earth during the last half-million years. His civilization has been here for only 10,000 years. Man is yet in his infancy and has a long period ahead of him on this planet. He will work out a higher integration and produce world-minded men and women.

The eternal religion, outlined in these pages, is not irrationat or unscientific, is not escapist or asocial. Its acceptance will solve many of our desperate problems and will bring peace to men of good will.

This is the personal philosophy which by different paths I have attained, a philosophy which has served me in the severest tests, in sickness and in health, in triumph and in defeat. It may not be given to us to see that the faith prevails; but it is given to us to strive that it should.

*S. Radhakrishnan*

EMBASSY OF INDIA
MOSCOW, U.S.S.R.

HANS-GEORG GADAMER (1900–2002) was the leading thinker in the field of 'philosophical hermeneutics', an approach to philosophy which revives and extends the old discipline of hermeneutics, the interpretation of texts. His book *Truth and Method* (1960) is the major statement of hermeneutical theory in the twentieth century; it has influenced literary criticism and theology as well as philosophy. Gadamer's collection of essays, *Reason in the Age of Science* (1982) is also widely admired.

# Hans-Georg GADAMER

*" Question and answer play back and forth between the text and its interpreter. "*

WHEN IN 1918, WITH THE FIRST WORLD War in its last year, I was graduated from the Holy Spirit *Gymnasium* in Breslau and enrolled in the Breslau University, I had no idea, as I looked around, that my path would eventually lead into the field of philosophy.

My father was a researcher in the natural sciences, and was basically averse to all book knowledge, although his own knowledge of Horace was excellent. During my childhood he sought in a variety of ways to interest me in the natural sciences, and I must say he was quite disappointed at his lack of success. Of course, the fact that I liked what he called those "chattering professors"

(*Schwätzprofessoren*) was clear from the beginning. Still, he let me have my way, although for the rest of his life he remained unhappy about my choice.

My studies in those days were like the first adventures in a long Odyssey. A whole range of things enticed me and I tasted many of them; and if, in the end, it was the philosophical interest that gained the upper hand, rather than my genuine interest in the study of literature, history, or art history, this was really less a turning away from one of these and towards the others so much as it was a gradual pressing further and further on into the discipline of scholarly work as such. In the confusion which the First World War and its end had brought to the whole German scene, to try to mold oneself unquestioningly into the surviving tradition was simply no longer possible. And the perplexity we were experiencing was in itself already an impetus to philosophical questioning.

In philosophy, too, it was obvious that merely accepting and continuing what the older generation had accomplished was no longer feasible for us in the younger generation. In the First World War's grisly trench warfare and heavy-artillery battles for position, the Neo-Kantianism which had up to then been accorded a truly worldwide acceptance, though not undisputed, was just as thoroughly defeated as was the proud cultural consciousness of that liberal age, with its faith in scientifically based progress. In a disoriented world, we who were young at that time were searching for a new orientation. In our search we were limited, in practice, to the intra-German scene, where bitterness, mania for innovation, poverty, hopelessness, and yet also the unbroken will to live, all competed with each other in the youth of the time. Expressionism was the reigning force in life as well as art at that time, and while the natural sciences continued their upswing—with the Einsteinian theory of relativity in particular causing a great deal of discussion—still, in those areas of study and research conditioned by world view, namely writing and scholarship, truly a mood of catastrophe was spreading more and more, and was bringing about a break with the old traditions. *The Collapse of German Idealism*, an oft-cited book of that time by Paul Ernst, was one side of the new 'mood of the times' (*Zeitgefühl*)—the academic side. The other and far more encompassing side of this mood found its expression in the sensational success of Oswald Spengler's *The Decline of the West* (1919). This romance, as I think it must be called, made up partly of scholarship and mostly of world-historical fantasy, was 'much admired, much reviled', but in the end it would seem to be just as much the inscription of a world-historical mood of pessimism as it was a genuine calling into question of the modern faith in progress and its proud ideal of proficiency and 'accomplishing things'. In this situation it is hardly surprising that a completely second-rate book of the times had a truly revolutionary effect on me: Theodor Lessing's *Europe and Asia*. This book, based on the wisdom of the East, called into question the whole of European accomplishment-oriented thinking. Regrettably, in a later and still more chaotic time, Lessing was assassinated by German nationalists. In any case, for the first time in my experience the all-encompassing horizon which I had grown into through birth, education, schooling, and, indeed, the whole world around me, was relativized. And so for me something like *thinking* began.

A number of significant authors had already given me a certain first introduction to thinking. I remember the powerful impression which Thomas Mann's *Observations of an Unpolitical Person* made on me during my final year of high school. His fanciful but enthusiastic opposition between art and life as it was expressed in *Tonio Kröger* also touched me deeply, and I remember being enchanted by the melancholy tone of Hermann Hesse's early novels. My first introduction to the art of conceptual thinking, on the other hand, came from Richard Hönigswald, whose chiseled dialectic elegantly, although a little monotonously, defended the transcendental-idealistic position of Neo-Kantianism against all psychologism. I very faithfully took down his lecture course, 'Basic Questions in the Theory of Knowledge', word for word in shorthand and then transcribed it into longhand. My two notebooks containing this lecture course have since been donated to the Hönigswald Archive in Würzburg, which was brought into being by Hans Wagner. In any case, these lectures offered me a good introduction to transcendental philosophy. So when in 1919 I came to Marburg I already had a fair preparation in transcendental philosophy.

In Marburg I was soon confronted with new academic experiences. Unlike the universities in the large cities, the 'small' universities of that time still led a real academic life—a 'life of ideas' as Humboldt meant that phrase—and in the philosophical faculty there was in every area and with every professor a 'circle' so one was soon drawn in several directions toward a variety of interests. At that time the critique of historical theology following in the footsteps of Karl Barth's *Commentary on the Letter to the Romans* (1919) was just beginning in Marburg, a critique which was later to become the so-called dialectical theology. Among more and more young people in those days, there was sharp criticism of the 'methodologism' of the Neo-Kantian school, and over against this, there was acclaim for Husserl's art of phenomenological description. But it was 'life-philosophy', above all— behind which stood the European event of Friedrich Nietzsche—that was taking hold of our whole feeling for life. And of course the problem of historical relativism connected with this preoccupied the minds of many young people, whose discussion of it related especially to the works of Wilhelm Dilthey and Ernst Troeltsch.

In addition to these theological and philosophical developments, it was about that time that the influence of the circle around the poet Stefan George, in particular, began to penetrate into the general academic world, and the extremely effective and fascinating books of Friedrich Gundolf brought a new artistic sensitivity into the scholarly interaction with poetry. Overall, everything that came out of the George circle—Gundolf's books as well as the Nietzsche book of Ernst Bertram, Wolters's skillful pamphlet rhetoric, Salin's crystalline delicacy, and finally, Erich von Kahler's exceptionally explicit declamatory attack on Max Weber's famous speech on 'Science as a Profession'—amounted to a single great provocation. These were the voices of a strongly held critique of the culture. And I had the feeling that, in this case, in contrast to similar tones of protest from other sides—which, in light of my being a typically dissatisfied beginning student, also gained a certain hearing from me—there was definitely something to it. A certain power seemed to stand behind these often monotonous declamations. The fact that a poet like George could, with the magical sound of his verse and the force of his personality, exercise such a powerful formative effect on human beings remained a nagging question for many thoughtful persons, and represented a never completely forgotten corrective to the play with concepts I was encountering in my philosophical study.

# The Truth of Art

I myself simply could not ignore the fact that the experience of art had something to do with philosophy. Philosophers in the German Romantic period, right up to the end of the idealistic era, held that art was the true instrument of philosophy, if not its superior adversary, and they found in this truth their all-encompassing task. Indeed, the price that the university philosophy of the post-Hegelian era had to pay for its failure to recognize this truth was barrenness. The same thing also held and holds for Neo-Kantianism, and indeed it applies also to positivism right up to the present-day new positivism. In my view then, and it remains my view today, the task of reclaiming this truth about the relevance of art to philosophy is something our historical heritage has assigned to us.

But certainly the task of appealing to the truth of art against the doubt which an historical relativism had already attached to the conceptual truth claims of philosophy was not an easy one. The experience of art constitutes a kind of evidence which is both too strong and at the same time not strong enough. It is too strong in the sense that probably no one would venture to extend their faith in scientific progress to the heights of art and try, for instance, to see in Shakespeare an advance over Sophocles, or in Michelangelo an advance beyond Phidias. On the other hand, the evidence of art is also too weak in the sense that the artwork withholds the very truth that it embodies and prevents it from becoming conceptually precise. In any case, by the time I was in Marburg, the form of cultural education—of the esthetic consciousness as well as of historical consciousness—had degenerated into the study of 'worldviews'. This did not mean, of course, that either art or the encounter with the historical tradition of thought had lost their fascination. On the contrary, the assertions of art, like those of the great philosophers, raised a claim to truth then more than ever, confused but unavoidable, which would not allow itself to be neutralized by any Kantian 'history of problems', nor to be subordinated to the rules of rigorous scientific exactitude and methodical progress.

Rather, the claim to truth at that time, under the influence of a new reception of Kierkegaard in Germany, called itself 'existential'. Existentialism dealt with a truth which was supposed to be demonstrated not so much in terms of universally held propositions or knowledge as rather in the immediacy of one's own experience and in the absolute unsubstitutability of one's own existence. Dostoyevsky, above all others, seemed to us to have known about this. The red Piper volumes of the Dostoyevskian novels flamed on every writing desk. The letters of van Gogh and Kierkegaard's *Either-Or*, which he wrote against Hegel, beckoned to us, and of course behind all the boldness and riskiness of our existential engagement—as a still scarcely visible threat to the romantic traditionalism of our culture—stood the gigantic form of Friedrich Nietzsche with his ecstatic critique of everything, including all the illusions of self-consciousness. Where, we wondered, was a thinker whose philosophical power was adequate to the powerful initiatives put forward by Nietzsche?

The new feeling that had arisen in that time was causing new ground to be broken also in the Marburg School of philosophy.[1] Paul Natorp, the

---

1. One of the four great schools of Neo-Kantian philosophy, the Marburg School is best known for the works of Hermann Cohen (1842–1918), Paul Natorp (1854–1924), Nicolai Hartmann, (1882–1950), and Ernst Cassirer (1874–1945).

brilliant methodologist of the Marburg School, who in his older days sought with muse-like enthusiasm to penetrate into the mystical unsayability of the primordially concrete, left behind lasting impressions. Natorp conjured up not only Plato and Dostoyevsky but Beethoven and Rabindranath Tagore, and also the mystical tradition from Plotinus and Meister Eckhart down to the Quakers. And no less impressive was the daemonism of Max Scheler, who, as guest lecturer in Marburg, demonstrated his penetrating phenomenological gifts, which had directed him into very new, unexpected fields of exploration. And also there was the cool acuteness with which Nicolai Hartmann, a thinker and teacher of imposing perseverance, sought to strip away his own idealistic past through critical argumentation. When I wrote my Plato dissertation and in 1922 received my doctorate far too young, I stood under the influence of Nicolai Hartmann, above all, who had come out in opposition to Natorp's system-oriented, idealistic style.

We also lived in the expectation of a new philosophical orientation, which was particularly tied to the dark, magical word, 'phenomenology'. But when Husserl himself, who with all his analytical genius and inexhaustible descriptive patience that continuously pressed on for final evidence, had envisioned no better philosophical support than a Neo-Kantian transcendental idealism, where was help for thinking to come from? Heidegger brought it. Some followers built their interpretation of Marx on Heidegger, others their interpretation of Freud on Heidegger, and all of us, in the end, our interpretation of what Nietzsche was. I myself suddenly realized from Heidegger that we could only repeat the philosophizing of the Greeks once we had forfeited that *fundamentum inconcussum* of philosophy on the basis of which Hegel had written his story of philosophy and the Neo-Kantians their history of problems—namely, *self-consciousness.*

# Heidegger and the Greeks

From that point on I had a glimpse of what I wanted—and obviously it had nothing to do with the idea of a new, all-encompassing system. For I had not forgotten Kierkegaard's critique of Hegel. In my early essay, 'On the Idea of System in Philosophy', written for the Festschrift celebrating Natorp's seventieth birthday, I attempted to refute the new idea that philosophy can be reduced to basic experiences that carry human existence and that philosophy can be explained somewhere beyond all historicism. Although a document of my immaturity, this essay also gave evidence of my new involvement with Heidegger and the inspiration he had already become for me. Because this essay appeared in 1924, it has sometimes been interpreted as an anticipation of Heidegger's turn against transcendental idealism—an interpretation which I think is completely wrong. As a matter of fact, the three months in the summer of 1923 that I was in Freiburg studying with Heidegger would in themselves scarcely have led me to this 'inspiration' if there were not all sorts of things already in place and ready to receive it. Certainly Heidegger was the one who permitted me to have the necessary distance from the work of my two other Marburg teachers: Natorp's construction of encompassing systems, and the naive objectivism of Hartmann's categorial research. That essay, at that point, was of course quite impertinent stuff. As I came to know more, I began to remain silent. In fact, at the time of my habilitation in 1928, I could present as philosophical publications in addition to my habilitation, only one other, equally impertinent publication, from 1923, on Hartmann's *Metaphysics of Knowledge*, published in *Logos*. I had in the meantime, however, been studying classical philology, and I was later able to develop from my entry paper in the philological seminar of Paul Friedländer, namely, 'The Aristotelian *Protreptikos* and Aristotelian Ethics from the Standpoint of their Developmental History', an essay which Richard Heinze accepted for publication in *Hermes*. It was a critique of Werner Jaeger. The success of this essay gained me recognition in philological circles—even though I professed to be a student of Heidegger.

What was it that so attracted me and others to Heidegger? At the time, of course, I could not tell you. Today I would put it as follows: In Heidegger the development of thought in the philosophical tradition came to life because it was understood as answers to real questions. The disclosure of the history of the motivation of these philosophical questions lent to them a certain inevitability. And questions that are understood cannot simply pass into one's stock of knowledge. They become one's own questions.

Indeed, it had also been the claim of the Neo-Kantian 'history of problems' approach to recognize in those problems one's own questions. But their claim to fetch back these supertemporal, 'eternal' problems in ever new systematic contexts was not shown to be correct, and these 'identical' problems actually were purloined with full naiveté from the building materials of Neo-Kantian and German Idealist philosophy. The objection lodged by historical relativist skepticism against such supposed supertemporality is persuasive, I think, and simply cannot be gainsaid. Only when I learned from Heidegger how to bring historical thinking into the recovering of our own questions, did this make the old questions of the tradition understandable and so alive that they became our own questions. What I am describing here I would today call the fundamental experience in hermeneutics.

Above all, it was the intensity with which Heidegger evoked Greek philosophy that worked on us like a magical spell. The fact that such a spell was more a counterexample than an example of what his own questioning was intending was something we were scarcely aware of at the time. Heidegger's *Destruktion* of Greek metaphysics was concerned, however, not just with the consciousness-based idealism of the modern age, but likewise with its origins in Greek metaphysics. Heidegger's 'destruction'[2] and radical critique also called into question the Christian character of theology as well as the scientific character of philosophy. What a contrast to the bloodless academic philosophizing of the time, which moved within an alienated Kantian or Hegelian language and attempted once again either to bring transcendental idealism to perfection or else to overcome it! Suddenly Plato and Aristotle appeared as co-conspirators and comrades in arms to everyone who had found that playing around with systems in academic philosophy had become obsolete—even in the form of that open system of problems, categories, and values, on the basis of which both the phenomenological research into essences, the history of problems, or the analysis of categories understood themselves. From the Greeks one could learn that thinking in philosophy does not, in order to be responsible, have to adopt as system-guiding the thought that there must be a final grounding for philosophy in a highest principle; on the contrary, it stands always under the guiding thought that it must be based on primordial world experience, achieved through the conceptual and intuitive power of the language in which we live. The secret of the Platonic dialogues, it seems to me, is that they teach us this.

Among German Plato scholars at that time it was Julius Stenzel whose work pointed in a direction similar to my own. Taking note of the aporiae of self-consciousness in which both idealism and its critics found themselves trapped, Stenzel observed in the Greeks the "restraining of subjectivity." This occurred to me, likewise, and even before Heidegger began to teach

---

2. (Note by the translator) *Destruktion* in Heidegger, as Professor Gadamer has emphasized in his essay on 'Destruktion und Dekonstruktion', does not primarily mean destruction but the polishing of a word or concept to regain its primordial meaning, or as here stated, "a critical relationship to the concepts in [present] philosophical terminology."

me, as being a superiority of the Greeks, yet it is a puzzling superiority in which out of self-forgetful surrender they abandoned themselves in boundless innocence to the passion of thinking.

Already very early, and on the same basis, I had taken an interest in Hegel, so far as I understood him, and precisely because I only understood him that far. Above all, his *Logic* possessed, for me, really something of Greek innocence, and the genial, but unfortunately poorly edited, *Lectures on the History of Philosophy,* provided a bridge to a nonhistorical but truly speculative understanding of Platonic and Aristotelian thinking.

# What I Learned from Heidegger

What was most important for me, however, I learned from Heidegger. And it was, above all, in the first seminar in which I participated, in 1923, when Heidegger was still in Freiburg, on the Sixth Book of the *Nicomachean Ethics.* At that time, *phronēsis,* the virtue of practical reason, that *allo eidos gnōseōs,* that other form of cognition, was for me truly a magical word. Certainly, it was an immediate provocation to me when Heidegger one day analyzed the demarcation between *techne* and *phronēsis* and then in reference to the sentence, *phronēseōs de ouk esti lēthē* (in practical reason there is no forgetting), explained, "That is conscience!" But this bit of spontaneous pedagogical exaggeration focussed on a decisive point, by means of which Heidegger himself was preparing for his new way of posing the question of Being in *Being and Time.*

What was by no means clear to me then was that Heidegger's remark could also be understood in a completely different way, namely as a covert critique of the Greeks. Then this saying means that only as a thought whose certainty of knowledge was unthreatened by any forgetting was Greek thought able to think the nonprimordial, the only apparently human phenomenon of conscience. For me, in any case, Heidegger's provocative remark stimulated me to make alien questions my own and at the same time made me aware of the anticipation within concepts.

The second essential point I gained from Heidegger's instruction was one which Heidegger demonstrated to me from Aristotle's text (in some private encounters), namely how untenable the alleged 'realism' of Aristotle was, and that Aristotle stood on the same ground of the logos which Plato had prepared in his discipleship to Socrates. Many years later—following a paper given in one of my seminars—Heidegger discussed with us the fact that the new common ground in the *logos,* and thereby in dialectical philosophizing, between Plato and Aristotle not only supports Aristotle's doctrine of the categories but also enables one to sort out the differences between *dynamis* and *energeia.*

What I have described above was, in reality, my first introduction to the universality of hermeneutics. This was not clear to me at the time. Only slowly did it dawn on me that the Aristotle that had been strongly pressed on us by Heidegger, an Aristotle whose conceptual precision was filled to the limit with intuition and experience, did not at all itself express the new thinking. Heidegger followed the principle put forward in Plato's *The Sophist,* that one should make the dialogical opponent stronger, so well that Heidegger almost appeared like an Aristotle brought back to life, an Aristotle who through the power of intuition and the boldness of his original conceptuality cast a spell over everyone. Nevertheless, the identification, to which Heidegger's interpretations forced us, posed a powerful challenge to me personally. I was acutely aware that my diverse studies up to that time, studies which had ranged through many areas, literature and art history, and even my studies in the field of ancient philosophy, in which I had written my dissertation, were of no use to me in coming to grips with this challenge. So I began a new and systematically laid out study of classical philology under the direction of Paul Friedländer, a plan of study in which, along with the Greek philosophers, the radiant figure of Pindar, who had been put in a new light by the new edition of Hölderlin, attracted me above all—not to mention ancient rhetoric, whose complementary function to philosophy dawned on me then and has accompanied me in the development of my philosophical hermeneutics. All things considered, I feel strongly indebted to these studies because they made the strong identification with Aristotle, to which Heidegger had invited us, ever more difficult on my part. For the more or less conscious *Leitmotif* of all my studies was: in becoming aware of the otherness of the Greeks to be at the same time loyal to them, to discover truths in their being-other that have perhaps been covered over but that perhaps were still today operative and unmastered. In Heidegger's interpretation of the Greeks, however, lay a problem that especially in the works after *Being and Time* (1927) kept bothering me. Certainly it was possible in terms of Heidegger's purposes at that time to contrast the existential concept of *Dasein* with the 'merely at hand' (*Vorhandenheit*), as its counterconcept and extremist derivation without differentiating between this Greek understanding of being and the 'concept of object in the natural sciences'.

But for me there lay in this a strong provocation to test the validity of this point in Heidegger, and from this stimulus I went so far as to immerse myself for a time in studying the Aristotelian concept of nature and the rise of modern science, above all in Galileo.

Of course, the hermeneutical situation which I took as a starting point was given through the shattering of the idealistic and romantic search for a restoration of unity. The claim to be able to integrate even the empirical sciences of modern times into the unity of philosophical sciences, a claim which found its expression in the concept of *Speculative Physics* (a journal carried this name!) was simply unfulfillable. Any new effort at an integrative claim obviously could not be a repetition of that earlier, failed attempt. However, in order to know more clearly the reasons for this impossibility, the concept of science in modern times must, for its part, present a sharper profile, and the Greek concept of 'science' based on the concept of purpose must do so as well, a concept which German Idealism had undertaken to renew. It is self-evident that Kant's *Critique of Judgment,* in particular its critique of teleological judgment, becomes significant in connection with this problem, and a number of my students have undertaken to work this out further.

For the history of Greek science is apparently quite different from the history of modern science. Plato has already succeeded in joining together the path of enlightenment, that is, the path of free research and rational explanations of the world, with the traditional world of Greek religion and traditional Greek view of life. Plato and Aristotle, not Democritus, held sway over the history of science in late antiquity, and this was by no means a history of scientific decline. In Hellenistic times specialized science did not have to defend itself against philosophy and its prejudices, but rather received its emancipation *by means of* Greek philosophy, through the *Timaios* and Aristotelian philosophy of nature, as I tried to show in a paper titled 'Is there Matter?' (1973). Actually, even the counterproject of Galileian and Newtonian physics remains conditioned by Greek philosophy. My study on 'Ancient Atomic Theory' (1935) is the only piece from this study-circle that I published at that time. It should help to correct the childish preference which modern science has held for the great unknown figure of Democritus. I should also add that this does not in the least detract from the greatness of Democritus.

But of course Plato was at the center of my studies. My first Plato book, *Plato's Dialectical Ethics,* based on my habilitation thesis, was an Aristotle book that got stuck, because my starting-point was actually Aristotle's two treatises on pleasure in the *Nicomachean Ethics*. However, the problem is scarcely solvable if one takes a genetic approach, so I argued that the problem should be posed in a phenomenological way. Even though I could not explain this juxtaposition historically-genetically, I wanted, if possible, to demonstrate that it could be justified anyway. But this could not be done without relating both treatises to the Platonic *Philebus;* and so it was with this intention that I undertook a phenomenological interpretation of this dialogue. In those days I was not yet able to appreciate the universal significance of the *Philebus* for the Platonic view of numbers and, in general, for the problem of the relationship of idea and 'reality'. Rather, the two things I had in mind both had to do with method: first, to understand the function of Platonic dialectic from a phenomenology of the dialogue, and second, to explain the teaching about pleasure and its forms of appearance from a phenomenological analysis of real phenomena found in life. The phenomenological art of description which I had tried to learn from Husserl (in Freiburg in 1923) and also from Heidegger was supposed to yield an interpretation of ancient texts that was oriented 'to the things themselves'. It had relative success and received some recognition, not of course from the specialized historians, who indeed always live in the delusion that it is trivial to understand what is simply there. What should be investigated, they think, is what lies behind it. So Hans Leisegang in his review of current Plato research in 1932 thrust my work aside with a disdainful reference to a sentence from my introduction: "Its relationship to historical criticism is then already a positive one, if such criticism—taking the view that no progress is going to be made from our interpretation—finds that what is said in our interpretation [of what the text says] is self-evident:" In reality, however, I was well grounded in classical philology. I had in the mid-1920s pursued a rigorous course of studies to become certified as a classical philologist and passed a state exam in it in 1927. I was habilitated in philosophy very soon thereafter (l928–29). What is at issue here is a contrast in methodological standpoints which I undertook to clarify later through my hermeneutical analyses— obviously without success according to all those who are not ready for the work of reflection but can only regard one's research as 'positive' if something new is produced (even if it remains as 'un-understood' as the old that it replaced).

# Plato under the Nazis

Nevertheless, it was a successful start. As a teacher of philosophy I learned new things every semester. In those days, even under the poverty-stricken conditions of a foundation-supported scholar or commissioned and authorized teacher [*Lehrbeauftragter*], my teaching could be completely in line with my own research plans. So I entered into Plato's thought ever more deeply. In this connection, I was greatly helped by working with Jakob Klein in the area of mathematics and number theory. It was in those times that Klein's classical treatise, *Greek Logistics and the Rise of Algebra* (1936) was first published. I certainly will not claim that these mathematics-oriented studies of mine, which extended over a decade, reflected in any meaningful way the horrific drama of the events of that time. At most they did so indirectly in that in light of the situation after 1933 I purposely abandoned a larger study of the Sophistic and Platonic doctrines of the state, although I did publish two partial aspects of it: 'Plato and the Poets' (1934) and 'Plato's Educational State' (1942).

Each of these essays has its story. The first little piece developed an interpretation of the *Republic* by which I still stand today as the only correct one: that the Platonic ideal state presents a conscious utopia which has more to do with Jonathan Swift than with political science. My publication of this essay in 1934 also documents my position vis-à-vis National Socialism with the motto placed at the beginning: "Whoever philosophizes will not be in agreement with the conceptions of the times." As a quotation from Goethe it was indeed well masked, as it was in continuity with Goethe's characterization of the Platonic writings. But if one does not want to make a martyr of oneself or voluntarily choose emigration, such a motto can nevertheless convey a certain emphasis to the understanding reader in a time of enforced conformity, an affirmation of one's own identity—similar to Karl Reinhardt's inscription at the end of the preface to his book on the Greek tragedian Sophocles: "In January and September 1933." Indeed, from that time on the fact that one strenuously avoided politically relevant themes (and publication in journals outside one's special field altogether) was in accord with the same law of self-preservation. It remains true even to this day that a state which, in philosophical questions, designates a single doctrine about the state as correct, must know that its best people will move into other fields where they will not be censured by politicians—which in effect means by laymen. In this case, it makes no difference whether they are black or red, no outcry can change anything. So I continued my work unnoticed and found gifted students, among whom I would like to mention here Walter Schulz, Karlheinz Volkmann-Schluck, and Arthur Henkel. Fortunately in those days, the policies of National-Socialistic politics, in preparation for war in the East, somewhat moderated their pressure on the universities, and so my academic opportunities, which for years had been nil, improved. After ten years working in Marburg as a *Dozent,* I finally attained the long-desired rank of professor at Marburg in the spring of 1937. In 1938, an offer of a chair in classical philology at Halle came, and shortly thereafter I received a call to the philosophical ordinariate in Leipzig, which confronted me with new tasks.

The second piece, 'Plato's Educational State', was written as a kind of alibi. It was already wartime. A professor of the Hanover Institute of Technology by the name of Osenberg had persuaded Hitler of the decisive role of science in the war effort and through this was given full powers to preserve and cultivate the natural sciences, and in particular to further develop talented younger people. This so-called 'Osenberg-action' saved the lives of many young researchers. It aroused the envy of scholars in the humanities and social sciences, until finally a clever Party member came up with the proposal of a 'parallel action'. This was an idea whose inventiveness would have done honor to Robert Musil![3] It went under the label, *der Einsatz der Geisteswissenschaften für den Krieg*—dedicating the humanities and social sciences to the war effort. The fact that what it had to do with in reality was the dedication of the war effort to the humanities and social sciences—and nothing else, really—was hard to miss. In order to avoid getting entangled in some co-operative project in the philosophical sector of this effort, where such wonderful themes as 'The Jews and Philosophy' or 'The German Element in Philosophy' were surfacing, I emigrated into classical philology. There everything was very mannerly, and under the protection of Helmut Berve an interesting collective work titled *The Heritage of Antiquity* was created which after the war one could find in an unchanged second edition. My contribution to it, 'Plato's Educational State', carried further my earlier study, 'Plato and the Poets', and also pointed in the direction of some of my more recent studies with its last words, *die Zahl und das Sein*—number and being.

# My Unobtrusive Behavior in the Third Reich

The only monograph I submitted for publication during the whole era of the Third Reich was *People and History in the Thinking of Herder* (1942). In

---

3. Musil (1880–1942) is best known for his fantastic and monumental novel, *The Man without Qualities.*

this study, what I principally tried to work out was the role of the concept of power in Herder's historical thinking. Of course, the study avoided every hint of relevance to the present. Nevertheless, it still offended some people, above all those who had made themselves heard on similar themes and who believed that a little more sychronization, working together, 'toeing the line' (*Gleichschaltung*), was not to be avoided. There is a particular reason why I am fond of this work. I had dealt with this theme for the first time in a lecture given in French to French officers in a prisoner-of-war camp. In the question period and discussion afterwards I said that an empire that extends itself beyond measure, beyond moderation, is *au près de sa chute*—near its fall. The French officers looked at each other meaningfully and understood. (I sometimes wonder if, in this macabre and unreal situation, I anonymously met one or another of my later French colleagues, of whom, indeed, many could have been there.) The political functionary who had accompanied me was, for his part, positively enthusiastic. Such mental clarity and reckless abandon, according to him, mirrored with particular effectiveness our consciousness of victory. (Whether he really believed this or was just playing along, I could not decide. In any case, he took no offense, and I even had to give my lecture again in Paris.)

During those years, if one wanted to avoid conflict with the Party, it was necessary to behave unobtrusively. The results of my studies I communicated only in lectures. There one could function basically in an open and unhindered way. In Leipzig I even gave lectures on Husserl undisturbed. Much of what I had worked on and developed during that period saw the light in works by my students, in particular I think of Karlheinz Volkmann-Schluck's excellent dissertation, 'Plotinus as Interpreter of Platonic Ontology" (1941).

Since I was professor in Leipzig and, after Theodor Litt's retirement, its only representative in the area of philosophy, I could no longer adjust my teaching to my own research interests and plans. In addition to the Greeks and their latest and greatest follower, Hegel, I had to mediate the whole classical tradition in philosophy from Augustine and Thomas Aquinas to Nietzsche, Husserl, and Heidegger—obviously, as half-philologist, I always stayed close to the text. In addition to this, in seminars I dealt also with difficult poetic texts, those of Hölderlin, Goethe, and above all, Rilke. Rilke was, thanks to the highly cultivated mannerism of his style, the true poet of the academic *Résistance*. Whoever talked like Rilke or like Heidegger, or who explained Hölderlin, stood on the margins and attracted those who also stood on the margins.

The last years of the war were naturally lived out in the grip of desperation and were very dangerous for everyone. Still, the intensive bombing which we had to survive and which left the city of Leipzig as well as the university—my means of livelihood—in ruins, also had its good aspects: the Nazi Party with its terror was further tied up by the emergency situation then developing. Instruction at the university, switching from one emergency space to another, was continued until shortly before the end of the war. When the Americans occupied Leipzig, I was in the midst of studying the newly published second and third volumes of Werner Jaeger's *Paideia*— which is also an odd fact, it seems to me, that this work of an 'emigrant' into the German language should be published by a German publisher in the years of highest war emergency. Total war? The inner schism of our country under a despotic regime made such things thinkable.

After the end of the war, I suddenly had, as Rector of the University of Leipzig, other things to do. Of course, to contemplate a genuine continuation of philosophical work had for years been unthinkable. Still, my weekends were free, and during them I wrote the majority of the interpretations of poetry that appear in volume two of my *Kleine Schriften*. It occurred to me that never before had I so easily worked and written as in these stringently limited hours, certainly an expression of the fact that during the unproductive political and administrative daily work of the rectorship something accumulated which then just poured itself out in this way. Other than this periodic outpouring in the interpretation of poetry, however, writing remained a torment for me. I had the terrible feeling that Heidegger was standing behind me and looking over my shoulder.

In the fall of 1947, after serving two years as rector, I accepted a call to Frankfurt am Main and therewith returned completely and entirely to my teaching and research—as much as working conditions at that time permitted. In the two years I was in Frankfurt, I tried to do my share to deal with the distressed situation of the students at the time not only through intensive hours of teaching but also through the editing of new editions with commentary of Aristotle's *Metaphysics: Book XII* (Greek and German) and also Wilhelm Dilthey's *Outline of the History of Philosophy*, both of which Klostermann Press brought out very quickly. Important at that time, too, was the great conference in Mendoza, Argentina, in February 1949, at which we could, on the one hand, get together with old Jewish friends, and on the other, make our first contact with the philosophers of other countries (Italy, France, Spain, South America).

# The Rise of Hermeneutical Philosophy

Receiving the call in 1949 to succeed to Karl Jaspers's chair in Heidelberg for me meant the beginning of a truly academic career in an academic world. Just as I was for twenty years student and *Dozent* in Marburg, I was to be active over forty years in Heidelberg, and in spite of the multiplicity of tasks involved in the years of rebuilding, which claimed time from all of us, it was possible for me to largely disburden myself from politics and university politics and to concentrate on my own work plans, which in 1960 finally reached a first conclusion in *Truth and Method*.

The fact that along with my passionate engagement as teacher I came to write a large book is due to a natural need I felt to ponder how the various paths of philosophizing which I retraced in my teaching could be made genuinely relevant to today by starting from the current philosophical situation. To arrange them into a historical process that is constructed a priori (Hegel) seemed to me just as unsatisfactory as the relativistic neutrality of historicism. I agree with Leibniz, who once said that he himself approved of nearly all he read. But in contrast with that great thinker, the stimulus of this experience did not lead me to feel I must create one great synthesis. Indeed, I began asking myself whether philosophy could still be placed under the rubric of such a synthetic task at all. Rather, for the continuation of hermeneutical experiences, must not philosophy hold itself radically open, captivated by what remains always evident to it, and use its powers to oppose all redarkening of what it has seen? . . . Philosophy is enlightenment, but precisely also enlightenment against its own dogmatism.

In fact, the rise of my hermeneutical philosophy must be traced back to nothing more pretentious than my effort to be theoretically accountable for the style of my studies and my teaching. Practice came first. For as long as I can remember, I have been concerned not to say too much and not to lose myself in theoretical constructions which were not fully made good by experience. Since as a teacher I continued to give of myself to the students and in particular to offer intensive contact to my closest students, work on my book had to wait for vacations. This work took almost ten years, and during this time I avoided as much as possible every distraction. When the book finally appeared—and only while it was at the press was the title, *Truth and Method*, chosen—I was really not sure whether it had not come too late and might really be superfluous. For I could already foresee that a new generation was coming up that was in the grip partly of technological expectations and partly the captive of feelings associated with the critique of ideology.

The title of the book was difficult enough. My colleagues in philosophy both in Germany and outside Germany expected it to be labelled 'Philosophical hermeneutics'. But when I suggested this as the title, the publisher asked: "What is that?" And in fact it probably was better at the time to banish that still strange word to the subtitle.

In the meantime at Heidelberg my persistently continued university teaching activities were bearing ever more fruit. Also, my old friend Karl Löwith returned from exile and taught along with me, creating a healthy tension. There were several years of highly fruitful interaction with Jürgen Habermas, whom we called to Heidelberg as a young *extraordinarius* after I had learned that Max Horkheimer and Theodor Adorno had gotten into an argument on his account. Well, whoever was able to separate those intellectual brothers-in-arms, Max and Teddy, even just a little bit, must really be something, and in fact the manuscript we requested confirmed the talent of the young researcher, which had been evident to me for some time. But of course there were also other students who had passionately given themselves up to philosophy. I brought a large group of students with me when I came from Frankfurt, among them Dieter Henrich, who also carried the stamp of his first experiences, which were of the Marburg arch-Kantians, Ebbinghaus and Klaus Reich. In Heidelberg, too, there were also many others who were active in teaching or research, such as Wolfgang Bartuschat, Rüdiger Bubner, Theo Ebert, Heinz Kimmerle, Wolfgang Künne, Ruprecht Pflaumer, J.H. Trede, and Wolfgang Wieland. Others came later from Frankfurt, where Wolfgang Cramer had a strong influence: Konrad Cramer, Friedrich Fulda, and Reiner Wiehl also, more and more students from other countries came and blended themselves into the circle of my students. From Italy, I especially remember Valerio Verra and Gianni Vattimo; from Spain, Emilio Lledo; and of course a great number of Americans, many of whom I met again during my many trips to America after 1968, now holding positions of responsibility. A special source of satisfaction has been the fact that from my closest circle of students many emerged who found that what they learned could be carried over into other fields, a good test of the idea of hermeneutics itself.

# Hermeneutics as Practice

What I taught above all was hermeneutic praxis. Hermeneutics is a practice, the art of understanding and of making something understood to someone else. It is the heart of all education that wants to teach how to philosophize. In it what one has to exercise above all is the ear, the sensitivity for perceiving prior determinations, anticipations, and imprints that reside in concepts. This goes for a good part of my work in history of concepts. With the help of the German Research Foundation I organized a series of colloquia on the history of concepts, and reported on them, and these have triggered a variety of similar endeavors. Conscientiousness and reliability in the employment of concepts requires a concept-history kind of awareness, such that one does not fall into the arbitrariness of constructing definitions, or the illusion that one can standardize philosophical speaking into certain obligatory forms. A consciousness of the history of concepts becomes a duty of critical thinking. I have sought in other ways to accomplish these tasks, for instance by bringing to life, in conjunction with Helmut Kuhn, the *Philosophische Rundschau,* a journal dedicated completely to critique. Helmut Kuhn's critical talent was something I had already learned to admire very early, before 1933, in the last issues of the old *Kantstudien.* Some twenty-three years of issues of the *Philosophische Rundschau* appeared under the strict leadership of my wife, Käte Gadamer-Lekebusch, until it was entrusted to other, younger hands.

But the centerpiece of all my activity in the Heidelberg years, as before, remained my teaching duties. It was only after my formal retirement in 1968 that I had time to present my ideas on hermeneutics in a wider circumference and in other countries, where they met with widespread interest— above all, in America. To that phase of my life I now turn.

# A Travelling Scholar

In 1968, when I retired from full-time teaching, I began a whole new life, a life of travel. Throughout the years of my teaching activities, I had always limited my travel for lecturing to the vacations, when I was free of classes. I felt that an excessive number of such events during the periods of time when I was teaching would weaken my presence at the lectern. Indeed, for this reason I had refused a number of earlier invitations to lecture in America. Also, of course, I was conscious of the fact that while I could manage with French quite well in Europe, the English-speaking world had remained basically inaccessible to me because of my limited skill with spoken English. My only contact with English had been through reading it. But on my retirement in 1968, I finally accepted an invitation from Vanderbilt University to visit the university and to present a paper on Schleiermacher at an international Schleiermacher colloquium. On the tour of lectures I gave after the symposium was over I had an opportunity to become acquainted with a considerable number of American universities and in the course of time I developed enough speaking ability in English to manage at least passably in it. As much as possible, I attempted to give my lectures in English and without manuscript, for, in my view, lecturing and especially teaching in the U.S. and Canada would be meaningless if I could not somehow give expression to my own style of thinking in English. In the periods of my presence in America and Canada during the years that followed, I placed our common heritage in Greek philosophy in the foreground of my teaching, and in this way I was able to link my teaching activity during my sojourns in America to my own research studies. I was also able to try out these studies of Greek philosophy in a variety of ways later on in Europe, for example, in Italy, Spain, France, Belgium, Holland, and Scandinavia.

After all the many trips I had made over the years in old Europe, which had necessarily been limited to academic vacations, my venture into the Anglo-Saxon world for longer periods of time certainly represented something new, and it brought with it many memorable experiences. Obviously, the first of these was learning little by little to overcome the language barrier, and here my fondness for lyric poetry was a great help. Through reading T.S. Eliot, William Butler Yeats, and Wallace Stevens, I experienced something of the music of the English language. The philosophical expectations I necessarily had in these journeys into the Anglo-Saxon world also posed new tasks in thinking. It was no surprise to me, of course, that analytic philosophy occupied the greatest share of the philosophical space there and that what was labelled 'Continental Philosophy' was eclipsed by it; nor did it surprise me that for this audience the German philosophy of our times was identified with Husserlian phenomenology, and Heidegger and hermeneutics were little known. As I learned to speak English a little better, albeit slowly, and got better acquainted with American philosophers, it became quite apparent to me that there were also quite viable bridges from analytic philosophy to hermeneutics. As a matter of fact, already very shortly after I had completed *Truth and Method* in 1960, I had myself begun to read the later Wittgenstein and found there much that had long been familiar to me. By that time, of course, the recognition of Wittgenstein's famous term, 'language games', was already widespread in Germany.

Another connecting link between my own heritage and that of the new continent, was theology. In both Catholicism and Protestantism, the existence of theological faculties signified the presence of Greek, and in the Catholic universities also Latin. Of course, I myself certainly claim no special competence as a theologian. But since Greek metaphysics has had such a profound influence on Christian dogmatics, especially through the adoption of Aristotle in such an encompassing way, the tensions resident in the Roman Catholic metaphysical concept of God as the highest being were long familiar to me. And on the Protestant side, there was in most of the Protestant theological faculties—whose exegetical subtleties I found extremely stimulating—a very good knowledge of the Greek language and of the Greek cultural world. And since the question 'How is it possible to speak about God?' was central to dialectical theology in Protestantism, their interest was philosophically concentrated above all on the nature of the divine instead of on Greek religious cults, and much more on Plato than on Aristotle. The issues and tensions involved here were already familiar to me from my studies of Greek philosophy—specially in terms of the participation of Platonism and Aristotelianism in the history of metaphysics—ever since the dialectical theology of the 1920s put theology in a state of suspense with the problem of speaking about God. And, finally, the task of again taking up the Greek problem of being, but now and under modern circumstances, must necessarily confront one with new challenges and tasks.

# The Wide Appeal of Hermeneutics

Just as in Germany, interest in hermeneutic philosophy on the new continent did not limit itself to departments of philosophy. Certainly it is everywhere evident that the great inheritance of Greek and Christian thinking in our age of science is not to be found only in departments of philosophy. And the part of that heritage we may call the hermeneutical approach has for a long time had its residence rights in several different fields. Thus, in my visits to America I could connect not only with theology but also with departments related to language and literature, especially comparative literature, departments which in the German language we sometimes refer to as the 'philological disciplines'. And still other disciplines quite different from these also began to acquaint themselves with the problems dealt with in hermeneutical philosophy, disciplines such as law and medicine, as well as the range of fields concerned with the problems of aesthetics. I believe one can say that the *Geisteswissenschaften,* as we call them in German, those disciplines which in English are labelled the 'humanities', and those which in

French are broadly called *Lettres,* have just as much inherited Western meta-physics as philosophy itself has. It makes a huge difference for our *Geisteswissenschaften,* for instance, that in English the word for *Wissenschaft* is 'science'! It makes a difference that earlier the term 'science' was not used at all in English in reference to humanities disciplines and even today is only used out of desperation. Basically, in English, 'the sciences' refers to the nat-ural sciences.

This fact, or this contrast, has had powerful consequences in the realm of philosophy itself. Language and words have a completely different place in the tradition of philosophy familiar to us than they do in the Anglo-Saxon tradition. Certainly it is true that within Anglo-Saxon philosophy, too, the heritage of the humanistic tradition lives on and is perceivable in its reigning concepts, but these concepts have no different function than they do in the linguistic formulations customary in the empirical sciences. If one wishes to formulate this difference in philosophical terms, I think one needs to go back to the scholastic opposition between nominalism and realism. In this opposition 'realism' means of course the realism of concepts. Here, it becomes immediately clear that the *language* of modern science is totally molded and determined by the nominalism we find described in scholasti-cism. For in the areas of research in the empirical sciences, word and con-cept are regarded as instruments, as merely a means of designating what their research is about and what its results are. This nominalistic view of concepts is so dominant in the modern period in general, even in the German tradition of philosophy, for instance—and, not least, even in German Idealism—that the language of their concepts was rarely the object of their philosophical inquiry. In 1918, when I myself began my philosoph-ical studies, the reigning Neo-Kantianism still always spoke the conceptual language of Kant, a language that in turn was derived from the scholastic metaphysics of the eighteenth century which transformed their Latin into German. I think that in the early decades of the twentieth century one was not aware that the project of phenomenology really entailed changing the meaning of 'concept' itself. For what was derived from Franz Brentano and continued by Frege, Husserl, Meinong, and others, was really directed towards a new discipline of thinking in which the concept is not merely an instrument and a medium of understanding but becomes the subject mat-ter of philosophy itself. It is also astonishing to find that, when one goes back to Hegel's *Science of Logic*—the last great attempt at a system in German Idealism—one encounters a logic that leads from 'being' to 'essence' and then to 'concept'. This 'domain' of the concept, then, is supposed to make up the unity of both being and essence. This unity does not have its right of residence just on one side, the side where our thinking is conducted; rather, it resides precisely in *both* the 'true being' of the subject matter (that is, in its concrete immediacy) as well as in its essence (its whatness, its truth). This is still reflected, I believe, in the meaning of the term *Inbegriff* (quintessence) in German linguistic usage, where this word refers to the whole essence of the thing being discussed and not only to that side of it which is grasped through our conceptual understanding.

In any case, it was a new experience for me when, in my first encounter with Heidegger, I heard the term *Begrifflichkeit* (conceptuality), and also when I learned, under the caption of *Destruktion*, a critical suspicion of the concepts resident in philosophical terminology. Slowly I became aware that the language customarily used in German philosophy was not just full of preconceptions and prejudices, but also full of depth and significance. Gradually I came to heed the speaking power of words, a power which still goes on speaking in every linguistic usage and in its antecedents. In sum, the language of philosophy itself began to speak again.

# The Greatness of Heidegger

This also involved a slow process of re-educating myself to a viewpoint in marked contrast to that found in the predominant theory of signs, with its instrumentalist view of their function. It was the young Heidegger who, as he recognized the prejudgments behind this reigning conceptuality, called it to account. He took from Kierkegaard the expression 'formal indications' and with it he brought into play the phenomenological principle of the self-showing of the thing itself. It no longer sufficed in philosophy, as it still does in science, to use the term 'the given' to link the necessary designation of a thing with what it designates. For in philosophy what is 'the designated'? How can a thing, for instance, be so given that we can also introduce a designation for it according to some random convention? And because conventional designation looks like a definition, it sometimes occurs even in philosophy.

My own view on this point, however, is very close to that of Wittgenstein, whose thinking I have in mind when I say that in thinking this is clearly not the way that words 'work'. The words we use in our speaking are much more familiar to us than this, so that we are in the words, so to speak. That is to say, words which are working never become objects. The 'use' of words in a language is not a 'using' at all. Rather, language is a medium, an element: Language is the element in which we live, as fishes live in water. In linguistic interaction we call it a conversation. We search for words and they come to us; and they either reach the other person or fail him. In the exchange of words, the thing meant becomes more and more present. A language is truly a 'natural language' when it binds us together in this way. Of course, in philosophy we constantly use words which do not belong to the natural language, and the same thing also applies to the sciences. There one calls such usages 'specialized expressions' or terminology. But the specialized term in the empirical sciences must claim to be a univocal designator in order to make it something confirmable through empirical testing, and fundamentally such a univocal meaning is appropriately fixable only in the symbolic language of mathematics.

On the other hand, in philosophy the use of language looks quite different. Each term we use contains a certain saying-power within itself. Our terms are not like signs that point to something but rather themselves tell something of their own origin and from this they form a horizon of meaning which is supposed to lead speaking and thinking beyond themselves to the thing meant. Consequently Heidegger has designated the task of philosophy precisely as a *Destruktion* of terms, and in so doing he was heeding the fundamental phenomenological principle that one should avoid all theoretical constructions and get back 'to the things themselves'. This had been Husserl's famous slogan, a directive which he himself carried out by means of a very finely differentiated use of the German language in those areas that were most his own, namely mathematical problems, logic, and the analysis of basic concepts like time and space. But when Heidegger entered into the teachings of phenomenology with Husserl, and as he learned from Husserl the highly descriptive technique of phenomenological analysis of concepts, the task of 'getting back to the things themselves' took on an entirely new dimension: that of a history of the ancestry of terms, a history in which the special terminology in philosophy is more or less covered over and in the background, and yet this history still speaks within and along with that term.

In his early years Heidegger had studied the work of Wilhelm Dilthey intensively, and through this he gained access to the great inheritance that had come to German philosophy from the Romantics, an inheritance otherwise basically unavailable, since it was very little present in the reigning Neo-Kantianism of that time. The enormous historical-cultural education which Dilthey had acquired as the biographer of Schleiermacher, and which—like Dilthey—the generation of followers had also acquired, stood the young Heidegger in very good stead. Certainly the Neo-Kantian philosophy of that time was not so completely oblivious and cut off from the so-called *Geisteswissenschaften* as analytic philosophy in the Anglo-Saxon realm has been. Something of the humanistic potential of Neo-Kantianism is, of course, evident in the philosophy of Ernst Cassirer. At that time, Cassirer represented something quite individual and special in Neo-Kantianism. In the end, however, he remained a disciple of the Marburg School, that is to say, of the systematic revival of Kantian thought, a school of thought which through and through placed itself under the factum of the natural sciences just as Kant had done in the *Prolegomena*. Nevertheless, Cassirer was characterized by an enormous flexibility, an astonishing familiarity with literature, and apparently a good bit of natural historical sense, so he was able to make a very fruitful application of transcendental philosophy to the historical world without falling back into scholastic terminology and concepts. Otherwise, the Neo-Kantian school was not particularly competent to undertake either a history of concepts or a history of their linguistic presuppositions. Granted, the relationship to the history of philosophy was essential to Neo-Kantianism throughout, but unfortunately Neo-Kantianism, as we noted earlier, understood the history of philosophy as a history of problems, and it held that there were invariant elements in the problems. Thus, one really did not have to bother about their origins at all, which in reality were derived from Hegelian logic; rather, they simply treated them as fixed categories which provided a foundation. Of course, on the other hand, one must also freely admit that in the wake of German idealism the unfolding of historical consciousness in Germany was so intensively cultivated that the Anglo-Saxon visitor before the First World War came to the conclusion that German philosophy was drowning in history. And perhaps with some justification this is precisely what one could say about the scholarly achievements of the majority of the philosophy professors at that time. They had become only an extension and special part of the Historical School, a school which, in the late history of German Romanticism, had been the pride of the German universities in the late nineteenth century.

The young Heidegger, however, was certainly no mere historian of philosophy. By education he was a theologian and by temperament truly a thinker. Anyone who was inspired by the appearance of Heidegger on the philosophical scene could no longer make a separation between philosophy and its history. Heidegger was even able to persuade Husserl that Aristotle had been a founder of phenomenology long before its modern founder, namely Husserl himself. Heidegger also had a gift for envisioning the basic experiences which Aristotle had turned over and over in his masterful way. Now, for once, Aristotle was no longer read through the eyes of Aquinas but rather from the raw materials that were present at the inception of Greek thought itself since Homer.

It was only logical that, in the end, as Heidegger passed through Aristotle, he began to pose the question of the beginnings of philosophy. As is well known, we possess only a few fragments that testify to the origins of Greek thinking. And even these were preserved primarily thanks to the interest Aristotle had awakened in those beginnings, making it possible for fragments of that early thought to be passed down to us through the centuries of late Greek times. But these Greek origins also hold a special significance from a hermeneutical standpoint. They were, in the strong sense of the word, an almost speechless beginning. Yes, there are citations, but precisely being a citation means that they have themselves been ripped out of the flux of thinking; the context in which these sentences were truly speaking is no longer given. All our philological reconstruction can never substitute for what belongs to the very nature of real speaking. So one has to say that the first philosophical texts of the Greeks that we possess are the Platonic dialogues and the so-called 'teaching treatises' of Aristotle.

Both of these texts, of course, immediately confront us with the fundamental hermeneutical problem of writtenness. Plato's dialogues are conversations *written down* by a great philosophical and poetic master, and yet we know from Plato himself in his famous 'Seventh Letter' that he did not leave behind a written presentation of his true teaching and did not want to. This means he has unequivocally confronted us with the necessity of a mimetic doubling, that is to say, by means of the written conversation to go back to the originally spoken conversation in which the thought found words—a task which can never be fully accomplished. Now certainly one can see quite well through the eyes of Aristotle what had been thought in this conversation. But once again one sees this only in the further mediation of reading a trace of Aristotle's spoken speech in the so-called 'texts' of the Aristotelian corpus that have been left behind. It is hardly necessary to add here, too, that the Latinizing of the Aristotelian terminology in Scholasticism confronts us with yet another task: namely, of thinking in a Greek way on the basis of Latin. One needs to take into account the effort the ancient Romans put into adopting Greek culture for themselves, and, indeed, also to take seriously the fact that even in ancient Rome in the early Christian era, say, around A.D.

200 or so, philosophy was not pursued in Latin but in Greek. One then begins to sense the significance of the far later step that the schools of Christian humanism took at the threshhold of the modern era, when the language of that cultural heritage was reshaped to fit the measure of the national languages. The word *Destruktion* in Heidegger traverses all the layers of this heritage, and it does so not in order to destroy something but to set something free.

The question which I would pose is: What is truly the language of philosophy? What language is the language of philosophy? Is there a 'language of philosophy' at all? In the end, as we ask these questions, we recognize that language is the task of philosophy itself, whatever it may be in its own living reality behind all these stages of its historical development; yes, even to recognize in it also the prelinguistic history of humanity in its potential still hidden beneath the ruins of a languageless past. What I am thinking of is not some kind of Indo-Germanic language such as that reconstructed by linguistic research as the basis for most languages in the various European cultures, nor is it anything like a primordial language. Rather, I have in mind the linguisticality, as such, through which and out of which languages are first able to form themselves at all and out of which have been formed the multiplicity of languages, even including those that are not within our own circle of culture.

And one point cannot be left out: that it is the context of problems surrounding *the indissoluble connection between thinking and speaking* which compels hermeneutics to become philosophy. One must always think in a language, even if one does not always have to think in the same language. Hermeneutics cannot evade claiming universality because language as linguisticality constitutes a human capacity inseparably linked with rationality as such. This only repeats here something Aristotle likewise emphasized: his argument had first to do with the universality of seeing and with the region of differences that were comprehended through seeing. But he also had to distinguish the sense of hearing, and about it he had to say that he knew no boundaries to hearing at all, because language is among the things one hears, and, as the *logos,* language encompasses simply everything. This is why the project of a hermeneutical philosophy ever and again must go back to Greek philosophy. In the language and the formation of philosophical concepts of the Greeks there still lives the immediacy of experience out of which those concepts were formed. The language of the sciences, indeed specifically this language, has been shaped in such a way that in the end it has led to the development of mathematics. But what holds even more strongly as regards the thinking of the Greek philosophers and the keen pleasure they took in questioning is that they created their thinking from *the language people spoke*. These philosophers profited from and built upon the artful development of the spoken language in Homeric and Hesiodic verse art, and they built upon rhetoric, which had flourished as a highly developed art through which the youth in their claim to education engaged in verbal battles with their peers. It is a language whose influence, through the alliance between rhetoric and dialectic, has continued over many centuries.

# What Is Philosophical Hermeneutics?

This is how the door to Europe was opened—and in the same century that Athens and the Greek culture of the *polis* had victoriously withstood the attack of the Persians. Hermeneutics and Greek philosophy have remained the two main foci of my work, and *Truth and Method* has been a center of discussion and critique over a period of over thirty-five years since its publication. In the remainder of this essay, then, I should like, first, in this section, to explore the context of factors which has motivated my thinking in hermeneutics, and in particular 'practical philosophy', and, in the final section, to make an effort at self-criticism in relation to *Truth and Method*.

First, there was the hermeneutics I developed in *Truth and Method*.

What was this *philosophical* hermeneutics? How did it differ from the hermeneutics that arose in the Romantic tradition with Schleiermacher, who deepened a very old *theological* discipline, and which reached a high point in Dilthey's *geisteswissenschaftliche* hermeneutics, a hermeneutics intended to serve as methodological basis for the humanities and social sciences? With what justification could my own endeavor be called a 'philosophical' hermeneutics?

Regrettably it is not a superfluous task to go into these questions, because many people have seen and do see in this hermeneutical philosophy a rejection of methodical rationality. Many others, especially after hermeneutics became a stylish slogan, and any and every kind of 'interpretation' called itself 'hermeneutical', misused the word and misunderstood the reason I had adopted this term. They reversed its meaning in that they saw it as a new methodology, through which they could justify methodological unclarity or furnish a legitimate cover for their ideology. Others, again, belonging to the camp of the critique of ideology recognize truth in it, but only half the truth. It is fine and good, they say, that preconceptual operativeness of tradition has now been recognized, but hermeneutics lacks the decisive thing, a critical and emancipatory reflection that would free it from tradition.

Perhaps it will shed some light on the situation if I present the motivation for my approach as it actually developed. In this way it may become clear that in reality, the method-fanatics and the ideology-critics are the ones who are not doing enough reflection. For the method-fanatics treat the rationality of trial and error—which is undisputed—as the ultimate measure of human reason; on the other hand, the ideology-critics recognize the ideological prejudice such rationality contains, but they do not sufficiently ponder the ideological implications of their own critique of ideology.

When I sought to develop a philosophical hermeneutics, it was obvious to me from the history of hermeneutics that the disciplines based on 'understanding' formed my starting point. But I supplemented these with something that had previously been left out of account, namely the experience of art. Both art and the historical disciplines present us with ways of experiencing in which our own understanding of existence is directly brought into play. Heidegger's unfolding of the existential structure of understanding offered me conceptual help in placing the problematic of 'understanding' in its proper breadth. He called this displaying of the existential structure of understanding a "hermeneutic of facticity," that is to say, in its self-interpretation as the human *Dasein* actually finds itself in 'factual' existence. Using Heidegger's analysis, my starting point was a critique of German Idealism and its Romantic traditions. On this basis it was clear to me that the inherited forms of consciousness that we have acquired historically in our education—what we call 'esthetic consciousness' and 'historical consciousness'— represent only alienated forms of our true historical being. The unique, originary experiences that are mediated through art and history cannot be grasped within these alienated forms. The tranquil distance from which a consciousness conditioned by the usual middle-class education enjoyed its cultural privileges does not take into account how much of *ourselves* must come into play and is at stake when we encounter works of art and studies of history.

So I sought in my hermeneutics to overcome the primacy of self-consciousness, and especially the prejudices of an idealism rooted in consciousness, by referring to the mode of 'game or play' [*Spiel*].[4] For when one plays

---

4. (Note by the translator) In German, the same word, *Spiel*, is used to mean both play and game. This translation sometimes uses one term, sometimes the other, depending on the context, and sometimes also 'playing the game', suggesting overtones of motion.

a *game*, the game itself is never a mere object; rather, it exists in and for those who play it, even if one is only participating as 'spectator'. In this context, I think, the inappropriateness of the concept of a 'subject' and an 'object' is evident, a point which Heidegger's exposition in *Being and Time* also made. That which led Heidegger to his famous 'turn' I for my part sought to describe in terms of our self-understanding coming up against its limits, that is, as the 'historically affected consciousness' which is 'more being than consciousness'.[5] What I formulated with this phrase was not so much a task to be accomplished in the practice of art history or historical scholarship—indeed, it did not primarily have to do with the methodical consciousness in these disciplines—rather, it was concerned exclusively, or at least principally, with the philosophical issue of accountability. It was in this connection that I asked: to what extent is method a guarantee of truth? It is the role of philosophy to make us aware that scholarship and method have a limited place within the whole of human *Existenz* and its rationality.

# The Hermeneutical Problem in the Sciences

My own undertaking was itself conditioned by an 'effective history'. Obviously it was rooted in a very definite German philosophical and cultural heritage. The so-called *Geisteswissenschaften* ('human sciences') in Germany had really never before so completely united in one package their scientific and their world-intuitive functions. Or, to put it more bluntly, they had never so fully and consistently concealed their ideologically conditioned interests behind the epistemological and methodological pretensions of their scientific procedures. The indissoluble unity of all human self-knowledge was expressed much more clearly elsewhere than Germany: in France through the broader concept of *lettres,* and in English in the newly introduced concept of 'the humanities'. What I wanted to bring about by insisting on the 'historically affected consciousness' was a correction of the self-concept of the historical human sciences, and here I include

---

5. Gadamer is making a pun that he has made before. The German word for 'consciousness', *Bewußtsein*, includes the word *Sein*, which means 'being'. Gadamer is suggesting that even when he uses the word 'consciousness' the emphasis should be on the *Sein* that contains historically conditioned structures and not on an empty, flickering awareness.

scholarship about art: that they are not 'sciences' in the manner of the natural sciences.

But bringing about the recognition of a 'historically affected consciousness' in the human sciences was not my only goal, for the full dimensions of what I have called "the hermeneutical problem" are much broader. In the natural sciences, too, there is something like a hermeneutical problematic. Their path, too, is not simply that of methodical, step-by-step progress. This has been persuasively shown by Thomas Kuhn and was already implied by Heidegger's 'The Age of the World Picture' as well as in his interpretation of the Aristotelian view of nature. Both make clear that the reigning paradigm is decisive for the questions research raises and for the data it examines, and these are apparently not just the result of methodical research. Galileo had already said, *Mente concipio.*[6]

Behind all this, however, a much broader dimension opens up, a dimension rooted in the fundamental linguisticality of human beings. In all human knowing of the world and in all orientation within the world, the nature of the moment of understanding has to be worked out, and in this way the universality of hermeneutics will become evident. Naturally, the fundamental linguisticality of understanding cannot mean that all experiencing of the world can only take place as and in language, for we know all too well those prelinguistic and metalinguistic inner awarenesses, those moments of dumbfoundedness and speaking silences in which our immediate contact with the world is taking place. And who would deny that there are real factors conditioning human life, such as hunger, love, labor, and domination, which are not themselves language or speaking, but which for their part furnish the space within which our speaking to each other and listening to each other can take place? This fact cannot be disputed; indeed, it is precisely these preconditions of human thinking and speaking which themselves make hermeneutic reflection necessary.

Furthermore, with a hermeneutic oriented to Socratic dialogue like mine one does not have to be reminded that *doxa* is not real knowing, and that the apparent agreement-in-understanding on the basis of which one lives and speaks is not always a real agreement. But even the discovery that something is only apparently the case, which Socratic conversation brings about, takes place within the element of linguisticality. Even the total break-

---

6. 'I conceive through the mind'. Galileo worked out his experiments in his mind before performing them physically.

down of communication, even misunderstanding and the famous admission that one does not know, presuppose that understanding is possible. The commonality that we call human rests on the linguistic constitution of our lifeworld. Indeed, every attempt by means of critical reflection and argumentation to bring suit against distortions in interhuman communication only confirms this commonality.

# Finding a Common Language

What I have called the hermeneutic aspect of human life and communication thus cannot remain limited to hermeneutic scholarship, or history, or texts; nor is it enough to broaden it to include the experience of works of art. Rather, as Schleiermacher had already known, the universality of the hermeneutical problem has to do with the whole universe of the rational; that is, with everything about which one can seek to communicate. Where communication seems impossible because one 'speaks different languages', hermeneutics is still not at an end. Precisely here the hermeneutical task is posed in its full seriousness, namely finding a common language. Even the common language is never a fixed given. It resides in the play of language between speakers, who must enter into the game of language so that communication can begin, even where various viewpoints stand irreconcilably opposed to each other. The possibility of communication between rational beings can never be denied. Even the relativism which seems to reside in the multiplicity of human languages is no barrier to reason, whose 'word' (or *logos*) all have in common, as Heraclitus was already aware. The learning of a foreign language and likewise even the first learning of language by children do not just involve the acquisition of the means of reaching an understanding. Rather, this learning represents a kind of preschematization of possible experience and its first acquisition. Growing into a language, then, is a path to knowledge of the world. Not only such 'learning' but every experience takes place in a constantly developing formation of our communicative knowledge of the world. In a much deeper and more universal sense than the great philologist, August Boeckh, meant it when he formulated it in reference to the work of philologists, experience is always an *Erkenntnis von Erkanntem*—a knowledge of something already known. For we live in what has been handed down to us, and this is not just a specific region of our experience of the world, specifically what we call the 'cultural tradition' which only consists of texts and monuments and which is able to pass on to us a linguistically constituted and historically documented sense. No, it is *the world itself* which is communicatively experienced and continuously entrusted to us as an always open-ended task. It is never the world as it was on its first day but as it has come down to us. Always present when we experience something, when unfamiliarity is overcome, where enlightenment, insight, and appropriation succeed, the *hermeneutic process* takes place in bringing something into words and into the common consciousness. Even the monological language of modern science attains social reality *only in this way*. It is because of this that the universality of hermeneutics, which Habermas has so resolutely disputed, seems to me to be well grounded. Habermas, in my opinion, never gets past an understanding of the hermeneutical problem one finds in German Idealism and he unjustly restricts my conception of tradition to the 'cultural tradition' in the sense that Theodor Litt used this term. The extended discussion between Habermas and myself of this question is documented in the 1971 volume published by Suhrkamp entitled *Hermeneutics and the Critique of Ideology*.

# Resisting the Expansion of the Perspective of Natural Science

In relation to our philosophical tradition, also, I believe we have a similar hermeneutical task. Philosophizing, too, does not just start from point zero but rather has to think further and speak further the language we speak. What this means today, just as it did in the days of the ancient sophists, is that the presently alienated language of philosophy must recover its original saying power and be led back to the uttering of what is meant and back to the things we have in common, the solidarities that are the bearers of our speaking.

Modern science has more or less blinded us to this task, and the generalizing of its perspective into philosophy should be resisted. In Plato's *Phaedo* Socrates puts forward the following demand: he would like to understand the structure of the world and the occurrences in nature in the same way he understands why he sits here in prison and has not taken the offer of flight—namely because he holds it *good* to accept even an unjust sentence against him. To understand nature as Socrates here understands himself, namely in terms of the Good, is a demand that in a certain way is fulfilled through Aristotle's teleological philosophy of nature. But this

Socratic demand is no longer accepted and has not been since the science that developed in the seventeenth century, which was the first real nartural science, a science that has in some measure made the control of nature possible. But in my view, precisely because of the nonunifiability of philosophy with the modern natural sciences, hermeneutics as philosophy does not have as much to learn from the theory of modern science as it does from the older traditions, which it needs to call back to memory.

One of these is the tradition of rhetoric, a tradition Giambattista Vico,[7] as the last representative of that older tradition, defended with strong methodological awareness against modern science, which he called *critica.* Already in my classical Greek studies during the 1920s I had been strongly interested in rhetoric, both as the art of speaking and in its theory. Rhetoric for a long time has not been sufficiently recognized. In the older tradition rhetoric was the bearer of esthetic concepts, as still becomes quite clear in Baumgarten's determination of esthetics. In any case, this point needs great emphasis today: the rationality of the rhetorical way of arguing, which admittedly seeks to bring emotions into play but works with arguments and with probabilities, is and remains far more a determining factor in society than the excellence of science. For this reason, in *Truth and Method* I expressly related myself to rhetoric and from many sides found corroboration—for instance, the work of Chaim Perelman, who takes legal practice as his starting point. This does not mean that I underestimate the importance of modern science and its application in the technical civilization of today. On the contrary, there are completely new problems of mediation that are posed by modern civilization. But the situation has not in principle been changed by this. The 'hermeneutical' task of integrating the monologicality of science into the communicative consciousness, which entails the exercise of practical, social, and political rationality, has only become more urgent with the rise of technological civilization.

In reality this is an old problem, one that we have been aware of since Plato. The statesmen, the poets, but also the real masters of the individual manual arts, were accused by Socrates of not knowing the 'good'. Aristotle has determined for us the structural difference involved here through his differentiation of *techne* from *phronēsis.* This difference cannot just be talked away. Even if this distinction allows of being misused, and even if the

---

7. Giambattista Vico (1668–1744) wrote the influential work, *The New Science,* which defended history as a legitimate field of knowledge that should not be depreciated by comparison with natural science, but is in some respects superior.

call for 'conscience' may itself often conceal unrecognized ideological commitments, it is still a misunderstanding of reason and rationality if one only recognizes them within the anonymity of science as science. So I was persuaded that the Socratic legacy of a 'human wisdom', had to be taken up again in my own hermeneutical theory-formation, a legacy which, when measured against the godlike infallibility of science, is, in the sense of *sophia*, a consciousness of not knowing. What Aristotle developed as 'practical philosophy' can serve as a model for this fallible and merely human wisdom. This is the second line of the ancient tradition that, in my view, needs to be renewed.

# Practical Science and Practical Philosophy

The Aristotelian project of a practical science seems to me to offer really the only scientific-theoretical model according to which the scholarly disciplines that are based on 'understanding' can be thought out. Through hermeneutic reflection on the conditions of understanding, it becomes clear that this type of understanding can best be articulated in a reflection that neither starts at a zero point nor ends in infinity. Aristotle made it clear that practical reason and practical insight do not possess the teachability of science but can be exercised in praxis, and this implies an inner link with the ethos—a point well worth remembering. The model of practical philosophy, then, must be put in place of these *theoria*, whose ontological legitimation can only be found in an infinite intellect, an intellect about which our experience of human existence, unsupported by revelation, knows nothing. This model must be invoked against all who would bend human reason into the methodical thinking that characterizes 'anonymous' science. To present and defend the model of rationality belonging to practical reason over against the perfection of a logical self-understanding specific to the sciences seems to me the true and authentic task of philosophy today, also, and precisely in view of the practical relevance of science to our life and survival.

'Practical philosophy' is much more than a mere methodological model for the hermeneutical disciplines. It also offers something like a substantive foundation for them. The special kind of method that belongs to practical philosophy follows from what Aristotle worked out as 'practical reason', a rationality possessing a specific conceptual character. Indeed, its structure cannot be grasped by means of the modern concept of science at all. Hegel, whose dialectic was successful in rehabilitating many traditional ideas, was also able to renew many of the truths of 'practical' philosophy, yet even the dialectical flexibility of Hegel threatens today to become a new, unconscious dogmatism of reflection. For the concept of reflection that serves as the basis for Habermas's 'critique of ideology' implies a highly abstract concept of coercion-free discourse which totally loses sight of the real conditions of human praxis.

I had to reject Habermas's recourse to psychoanalysis as illegitimately taking the therapeutic situation of psychoanalysis for the program of critique of ideology. In the realm of practical reason there is simply no analogy to the 'knowing' analyst who guides the productive reflective processes of the analysand. With regard to the question of reflection, it seems to me that Brentano's differentiation of reflexive self-awareness from objectivizing reflection, a distinction that goes back to Aristotle, is still superior to what we find in the heritage of German Idealism. The same thing applies, in my view, also with regard to the demand for transcendental reflection that Karl-Otto Apel and others have directed at hermeneutics.

So I have to say that the dialogues of Plato, even more than the works of the great thinkers of German Idealism, have left their stamp on my thinking. These dialogues are my constant companions, and what a unique company they are! However much we moderns may have been taught by Nietzsche and Heidegger about how Greek concepts have anticipated everything from Aristotle to Hegel and up to modern logic, so that they constitute a boundary beyond which our own questions remain without answers and our intentions unsatisfied, it is still Plato's dialogical art which serves as an antidote to the illusion of superiority which we think we possess as inheritors of the Judeo-Christian tradition. Admittedly it was also Plato who, with the doctrine of ideas, the mathematization of nature, and the intellectualizing of what we would call 'ethics', laid the foundation for the metaphysical conceptuality of our tradition. But at the same time he mimetically limited all his assertions, and just as Socrates knew how to do this with his dialogue partners by using irony, so also Plato through his art of dialogical poetry, robbed his reader of his assumed superiority. To philosophize *with* Plato, not just to criticize Plato, that is the task. To criticize Plato is perhaps just as simple-minded as to reproach Sophocles for not being Shakespeare. This may seem paradoxical, but only to someone who is blind to the philosophical relevance of Plato's poetic imagination.

# Knowing that We Do Not Know

Of course, one must first learn to read Plato mimetically. In our century some things have happened that make this a little easier, especially through Paul Friedländer's great study, but also through many other inspired but sometimes not so well-grounded books from the circle of the poet Stefan George[8] (by Heinrich Friedmann, Kurt Singer, and Kurt Hildebrandt, for instance), as well as the works of Leo Strauss and his friends and students. The task, however, is far from accomplished. It consists of relating the conceptual assertions one encounters in conversations as exactly as possible with the dialogical reality out of which they grow. For one finds there a 'Doric harmony' of deed and speaking, of *ergon* and *logos*, which has to do not just with the words. Rather, it is the authentic spirit of the Socratic dialogues. They are in the literal sense, *hinführende Reden*—speeches that take you somewhere. Only in these does Socrates open his heart to us and let us know what he really intends, not in his art of refutation that often works sophistically and drives his partners into terrible entanglements.

Yes, if only human wisdom were such that it could pass from one person to another like water over a thread of wool (*Symposium*, 175d). But human wisdom is not like this. It is the awareness of not-knowing, *docta ignorantia*. Through it the other person with whom Socrates is having the conversation, is convicted of his own not-knowing—and this means that something dawns on him about himself and about his living in only pretended knowledge. Or, to put it in the clearer formulation from Plato's *Seventh Letter:* Not just his thesis but his soul is refuted. This applies not only to the young men who believe themselves to be friends and yet do not know what friendship is (in the *Lysis*), as well as to the famous generals (in the *Laches)*, who believe they embody in themselves bravery, the virtue of soldiers, or the ambitious statesmen (in the *Charmides)*, who think they possess a knowledge superior to that of all others. It applies, likewise, to all those who follow the professional teachers of wisdom, and in the end it even applies to the simplest citizen who must make himself and others believe that he is a just person as salesman, dealer, banker, or craftsman. Apparently, then, a specialized knowledge is not what is involved here but another kind of knowing, a

---

8. Stefan George (1868–1933) was a charismatic and influential German poet who sought to revive German poetry and reverse the decline of literary German.

knowing that is beyond all specialized competences and beyond all claims to superiority in knowledge, a knowing beyond all otherwise recognized *technai* and *epistemai*. This other knowledge means a 'turning to the idea'—a turning to that which lies behind all the mere positings of supposedly knowledgeable persons.

But this means that in the end Plato does not have a doctrine that one can simply learn from him, namely the 'doctrine of ideas'. And if he criticizes this doctrine in his *Parmenides,* this also does not mean that at that time he was beginning to have doubts about it. Rather, it means that the acceptance of the 'ideas' does not designate the acceptance of a doctrine so much as of a line of questioning that the doctrine has the task of developing and discussing. That is the Platonic dialectic. Dialectic is the art of having a conversation, and that includes the art of having a conversation with oneself and fervently seeking an understanding of oneself. It is the art of thinking. But this means the art of seriously questioning what one really means when one thinks or says this or that. In doing so, one sets out on a journey, or better, is already on the journey. For there is something like a 'natural disposition of man towards philosophy'. Our thinking is never satisfied with what one means in saying this or that. Thinking constantly points beyond itself. The work that goes on in a Platonic dialogue has its way of expressing this: it points towards the One, toward Being, the 'Good', which is present in the order of the soul, in the constitution for the city, and in the structure of the world.

# The History of Metaphysics as the History of Platonism

Although Heidegger interprets the acceptance of Plato's doctrine of ideas as the beginning of the forgetfulness of Being, a forgetfulness which reaches its peak in a thinking merely in terms of representation and objectivation, and in a will to power which dominates the era of technology, and although his understanding that even the earliest Greek thinking of Being is a preparation for the forgetfulness of Being that occurs in metaphysics is consistent enough with this, I would argue that the authentic meaning of the Platonic dialectic of ideas is ultimately something quite different from all this. The fundamental step of going beyond all existing things in Plato is a step beyond a 'simplistic' acceptance of the ideas; thus, it ultimately represents a countermovement *against* the 'metaphysical' interpretation of Being as merely the being of beings.

Actually, the history of metaphysics could be written as a history of Platonism. Its stages would be, say, Plotinus and Augustine, Meister Eckhart and Nicholas of Cusa, Leibniz, Kant, and Hegel; which means, of course, all those great efforts of Western thought to *go questioningly back behind* the substantial being of the Form and thus behind the whole metaphysical tradition. And in this respect, the first Platonist in the series would be none other than Aristotle himself. To defend this view, and thus to oppose the common interpretation of Aristotle's criticisms of the doctrine of ideas, and to attack also the substance metaphysics of the Western tradition, has been the goal of my writing in this area. By the way, I do not stand all alone in this; Hegel also held such a view.

To make good my point would not be some kind of merely 'historical' undertaking. For certainly my intention would not be to supplement the Heideggerian history of the increasing forgetfulness of being with a history of the remembering of being. That would not be meaningful. Indeed, it is certainly appropriate to speak of an increasing forgetfulness. In my view, Heidegger's great achievement was to have shaken us out of too full a forgetfulness by asking in earnest: what is being? I myself recall how in 1924 Heidegger ended a semester seminar on Cajetan's *De Nominum Analogia* with the question "What is that, Being?" and how we looked at each other and shook our heads over the absurdity of the question. In the meantime, we have all been reminded, in a certain sense, of the question of being. Even the defenders of the traditional metaphysical tradition, those who wish to be critics of Heidegger, find they are no longer captive to a self-evident understanding of being, an understanding grounded in the metaphysical tradition and accepted without question. Rather they now defend the classical answer as an answer, which means that they have again recovered the question as a question.

# The End of History

Everywhere that philosophizing is attempted, one finds in this attempt a recollection of being takes place. In spite of this fact, however, it seems to me there is no history of the recollection of being. Recollection has no history. There is not an increasing recollection in the same way that there is an increasing forgetfulness. Recollection is always what comes to one, and comes over one, so that something that is again made present to us offers, for the space of a moment, a halt to all passing away and forgetting. But recollection of being is not a recollection of something previously known and now present once again; rather, it is recollection of something previously asked, the reclaiming of a lost question. And a question which is asked again is no longer recollected; it becomes a question again and is now asked anew. It is no longer a recollection of something that was once asked—it is posed anew. In this way, questioning reconceptualizes—destroys but also preserves in a higher form—the historicity of our thinking and knowing. In this sense philosophy has no history. The first person who wrote a history of philosophy, that was really such, was also the last to do so—Hegel. And in Hegel, history was cancelled and fulfilled in the presence of absolute spirit.

But is this *our* present? Is Hegel still present also for us? Certainly one ought not to dogmatize and take what Hegel meant in a narrow sense. When he spoke of the end of history which is to be reached through the freedom of everyone, he meant that history is at an end only in the sense that no higher principle can be put forward than the freedom of everyone. The increasing unfreedom of everyone, which has begun to characterize Western civilization—perhaps its inescapable destiny—would constitute for Hegel no valid objection to the principle of freedom. Indeed, he would say, 'So much the worse for the facts'. At the same time, I would ask, against Hegel: Is the first and last principle in which the philosophical thinking of being culminates really 'spirit'? Certainly, the critique of the young Hegelians was polemically directed against this. But it is my conviction that Heidegger has been the first thinker since Hegel to present us with a positive alternative possibility, a possibility that gets beyond mere dialectical reversal. This is Heidegger's point: truth is not the total unconcealment whose ideal fulfillment would in the end remain the presence of absolute spirit to itself. Rather, Heidegger taught us to think of truth as an unconcealing and a concealing at the same time. The great efforts at thinking in the tradition, efforts in which we feel ourselves over and over again to be addressed and expressed, all stand in this tension. What is asserted is not everything. Indeed, it is the unsaid that first makes it, and lets it be, a word that can reach us. This seems to me to be compellingly true. The concepts in which thinking is formulated stand silhouetted like dark shadows on a wall. They work in a one-sided way, predetermining and prejudging. One thinks, for instance, of Greek intellectualism, or of the metaphysics of will in German Idealism, or the methodologism of the Neo-Kantians and Neo-Positivists. In a process of which they were not aware, each of these formulated its highest principle without realizing its anticipatory entrapment in its own concepts.

For this reason every dialogue we have with the thinking of a thinker we are seeking to understand remains an endless conversation. It is a real conversation, a conversation in which we seek to find 'our' language—to grasp what we have in common. Consciously taking up a historical distance from one's partner and placing the partner in an historically surveyable course of events must remain subordinate movements of our effort to achieve understanding. As a matter of fact, they represent a self-assurance by which one actually closes oneself off from one's partner. In a conversation, on the other hand, one seeks to open oneself to him or her, which means holding fast to the common subject matter as the ground on which one stands together with one's partner.

But if this is the case, then the goal of preserving one's own 'position' is in a jam. On the other hand, if one takes such a dialogical endlessness to its most radical extreme, does it not entail a complete relativism? But again, if this were so, would not this position itself be trapped in the well-known self-contradiction of all relativism? In the end, I think, the way such a dialogue goes is very much like the way we acquire our experiences in life: a fullness of experiences, encounters, instructions, and disappointments does not just conjoin everything in the end to mean that one knows everything; rather it means that one is initiated and at the same time has learned a bit of modesty. In a central chapter of my book *Truth and Method* I have defended this 'personal' concept of experience against the deformation the concept of experience has suffered in being institutionalized in the empirical sciences. In this I feel myself akin to Michael Polanyi. 'Hermeneutic' philosophy, as I envision it, does not understand itself as an 'absolute' position but as a path of experiencing. Its modesty consists in the fact that for it there is no higher principle than this: holding oneself open to the conversation. This means, however, constantly recognizing in advance the possibility that your partner is right, even recognizing the possible superiority of your partner. Is this too little? This seems to me to be the only kind of integrity one *can* demand of a professor of philosophy—but it is one which one *ought* to demand.

It seems to me evident that we cannot get around the original dialogic of human being in the world and having a world. This holds even if one is demanding some kind of final accountability or ultimate foundation—or for the self-realization of the spirit. The path of Hegel's thought, above all, should be examined afresh. Heidegger has uncovered the Greek roots of the tradition of metaphysics, and he has at the same time recognized a radical allegiance to the Greeks in Hegel's dialectical dissolution of traditional concepts as carried out in the *Science of Logic*. But Heidegger's *Destruktion* of metaphysics has not, in my view, robbed metaphysics of its importance today. In particular, Hegel's powerful speculative leap beyond the subjectivity of the subjective Spirit established this possibility and offered a way of shattering the predominance of subjectivism. Was Hegel's intention not the same as that in Heidegger's turn: away from the transcendental principle of the self? Was it not Hegel's intention, also, to surpass the orientation to self-consciousness and the subject-object schema of a philosophy of consciousness? Or are there still differences that remain? Do not my orientation to the universality of language and my insistence on the linguisticality of our access to the world, both of which I share with Heidegger, really constitute a step beyond Hegel, or are they a step back behind Hegel?

I could, in fact, say, as a first determination of the site of my own effort at thinking, that I have taken it on myself to restore to a place of honor what Hegel termed 'bad infinity'—but with a decisive modification, of course. For in my view the unending dialogue of the soul with itself which thinking is, is not properly characterized as an endlessly refined determination of the objects that we are seeking to know, either in the Neo-Kantian sense of the infinite task or in the Hegelian dialectical sense that thinking is always moving beyond every particular limit. Rather, here I think Heidegger showed me a new path when, as a preparation for posing the question of being in a new way, he turned to a critique of the metaphysical tradition—and in doing so found himself 'on the way to language'. This way of language is not absorbed in making judgments and examining their claims to objective validity; rather, it is a way of language that constantly holds itself open to the whole of being. Totality, in my view, is not some kind of objectivity that awaits human determination. In this respect, I find Kant's critique of the antinomies of pure reason to be correct and not superseded by Hegel. Totality is never an object but rather a world-horizon which encloses us and within which we live our lives.

# Logical Analysis versus Reading

I did not need to follow Heidegger, who based himself on Hölderlin against Hegel and who interpreted the work of art as a primordial occurrence of truth, to find in the poetic work a corrective for the ideal of an objective determination of truth, or in order to recognize the hubris that resides in concepts. On the contrary, this was already clear to me in my own first efforts at thinking. From that time on, the poetic work offered my own hermeneutic orientation constant food for thought. Likewise, the hermeneutical effort to think the nature of language in terms of dialogue—inevitable for me as a lifelong student of Plato—ultimately signified that every formulation one might make was in principle surpassable in the process of conversation. The rigid fixing of things in terminology, which is fully appropriate in the realm of modern science and its effort to put knowledge into the hands of its anonymous society of investigators is peculiarly suspect in relation to the realm of motion called philosophical thought. The great Greek thinkers were able to preserve the flexibility of their own language even when it was occasionally carried out in conceptually fixed terms, say, in thematic analysis. On the other hand, there is Scholasticism: ancient, medieval, modern—and the most recent. It follows philosophy like its shadow. That is why the true rank of a thinker or of thinking is almost determinable according to how far the thinker or the thinking is able to break through the fossilization represented by the usages inherited in his or her philosophical language. Fundamentally, Hegel's programmatic effort at this, which in his hands became the dialectical method, had many predecessors. Even a thinker as ceremonially minded as Kant, who constantly had in mind the Latin language of late Scholasticism, established his 'own' language, a language which certainly avoided neologisms but in which the traditional concepts gained new applications and new meaning. Likewise, Husserl's higher rank as compared with the contemporary and older Neo-Kantianism consists precisely in the fact that his intellectual powers of intuition welded together the inherited technical expressions and combined them with the descriptive elasticity of his vocabulary into the unity of a personal style. And Heidegger did not hesitate to appeal to the example of Plato and Aristotle to justify the novelty of his use of language, and he is, by the way, far more followed now than the initially provocative effect and public amazement would have allowed one to expect. Philosophy, in contrast to the sciences and also to practical life, finds itself in a peculiar kind of difficulty. The language we speak in everyday use is not created for the purpose of philosophizing. Philosophy continually finds itself in a state of urgent linguistic need. This is constitutive of philosophy, and this calamity, this distress, becomes all the more felt, the more boldly the philosophizer is breaking new paths. One generally marks oneself as a dilettante in thinking if one arbitrarily introduces terms and zealously 'defines one's concepts'. Rather, the true philosopher often awakens the intuitive power already resident in language, and every linguistic zeal, or even linguistic violence, can be in place if only this can be accepted into the language of those who would think along with the philosopher, think further with him, and that means if the words are able to push forward, extend, or light up the horizon of communication.

It is unavoidable that philosophy, which never finds its object already at hand but must itself provide it, does not move within systems of propositions whose logical formalization and critical testing for conclusiveness and univocity might somehow deepen its insights. Such a way with language will create from the world no 'revolution', not even that proclaimed by the analysts of ordinary language. To illustrate this point with an example, if one analyzes with logical methods the arguments in a Platonic dialogue, shows inconsistencies, fills in gaps, unmasks false deductions, and so on, one can achieve a certain gain in clarity. But does one learn to read Plato by proceeding in this way? Does one make his questions one's own? Does one succeed in learning from Plato instead of just confirming one's own superiority? What applies to Plato in this case applies by extension to all philosophy. Plato has in his *Seventh Letter* rightly described this, once and for all: the means one uses for philosophizing are not the same as philosophizing itself. Simple logical rigor is not everything. Not that logic does not have its evident validity. But the thematization in logic restrains the horizon of questioning in order to allow for verification, and in doing so blocks the kind of opening up of the world which takes place in our own experience of that world. This is a hermeneutical finding which I believe in the end converges with what we find in the later Wittgenstein. In his later writings he revised the nominalistic prejudices of his *Tractatus* in favor of leading all speaking back to the context of life-praxis. Of course, the result of this proposed reduction of philosophy to a praxis-context remained for him a negative one. It consisted in a flat rejection of all the undemonstrable questions of metaphysics rather than in a *winning back* of these undemonstrable questions of metaphysics, however undemonstrable they might be, by detecting in them the linguistic constitution of our being-in-the-world. For this, of course, far more can be learned from the words of the poets than from Wittgenstein.

# Poetic Truth Is Inexhaustible

In the case of poetry, one thing is undisputed: conceptual explication is never able to exhaust the content of a poetic image. No one contests this. Indeed, this point has been recognized at least since Kant, if not earlier with Baumgarten's discovery of poetic truth as *cognitio sensitiva*. From a hermeneutic perspective this has to be of special interest. In the case of poetry, the mere separation of the esthetic from the theoretical, and the freeing of poetry from the pressure of rules or concepts is not enough. For poetry is still a form of speech in which concepts enter into a relationship with each other. So the hermeneutical task is to learn how to determine the special place of poetry in the constraining context of language, where a conceptual element is always involved. The question is: in what manner does language become art? I do not pose this question here just because the practice of interpretation always has to do with forms of speaking and forms of text and because in poetry also one has to do with a linguistically created work or composition, that is, with a text. Rather, it is because poetic compositions are text in a new kind of sense: they are text in an 'eminent' sense of that word—namely, 'eminent text'. In this kind of text language emerges in its full autonomy. Here language just stands for itself; it brings itself to stand before us, whereas normally its words are taken over by the intention in the speech and then after being used are just left behind. One could say that, in a sense, the words simply disappear into their function.

Here we have a hermeneutical problem with a difficulty of its own, for through poetry a special kind of communication takes place. In a poem, with *whom* does the communication take place? Is it with the reader? With *which* reader? Here the dialectic of question and answer which is always the basis of the hermeneutical process and which corresponds to the basic structure of dialogue undergoes a special modification. The reception and interpretation of poetry appears to imply a dialogical relationship of its own special kind.

This becomes especially evident when one studies the specific character of the various kinds of speaking. First, the poetic word displays a wide scale of differentiation in the dialogical relationship; for instance, epic, drama, and lyric poetry. But there are also other kinds of speaking in which the basic hermeneutical relationship of question and answer undergoes funda-mental modifications. I am thinking, for instance, of the various forms of religious speaking, such as proclaiming, praying, preaching, blessing. One could also mention the mythic saga, the legal text, and even the more or less stammering language of philosophy. All of these involve the hermeneutical structure of application with which I have increasingly occupied myself since the publication of *Truth and Method*. I believe I have been able to get closer to what is involved here by approaching the problem from two sides: first, from my studies of Hegel, in whom I have pursued the role of the linguistic in relation to the logical, and second, from the side of modern hermetic poetry, to which I have dedicated a book, choosing Paul Celan's '*Atemkristall*' as the object of the commentary. Reflection on them has served to remind me, and can constantly serve to remind us all, that Plato was no Platonist and philosophy is not scholasticism.

# *Truth and Method* Reconsidered

Now that more than three decades have passed since the appearance of *Truth and Method* in 1960, perhaps the time has come to ponder the consistency of a project that brought together several different investigations from several different sides and attempted to weld them into a philosophic statement. So I would like in this final section to make an effort at self-criticism. Do the investigations I undertook in *Truth and Method* constitute the unity of a philosophical whole, or can one perceive glaring gaps in them, inconsistencies in the line of argument as a whole, or structural deficiencies? Has the form of their presentation here and there gotten out of date?

Quite certainly it may seem outdated today to lay the emphasis just on the historical and the philological disciplines within the *Geisteswissenschaften*. In an era of 'social sciences' and of structuralism and linguistics, an effort to link up with the Romantic heritage of the historical school can no longer seem sufficient. The limited range of experience with which I began may to some degree account for this. Nevertheless, the intention of all my work has been directed toward the universality of the hermeneutical experience, and if this experience is really a universal, it ought to be reachable from any starting point.

Doubtless the image of the natural sciences that I had in mind when I conceived my hermeneutical ideas for *Truth and Method* was quite one-sided. It is now clear to me in this respect that a whole broad field of hermeneutical problems has been left out, a field which goes far beyond the range of my own knowledge of the processes and procedures of current scientific research. It is really only in the historical-philological disciplines that I have gotten far enough along to participate here and there in the work of genuine research. In cases where I cannot study the original work done, I do not feel that I am justified in wanting to make the researcher aware of what he is doing and what is going on with him. The validity of hermeneutical reflection, after all, depends on the experience that must arise out of concrete hermeneutical praxis.

Nevertheless, the fact that a hermeneutical problematic is present in the natural sciences was already clear to me when I read Moritz Schlick's convincing critique of the dogma of protocol sentences in 1934. When the ideas for my book were developed in the 1930s, which was a time when circumstances entailed an increasing isolation, physicalism and the unity of science were the official image that was pressed upon us. At that time, the 'linguistic turn' in Anglo-Saxon philosophical thinking was not yet even on the horizon. Only after I had completed the path of thought that led to *Truth and Method* did I have time to study the work of the later Wittgenstein, for instance, and only much later did I realize that Karl Popper's critique of positivism also contained motifs similar to those in my own orientation.

So I am only too aware of the way in which the points of departure in the formation of my thinking were captive to the times. It is the task of the younger generation to take into account the changed conditions for hermeneutical praxis, and fortunately this has happened. The critiques that have arisen over the years have prompted lively discussion on many sides.

As I look back today, I see one point in particular where I did not achieve the theoretical consistency I strove for in *Truth and Method*. I did not make it clear enough how the two basic projects that were brought together in the concept of 'play' harmonized with each other and how they contrasted with the subjectivism of modern thinking. On the one hand, there is the orientation to the game we play with art and on the other hand the grounding of language in conversation, the game of language. With this, the further and decisive question arises as to whether I succeeded in making it fully clear that the hermeneutic dimension goes beyond the sort of thinking that is based on consciousness, that is, beyond what German philosophy calls 'self-consciousness'. This entails showing that the otherness of the Other is not overcome in understanding, but rather preserved. What I needed to do was go back to my concept of game once again and place it within an ontological perspective that had been broadened by the universal element of linguisticality.

In other words, I needed to unite the game of language more closely with the game art plays, which I had designated as the model for hermeneutics. It was certainly obvious that one could think the universality of linguistic world-experience under the model of playing a game. Indeed, already in the foreword to the second edition of *Truth and Method* (1965), as well as in the closing pages of my 1963 essay on 'The Phenomenological Movement', I referred to the convergence of my concept of 'game' with the concept of language-game in the later Wittgenstein.

# Meaning and Language-Games

To say that learning to speak a language is a 'learning process' is really only a manner of speaking. In reality, it is a game of imitation and of exchange. The apprehending child's natural urge to imitate, to form sounds, either in imitation or out of sheer pleasure, is combined in that child's mind with the illuminating flash of meaning. No one can really say how the child's first understanding of meaning comes about. There are always prelinguistic experiences of meaning that have been going on long before that moment, and surely also the exchange of looks and gestures, so all the crossings over from prelinguistic to linguistic understanding flow smoothly. Equally ungraspable is how the result is arrived at. So no one can quite figure out what the term from present-day linguistics, namely 'linguistic competence', really means. Apparently whatever it means cannot be objectively described as the possession of an inventory of what is linguistically correct. Rather, what the term 'competence' means is that the linguistic capacity has been developed in a person who speaks and cannot be described simply in terms of the application of rules or merely as the rule-governed management of language. One must instead view this competence as the fruit of an unencumbered—within limits—practice of speaking. A central part of my own endeavor, in contrast to the concept of linguistic competence, has been to demonstrate hermeneutically the universality of linguisticality. For I regard learning to speak and the acquiring of an orientation to the world as inseparably woven together in the fabric making up the history of the cultural development of humankind. This may be a never-ending process, and it is on the basis of *this* that one acquires at the same time something like linguistic 'competence.' It may be instructive to compare this process to that of learning a foreign language. In general, we can only speak here of *approaching* so-called speaking competence, except in the case of someone who has over a long period of time fully and completely entered an environment in which the foreign language is spoken. Generally, competence is only achievable in one's own mother tongue, or the language one spoke where one lived and grew up as a child. This confirms the fact that one learns to interact with the world through one's mother language, and conversely, the first development of one's own capacity to speak begins to be articulated within one's orientation in the surrounding world.

The question, then, is how the playing of the language-game, which is for each person also the playing of the world-game, goes together with playing the artwork-game. How do both relate to each other? It is clear that in both cases, I think, that linguisticality is incorporated into the hermeneutical dimension. I believe I have rather persuasively shown in *Truth and Method* that the understanding of what is spoken must be thought of in terms of the dialogical situation, and that means ultimately in terms of the dialectic of question and answer. That is always the situation in which one makes oneself understood, and through which one articulates the world both sides hold in common. I have moved a step beyond the logic of question and answer as Collingwood had developed it, in that not only does one's world orientation, as he held, find expression in what develops between the speaking of question and answer; it also happens to us *from the side of the things that are the topic of conversation*. That is to say, the subject-matter 'raises questions'. Likewise, question and answer play back and forth between the text and its interpreter. That the text is written does not, as such, change the basic problem-situation at all. It is always the *matter* which is being spoken about: is it this way or that? A written communication, such as a letter, is merely the continuation of a conversation by other means. Also a book, as it waits for the reader's answer to it, is the opening of such a conversation. Something 'comes into words' in it.

# The Ceaseless Dialectic of Question and Answer

But how is it with the artwork, and especially with the linguistic work of art? How can one speak here of a dialogical structure of understanding? The author is not present as an answering partner, nor is there an issue to be discussed as to whether it is this way or that. Rather, the text, the artwork, stands in itself. Here the dialectical exchange of question and answer, insofar as it takes place at all, would seem to move only in one direction, that is, from the one who seeks to understand the artwork, the one who interrogates it and himself/herself and listens to the answer of the work. As this one, which he is, he may, like any thinking person, be both questioner and answerer at the same time, just as in a real conversation between two people. But this dialogue of the understanding reader with himself seems not to be a dialogue with the text, which is already fixed and definitively given. Or is this really the case? Is there any text at all that is definitively given?

The dialectic of question and answer does not here come to a stop. On the contrary, the work of art distinguishes itself in that one never completely understands it. That is to say, when one approaches it questioningly, one never obtains a final answer that one now 'knows'. Nor does one take from it relevant information, and that takes care of that! One cannot fully harvest the information that resides in an artwork so that it is, so to speak, consumed, as is the case with communications that merely advise us of something. Apprehending a poetic work, whether it comes to us through the real ear or only through a reader listening with an inner ear, presents itself basically as a circular movement in which answers strike back as questions and provoke new answers. This is what moves us to tarry with a work of art, of whatever kind it may be. To be tarrying is clearly the distinguishing mark of the experience of art. An artwork is never exhausted. It never becomes empty. Conversely, we define every piece of non-art that is merely imitation or cheap sensationalism precisely through the fact that we find it 'empty'. No work of art addresses us always in the same way. The result is that we must answer differently each time we encounter it. Other susceptibilities, other attentivenesses, other opennesses in ourselves permit that one, unique, single, and self-same unity of artistic assertion, to generate an inexhaustible multiplicity of answers. It is a mistake, I think, to try to make this endless multiplicity a denial of the unshakable identity of the work. What this seems to me to be saying, against the reception-aesthetics of Hans-Robert Jauss as well as the deconstructionism of Jacques Derrida (both of which come very close to doing this), is: to hold fast to the identity of sense of a text is neither a falling back into the vanquished Platonism of a classicistic aesthetics nor is it an entrapment in metaphysics. The work, the text we read, is not something we dream up.

# In Defense of 'Bad Infinity'

Likewise, one may ask whether my own endeavor to bring together the *difference* of understanding and the *oneness* of the text or work and in particular whether my holding fast to the concept of a 'work' in the realm of art do not themselves presuppose a metaphysical concept of identity: if reflection by a hermeneutic consciousness also leads us to recognize that to understand at all is always to understand differently, is one really doing justice thereby to the resistance and inscrutability that characterize the work of art? Can the example of art really provide a framework within which a universal hermeneutics could be developed?

I answer: this was really the starting point of my whole hermeneutical theory. The artwork is a challenge for our understanding because over and over again it evades all our interpretations and puts up an invincible resistance to being transformed into the identity of the concept. This is a point I think one could already have learned from Kant's *Critique of Judgment*. It is for this reason that the example of art has the function of leading the way, a function which the first part of *Truth and Method* (on esthetic consciousness) possesses for my whole project of a philosophical hermeneutics. This becomes completely clear if one is to let 'art', in all the endless multiplicity and diversity of its 'assertions', be accepted as true.

From the beginning I have regarded myself as a defender of what Hegel called 'bad infinity', which keeps me in a kind of nearness, albeit tense, to Hegel. In any case, the chapter in *Truth and Method* that dealt with the limitations of *Reflexionsphilosophie* and then passed over to an analysis of the concept of experience tried to make this point clear. There I go so far as to play off a concept that Hegel used polemically against others, namely *Reflexionsphilosophie,* against Hegel himself: in his dialectical method I see a dubious compromise with the scientific thinking of modernity. When, in his dialectic, he takes the external reflection of ongoing experience up into the self-reflection of thought in the way he does, this remains in the end a reconciliation within thought itself.

On the other hand, one can hardly escape the inner enclosedness of an idealism based on consciousness and the whirlpool of its movement of reflection that sucks everything up into immanence. Was Heidegger not right when he himself left behind the transcendental analytic of *Dasein* and the approach he called the "hermeneutic of facticity"? Also, in relation to this turn in Heidegger's thought, how have I tried to find a path of my own?

First, I took as a starting point Wilhelm Dilthey and his question about establishing the methodological foundations of the human sciences and I critically contrasted my own view with it. Taking this path, I must admit, has made defending the universality of the hermeneutical problem, about which I have been concerned from the beginning, much more difficult.

Indeed, one has the feeling at a number of points in the argument in *Truth and Method*, that my taking the 'historical' human sciences as a starting point is rather one-sided. In particular, the argument for the significance of temporal distance, as persuasive as it is in itself, was a poor preparation for discussing the fundamental significance of the otherness of the other and the fundamental role played by language as conversation. It would have been more in tune with the subject matter, I think, to speak of distance and its hermeneutic function in a more general way. After all, interpretive distance does not always have to be historical distance; it is also not always the distance in time as such that enables us to overcome false over-resonances and distorted applications. Even in simultaneity, distance can function as an important hermeneutical element; for example, in the encounter between persons who try to find a common ground in conversation, and also in the encounter with persons who speak an alien language or live in an alien culture. Every encounter of this kind allows us to become conscious of our own preconceptions in matters which seemed so self-evident to oneself that one could not even notice one's naive process of assuming that the other person's conception was the same as one's own, an assumption which generates misunderstanding. Here my insistence on the primary significance of conversation has become important in ethnological research, especially as regards the questionable validity of its questionnaires technique. Nevertheless, where temporal distance does play a role, it remains true that it still offers a special critical help. Certain changes often only then become apparent and certain differences only become accessible to observation with temporal distance. Think, for instance, of the difficulty of evaluating contemporary art, a difficulty which I had in mind especially in my own argument for the importance of temporal distance.

## "What About Thrownness?"

Without question, such considerations as these do extend the significance of distance. Still, they remain within the context of a theory of the humanities and social sciences—the *Geisteswissenschaften*. But the deepest impulse of my hermeneutical philosophy was something other than this. The philosophical context into which I was born was that of subjective idealism and its crisis, which during my youth erupted with the re-appropriation of the Kierkegaardian critique of Hegel. This critique gave the meaning of understanding a completely different sense. According to Kierkegaard, it is the other who breaks into my ego-centeredness and gives me something to understand. This Kierkegaardian motif guided me from the beginning, and entered completely into my 1943 lecture, 'The Problem of History in Modern German Philosophy'. When Heidegger had read that little work in typescript, he nodded approvingly, but immediately countered with the question, "And what about thrownness?"[9] The sense of Heidegger's question was that in the collective meaning of thrownness one finds a sufficient counterinstance to the illusion of a full self-presence and self-consciousness. But what I had in mind was the special autonomy of the other person, and so quite logically I sought to ground the linguisticality of our orientation to the world in conversation. And when I did this I found that a complex of questions opened up to me which had already, long before my first efforts, been addressed by such thinkers as Søren Kierkegaard, Friedrich Gogarten, Theodor Haecker, Friedrich Ebner, Franz Rosenzweig, Martin Buber, and Viktor von Weizsäcker.

This comes to light today when I try to think over my own relationship to Heidegger and my ties to his thought. My critics have viewed this relationship in quite different ways. In general, they focus on my use of the concept of 'historically affected consciousness'. The fact that I make use of the concept of 'consciousness' at all, a term whose ontological bias Heidegger had clearly demonstrated in *Being and Time,* to me only represented an accommodation to what seemed a natural usage of language. Certainly this also gave the appearance that I remained captive to the standpoint of the early Heidegger, which took a *Dasein* concerned with its being and characterized by an understanding of being as its starting point. Of course, the later Heidegger expressly tried to overcome the transcendental-philosophical view of the self found in *Being and Time.* My own intention in introducing the concept of historically affected consciousness, however, was precisely to blaze a trail *to* the later Heidegger. When Heidegger's own thinking pressed beyond the conceptual language of metaphysics, he fell into a *Sprachnot*—lack or need of language—which led him to borrow the language of Hölderlin and to adopt a half-poetic diction. In a recent collection of my shorter works on the later Heidegger which I have titled *Heidegger's Ways,* I have tried to make it clear that the use of language in the later Heidegger does not represent a drifting off into poetry but rather is situated completely in tune with the thinking which led him into a whole new line of questioning.

The end of my apprenticeship to Heidegger coincided with his departure from Marburg and return to Freiburg in 1928, and with the beginning of my own teaching activities in Marburg. Then in 1936 came Heidegger's three Frankfurt Lectures which are today known as *The Origin of the Artwork.* I

---

9. "Und was ist es mit der Geworfenheit?"

journeyed to Frankfurt to hear them when they were first given. In these lectures, it was the concept of the 'Earth' with which Heidegger dramatically transgressed the limits of German philosophical vocabulary once again, a vocabulary he had in his lectures long been renewing and filling with vitality after it had so long dwelt outside the linguistic spirit of the German language. These three lectures so closely addressed my own questions and my own experience of the proximity of art and philosophy that they awakened an immediate response in me. My philosophical hermeneutics seeks precisely to adhere to the line of questioning of this essay *and the later Heidegger* and to make it accessible in a new way. In seeking to achieve this goal I reluctantly retained the concept of consciousness, against whose function as an ultimate ground for thought Heidegger had directed his ontological critique. Still, I sought to limit this concept within itself. Heidegger doubtless saw in my use of this term a falling back into dimensions of thought he had gone beyond—even if he certainly also did not overlook the fact that my intention pointed in the direction of his own thinking. In any case, I must leave it to others to decide whether the path I have followed can claim to have kept up, at least to some degree, with Heidegger's own ventures in thinking. But I think one can at least say today that there is an aspect of my own path which makes more identifiable the significance of some of the endeavors of thought in the later Heidegger and which points to something that could not have been done in simply following Heidegger's own lead in thought. Obviously one must read my chapter in *Truth and Method* on historically affected consciousness in the right way. One should not see in it merely a modification of self-consciousness; say, something like an awareness of the way history is working on us; nor even something upon which one could base a new hermeneutical method. Rather, through this term one has to recognize the *limitation* placed on consciousness by history having its effect—that is effective history, the history within whose effects we all exist. It is something that we can never completely go beyond. The historically affected consciousness is, as I said then, really "more being than consciousness."

Therefore I cannot see that it makes sense to regard my continuing to make use of the traditional concepts of philosophy as an inconsistency in my project of thinking, as some of the best among the younger critical participants in hermeneutics have done, such as Thomas Seebohm, Heinrich Anz, or Manfred Frank. This kind of argument, by the way, is similar to the one that Derrida turned against Heidegger. According to Derrida, in Heidegger the overcoming of metaphysics failed; it was really

Nietzsche who succeeded in accomplishing this. In such argumentation, the more recent French reception of Nietzsche quite logically ends up in disintegrating the question of being and even the question of meaning as such.

# There Is No 'Language of Metaphysics'

Now I must myself take issue with Heidegger when he says that we have to go beyond the language of metaphysics. I insist that there simply is no 'language of metaphysics'. There are only *concepts* in metaphysics whose content is determined by the usage of these words, just as with all words. The concepts in which our thinking moves are no more governed by some rigid rule of fixed pregivenness than the words used in our everyday language. The language of philosophy, even when it carries such a heavy load of tradition, as is the case in the language used in Aristotelian metaphysics and is translated into Latin, still seeks ever and again the fluidity that belongs to all statements that are offered in language. Even in Latin, old meanings can be transformed into new, as happens in the works of Nicolas of Cusa, whose genius I have long admired. Such a transformation of meaning need not necessarily take place through some method in the style of Hegelian dialectic or through Heideggerian linguistic force and violence. Even the concepts which I myself have used gain new senses and definitions through being used in the context in which I apply them. And the concepts I have used, by the way, are really not so much those of classical Aristotelian metaphysics as it has been newly unlocked for us through Heidegger's ontotheology. Far more, they belong to the Platonic tradition: for instance, expressions like *mimesis, methexis, participatio, anamnesis, emanatio*— many of which I have often made use of in such modifications as *Repräsentation*—*are* all terms deriving from Plato. In Aristotle they occur only as expressions he is criticizing, and thus they do not belong to the conceptuality of metaphysics in the form metaphysics later takes in the school founded by Aristotle.

In this regard, I am finally touching on a point where my deviation from Heidegger's thought is genuine, and it is a point which holds for a considerable part of my work in ancient philosophy, especially my Plato studies. (I have the satisfaction, by the way, of knowing that precisely the essays on

Plato which are now in Volume 6 and in part in Volume 7 of my collected works, meant something to Heidegger in the last years of his life.) In these studies I argue that Plato may *not* be read as the preparation for or the forerunner of ontotheology. (And, by the way, it is only because Plato was *not* a preparation for ontotheology that Paul Natorp's accentuation—indeed, overaccentuation—of the nearness of Plato to Kant was possible at all.) Even the metaphysics of Aristotle contains other dimensions than those Heidegger unlocked in his work. In this, I believe I was able to refer Heidegger to certain limits in his own interpretations. I am thinking especially of Heidegger's early fondness for referring to "the famous analogy." He liked to speak in this vein in the Marburg period. He welcomed the Aristotelian teaching of *analogia entis*—the analogy of being—from early on as a brother-in-arms against the dream of a final grounding, a project which Husserl presided over somewhat in the style of Fichte. Also, Heidegger is carefully distancing himself from Husserl's transcendental self-interpretation when he commonly uses a term like 'equiprimordial'—surely an echo of the 'analogy of being' slogan and at bottom another element in Heidegger's movement toward a more hermeneutical phenomenological idiom. It was not just Aristotle's criticism, based on his concept of *phronesis*, of Plato's 'Form of the Good', then, that put Heidegger onto his own path. He received other impulses from the center of Aristotelian metaphysics itself and indeed directly from Aristotle's *Physics*, as Heidegger's treatise on the *Physics*, so rich in perspectives, clearly shows. Just from this fact it becomes evident why I have assigned the dialogical structure of language such a central role. What I had to learn from the great dialoguer Plato, or rather from the Socratic dialogue that Plato poetically created, was that the monologue structure of scientific consciousness never permits philosophical thought to achieve what it intends. My interpretation of the excursis in Plato's *Seventh Letter* it seems to me, stands above all the critical debates about the authenticity of this letter. Only from this letter does it become completely understandable why the language of philosophy developed from that time on in constant conversation with its own history: at first it was through writing commentary, correcting, and varying it; then, with the rise of historical consciousness moving into a new tension between historical reconstruction and speculative transformation. So the language of philosophy remains the dialogue, even when this dialogue is carried on over the distance of centuries and even millennia. The texts of philosophy are for this reason not really texts or works so much as contributions to a conversation going on through the ages.

# Identity and *Différance*

Perhaps this is the place to say something about identity and difference, or *différance*, if you will[10]—starting with Husserl. Husserl's phenomenology of time-consciousness attempts to describe the temporal foundation for objective validity. This is undoubtedly Husserl's intention, and it has a certain persuasive power. *Identity;* in my view, is not placed in jeopardy when one rejects Husserl's idea of an ultimate transcendental grounding and also his recognition of the transcendental ego and its temporal self-constitution in the *Logical Investigation* as the ultimate instance of grounding.

The identity of the ego, as the identity of a meaning that is constructed between partners in a dialogue, remains untouched by this argument, in my opinion. It is obviously correct that no understanding of one person by the other can ever achieve complete coverage of the thing being understood. Here hermeneutical analysis must clear away a false model of understanding and of agreement-in-understanding. An agreement in understanding never means that difference is totally overcome by identity. When one says that one has come to an understanding with someone about something, this does not mean that one has absolutely the same position. The German phrase meaning 'one comes to an agreement'—*man kommt überein*—expresses it very well. Or, appealing to the genius of the Greek language, it is a higher form of *syntheke,* a word that means a putting-together, as in an agreement or treaty. In my view it is just the opposite of a right procedure if one isolates the elements of speaking, of *discours,* and makes them the object of critique. In this case, yes, the same is no longer the same, so one can understand why a person who is fixated on 'signs', has to speak of *différence* or *différance.* In the absolute sense of meaning, no sign is identical with itself. Derrida's critique of Platonism in Husserl, which he finds in the *Logical Investigations* and in the concept of intentionality in *Ideas I,* is correct. But this point was clarified long ago by Husserl himself. It seems to me that a clear line leads directly from the concepts of passive synthesis and anonymous intentionality to the hermeneutical experience. And in it, everyone agrees with my dictum—at least everyone who has shaken off the compulsion to method in the transcendental way of thinking—that "if one understands at all, one understands *differently.*"

---

10. Gadamer is referring to Jacques Derrida's deliberate mis-spelling of the French word, *différence,* to make a philosophical point.

The concept of literature in relation to the complex of questions that makes up hermeneutics has been a preferred theme of my studies throughout the decades since I completed *Truth and Method*. Volumes 8 and 9 of my collected writings contain essays on the theory of literary interpretation as well as interpretations of such writers as Goethe, Hölderlin, Rilke, Kleist, Stefan George, Paul Celan, and others. Also, in Volume 2 one finds two essays from the decade of the 1980s that are related to the literary text: 'Text and Interpretation' attempts to draw together several of my ideas on the literary text, and 'Destruktion und Dekonstruktion' deals with the recent debate about deconstruction, a term which, through Derrida's use of it, has had an important influence on literary theory. As I have already noted, in *Truth and Method* I had not yet defined with enough precision the necessary difference between the game of language and the game of art. As a matter of fact, the relationship between language and art is nowhere so graspable as it is in the case of literature, which is speech—and also writing.

# Reading and Reproduction

It is significant that since antiquity poetics appears alongside rhetoric; then, with the spread of reading culture—which was taking place already in the age of Hellenism and of course much more fully in the age of the Reformation—the written, the *litterae* [letters], gets combined with the concept of 'text'. This means that reading moves to the center of hermeneutics and of interpretation. Both hermeneutics and interpretation serve *reading*, for reading is at the same time *understanding*. So when one is dealing with a literary hermeneutics, one is dealing primarily with the *nature of reading*. One may be fully convinced of the primacy of the living word and of the primordiality of language as it lives in speech; nevertheless, one must acknowledge that reading possesses an even wider circumference. This circumference justifies the very broad concept of literature that I have suggested, in a very preliminary way and awaiting future development, at the end of the first part of *Truth and Method*.

Here I think we need to go into the difference between reading and reproduction. I cannot go as far as Emilio Betti does in his theory of interpretation when he totally separates understanding and reproducing. What I must insist on, in this regard, is that it is *reading*, not reproduction, which truly defines the way we experience the artwork itself. I hold that just as the poetic text is 'text' in the 'eminent' sense of that word, the experience of the artwork shows us what 'reading' in the 'eminent' sense of the word, is.

Reading, I believe, is really the basic form in which all encounter with art takes place. Reading takes place not only in relation to texts, then, but also in relation to pictures, sculpture, and buildings.

Reproduction, however, is something quite different from this, since it has to do with a new realization of something through using the sensory materials of sounds and sound-shadings; and this being so, it has to do with something like a new creation. Certainly a reproduction seeks to bring the work authentically to appearance—the drama on the stage or the musical score through the making of sounds—and this living reproduction rightly carries the name of 'interpretation'. Precisely because of this, the link in interpretation has to be maintained between reproduction and the cultivation of reading. For to reproduce something is also to understand it, even if it is also more than this. So reproduction is not a matter of free creation; rather it is only an *Aufführung* (performance or production, literally 'up-leading'), as the German word so clearly expresses it, a realization by means of which the understanding of a firmly fixed work is led up into the form of a new, real entity. With reading, however, it is a different story, since the sensory reality of the meaning culminates in all its reality in the performance of reading itself, not in something else that happens subsequent to it. So the fulfillment of the event of understanding in the case of reading does not entail—as it does in the case of reproduction—being realized in a new sensory appearance.

Reading aloud demonstrates quite clearly, I think, that reading is a completion-of-meaning which is one's own and is fulfilled within itself in the same act of fulfillment. We can also see from this example that reading is essentially different from a theatrical or musical performance, production, or reproduction. And this applies all the more to 'silent reading', or even when this is articulated out loud as one reads, as was self-evidently the case in classical antiquity. In fact, silent reading is a full completion of meaning, although it is only carried out in a schematizing way by intuition. It remains open to various kinds of imaginative filling out. I once illustrated this point by referring to the work of Roman Ingarden.[11] The same thing also applies

---

11. (Note by Gadamer) In the case of music, the relationship of reading and reproduction is a special question. One would certainly concede that music is not experienced in the reading of the notes, and this constitutes a difference from the reading of literature. And drama is intended for performance rather than merely reading. Even the epic existed in an external sense before it was given to the bard. Nevertheless, essential differences remain. One has to make the music, and the listener must go along with the music.

to someone reciting a text. The good reciter cannot for an instant forget that he or she is not the real speaker but is serving the process of reading. Although reciting a text is a reproduction and representation for another person, and thus includes a new realization in the sensory world, it still remains enclosed within the intimacy of the reading process.

In connection with these various distinctions, we need to clarify a question I have tried over and over again to think through: what role in the hermeneutic process does the intention of the author play? In the usages of everyday speaking, where it is not a matter of passing through the fixity of writtenness, I think it is clear: one has to understand the other person's intention; one must understand what the other person is saying as he or she meant it. The other person has not separated himself from himself, so to speak, into a written or whatever other form of fixed speech, and conveyed or delivered it to an unknown person, who perhaps distorts through misunderstanding, willful or involuntary, what is supposed to be understood. Even more, one is not separated physically or temporally from the person one is speaking to and who is listening to what one says.

How well this other person understands what I want to say is even shown by how the person addressed deals with it. The thing that is understood is thus lifted out of the indeterminacy of just moving in a certain direction of meaning and given a new determinacy, which allows it to be understood or misunderstood. That is what happens in a conversation: the thing meant is articulated, and through this articulation it becomes something one has in common. The individual expression is always embedded in a communicative event and may not be understood as a purely individual thing. Discussion of the 'mind of the author', therefore, really only plays a hermeneutical role where one is not dealing with a living conversation but with fixed expressions, or texts. In this latter case, the question is: does one understand *only* insofar as one goes back to the author or originator? Does one understand enough if one just goes back to what the author had in mind? And what about when this is simply not possible because one knows nothing about the author?

On this point, it seems to me traditional hermeneutics has still never fully overcome the consequences of psychologism. In all reading and all understanding of writing one is dealing with an event or process through which what has been fixed into the text is elevated into a new assertion and must be concretized anew. Now the nature of true speaking is such that what is meant constantly goes beyond what is said. For this reason it seems to me that to hypostatize the intention of the speaker as the measure of understanding constitutes an ontological misunderstanding that one does not realize. It assumes that one could just somehow reconstruct this intention once again through a kind of identification and reproduction, and *only then* turn to the words as a standard of meaning. But as we have seen, reading is not a process of reproduction that permits a comparison with the original intention. To assume that it can do so is to make an epistemological assumption that has been refuted by phenomenological research—namely, that we have before our consciousness a kind of image of the actual thing that is meant, a so-called *Vorstellung*, that is, a representation. But in my view, all reading goes beyond the hardened trace of the word to the sense of the text itself. It does not re-enact the original process of producing the meaning, a process which one would understand as a mental event or event of expression; nor does reading testify to the thing meant otherwise than from the word-trace. This includes, too, that when one understands what another person says, this is not only something meant, it is also something shared, something held in common. When one brings a text to speak through reading, even if such reading be without any audible articulation, one takes up the meaning that resides in the line of meaning that the text has and builds it into the universe of meaning which the reader himself or herself has already opened up. Ultimately this substantiates an insight of the Romantics which I have also taken up: that all understanding is already interpreting. Schleiermacher once put it quite explicitly:

"Interpretation [*Auslegen*] is distinguished from understanding [*Verstehen*] only in the way that speaking out loud is distinguished from inner speaking." This does not mean, however, that inner speaking attains the same degree of articulalion as the given text, but rather the opposite: that speaking aloud can never fully express one's intended meaning.

The same thing holds for reading. What we call reading means to read with understanding. So reading itself is already an interpretation of what is meant. And thus reading is the basic structure that is common to all carrying out, all realization, of meaning. Even if reading is not a reproduction process, every text one reads is only realized in understanding. It therefore also holds that for the text about to be read, the reader who gives the work its full presentness will experience an increase in being. Even when it is not a reproduction on the stage or at the podium, this seems to be the case.

# Hermeneutics and History

In 'Text and Interpretation' I analyzed in some detail the various forms of text with which hermeneutics deals. Yet the special case of the historical requires a further discussion here. In *Truth and Method* I started with the presupposition that historical research is in its final sense interpretation, and thus a performance and a fulfillment of meaning. Even if one starts with this presupposition, however, one has to ask whether the relationship of the historian to the text that is to be researched, namely history itself, is not a different relationship from that of the philologist to the text. The resistance of historians to my arguments in *Truth and Method* made me aware that I had assimilated too closely the historian's special type of understanding to the type of understanding of the philologist. As I now see it, this is not just a question of the scale of what I undertook in *Truth and Method*. History is not just philology writ large, as I suggested there. Rather, in the two cases, there is in play a quite different sense of *text*, and therewith also of what understanding the text means.

The whole of the past, which one may take to be the ultimate object of historical understanding, is not text in the same sense of the word as the individual textual structure is *a text* for the philologist. Is the totality of history ever given for the historian in the same way as a concrete text is given to the philologist? For the philologist, the text, and especially a poetic text, is there in front of its interpreter like a fixed given that precedes every new interpretation. The historian, on the other hand, has first to reconstruct his basic text, namely history itself. Certainly one cannot draw an absolute line of separation here. The historian, for instance, must first understand the literary or whatever texts that are found, just as the philologist does. And it is equally the case that the philologist often must first reconstruct and review the authentic texts in order to understand them at all, and in understanding these the philologist will let historical knowledge be included in philological work exactly as in his trade he will take into account every possible other knowledge. Also, the view of understanding and of meaning is not the same in both cases. The meaning of a text for a philologist has to do with what the text wants to say. The meaning of an event for a historian, on the other hand, is something that the historian reconstructs on the basis both of texts and other evidence, for a reading which perhaps can even force a transformation of the interpretation one had originally anticipated.

# Joy in Meaning

For the sake of clarification, I would like to introduce here a meaning of the term philology that could be the literal translation of the Greek word: philology is 'taking joy in the meaning which is expressed'. In my view, this is just as much the case whether this joy is expressed in the form of a language construct or in some other form. Art, too, as a carrier of meaning, is the object of philology, as well as works of science and philosophy. But even in this broadest sense of philology, as that which understands meaning, philology is still different from history, however much history also seeks to understand meaning. As scholarly disciplines, both history and philology use the methods of their discipline. But insofar as one is dealing with a *text*, even texts of the most varied type and stature, these texts are not only to be understood by taking the path of methodical research. Every text has always already found its reader *before* scholarship comes into the picture. The difference between joy in a meaning that is expressing itself and research that is directed toward a meaning that is concealed already articulates the larger realm of meaning in which actually both ways of understanding move. On the one hand, there is the delight in the expressed meaning as it strikes the 'reader'—and, of course, the concept of the reader can easily be extended to the understanding of all kinds of arts. On the other hand, there is also the reader's vague knowledge of her or his own home and origin, that is to say, of the historical depths that belong to one's own present moment. The interpretation even of a text whose meaning is clearly expressed, is always also related back to the interpreter's prior understanding and fulfills itself in the enlargement of that understanding.

Likewise, the sense of the text of history is always already determined, partly through the interpreter's own personal life-history and partly through that which everyone knows by virtue of a knowledge that has been shaped into what it is by culture. Long before historical research begins its methodical work, the historian has formed such a unified image of history, an image that encompasses the whole content of the heritage. Since a certain historicity belongs to all of us as we acquire our knowledge at school, or even before this, the tie in the ribbon of life that links together critical-historical research and the tradition and heritage is never broken. Only a person who imagines him- or herself to be a mere spectator of world history, may seek to blot out his or her own individuality, as the nineteenth-century historian, Ranke, sought to do. But such a person still remains, like Ranke, a child of his own time and of his own homeland. Neither the philologist nor the historian can know the conditioning elements at work in his or her own understanding, which in a way lies ahead of them and thereby beyond their own methodical control. This applies to both of them, but not in the same way in both cases. For the philologist, the simultaneity of meaning that is asserted in the text is constructed through his or her interpretation (when it succeeds). On the other hand, the successful historian undertakes the construction and destruction of meaning—contexts, which amounts to a constant process of correction and emendation, a destruction of legends, a discovery of falsifications, a constant breaking up of former constructions of meaning—for the sake of a meaning they seek that lies behind them. In such a process, he or she is never able to get back to the simultaneity of an evidential meaning.

My studies since *Truth and Method* have also taken me in another quite different direction: into practical philosophy and the problems of the social sciences. The critical interest that Jürgen Habermas showed in my work during the 1960s itself gained critical significance for me and drew my interest into these areas. Habermas's critique and my countercritique first made me aware of the critical dimension into which I had entered when I went beyond the realm of text and interpretation and attempted to move in the direction of the linguisticality of all understanding. This prompted me again and again to go more deeply into rhetoric and the role that rhetoric has had in the history of hermeneutics, a role which relates to a far greater degree to the form of existence of society as such.

Finally, this same kind of problem has compelled me to work out and define more sharply the theory-of-science dimensions that are specific to a hermeneutic philosophy, in which understanding and interpreting as well as the procedures of the interpretive sciences would find their legitimation. In doing this, I once again took up a question which I have been intensively interested in since my earliest beginnings: what is practical philosophy? How can theory and reflection deal with the realm of praxis when praxis does not tolerate distance but rather calls for engagement? This question has deeply touched me from very early on, at first through the existential pathos of Kierkegaard. In addition, I have oriented my thinking to the model of Aristotelian practical philosophy. I sought to avoid the absurd model of a theory and its application which had one-sidedly determined the praxis-concept at the basis of the modern concept of science. Here, Kant has introduced the self-criticism of the moderns. In Kant's *Foundation for a Metaphysics of Morals* I believed I had found, and I still believe this today, what is, within limits, an unshakable truth. Certainly it is only partial insofar as it is reduced to an imperative ethics. It is that the impulses to enlightenment should not lead to a social utilitarianism. Otherwise one cannot defend it against Rousseau's criticism, which Kant confessed was for him decisive.

Behind this whole issue, I think, lies the old metaphysical problem of the concretizing of the general. I had this problem in mind already in my earliest studies of Plato and Aristotle. The first document of my thinking in this regard was written in 1930 although it remained unpublished until 1985, when it found a place in the fifth volume of my collected works under the title 'Practical Knowledge'. There I have worked out the nature of *phronesis* in close reference to the sixth book of Aristotle's *Nicomachean Ethics,* taking up initiatives I received from Heidegger. In *Truth and Method* this problem moves to the center. Aristotelian practical philosophy has in the years since that early essay been taken up from many different sides. It seems to me indisputable that it is genuinely relevant today. In my view this has nothing to do with the political omens variously connected today with what is called Neo-Aristotelianism. What practical philosophy is remains a real challenge for the concept of science within the thinking of modernity as a whole, a challenge that one ought not to ignore. What we can learn from Aristotle is that the Greek concept of science, *episteme* means knowledge through reason. This means that science, for the Greeks, had its model in mathematics and did not encompass the empirical. Modern science, on the contrary, corresponds less to the Greek concept of science, namely *episteme,* than to the Greek concept of *techne.* In any case, for Aristotle, practical and political knowing represent a fundamentally different type of knowing than all the teachable forms of knowledge and their 'practical' applications. It is this *practical knowledge* which, in reality, assigns and opens the space for each scientifically grounded capacity to do things. This was already the meaning of the Socratic question about the Good, a meaning to which both Plato and Aristotle held firmly. Whoever believes that science, thanks to its indisputable competence, can serve as a substitute for practical reason and political reason, misunderstands the real conditions under which human beings have to organize and design human life. Only practical wisdom is capable of employing science, like all human capacities, in a responsible way.

Now certainly practical philosophy is not itself such a rationality. It is philosophy; which means it is a kind of reflection, or to be more precise, it is a reflection on what a human organization and shape of life is or can be. In the same sense, a philosophical hermeneutics is not itself the art of understanding but only the philosophy of understanding. But both the practical wisdom and philosophical hermeneutics arise out of praxis and are a waste of time without it. That is the special meaning of *Wissen* and *Wissenschaft*—knowing and science—for which hermeneutical philosophy sought to bring a new legitimation. Both in and after *Truth and Method* this has been the goal to which my work has been dedicated.

*Hans-Georg Gadamer*

JEAN-PAUL SARTRE (1905–1980) the leading French philosopher of the twentieth century, was also a highly prominent writer of fiction, a playwright, biographer, and political polemicist. A phenomenologist in the tradition of Husserl
and Heidegger, he became popularly known as the prophet of Existentialism.
Sartre is also well-known because of his lifelong partnership with Simone de
Beauvoir, whose memoirs are largely concerned with him. His most brilliant
philosophical work is *Being and Nothingness* (1943); his most esteemed novel
is *Nausea* (1938). The following are edited transcripts of taped interviews,
given in 1975 when Sartre was already almost blind. The interviewers are
Michel Rybalka, Oreste F. Pucciani, and Susan Gruenheck.

# Jean-Paul SARTRE

## "To me, philosophy is everything. It is the way one lives."

RYBALKA: *R.D. CUMMING MAKES THE following observation. You, M. Sartre, have left a kind of literary testament in the form of your autobiography,* Words. *You have hinted at what might be your political testament with* We're Right to Revolt, *but until now you have not yet taken such a retrospective look at your own philosophy.*

SARTRE: This is precisely what I have begun with Simone de Beauvoir: a book that would be a sequel to *Words* in which I take the position of someone drawing up a philosophical testament. This book will follow a topical procedure, not the chronological order of *Words*.

RYBALKA: *There is a period in your life concerning which we know relatively little, the one dating roughly from 1917 to 1930, in other words, from the end of what you have written about in* Words *to the beginning of Simone de Beauvoir's memoirs. My first question may seem rather trite: Your initial intention was to write, that is, to do literary work. How did you come to do philosophy?*

SARTRE: I was not at all interested in philosophy in my last years at high school. I had a teacher named Chabrier, whom we nicknamed 'CucuPhilo'. He did not arouse in me the slightest desire to do philosophy. Nor did I acquire that desire in *hypokhâgne*:[1] my teacher, by the name of Bernes, was inordinately difficult and I did not understand what he was talking about.

It was in *khâgne* that I made up my mind, under a new teacher, Colonna d'Istria. He was a cripple, a very small and deformed man. The story went around in class that he had been in a taxi accident and that the crowd had moved in around him saying, 'How horrible!' Actually, he had always been like that.

The first essay topic that he assigned, advising us to read Bergson, was: 'What Does Duration Mean?'. I therefore read Bergson's *Essay on the Immediate Data of Consciousness* and it was certainly that which abruptly made me want to do philosophy. In that book I found the description of what I believed to be my psychological life. I was struck by it, and it became a subject for me on which I reflected at great length. I decided that I would study philosophy, considering it at that point to be simply a methodical description of man's inner states, of his psychological life, all of which would serve as a method and instrument for my literary works. I still wanted to continue writing novels and, occasionally, essays; but I thought that taking the *agrégation* exam in philosophy and becoming a professor of philosophy would help me in treating my literary subjects.

---

1. This is the name for the first year of preparation for the entrance examination to the Ecole Normale Supérieure (the elite school in Paris). *Khâgne* is the second and final year of such preparation.

RYBALKA: *At that time you already saw philosophy as a foundation for your literary work. But didn't you also feel a need to invent a philosophy to account for your own experience?*

SARTRE: Both were involved. I wanted to interpret my experience, my 'inner life' as I called it then, and that was to serve as a basis for other works that would have dealt with I don't quite know what, but assuredly purely literary things.

RYBALKA: *Thus in 1924, when you entered the Ecole Normale, you had made your choice?*

SARTRE: I had made my choice: I was going to study philosophy as my teaching discipline. I conceived of philosophy as a means, and I did not see it as a field in which I might do work of my own. Undoubtedly, so I thought at the time, I would discover new truths in it, but I would not use it to communicate with others.

RYBALKA: *Could your decision be described as a conversion?*

SARTRE: No, but it was something new which made me take philosophy as an object for serious study.

As the basis and foundation for what I was going to write, philosophy did not appear to me as something to be written by itself, for its own sake; rather, I would keep my notes, et cetera. Even before reading Bergson, I was interested in what I was reading and I wrote 'thoughts' which seemed to me philosophical. I even had a physician's notebook, arranged in alphabetical order, that I had found in the subway, in which I wrote down those thoughts.

RYBALKA: *Let's go back. Was there a philosophical tradition in your family?*

SARTRE: Absolutely not. My grandfather, who taught German, knew nothing about philosophy. In fact, he made fun of it. For my stepfather, an engineer graduated from the Ecole Polytechnique, philosophy was only, in some sense, philosophy of science.

RYBALKA: *Was your decision influenced by friends such as Nizan?*

SARTRE: No, although Nizan—I don't know why—studied philosophy at the same time as I, and he too obtained the *agrégation* several years later. He made the change at the same time I did, and for him philosophy played more or less the same role as for me.

RYBALKA: *Didn't you discuss it with each other?*
SARTRE: Obviously, we did.

PUCCIANI: *What was it in your first reading of Bergson that awakened your interest in philosophy?*
SARTRE: What struck me was the immediate data of consciousness. Already in my final year at high school, I had had a very good teacher who steered me a bit toward a study of myself. From then on, I was interested in the data of consciousness, in the study of what went on inside my head, in the way ideas are formed, how feelings appear, disappear, and so on. In Bergson, I found reflections on duration, consciousness, what a state of consciousness was, and the like, and that certainly influenced me a great deal. However, I broke away from Bergson very quickly, since I stopped reading him that same year in *khâgne*.

RYBALKA: *And you attack him rather harshly in* Imagination, *for which Merleau-Ponty reproached you.*
SARTRE: I was never a Bergsonian, but my first encounter with Bergson opened up to me a way of studying consciousness that made me decide to do philosophy.

PUCCIANI: *Even at that time you already thought that literature needed to be based on something?*
SARTRE: That's right. What was new for me was the idea of literature having philosophical foundations, foundations concerning the world and 'the interior life', the life of consciousness, concerning general topics which I thought were of interest only to philosophers.

RYBALKA: *In one of your early writings, you describe yourself as determined to write only about your own experience. Did you have the same intention in philosophy?*
SARTRE: Of course. I thought that my experience was the universal experience of man. That was my starting point, and then my studies naturally gave more importance to philosophy. At the Ecole Normale, I wrote works intended to be both literary and philosophical, which is very dangerous; one should never do that. But anyway, that is how I began, by writing novels of a sort, myths that in my eyes had a philosophical meaning.

RYBALKA: *You once told me that you considered your unpublished work, 'The Legend of Truth' to be a literary work. I read and re-read the manuscript with Michel Contat and we came to the conclusion that it is more philosophical than literary.*

SARTRE: At that time I considered 'The Legend' to be literary, and yet the content obviously tended to be philosophical.

RYBALKA: *Nevertheless, we still have two philosophical texts from that period: your thesis on the image for your Diploma of Higher Studies and your essay on the theory of the State.*

SARTRE: Those are very small and trivial things.

RYBALKA: *And yet, your interest in the image . . .*

SARTRE: The thesis on the image had some importance, but I did not really expand my ideas on the question until later.

RYBALKA: *But why this particular interest rather than some other?*

SARTRE: Because, in my mind, philosophy ultimately meant psychology. I got rid of that conception later. I was surprised a moment ago to learn that some of the contributors speak of my psychology. There is philosophy, but there is no psychology. Psychology does not exist; either it is idle talk or it is an effort to establish what man is, starting from philosophical notions.

RYBALKA: *That, by the way, is the point of view of Amedeo Georgi. He sees only behaviorism in psychology today and he considers that you, on the contrary, have provided the groundwork for true psychology. When did you reject traditional psychology?*

SARTRE: In my book, *Sketch for a Theory of the Emotions*, which is still psychology, I try to explain that our conception of psychology does not correspond to true psychology, and in *The Imaginary* I go beyond what is ordinarily called psychology.

PUCCIANI: *For your Diploma in Higher Studies you worked with Professor Henri Delacroix.*

SARTRE: He was a professor of psychology, as a matter of fact.

PUCCIANI: *What sort of relationship did you have?*

SARTRE: We were on good terms, but I had little esteem for him. He was there to grant my diploma, that's all. He had written some works on language that were worthless. He was a professor at the Sorbonne like a hundred others every year. He was rather well known, I don't know why, but he had no influence on me.

RYBALKA: *Since we are talking about influence, what philosophers interested you after Bergson?*

SARTRE: Well, they were classical philosophers: Kant, Plato very much, above all Descartes. I consider myself a Cartesian philosopher, at least in *Being and Nothingness.*

RYBALKA: *Did you study these authors systematically?*

SARTRE: Quite systematically, since I had to take the required courses for the *licence* and the *agrégation.* The development of my ideas on philosophy was related to what I was taught in high school and at the Sorbonne.[2] I didn't come to philosophy independently of the courses I had: Colonna d'Istria assigned me that essay on Bergson, Delacroix directed my thesis . . . The philosophers I liked, Descartes and Plato, for example, were taught to me at the Sorbonne. In other words, the philosophical education I received all those years was an academic education. That is natural, since it leads up to the *agrégation.* Once one has passed the *agrégation,* one becomes a professor of philosophy and everything is settled.

RYBALKA: *Were you influenced by Nietzsche?*

SARTRE: I remember giving a seminar paper on him in Brunschvicg's class, in my third year at the Ecole Normale. He interested me, like many others; but he never stood for anything particular in my eyes.

RYBALKA: *That seems a bit contradictory. On the one hand, one senses that you were somewhat attracted, since in* Empedocles *you identified with Nietzsche, with the characterization "the lamentable Frederic." On the other hand, during the same period, you threw water bombs on the Nietzscheans of the Ecole Normale, yelling: "Thus pissed Zarathustra."*

---

2. The Sorbonne is France's leading university.

SARTRE: I think they go together. In *Empedocles* I wanted to take up again, in the form of a novel, the Nietzsche–Wagner–Cosima Wagner story, giving it a far more pronounced character. It was not Nietzsche's philosophy that I wished to portray but simply his human life, which made him fall in love with Cosima during his friendship with Wagner. Frederic became a student at the Ecole Normale and ultimately I identified with him. I had other referents for the other characters. I never finished that little novel.

RYBALKA: *And Marx?*
SARTRE: I read him, but he played no role at that time.

PUCCIANI: *Did you also read Hegel then?*
SARTRE: No. I knew of him through seminars and lectures, but I didn't study him until much later, around 1945.

RYBALKA: *As a matter of fact, we were wondering at what date you discovered the dialectic?*
SARTRE: Late. After *Being and Nothingness*.

PUCCIANI: *[surprised] After* Being and Nothingness?
SARTRE: Yes. I had known what the dialectic was ever since the Ecole Normale, but I did not use it. There are passages that somewhat resemble the dialectic in *Being and Nothingness*, but the approach was not dialectical in name and I thought there was no dialectic in it. However, beginning in 1945 . . .

RYBALKA: *There are one or two contributors who maintain that you were a dialectician from the start . . .*
SARTRE: That's their affair. I didn't see things that way.

PUCCIANI: *But isn't there, after all, a dialectic of 'in-itself' and 'for itself'?*
SARTRE: Yes. But then, in that case, there is a dialectic in every author's work; we find everywhere contradictions that oppose each other and are transformed into something else, et cetera.

RYBALKA: *You have often been criticized for not being interested in scientific thought and epistemology. Did they have a place in your education?*

SARTRE: Yes. I had to study them in high school and at the Ecole Normale (where much attention was paid to the sciences), and afterward, for my own courses, I had to read particular works. But I never found them terribly absorbing.

PUCCIANI: *And Kierkegaard, when did you discover him?*

SARTRE: Around 1939–1940. Before then I knew he existed, but he was only a name for me and, for some reason, I did not like the name. Because of the double *a*, I think . . . That kept me from reading him.

To continue this philosophical biography, I would like to say that what was very important to me was realism, in other words, the idea that the world existed as I saw it and that the objects I perceived were real. At that time this realism did not find its valid expression, since, in order to be a realist, one had to have both an idea of the world and an idea of consciousness—and that was exactly my problem.

I thought I had found a solution or something resembling a solution in Husserl, or rather in the little book published in French on the ideas of Husserl.

RYBALKA: *Lévinas's book?*

SARTRE: Yes. I read Lévinas a year before going to Berlin. During the same period, Raymond Aron, who had just come back from Germany, told me, for his part, that it was a realist philosophy. That was far from accurate, but I was simply determined to learn about it and I went to Germany in 1933. There I read the *Ideas* in the original text and I really discovered phenomenology.

RYBALKA: *There are some who see a phenomenologist Sartre and some an existentialist Sartre. Do you think this distinction is justified?*

SARTRE: No, I don't see any difference. I think they were the same thing. Husserl made the 'I' of the 'ego' a datum within consciousness, whereas in 1934 I wrote an article called 'The Transcendence of the Ego', in which I held that the ego was a sort of quasi-object of consciousness and, consequently, was excluded from consciousness. I maintained that point of view even in *Being and Nothingness*. I would still maintain it today; but at this stage it is no longer a subject of my reflections.

PUCCIANI: *This question concerning the ego presents a problem for many of your critics.*

SARTRE: Such critics are adhering to tradition. Why should the ego belong to an inner world? If it's an object of consciousness, it's outside; if it's within consciousness, then consciousness ceases to be extra-lucid, to be conscious of itself, in order to confront an object within itself. Consciousness is outside; there is no 'within' of consciousness.

PUCCIANI: *The difficulty stems from the fact that it is not a thing . . .*

SARTRE: No, it's not a thing. But you're not a thing either and yet you are an object of my consciousness. Subjectivity is not in consciousness; it *is* consciousness. Through this, we can restore one meaning of consciousness as objectified in the subject. The ego is an object that is close to subjectivity, but it is not within subjectivity. There can be nothing within subjectivity.

PUCCIANI: *Simone de Beauvoir wrote that this continues to be one of your firmest convictions. Is it a conviction or a fact?*

SARTRE: I consider it a fact. In non-reflexive thought, I never encounter the ego, my ego; I encounter that of others. Non-reflexive consciousness is absolutely rid of the ego, which appears only in reflexive consciousness, or rather in reflected consciousness, because reflected consciousness is already a quasi-object for reflexive consciousness. Behind reflected consciousness, like a sort of identity shared by all the states that have come after reflected consciousness, lies an object that we will call 'ego'.

RYBALKA: *In your early philosophical writings, for example when you were writing* Imagination *or* The Psychology of Imagination, *did you have any stylistic ambitions?*

SARTRE: I *never* had any stylistic ambition for philosophy. Never, never. I tried to write clearly, that's all. People have told me there are passages that are well written. That's possible. Ultimately, when one tries to write clearly, in some sense one writes well. I am not even proud of those passages, if there are any. I wanted to write as simply as possible in French, and I did not always do this, as, for example, in the *Critique of Dialectical Reason*—which was due to the amphetamines I was taking.

RYBALKA: *How would you define 'style'?*

SARTRE: Style is, first of all, economy: it is a question of making sentences in which several meanings co-exist and in which the words are taken as allusions, as objects rather than as concepts. In philosophy, a word must signify one and only one concept. Style is a certain relation of words among themselves which refers back to a meaning, a meaning that cannot be obtained by merely adding up the words.

PUCCIANI:  *In this respect, then, if we employ the distinction set down in* What Is Literature?, *style would come closer to poetry than to prose.*
SARTRE:  Certainly.

RYBALKA:  *The question is often raised as to whether there is a continuity or a break in your thought.*
SARTRE:  There is an evolution, but I don't think there is a break. The great change in my thinking was the war, 1939–1940, the Occupation, the Resistance, the liberation of Paris. All that made me move beyond traditional philosophical thinking to thinking in which philosophy and action are connected, in which theory and practice are joined: the thought of Marx, of Kierkegaard, of Nietzsche, of philosophers who could be taken as a point of departure for understanding twentieth-century thought.

PUCCIANI:  *When did Freud come into the picture?*
SARTRE:  I had known about Freud ever since my philosophy class and I read several of his books. I remember having read *The Psychopathology of Everyday Life* in my first year at the Ecole Normale and then, finally, *The Interpretation of Dreams* before leaving the Ecole Normale. But he ran counter to my way of thinking, because the examples he gives in the *Psychopathology of Everyday Life* are too far removed from rational, Cartesian thinking. I talked about that in the interview I gave to the *New Left Review* in 1969.

Then, during my years of teaching, I went deeper into the doctrine of Freud, though always separated from him, by the way, because of his idea of the unconscious. Around 1958, John Huston sounded me out on doing a film about Freud. He picked the wrong person, because one shouldn't choose someone who doesn't believe in the unconscious to do a film to the glory of Freud.

I think you had a look at my manuscript, didn't you?

RYBALKA:  *Yes, I looked through it. It is a rather imposing manuscript, about 800 pages.*
SARTRE:  I wrote a complete script. In order to do it, I not only re-read Freud's books but also consulted commentaries, criticism, and so forth. At that point, I had acquired an average, satisfactory knowledge of

Freud. But the film was never shot according to my script, and I broke off with Huston.

RYBALKA: *R.D. Cumming says you have a tendency to exaggerate the discontinuity in your thought: you announce every five or ten years that you are no longer going to do what you have been doing. If we take the example that you gave a moment ago—the little notebook you had when you were a student, which became the notebook of the Self-Taught Man in* Nausea[3]—*it's obvious that you were thinking in opposition to yourself*

SARTRE: But it's not like that! I was thinking in opposition to myself in that very moment of writing, and the resulting thought was in opposition to the first thought, against what I would have thought spontaneously.

I never said that I changed every five years. On the contrary, I think that I underwent a continuous evolution beginning with *Nausea* all the way up to *The Critique of Dialectical Reason*. My great discovery was that of sociality, during the war, since to be a soldier at the front is really to be a victim of a society that keeps you where you do not want to be and gives you laws you don't want. Sociality is not in *Nausea*, but there are glimpses of it . . .

RYBALKA: *However, in* Words *you say: "I transformed a quiet evolutionism into a revolutionary, discontinuous catastrophism."*

SARTRE: [continuing what he was saying] At that time, having become aware of what a society is, I returned from being a prisoner of war to Paris. There I encountered a society occupied by the Germans, which gave a stronger and, I might say, more experimental character to my knowledge of the social phenomenon.

RYBALKA: *And in terms of the social phenomenon,* Being and Nothingness *was the end of a period in your life?*

SARTRE: Yes, it was. What is particularly bad in *Being and Nothingness* is the specifically social chapters, on the 'we', compared to the chapters on the 'you' and 'others'.

RYBALKA: *Then do you think you deserved to be reproached for idealism, as has rather frequently been charged?*

SARTRE: No, not idealism but rather, bad realism. That part of *Being and Nothingness* failed.

---

3. *Nausea* was Sartre's first novel, published in 1938. Many critics believe it is his best.

PUCCIANI: *One often has great difficulty with your analyses of love, of the 'for-others'. You yourself have said that in* Being and Nothingness *you depicted above all negative love.*

SARTRE: Yes, certainly. Beginning with *Saint Genet* I changed my position a bit, and I now see more positivity in love.

PUCCIANI: *Sadism and masochism are quite normal aspects of human love.*

SARTRE: Yes, that was what I wanted to say. I would still maintain the idea that many acts of human love are tainted with sadism and masochism, and what must be shown is what transcends them. I wrote *Saint Genet* to try to present a love that goes beyond the sadism in which Genet is steeped and the masochism that he suffered, as it were, in spite of himself.

RYBALKA: *Maurice Natanson has asked the question: "Does the 'for-itself' have a plural or a gender?"*

SARTRE: That relation is not in *Being and Nothingness*, as a matter of fact. It is in *The Critique of Dialectical Reason.*

RYBALKA: *In this connection, do you consider the notion of scarcity to be ontological?*

SARTRE: No, nor is it anthropological. If you like, it appears as soon as there is animal life.

RYBALKA: *Does the 'for-itself have a plural or a gender?*

SARTRE: No, obviously not. There is always and only the 'for-itself': yours, mine. But that does not make several 'for-themselves'.

PUCCIANI: *The strength of your system is that it is grounded in ontology. How did you arrive at your notion of ontology?*

SARTRE: I wanted my thought to make sense in relation to being. I think that I had the idea of ontology in mind because of my philosophical training, the courses I had taken. Philosophy is an enquiry concerning being and beings. Any thought that does not lead to an inquiry concerning being is not valid.

PUCCIANI: *I quite agree. But I would remind you that some scientific thought—the philosophers of the Vienna Circle, for example—completely denies any notion of being as a sort of daydream.*

SARTRE: I know that, and that is exactly what I mean: when one begins with being, one is doing philosophy. In other words, I do not believe that the thought of the Vienna philosophers, and that of people close to them, is valid. Nor do I believe that it yielded valid results later on. One must either begin with being or go back to it, as Heidegger did. Whatever the case, being must be called into question, and that leads to more detailed thinking on current philosophical problems.

RYBALKA: *As Natanson asks, must one have a retrospective point of view and can one discuss* Being and Nothingness *today without entering into dialectics?*

SARTRE: That raises a difficult problem, the problem of knowing how to interpret a dead philosopher who had several philosophies. How should one speak of Schelling, let's say? What value should be placed on his early philosophy and how should it be understood in relation to his later thought? To know exactly what are the sources of an early philosophy insofar as it is early and the sources of the later philosophy—to know how much the early one plays a part in the later one—that's a very difficult question, which I have not yet entirely answered.

PUCCIANI: *But without a fundamental ontology, I wonder if you could have raised the social problem in the way you did in the* Critique.

SARTRE: I think not. That's really where I differ from a Marxist. What in my eyes represents my superiority over the Marxists is that I raise the class question, the social question, starting from being, which is wider than class, since it is also a question that concerns animals and inanimate objects. It is from this starting point that one can pose the problems of class. I'm convinced of that.

RYBALKA: *To go back a little, I would like to ask you, with regard to the imagination, if you still maintain the analogon theory that has so often been contested.*

SARTRE: Yes, I still maintain it. It seems to me that if I had to write on the imaginary, I would write what I wrote previously.

PUCCIANI: *Philosophers have a great deal of trouble understanding the relation between the analogon and the mental image, when the mental image is the analogon of something else.*

SARTRE: Yes, but that is the definition of the mental image itself, to be always the analogon of something else.

PUCCIANI: *And this something else is found in the real world?*
SARTRE: Yes, I can have an image of Simone de Beauvoir, even though she is not here at this moment.

PUCCIANI: *Do you have both an analogon of Simone de Beauvoir and a mental image of her?*
SARTRE: No. The analogon is part of the intention that makes up the mental image. There's no separate mental image that would be the act of consciousness. There is an intention of Simone de Beauvoir through the analogon, and this intention is on the level of the image. That is what we call the image, but it is an intention, the intention by way of the analogon.

RYBALKA: *You have said that in your book on Flaubert you were in part taking up again* The Psychology of Imagination.
SARTRE: That's correct. I give it more . . . rather, I develop it somewhat differently. *Flaubert* is *The Psychology of Imagination* at seventy years of age, while *The Psychology of Imagination* was at thirty.

RYBALKA: *I read in an interview that it was Groethuysen who asked you to add the final chapter to* The Psychology of Imagination, *the one concerning the status of the esthetic object.*
SARTRE: Originally, I did not plan to do such a broad *Psychology of Imagination*. I wanted to do it only on the level of the analogon. In fact, I was not happy with that last chapter, because an entire book should have been done on it.

RYBALKA: *There were rumors that you originally considered doing a thesis on Husserl.*
SARTRE: That's completely untrue. Moreover, I never thought that *The Psychology of Imagination* was going to be a thesis, even if I may have said so in conversation.

RYBALKA: *One often asks what is the place of esthetics in your philosophy. Do you have an esthetics, a philosophy of art?*

SARTRE: If I have one—and I do have somewhat of one—it is entirely in what I have written and can be found there. I judged that it was not worthwhile to do an esthetics the way Hegel did.

RYBALKA: *That was never your ambition?*
SARTRE: Never.

PUCCIANI: *Your esthetics is implicit; it is everywhere and at times it becomes explicit.*
SARTRE: That's it, exactly. In *Saint Genet*, in *Flaubert*, one would find more specific things because I am dealing with an author, but in fact it is everywhere. I never wrote a book on aesthetics and I never wanted to write one.

PUCCIANI: *Was there a reason for that?*
SARTRE: No. I chose to talk about what interested me most.

# Sartre Replies to Charles Tenney

RYBALKA: *Charles Tenney has written that "Sartre could have produced a first-rate aesthetics; he could have become an art critic." Tenney makes a distinction between esthetic materials and non-esthetic materials and he finds that the latter (Marxist interpretation, autobiography, sociology) have been gradually invading your work.*
SARTRE: But everything is esthetic. It is incongruous to suppose that some material could be non-esthetic.

RYBALKA: *Tenney brings up a question that you have often been asked: "Sartre insists on the darker aspects of humanity. Shouldn't he have offset that by a study of light and joy?"*
SARTRE: And abundance, and so forth. Well, no, because they are not situated on the same plane. Tenney seems to assume that men are made half-good and half-bad and that someone who speaks of the bad half without talking about the good half has only seen half of humanity. But that is his idea. Things are not at all like that!

It seems to me that this kind of question is no longer relevant, and it is brought up again by people who have not read anything after *Being and Nothingness*.

RYBALKA: *Tenney raises another question: "In recent years, Sartre has been especially interested in psychoanalysis and Marxism. Does he now consider poetry, painting, and music as insignificant or less important?"*

SARTRE: That's inept. Why? One can concern oneself with psychoanalysis and Marxism and still have other areas of interest.

RYBALKA: *A final question from Tenney: "Does Sartre maintain the distinction between prose and poetry?"*

SARTRE: But that is a distinction that exists of itself. Prose and poetry have different aims and different methods. I still maintain what I wrote on this subject—more or less.

RYBALKA: *However, you have slightly modified the distinction that you made . . .*

SARTRE: Yes, a little. In *Flaubert*, for example. But the distinction remains true. If we push it to its limits, I see prose and poetry as two poles within an overall idea of literature. Moreover, it was in *What Is Literature?* that I made the distinction.

PUCCIANI: *But the writers of the 'New Novel' brought the novel closer to poetry and were able to attack your conception of literature.*

SARTRE: They did not fail to do so, by the way. But the New Novel has disappeared. It attempted to take a position it could not maintain. Personally, I liked some of Robbe-Grillet's novels very much, as well as a few of Butor's.

PUCCIANI: *So, artistic prose would come closer to poetry, and purely signifying prose would be true prose . . . ?*

SARTRE: That's right. But artistic prose is also removed from poetry so far as meaning and signification are concerned. There one would have to go much further.

RYBALKA: *Given the difficulties raised by this distinction between prose and poetry, do you think it is operative?*

SARTRE: Yes, but one must know how to use it, and most literary critics do not.

GRUENHECK: *Have you ever thought of doing a philosophy of language?*

SARTRE:  No. Language must be studied within a philosophy, but it cannot be the basis for a philosophy. I think that a philosophy of language could he drawn out of my philosophy, but there is no philosophy of language that could be imposed upon it.

GRUENHECK:  *To continue on the literature/philosophy problem, do you still see literature as communication?*

SARTRE:  Yes. I can't even imagine what else it might be. One never publishes anything that is not for others.

RYBALKA:  *And yet, in your own work, you have gradually reduced the role of literature, whereas originally philosophy was simply intended to serve as a foundation for literature.*

SARTRE:  Philosophy has always served that purpose; there's no doubt about it—to the extent of becoming indistinguishable from it. *Words*, for example, is a work which has philosophical underpinnings but which is purely literary. It is the story of a man who remembers what happened when he was a child.

RYBALKA:  *Couldn't* Words *be considered part of a larger undertaking? Starting in 1953, you began to work out a threefold project: autobiographical with* Words, *biographical with* The Family Idiot, *theoretical with the* Critique—*and those three projects complemented each other.*

SARTRE:  Yes, I had those three projects, but I did not see them through to the end and they will never be completed. I did not finish *Words*. I am continuing it now with Simone de Beauvoir, but in a different way. I will never finish the *Critique*, which was supposed to have a second volume on history. I will not finish *Flaubert*; it is too late now.

RYBALKA:  *And yet when I saw you some time ago, you were absolutely determined to finish it.*

SARTRE:  There is my eyesight. . . and the *Flaubert* is very difficult. There are also those television programs I am preparing. I cannot see what I write and therefore I cannot correct it. I can't re-read; someone must re-read it to me. Those are the worst possible conditions for writing. Other methods have been suggested to me: I have a tape recorder over there. If you press the button, it starts talking. Either I'm too old to learn that or it is not very ingenious—I don't know which. In any case, it does not replace the act of crossing out a word and putting in a new one above it.

RYBALKA:  *I suppose that those who are used to a tape recorder no longer know how to write.*
SARTRE:  That's what I think. [Laughter]

RYBALKA:  *Robert Champigny points out that your early novels were already marked "to be continued" and he adds, without knowing about your eyesight: "If Sartre finishes the* Flaubert *we should have to offer him our condolences." [Laughter]*
SARTRE:  He is right in saying that. There is something that goes beyond my eyesight. I took notes on the fourth volume of the *Flaubert* before my eyes became weak. They were read back to me; they were not first-rate. Something had stopped.

RYBALKA:  *In this regard, you have said that someone else, having read the first three volumes, could write the fourth. Then what is your role in your own written works? [Laughter]*
SARTRE:  That someone else could not have written the first three volumes! The fourth book can be deduced or induced from the first three and, incidentally, people have already given me dissertations written after reading my *Flaubert*.

RYBALKA:  *Do you think that the philosopher, like the writer, has an individual experience to transmit?*
SARTRE:  No . . . well, perhaps. His role is to show a method whereby the world can be conceived starting at the ontological level.

GRUENHECK:  *Cumming has attempted to prove that this method, in your work, has always been dialectical. It is first a method for defining things; then it becomes a way of exploding the image in consciousness; and, finally, it appears as a dialectic of social classes. The truth always arises from such an explosion, from the displacement, the gap between opposing elements.*
SARTRE:  You will find that in any philosopher, even in a non-dialectician. After all, the dialectic is more complicated than that. I tried to give an account of it in the *Critique*.

At first I was a non-dialectician, and it was around 1945 that I really began to concern myself with the problem. I delved deeper into the dialectic beginning with *Saint Genet* and I think that the *Critique* is a truly dialectical work. Now it is always possible to amuse oneself by showing that I was previously a dialectician without knowing it; one can show that Bergson was Bergsonian at age six when he ate jam and toast. [Laughter]

GRUENHECK: *Cumming uses as an example of a nascent dialectic your article 'How a Good American Is Made', in which you describe a twofold process of disintegration and reintegration.*

SARTRE: It is a process that resembles the dialectic, but I do not think that one becomes a dialectician just like that, by providing an example, a particular thought. One becomes a dialectician when one has posited what the dialectic is and tries to think dialectically.

PUCCIANI: *One is a dialectician when one thinks a totality.*

SARTRE: That's right, a totality with lots of contradictory relationships within the whole and an interconnection of the whole that comes from the shifting of all these particular contradictions. If one has a thought that contains an opposition between two terms and a third element that goes beyond them both, it is an ordinary thought of which the dialectic has indeed taken advantage but which is non-dialectical for most people who use it. People do this all the time.

GRUENHECK: *Cumming says that the synthesis must be the inert because, once synthesized, a thing becomes a product. His idea of the dialectic is, I believe, one of movement, of continual displacement without synthesis.*

SARTRE: That is one conception.

GRUENHECK: *Do you think that syntheses exist?*

SARTRE: Yes—at least partial syntheses. I demonstrated that in the *Critique of Dialectical Reason.*

GRUENHECK: *You would reject an absolute synthesis, I suppose?*

SARTRE: Absolute, yes. But a synthesis of a historical period, for example, no. Our time is its own synthesis with itself. That is what I would have explained in the second volume of the *Critique*. Certainly one must go beyond the type of synthesis that was available to me in the first volume in order to arrive at syntheses touching oneself and others. We can, at every moment, each one of us, make syntheses. For example, I can make a synthesis of you three and, in some way, place myself in it, and you can do the same thing. But these syntheses are not at all on the same level as the synthesis of the whole, and one person alone can never accomplish that. If there were six of us, we could start over. But if there were a thousand of us, it would no longer have much meaning. Only individuals can take several individuals to make a group but not the totality, since they would have to place themselves within it. It's therefore necessary to look for another way of conceiving these latter syntheses. That is what I tried to do when I was working on the second volume of the *Critique,* but it was not finished.

PUCCIANI: *In* Being and Nothingness, *however, you say that consciousness is synthesis.*

SARTRE: Yes, of course. But it is the consciousness of everyone that is the synthesis of what he sees. I am synthesis in relation to everything I see, in relation to you three, but to you three in your relation to me. But I am not a synthesis of what happens in the street that I do not see. [*At this moment in the interview, there is a wail of sirens from the street.*] Since I believe only in individual consciousness and not in a collective consciousness, it is impossible for me to provide, just like that, a collective consciousness as historical synthesis.

PUCCIANI: *That would be providing what one wished to find.*
SARTRE: Obviously.

# The End of Marxism

RYBALKA: *You have defined the* Critique of Dialectical Reason *as a work opposed to the Communists and yet endeavoring to be Marxist.*

SARTRE: Opposed to the Communists, certainly. But Marxist is a word that I used a bit lightly then. At that time I considered the *Critique* to be Marxist. I was convinced of it. But I've changed my mind since then. Today I think that, in certain areas, the *Critique* is close to Marxism, but it is *not* a Marxist work.

RYBALKA: *In* Search for a Method *you differentiate between ideology and philosophy, and that is a distinction which bothers people.*

SARTRE: That is because they all want to be philosophers! I would still maintain the distinction, but the problem is very complex. Ideology is not a constituted, meditated, and reflected philosophy. It is an ensemble of ideas which underlies alienated acts and reflects them, which is never completely expressed and articulated, but which appears in the ideas of a given historical time or society. Ideologies represent powers and are active. Philosophies are formed in opposition to ideologies, although they reflect them to a certain extent while at the same time criticizing them and going beyond them. Let us note that, at the present time, ideology exists even in those who declare that ideology must be brought to an end.

PUCCIANI: *I myself was bothered by your distinction. I saw the existentialism of the* Critique *as an attempt at synthesizing Marxism and going beyond it, whereas you said that existentialism was only an enclave of Marxism.*
SARTRE: Yes, but that was my mistake. It cannot be an enclave, because of my idea of freedom, and therefore it is ultimately a separate philosophy.
I do not at all think that ultimately this philosophy is Marxist. It cannot ignore Marxism; it is linked to it, just as some philosophies are linked to others without, however, being contained by them. But now I do not consider it at all a Marxist philosophy.

RYBALKA: *Then what are the elements that you retain of Marxism?*
SARTRE: The notion of surplus value, the notion of class—all of that reworked, however, because the working class was never defined by Marx or the Marxists. It is necessary to re-examine these notions, but they remain valid in any case as elements of research.

RYBALKA: *And today you no longer consider yourself a Marxist?*
SARTRE: No. I think, by the way, that we are witnessing the end of Marxism and that in the next hundred years Marxism will no longer take the form in which we know it.

RYBALKA: *Theoretical Marxism, or Marxism as it has been applied?*
SARTRE: Marxism as it has been applied, but it was also applied as theoretical Marxism. Since Marx, Marxism has existed, living a certain life and at the same time growing old. We are now in the period in which old age moves toward death. Which does not mean that the main notions of Marxism

will disappear; on the contrary, they will be taken up again . . . but there are too many difficulties in preserving the Marxism of today.

RYBALKA: *And what are those difficulties?*
SARTRE: I would simply say that the analysis of national and international capitalism in 1848 has little to do with the capitalism of today. A multinational company cannot be explained in the Marxist terms of 1848. A new notion has to be introduced here, one which Marx did not foresee and which therefore is not Marxist in the simple sense of the word.

PUCCIANI: *And the* Critique *therefore already goes beyond Marxism?*
SARTRE: In any case, it is not on the level where it was placed, that of a simple interpretation of Marxism with a few alterations here and there. It is not opposed to Marxism. It's really non-Marxist.

PUCCIANI: *You go beyond Marxism with the idea of seriality, of the practico-inert, through new ideas that have never been used.*
SARTRE: Those are notions that seem to me to have come out of Marxism, but which are different from it.

RYBALKA: *And what would be this philosophy of freedom that is being born today?*
SARTRE: It's a philosophy that would be on the same level as Marxism, a mixture of theory and practice—a philosophy in which theory serves practice, but which takes as its starting point the freedom that seems to me to be missing in Marxist thought.

RYBALKA: *In recent interviews, you seem to have accepted the term 'libertarian socialism'.*
SARTRE: It's an anarchist term, and I keep it because I like to recall the somewhat anarchist origins of my thought.

RYBALKA: *You once said to me: "I have always been an anarchist," and you declared to Contat: "Through philosophy I discovered the anarchist in me."*
SARTRE: That is a bit hasty; but I have always been in agreement with the anarchists, who are the only ones to have conceived of a whole man to be developed through social action and whose chief characteristic is freedom. On the other hand, obviously, as political figures the anarchists are somewhat simple.

RYBALKA: *On the theoretical level as well, perhaps?*
SARTRE: Yes, provided that one considers only the theory and deliberately leaves aside some of their intuitions which are very good, specifically those on freedom and the whole man. Sometimes those intuitions have been realized: they lived in common, they formed communal societies, for example, in Corsica around 1910.

RYBALKA: *Have you been interested recently in those communities?*
SARTRE: Yes, I read that in the book on the anarchists by Maitron.

RYBALKA: *In your television programs are you planning to adopt an anarchist view of history?*
SARTRE: Anarchist, no; but we will talk about anarchism.

RYBALKA: *You have not said much about what socialism could be, and I surmise you have reproached yourself for having insufficiently outlined socialist society.*
SARTRE: That is correct, but I do not reproach myself severely, because it is not up to people now to do so. We can indicate the basis and the principles, but we cannot think through such an alteration of society. We know in what direction we are going, the direction of the freedom that must be given to men . . .

RYBALKA: *If you had to choose today between two labels, that of Marxist or that of existentialist; which would you prefer?*
SARTRE: That of existentialist. That's what I just told you.

RYBALKA: *Wouldn't you prefer another term that would better render your position?*
SARTRE: No, because I didn't look for it. I was called an existentialist and I took on the name, but I didn't give it to myself.

# Lived Experience

RYBALKA: *The notion of lived experience [vécu] that you use in the* Flaubert *remains rather vague and you have not yet theorized it . . .*
SARTRE: I think that would have come, little by little, in the volume on *Madame Bovary*. But it is difficult to go very far in this area, because it

means really 'breaking into' the other. I can talk about *my* lived experience, but only riskily can I reconstitute yours.

PUCCIANI: *Wouldn't a theory of lived experience require you to reconsider the notion of consciousness? Because lived experience seems at times to be a reply to the Freudian unconscious.*

SARTRE: It is to some degree a reply to the Freudian unconscious, a way of showing that a host of complex intentions that Freud placed in the unconscious can be found in lived experience. That is certainly part of it. It is also the fact that we constantly have in ourselves states that we can understand if we take time, but that we do not understand. These states are full of richness, but they do not yield it. They come and go, there is nothing mysterious about them, nothing unconscious. It's simply that they retain and contain in themselves a richness that is undeveloped, that one understands but does not develop.

PUCCIANI: *That is "understanding without understanding," as you say in the* Flaubert?

SARTRE: Exactly. Lived experience is just that.

PUCCIANI: *It is thus a question of a reflection that is pushed to genuine understanding and even farther, to become knowledge.*

SARTRE: Yes, *if* that happens.

PUCCIANI: If *that happens?*

SARTRE: Because with most people that does not happen. And then there are those who try to do it and fail, and those who sometimes succeed.

PUCCIANI: *Would this change the theory of consciousness as it is formulated in* Being and Nothingness? *For example, wouldn't lived experience call into question the perfect translucidity of consciousness?*

SARTRE: I don't think so. In theory, it would not have any effect on it. In practice, obviously, the states that are 'understood without being understood' are not . . .

PUCCIANI: *Wouldn't lived experience introduce opacity into consciousness?*

SARTRE: No, for to be 'understood without being understood' assumes that the object is not a pathos, is not something thick and opaque, but is grasped. Only we do not have the words, the divisions, that would enable us to describe all the richness that this object has. If you like, it is a compression of consciousness. What would remain to be done would be to create centers, subdivisions and so forth, that would make the object a whole that is completely clear to the other. In the end, to be understood without being understood is to be understood by me without being able to make it understood by the other.

PUCCIANI: *Wouldn't that be that switching of the position of consciousness that goes from perception to imagination? There are two different theses and we retain in us the product of these two theses.*
SARTRE: Exactly. Frequently even the understanding will be achieved in a different language from that of 'understanding without understanding'.

PUCCIANI: *Thus, in some sense, lived experience would be a kind of imaginary within us.*
SARTRE: Exactly.

PUCCIANI: *Then a theory of forgetting would also be necessary?*
SARTRE: That has often tormented me, but I did not do it. Why? Because I did not know *how* to do it. There are plenty of problems pestering me that I have not resolved.

PUCCIANI: *Isn't forgetting an annihilation?*
SARTRE: No, because one can recall things that one has forgotten. There is perhaps a movement toward annihilation, but with many degrees before annihilation.

RYBALKA: *Are there other problems, like the one of forgetting, that you have not treated?*
SARTRE: Social problems . . .

RYBALKA: *Do you consider that your work is finished?*
SARTRE: Yes. You've come at the right time! You have found a dead man who isn't dead!

RYBALKA: *That's going too far . . .*
SARTRE: Listen, I can no longer write and there are things that one cannot do at age seventy. But I can do television programs, for example.

RYBALKA: *By the way, how are those programs working out?*

SARTRE: I don't know. As you know, the programs are an attempt to outline the history of France from my birth to my seventy years of age. Originally, they were to be placed under the category of 'documentaries'. But I find the word very unsatisfactory, because a life within seventy years of history is not a document. Now the name 'Drama' has been proposed to me, and the directors of the program and I have accepted it, for that will make it possible to get things moving. Television has more money for dramatic programs and, moreover, the name allows for the imaginary side involved in reconstructing seventy years of history.[4]

RYBALKA: *Many people who write about you say that your thought is essential but that you have not always pursued your intuitions and you have left obscurities and difficulties.*

SARTRE: That's true; but I think it is an extremely severe and even very partial view of things to imagine that a man is obliged to pursue any idea he has launched down to its smallest details. That was not my work; that was not my role. What I wanted to do was to discuss as many problems as possible starting from ontology.

RYBALKA: *That is what makes your work open-ended . . .*

SARTRE: Yes, open-ended, absolutely open-ended. That is one of the reasons why I said that anyone could continue it on any level, that anyone could, for example, finish *Flaubert*.

RYBALKA: *On the other hand, in many people, especially the young, there is an adherence to your thought that leads to doing exactly what you have done, in the same context and in your own language . . .*

PUCCIANI: *There is a spell cast by your thought. It takes a long time to free oneself from it. If one wishes this thought to be an instrument, one must get perspective on it at a distance.*

SARTRE: You are right.

PUCCIANI: *But before getting to that point; one is under its spell.*

SARTRE: Yes. That is what I wanted. [*Laughter*]

---

4. Having concluded that the working conditions proposed to him were unacceptable, Sartre finally abandoned this TV project at the end of September 1975.

# Never a Marxist

GRUENHECK: *Listening to you talk, I have the impression that you continue to reflect as a phenomenologist. Have you ever left phenomenology?*

SARTRE: Never. I continue to think in those terms. I have never thought as a Marxist, not even in the *Critique of Dialectical Reason*.

PUCCIANI: *Would it be fair to say that Marx provided you with ideas that you have treated in your own way?*

SARTRE: If you like, yes. At one time I even thought that one could not do without some of Marx's ideas, that it was absolutely necessary to go through Marxism in order to go farther. But now I no longer think that altogether.

PUCCIANI: *You have not by-passed Marx; you have gone right through.*

SARTRE: Yes, that's right.

PUCCIANI: *I see many people today trying to go beyond Sartre without going through Sartre's thought.*

SARTRE: Ha-ha!

RYBALKA: *What is interesting is to grasp to what extent your thought is the thought of a historical time, how you are contemporaneous. In other words, how have you 'programmed' yourself in relation to the philosophical thought of the time?*

SARTRE: That's a difficult question. *Being and Nothingness* was phenomenology and existentialism . . . existentialism is the wrong word . . . let us say the philosophy of Heidegger and Husserl. I took from them what appeared to me to be true and I tried to develop my own ideas from there. For example, I took Husserl for a realist, which he is not; that is a philosophical error. He is much closer to Kant.

RYBALKA: *In short, you took a pseudo-Husserl as Merleau-Ponty took from you a pseudo-Sartre?*

SARTRE: That's right.

RYBALKA: *At the present time, Marxism is being contested by some. Are you in sympathy with them?*

SARTRE:  That depends. I am in sympathy with the ones called 'les Maos', the militants of the Proletarian Left with whom I directed *The People's Cause*. They were Marxists in the beginning, but they have done what I did: they are not Marxists any longer, or they are much less so than before. Pierre Victor, for example, with whom I am working on these television programs, is no longer a Marxist, or at least he envisions the end of Marxism.

RYBALKA:  *Some critics attempt to find in you a Maoist philosopher.*
SARTRE:  That is absurd. I am not a Maoist. That is meaningless, by the way. When I was writing *Being and Nothingness*, Mao was seldom talked about.

    For some groups it had a meaning, though very vague: they imagined certain forms of socialist life such as had been seen or believed to have been seen in China, and they wanted to apply them here. These groups were Maoist when Mao's face had not yet appeared on the front page of *The People's Cause*; they ceased to be when Mao's face did appear.

RYBALKA:  *It always seemed to me that in French Maoists there was ten percent Mao and ninety percent something else that is not very easy to define.*
SARTRE:  Difficult to define but interesting. That is what we tried to do in *We're Right to Revolt*.

RYBALKA:  *Some people who recently returned from Portugal told me that your work is widely read there, that it is being read in buses and even sold in dairy shops.*
SARTRE:  Sartre next to jars of cream—that's very good. I just spent Easter vacation in Portugal, and a translation of *We're Right to Revolt* has recently been published there.

PUCCIANI:  *And what do you think of the revolution that has taken place there?*
SARTRE:  What is interesting is not so much the military that has taken power or the political parties, but rather the people, that is, the creativity of the masses. They have self-management there; groups create entire hospitals by occupying buildings and even palaces and mobilizing the whole district. They are taking action with the support of the population and are forming a people's power.

PUCCIANI: *Were you surprised by the relative defeat of the French Communist Party in the April elections?*

SARTRE: No, it was expected. The Communist Party is powerful because it works in connection with the military and controls the press and the television. It is opposed to the socialists and it is not well liked among the people.

RYBALKA: *Is the socialist party really playing into the hands of the right wing?*

SARTRE: It is the old Social-Democrat party. One cannot have sympathy with it.

RYBALKA: *Do you think this third power, the people's power, that you spoke of in your interview in* Libération, *is truly important?*

SARTRE: It exists and it is very interesting. It is not a party but rather people who are reacting to their own difficulties and problems in a socialist manner.

RYBALKA: *Do you foresee this sort of people's power in France?*

SARTRE: Yes, but for the moment we have suffered a setback. It is such a people's power that we would like to encourage through the television programs.

RYBALKA: *One critic of your work has been struck by the status you give to the historical neurosis of the nineteenth century in Volume 3 of* Flaubert. *He considers it a discovery and would like to know what is the status of this inventive power. At what moment does a discovery take place? For example, when did the idea of programmation or that of historical neurosis occur to you?*

SARTRE: I don't know. It comes in the course of my reflections, but I cannot say at what moment it appears.

RYBALKA: *Some of us wonder how you invent hypotheses.*

SARTRE: That we do not know. It comes, we cannot say how.

RYBALKA: *Is it the text that gives you a thesis of interpretation and leads you to be ideologically creative? Another idea is that today we can keep philosophy from being closed by the use of texts.*

SARTRE: That is correct. I agree on that score.

RYBALKA: *Is that the reason you chose to make your* Flaubert *an example of concrete philosophy?*

SARTRE: Yes. But we do not know how ideas arise. How a specific idea came to me, I no longer know.

# Unfinished Works

RYBALKA: *Many critics raise a problem concerning the works that you did not complete. What is your position now concerning those works?*

SARTRE: I did finish some works. But there are many that I will not finish: *Being and Nothingness*, which was to include an ethical sequel that will never be done, at least not in that form; the novel *Roads to Freedom*, the *Critique of Dialectical Reason, Flaubert.*

*Roads to Freedom*,[5] for example, has been completely forgotten. I do not attach great importance to it now; I don't think it was good.

RYBALKA: *Didn't you take the project for the novel up again in other forms in* Flaubert, *insofar as you wanted to make it a true novel? Wasn't there some sort of transfer there?*

SARTRE: Not at all. Volume 4 of *Roads to Freedom* was not a true novel; it was a false novel that contained many imaginary or false circumstances unrelated to *Flaubert*. When I thought of the true novel it was rather in the sense that it was impossible to write an untrue novel and that it was necessary to raise questions about characters that had existed.

RYBALKA: *As regards the incomplete works, do you have a feeling of regret or of necessity?*

SARTRE: Necessity. It stopped there. I feel perhaps some regret about the *Critique of Dialectical Reason*, which I could have finished. But it did not happen. Well, that's too bad.

RYBALKA: *In many cases, the manuscripts still remain . . .*

SARTRE: . . . which convey what might have been a continuation . . .

---

5.  This work is really a projected series of four novels, of which three were published and were very popular: *The Age of Reason* (1945), *The Reprieve* (1947), and *Iron in the Soul* (1949).

RYBALKA: *... and that you are not particularly anxious to see published for the moment, I believe?*
SARTRE: It is not worth the trouble. If it amuses people after my death . . . [*Laughter*].

RYBALKA: *And yet, Michel Contat and I do plan to publish the manuscripts dealing with the novels.*
SARTRE: I don't care. Or rather, it no longer interests me.

RYBALKA: *Publishing the philosophical manuscripts seems to me to be somewhat urgent: those concerning the* Ethics, *the second volume of the* Critique, *Volume 4 of* Flaubert, *and so on. In general, they are highly valuable. Why not consider that they, too, are part of the domain of the Other?*
SARTRE: They can be published later.

# Concerning Animals

RYBALKA: *There's a question that comes up several times and is perhaps best put by Robert Champigny, who accuses you of human racism, of anthropomania. What bothers him about your famous statement in* The Communists and Peace, *"An anti-Communist is a dog," is not the political idea expressed . . .*
SARTRE: It's the dog?

RYBALKA: *It's the dog. [Laughter]*
SARTRE: Really, I don't think one can conclude from that statement that I have something against dogs. I used a quite ordinary expression there.

RYBALKA: *Champigny wrote a whole book to reproach you for that.*
SARTRE: A whole book! That's a lot.

RYBALKA: *He is not the only one who raises the problem.*
SARTRE: This is the first time I have heard about it.

RYBALKA: *Alluding to the passage in* The Family Idiot, *where you describe the dog, he notices a certain evolution. From a general standpoint, it raises the problem of consciousness.*
SARTRE: I think animals have consciousness. In fact, I have always thought so. There is no evolution in that.

RYBALKA:  *What status would their consciousness have in relation to man?*

SARTRE:  That is an extremely difficult problem, and I would not know how to answer. I know that animals have consciousness, because I can understand their attitude only if I admit a consciousness. What is their consciousness? What is a consciousness that has no language? I have no idea. Perhaps we will be able to determine that later on, but more will have to be known about consciousness.

PUCCIANI:  *All the same, animals do have a kind of language, not an articulated language, but the possibility of communicating in another way.*

SARTRE:  Certainly, but that still poses problems.

PUCCIANI:  *This question amuses me because my students are always asking me: Where are the animals in* Being and Nothingness?

SARTRE:  They are not in it, because I consider that what is said about animals in animal psychology is generally stupid or, in any case, absolutely unconnected to the conscious experiences that we have. Animal psychology has to be redone, but it is difficult to say on what foundations.

PUCCIANI:  *At the present time, very interesting research is being done in the United States on monkeys. They are being taught to type on a machine. They can think symbolically even though they cannot speak.*

RYBALKA:  *Do plants have consciousness?*

SARTRE:  I have absolutely no idea. I don't think so. I don't think that life and consciousness are synonymous. No, for me, consciousness exists where we notice it; and there are animals that do not have it, protozoa, for example. Consciousness appears in the animal kingdom at a certain moment: in men; surely also in monkeys. But how does it appear and what is it?

RYBALKA:  *There is a problem that is very bothersome to the Americans (who have a solid naturalist tradition), namely, ecology. Have you reflected on it?*

SARTRE:  No.

PUCCIANI:  *Some Americans have developed the idea that today the question of classes is completely secondary in relation to the question of the species: we live in Nature, which is the source of production and where the relations of production are less important.*

RYBALKA:  *One even uses the phrase 'Capitalism mystifies biology'.*

SARTRE: That does not appear to me to be serious thinking. The development of the human species has placed it in conditions that are no longer natural, but it nevertheless retains relations to Nature. The real problems of the human species today, the problems of class, capital, and so on, are problems that have no relation to Nature. They are posed by the human species in its historical movement, and that leaves Nature outside of them.

PUCCIANI: *I would agree, but what concerns these ecologists is that we are now in a situation in which we risk exhausting the resources of Nature, or of spoiling them completely. In several years there will be no more air for us to breathe.*

SARTRE: That is rather likely. In that case, there are two alternatives: the first is that as resources have been exhausted, we will have invented something else, which could happen; the other is that we will disappear, which could also happen. I never thought that the human species was infinite.

RYBALKA: *To the Americans, you are often the philosopher of anti-Nature.*

SARTRE: I am an anti-Nature philosopher, but only in certain respects. I know that in the beginning there was Nature, which directly influenced man. It is certain that primitive men had real relations with Nature, as orang-utans or ants do. This relation still exists, even today; but it is surmounted by other relations that are no longer material ones, or at least by relations in which Nature no longer plays the same role.

PUCCIANI: *The ecologists think that everything in Nature has been politicized and that a possible repercussion of this might affect the essential vitality of the human species.*

SARTRE: I think so too. It could end in the death of the species.

RYBALKA: *It seems to me, however, that ecology, as it is often advocated, is mystifying thought insofar as it does not bring in the class struggle and claims to be universal.*

SARTRE: Yes. It is in the domain of class struggle, in the domain of contemporary societies that one can see the real problems. The problems of Nature come in below these domains.

PUCCIANI: *Some who begin with ecology go on to assert that today everyone is proletarized, that there is only one universal class, which is the working class . . .*

SARTRE: That seems to me an exaggeration. For example, I do not consider us here to be proletarians. I have many relations with the proletariat and much sympathy for it, but I do not think the work we are doing here can be defined as the work of proletarians.

# Scarcity and Need

RYBALKA: *. . . The contention is nevertheless interesting, because it shows a whole new orientation of the former American New Left toward the ecology movement.*

*Let us go on to another question. Frequently your critics allege that you give too much importance to the notion of scarcity, that you accord it an overemphasized status compared with other elements of Marxist thought.*

SARTRE: It is not Marxist thought. Marx did not think that primitive man or feudal man lived under the rule of scarcity. He believed that they did not know how to use resources, but not that they were living in scarcity. This notion has been introduced into philosophy by others besides me, and I do not owe it to Marx. I consider that scarcity is the phenomenon in which we live. It is impossible to suppress it without changing the conditions of existence, of what is real, of intelligence . . . Even here, among ourselves, there is scarcity in our conversation: scarcity of ideas, scarcity of understanding. I may not understand your questions or may answer them badly—that, too, is scarcity.

PUCCIANI: *How is that? I don't understand.*

SARTRE: Well, a moment ago we were talking about ecology, about which I know practically nothing. There is therefore a certain scarcity in relation to ecological theory, scarcity in relation to me. The answers I gave, although I consider them to be true as regards the relation between Nature and capitalist man today—those answers are still scarce compared to the specific questions that an ecologist would ask me. There is scarcity on every level and from every point of view. You asked me a while ago how I came upon an idea. An idea is also a scarcity. Then how can such a scarcity appear in the midst of perceptions and imaginings . . . ? That question . . .

RYBALKA: *Is scarcity linked to desire, or to need?*

SARTRE: Sometimes to need, sometimes to desire. Inasmuch as a cause, any cause whatsoever, makes us need a certain substance or a certain object, that object is not given in the proportion that we need it: that is scarcity.

RYBALKA: *Doesn't scarcity thus tend to become an ontological category rather than an historical one? Oscar Wilde said, for example: "Wherever there is a demand, there is no supply."*

SARTRE: It is not an ontological notion, but neither is it simply a human notion or an empirical observation. It is drawn from the ontological side, but it is not ontological, because the human beings we are considering in the world are not to be studied only ontologically or on the level of particular abstract ideas, as some philosophies or particular ontologies do. They must be studied empirically as they are. And, on this level, one observes that a man is surrounded by scarcity, whether it be the toy that is not available to the child when he wants it or the food supplies that a human group demands and of which there is only a portion. In any case, there is a difference between supply and demand that arises from the way man is made, from the fact that man demands more, whereas the supply is limited.

RYBALKA: *We are clearly seeing today that the idea of abundance that was once current in the United States is a mystifier.*

SARTRE: Absolutely. Totally. We live in a world of scarcity, and from time to time we may imagine that we have found abundance by changing the nature of our desires. Not having what is necessary in one domain, we shift our desire to another. But it is all the same scarcity that lies at the origin of this conception.

PUCCIANI: *However, I always understood scarcity in the* Critique of Dialectical Reason *as a fact of social oppression.*

SARTRE: It is always a fact of social oppression. But there are other scarcities that arise solely from the relation of man's demand—a free demand, in no way imposed by someone else—to the quantity of what is given.

PUCCIANI: *But if there is an objective lack, is this also scarcity?*

SARTRE: Of course. In fact originally that is what scarcity was. Desire, will, the necessity to use such and such an object as a means, create a demand that may sometimes be unlimited, whereas the object in demand is limited in quantity in a territory or on the globe. Thus, for me, scarcity is a phenomenon of existence, a human phenomenon, and naturally the greatest scarcity is always the one based on social oppression. But scarcity is at the bottom of it. We create a field of scarcity around us.

PUCCIANI: *In the* Critique, *I thought need was the basic condition which after-ward gave rise to scarcity.*

SARTRE: Indeed, but need is not an oppression; it is a normal biological characteristic of the living creature, and he creates scarcity. In any case, the need of an animal or of primitive man for a certain object—for example, for food—does not make the object appear where he is. Thus, we must consider that the need is greater than the way in which the space surrounding us is constituted, which forces us to seek the object we lack elsewhere. As soon as this begins, there is struggle, the building of roads and a new construction of the field that surrounds us.

PUCCIANI: *Could one generalize and say that need is natural whereas scarcity is social?*

SARTRE: Need is natural, but that does not mean that the object of our desires is there. Scarcity is social to the extent that the desired object is scarce for a given society. But strictly speaking, scarcity is not social. Society comes after scarcity. The latter is an original phenomenon of the relation between man and Nature. Nature does not sufficiently contain the objects that man demands in order that man's life should not include either work, which is struggle against scarcity, or combat.

RYBALKA: *Do you see a possible end to scarcity?*

SARTRE: Not at the moment.

RYBALKA: *And what of the socialism we were talking about last time?*

SARTRE: It would not lead to the disappearance of scarcity. However, it is obvious that at that point ways of dealing with scarcity could be sought and found.

GRUENHECK: *When I study Heidegger with my students, they are often wary of him because of the position he took at one point in favor of Naziism in Germany, and they wonder if one can take a philosopher seriously who acts in such a way in the political sphere.*

SARTRE: In the case of Heidegger, I would not take him seriously; but I don't know if it is because of his character or because of his social action. And I don't know if one is the result of the other. I do not think that Heidegger's character, his way of entering into social action, trying not to compromise himself while at the same time giving certain assurances to the Nazis, justifies great confidence. It is not for his Naziism that I would reproach him, but rather for a lack of seriousness. His attitude showed a compliance with the regime in power in order to continue teaching his courses more than an awareness of any value that Naziism claimed to have.

PUCCIANI: *But why wouldn't you reproach him for his Naziism?*

SARTRE: I'm quite willing to reproach him for that. It wouldn't bother me in the least. [*Laughter*] You know I am not that fond of Heidegger. What I have said is simply the impression I had when I saw him. Heidegger's political ideas were of no importance, and he was doing philosophy almost in opposition to politics. But perhaps I am mistaken. In any case he was wrong, very wrong to adhere to Naziism, even discreetly as he did. It is possible that Naziism was a philosophy or political theory in which he really believed. But I think not. And this neither brings me closer to nor separates me farther from his philosophy.

GRUENHECK: *Do you think that one can do philosophy without taking politics into account?*

SARTRE: In Descartes's time, perhaps, but today it is impossible to do philosophy without having a political attitude. Of course, this attitude will vary according to the philosophy; but it is impossible to avoid having one. Every philosopher is also a man and every man is political.

For a long time, philosophy was a kind of thought by which one tried to escape from the conditions of life, especially from those that created the obligation to be political. There was the man who was alive, who slept, who ate, who clothed himself, and this man was not taken into account by the philosopher. He studied other areas, from which politics was excluded. Today the concern of philosophers is the man who sleeps, eats, clothes himself, and so on. There is no other subject matter, and the philosopher is forced to have a political position, since politics develops at this level.

# Sartre Replies to Ivan Soll

PUCCIANI: *Here is Soll's first point: Sartre uses above all Freud's first topology and fails to take into account the second. In so doing, he distorts the Freudian model into an ego, a censor, and an id.*

SARTRE: I didn't know that that was called a topology, but I think I tried to take everything into account.

PUCCIANI: *Soll's second point: Sartre's thought is a kind of strategy—the word is mine, not Soll's—designed to save the theory of consciousness in opposition to the Freudian theory of the unconscious. Sartre maintains that consciousness is equivalent to psychic reality. He puts forth a theory of consciousness that requires a theory of mind.*

SARTRE: I never maintained that consciousness was equivalent to psychic reality. Indeed, I consider that consciousness is a psychic reality; but I do not consider that all psychic reality can be defined by consciousness. One has only to look at what I have written on the subject. There are plenty of facts that appear to consciousness that are not themselves consciousness. Consciousness is only consciousness *of* and the objects are outside consciousness and transcendent. Thus it is impossible to say that consciousness is the only reality.

PUCCIANI: *Third point: Sartre develops the theory of the pre-reflexive cogito in order to explain unconscious psychic processes. Thus consciousness becomes, according to Sartre, "the generic category of various psychic processes."*

SARTRE: To me that is meaningless. Consciousness is not a generic category.

PUCCIANI: *Fourth point. By consciousness, Sartre means any intentional psychic process. Judgment, desire, intention, emotion, and so forth are all conscious a priori; therefore there is no unconscious. That leaves the empirically known mental processes. How can they be explained? That would be the role of pre-reflexive consciousness or bad faith.*

SARTRE: Certainly, I explain a number of so-called unconscious states in that way.

PUCCIANI: *But, according to Soll, bad faith fails as a criterion for criticism of Freud, because Freud himself had abandoned the unconscious system in his second topology. And even in the first topology, the censor was not a lie to oneself, bad faith, conscious in order not to be conscious, the duper-duped, but simply duper or a duped pre-conscious. The Sartrean conditions for lying were fulfilled: it was a question of an interpersonal lie on an intrapsychic level.*

SARTRE: This comparison between Freud and me in this area seems to me absurd. I did not create the theory of bad faith in order to argue against

Freud, nor in connection with the works of Freud, but because it appeared to me to be true. Moreover, to talk about the lie told by the conscious to the unconscious is simply to reduce the nature of the lie to someone who knows the truth and conceals it and someone who does not know the truth and from whom it is concealed. This ordinary, commonplace conception of the lie is only partly true. There are persons who know the truth and from whom one conceals it nevertheless, and there are persons who conceal a truth they know. At this point, there is no longer liar and lied-to, but each is liar and lied-to at the same time. This conception is much more complex but also much more true.

Soll abolishes consciousness as I tried to define it, that is, precisely the liar/lied-to at the same time, which is to say, consciousness as relation to self. He turns this relation into a relation to others, and it is consequently impossible to keep it within consciousness.

PUCCIANI: *I noticed that none of the criticisms we are considering here seems to take into account the circuit of selfness, although this characterizes the consciousness that needs to be a consciousness in order to be consciousness, and which can then constitute itself as an ego. It is starting from the circuit of fundamental selfness that consciousness becomes a structure of being.*
SARTRE: Of course.

PUCCIANI: *Soll next attacks the pre-reflexive cogito: Sartre's chief argument is a true* reductio ad absurdum. *The notion that an unconscious consciousness would be absurd fails in face of the fact that such a consciousness exists. I am conscious of this table, but I am simultaneously unconscious of other objects that are not in my visual field. Here is a consciousness that is both conscious and unconscious, unless we specify that it concerns the same object. There are therefore unconscious intentional processes, and the thesis of the unconscious is not absurd. It is not contradictory to say that one desires something without being conscious of desiring.*
SARTRE: But the example he provides is absurd. I am indeed unconscious at this moment of the St. Lazare Station, which is not in my perceptual field. But if I am unconscious of it, it is not because of consciousness, it is because of my position in the perceptual field and in the existential field. I may be conscious of it tomorrow, which does not mean that it is unconscious and acting at this moment. I am not in relation to the St. Lazare Station. If I am, I am in some way conscious of it. If I am waiting for the moment when a taxi will drive me there, I am conscious of the

St. Lazare Station. But in the meantime, there is no relation to it and therefore I am not conscious of the St. Lazare Station.

PUCCIANI: *Soll continues. Sartre demonstrates his theory of the pre-reflexive cogito by an example, that of counting cigarettes. But this example is valid only in certain cases, whereas it must be shown to hold in all cases. Moreover, the example is badly formulated: Sartre gives it in the present tense, whereas it should have been done in the past tense, since it involves a memory. Therefore, there is no need here either for the pre-reflexive cogito or for a positional self-consciousness.*

SARTRE: I don't remember the example of the cigarettes.

PUCCIANI: *It is in* Being and Nothingness *where, taking twelve cigarettes, you explain how you have arrived at that number. Soll claims that you should have said, 'I was counting cigarettes' and not 'I am counting cigarettes', which falsifies the whole example.*

SARTRE: Indeed. It is now that I count them. Obviously, I should not have said, 'I have arrived at twelve' but instead, 'For the moment, I have counted four and there remains a group to be counted'. [*Laughter*]

PUCCIANI: *Next, Soll wonders if there are certain cases in which a non-positional self-consciousness would be required. In* The Transcendence of the Ego, *the object of reflexive consciousness contains the 'I'. The 'I' appears in every memory and is the universal possibility of reflecting in memory. Can one truly say that the object of reflexive consciousness contains the 'I'?*

SARTRE: Not necessarily. Reflexive consciousness contains the 'I' but outside itself; it manifests the 'I'.

PUCCIANI: *Then where does the 'I' come from?*

SARTRE: That's just the point: it is not there. There must be some confusion here between reflected consciousness and reflexive consciousness.

PUCCIANI: *Soll goes on: Why must the memory depend on previous self-consciousness? Cannot a simple awareness of an object leave memory traces? A non-thetic consciousness of self is not necessary to explain a non-thetic memory; if the 'I' that is attached to the memory is not present in original consciousness, one cannot explain how the 'I' enters the memory. The pre-reflexive cogito does not shed any light on the mechanism of memory.*

*How can a non-reflexive consciousness explain the fact of counting cig-*
*arettes—I would add, in the past—whereas I was counting them without*
*reflecting and my reply was a kind of memory? Haven't we an unconscious,*
*unrepressed process here, as Freud would call it, a pre-conscious or latent*
*process which can easily be brought to consciousness? This would avoid the*
*Sartrean paradox of a conscious memory before the act of remembering.*
*According to Freud, one can become conscious of something for the first*
*time in memory. His terminology is more natural.*

SARTRE: I am astonished. That is not what I said. One can criticize what I
said, but that is not what I said. For example, there is no ego in consciousness any more than there is an 'I'. In *Being and Nothingness* I firmly
insisted on the fact that the 'I' and the ego were part of the system of
objects, the system of things that are outside consciousness.

# Sartre Replies to Lee Brown and Alan Hausman

PUCCIANI: *The two positions [of Sartre and Freud, mentioned in the article by*
*Brown and Hausman] are in agreement in that the patient comes to know*
*what he did not know, and one could even make Freud admit, although in*
*a weak sense, that the patient knew it from the beginning.*

SARTRE: It is Freud who must decide on that, but I don't think that for him
the patient knew from the start; he knew it in some way, but he did not
know it consciously. Whereas, indeed, in my study of bad faith one
could say that he knew it from the beginning. The comparison is
forced.

PUCCIANI: *For Brown and Hausman, where Sartre speaks of a distinction*
*between knowledge and consciousness, Freud speaks of a distinction*
*between conscious and unconscious. It is a question of terminology.*

SARTRE: That is rather simple and facile. Yet it is true that, for me, the idea
of knowledge is given at the start, that it is a work performed on data
already existing for consciousness. There is a kind of original vision of
things that can be made known by working upon this content. However,
I do not see what could be said similarly for Freud.

PUCCIANI: *Brown and Hausman conclude, after a four-point argument, that Freud and Sartre leave us with the dilemma of a psyche that both knows and does not know its symptoms.*

SARTRE: Yes, but that is because in this case knowledge does not have the same meaning at the beginning as at the end. The psyche knowing its symptoms means one thing and the psyche not knowing its symptoms means something else. At the beginning, we have a kind of non-thetic, undeveloped, non-affirmative knowledge and we can, by certain methods, arrive at an affirmative, definite knowledge with distinctions, judgments, and so forth. These two kinds of knowledge have almost no relation to each other. It is going from the former to the latter that requires the greatest effort, both for the analyst and, very simply, for the individual who thinks.

You were asking me a moment ago how an idea comes to me. Well, it comes in the same way: at first one has a vague, completely unasserted idea and then one attempts to determine it, to create functions. At this point one attains an awareness that is already beyond the pure consciousness-feeling that one had in the beginning. At first one has something that I would call not knowledge but intuition, and in a sense knowledge is radically different from what is given by this original intuition. It clarifies things that were not clarified; it amplifies others; it tones down some that were more apparent in the beginning. It retains a certain relation to the original intuition, but it is something else. This is what has been misunderstood in this article, I believe.

# Sartre Replies to Amedeo Giorgi

GRUENHECK: *Amedeo Giorgi attempts to show that there exists in your work a systematic psychology, a metapsychology that radicalizes our understanding of psychology because it objectifies the psychic without transforming it into a thing. He wonders if the psychic could be characterized as 'being-in-tension' and if it would thus form a third category situated between the for-itself and the in-itself.*

SARTRE: That is more or less what I did, but I did not consider it of major importance. It is true that, on the whole, one can compare a feeling to the in-itself, but obviously it is something other than the in-itself of a table or of a chair.

GRUENHECK: *Going on to the problem of method, Giorgi distinguishes three approaches: first, the phenomenology of Husserl that would be a complete reduction (progressive method); then an empirical psychology in which there would be no reduction at all (regressive method); finally, your phenomenological psychology that would be partly a reduction and partly empirical, thus constituting a progressive-regressive method.*

SARTRE: That is a bit oversimplified, but I accept the idea of a progressive-regressive method.

GRUENHECK: *For a phenomenological psychology?*

SARTRE: Yes, and for all human endeavors. I talked about the progressive-regressive method in *The Problem of Method*, but perhaps that has nothing in common with this except the terms. I do not think my psychology is partly empirical in the sense he gives the word.

GRUENHECK: *Is your existential psychoanalysis a psychology?*

SARTRE: No. Quite frankly, I do not believe in the existence of psychology. I have not done it and I do not believe it exists. Even the little book that I wrote on the emotions is not psychology, because in it I am forced to return to the nature of consciousness to explain the simplest emotion. I consider that psychology does not exist except in the sense of the empirical psychology that one does in novels, for example, when we see a future assassin thinking about killing his victim an hour before he puts him to death.

# Sartre Replies to Risieri Frondizi

PUCCIANI: *To go on to another problem, Risieri Frondizi considers your ethical work to be above all negative, and feels that one ends up falling into moral indifference. It is a fact that freedom is a necessary but not sufficient condition for a moral human life of significance and creativity; the Sartrean man goes drifting off on the stream of freedom. How, asks Frondizi, can one avoid this moral indifference?*

SARTRE: I have never had an ethics of indifference. That is not what makes ethics difficult, but rather the concrete, political problems that have to be solved. As I already said in *Saint Genet*, I think that at present we are not in a position . . . society and knowledge are not such that we can rebuild an ethics that would have the same kind of validity as the one we have gone beyond. For example, we are unable to formulate an ethics on the Kantian level that would have the same validity as Kantian ethics. It cannot be done because the moral categories depend essentially on the structures of the society in which we live, and these structures are neither simple enough nor complex enough for us to create moral concepts. We are in a period without ethics, or, if you like, there are ethical theories but they are obsolete or they depend on each other.

RYBALKA: *Isn't it impossible to live morally today?*
SARTRE: Yes. It has not always been impossible, will not always be, but it is today. Whereas a 'morale' is necessary for man and such is still possible, there are periods in which it is unrealizable, because too many contradictions exist and ideas are too confused. We are in one of those periods.

RYBALKA: *What I would reproach Frondizi for is that, insofar as your writings are concerned, he stopped in 1949.*
SARTRE: But they all stop too soon. I think that a study of my philosophical thought should follow its evolution. But no, they don't do it. It's odd.

# Sartre Replies to Hazel Barnes

PUCCIANI: *For Hazel Barnes, your materialism, the materialism of the* Critique, *implicitly is or assumes a metaphysics of Nature. You were stopped by that question, but you yourself have said that it was not your affair. However, you have to explain the problem of man in his relation to Nature or risk exposing yourself to the same criticisms that you level against the Marxists. Barnes concludes with the following conjecture: If the expression 'dialectical materialism' had not been adopted by a purely Marxist context, shouldn't we have to qualify Sartrean materialism precisely as 'dialectical materialism'?*
SARTRE: To attempt to do so leaves me a little cold.

PUCCIANI: *Barnes considers that you assume a materialism without providing the metaphysical grounds for it. She also cites a passage of the* Critique *where you say: "We shall accept the idea that man is one material being among others and that as such he does not enjoy any privileged status. We shall not refuse a priori that a concrete dialectic of Nature may one day disclose itself."*

SARTRE: Yes, but by that I mean that, if it were disclosed, the dialectic of Nature would go from the strictly physical object to the animal and to man, thereby indicating the material sources of what has thus far been irreducible in man: for example, consciousness. A dialectic of Nature would have to account for that; but since this dialectic does not exist and since I do not intend to do it, the problem remains unchanged. If it exists, we will have accounted for the material aspect of the conscious phenomenon, the material aspect that is behind consciousness.

PUCCIANI: *Barnes takes four statements from your philosophy:*

*"Man loses himself as man in order that God may be born."*

*"Man loses himself so that the human thing may exist."*

*"The for-itself is the in-itself losing itself as in-itself in order to find itself as consciousness."*

*"All this happens as if the for-itself has a passion to lose itself so that the affirmation 'world' might come to the in-itself"*

*Does not the in-itself seem to have produced something, and do not these statements, especially the third and the fourth, have metaphysical implications? Does not the analysis of motion in* Being *and* Nothingness *as "pure disorder of Being," "the malady of Being," "the clue to the alteration of the for-itself" reflect a metaphysics?*

SARTRE: In all of those cases, yes. But it is not up to me to deal with it. I don't wish to deal with it. I do not have the necessary knowledge. I am not competent to do it. I can simply point out the various elements and the questions that would be raised.

PUCCIANI: *To conclude, Barnes raises four questions. Here is the first: What is the nature of the in-itself or of matter?*

SARTRE: Matter is not exclusively the in-itself precisely because, if one is a materialist, one considers that consciousness itself is part of matter. Therefore it is not the in-itself. Both the for-itself and the in-itself must be included in materialism.

PUCCIANI: *In the* Critique, *consciousness belongs to matter.*

SARTRE: Exactly, but in the question that was asked it does not.

PUCCIANI: *What must be the being of matter if this being is capable of giving rise to a being that nihilates it, that is free of it, but without ceasing to be matter?*

SARTRE: That is true in a sense, but not quite in those terms.

PUCCIANI: *Sartre admits that Nature could conceal a kind of dialectic. Then how can the in-itself be simple plenitude?*

SARTRE: But Nature is not exclusively the in-itself. A plant that is growing is no longer altogether in-itself. It is more complex. It is alive.

PUCCIANI: *To what extent is it necessary to identify in-itself and matter?*

SARTRE: The in-itself is one kind of matter. But a man cannot be reduced to the in-itself precisely because he is conscious, and consciousness has been defined as a for-itself. That seems clear to me.

RYBALKA: *Barnes also asks what the relations are between consciousness and the brain and reasoning.*

SARTRE: That is a problem I studied for several years at the time of *Being and Nothingness* and afterward. I tried to deal with it, but I did not finish it. I was not interested in doing a study on the relations of consciousness and the brain, because I first wanted to define consciousness. That is enough for one man's lifetime. I wished to define it as it presents itself to us, for you, for me. In so doing, I wanted to posit a definite object which others would then have to try to explain within a materialist system, that is, to study its relation to the brain.

More generally, what I have noticed in the articles you are summarizing is that there is one thing the authors do not recognize: one chooses a kind of work and one does it. One can do certain things somewhat alongside, but one will not go into domains that are not among those chosen at the outset. One can try to show how they are related to the domain one is studying, but one does not study them in themselves.

RYBALKA: *Indeed, there are quite a few articles that lose sight of the overall view of your work, and they represent the work of specialists. Someone who does psychology, for example, would like to draw you into his domain and will find inadequacies that concern him rather than you.*

PUCCIANI: *In my own contribution I emphasize that, in your philosophy, it has always been a question of the priority of problems.*

SARTRE: Absolutely.

PUCCIANI: *Very often in reading these critical essays, I have the impression that they are telling you it would have been better had you begun with the Flaubert.*

SARTRE: That's childish. One does not begin with what one wishes.

# Sartre Replies to Charles Tenney

GRUENHECK: *In his essay on esthetics, Professor Tenney raises a question that I find interesting: for Sartre, the ontology of freedom seems to have been replaced by a philosophy of* engagement *that places heavy sociopolitical obligations on the artist. Does the artist thereby lose his privilege of free creation?*

SARTRE: I do not consider that there has been such a shift from freedom to *engagement.* I still speak of freedom, and the *engagement,* if there is one, is the result of freedom. On this issue I have not changed since *Being and Nothingness.* Consequently, I do not understand the question.

GRUENHECK: *Tenney is speaking of socialist art or revolutionary art as it is practiced in socialist countries.*

SARTRE: I never believed in that kind of art. For example, I do not at all believe in literature as it is viewed by the writers in Moscow. I hope the author does not see anything like that in my esthetics, for he would be very much mistaken.

GRUENHECK: *Tenney would like to know if in general, sociopolitical responsibilities do not infringe upon the freedom of the artist.*

SARTRE: No. According to my view, responsibility necessarily arises from freedom. I can conceive of a responsibility only in someone who is free. If he is not, if he is constrained or forced to accept a responsibility, that responsibility is worthless. The only responsibility that counts is the one that is freely assumed. Therefore, I do not see what is interesting in his question. He begins by thinking that I have changed—and that is his point of view, not mine—and he asks me if, starting from this change, I can say whether engagement infringes on freedom. He is the one who is making this distinction, not I. Therefore, I cannot answer. I maintain my principles, and in any case my esthetics, if there is one, stems from the idea of freedom and not from the idea of *engagement,* which is a by-product of freedom, a necessary by-product.

PUCCIANI: *In his article, Tenney says, by the way, that the ontology of Sartre has changed.*

SARTRE: No, it has not changed. *Being and Nothingness* deals with ontology, not the *Critique of Dialectical Reason.*

PUCCIANI: *He speaks of an ontology that has been sapped, thinned out, and is no longer holding together because its back has been broken.*

SARTRE: That must be my second ontology. I don't believe that I broke the back of the first. [*Laughter*]

PUCCIANI: *And then he discusses Sartrean esthetics without mentioning either the analogon or the real center of irrealization.*

SARTRE: Then what does he talk about?

GRUENHECK: *He lists six elements that compose your esthetics . . .*

*Sartre's esthetics must be measured against philosophies that are productive and comprehensive, not reductive and niggling.*

*The Sartrean esthetic tends to repudiate the traditional esthetics of representative objects, that is, the imitation of Nature in classical, romantic, and realistic works of art. It also rejects most official or 'museum' art.*

*The Sartrean esthetic tends to embrace an art that is open, not closed; dynamic, not static; suggestive, not fixed.*

*But presumably the Sartrean esthetic has never been formalized. It must be inferred from statements scattered throughout his works, as well as from certain features of his total philosophy.*

*The chief components of an esthetics drawn from Sartre's total philosophy would appear to be:*

*1. The* situation, *that is, the place, historical time, environmental instrumentalities, fellow humans, and ultimate debility that must be expected and surpassed if I am to create art.*

*2. The* project, *that is, my choice of being and my leap ahead into the realm of possibles. Art always begins as a project or in a project.*

*3. The use of* bracketing, *the Husserlian abstention. This is especially relevant to esthetics, because in order to enter the realm of art I must eliminate the natural view of things. Phenomenological brackets make possible the detachment and autonomy of imagined objects.*

*4. The* imagined object, *which derives from both the plenum of being and the nothingness of images. It is in these terms that I must define and create a work of art.*

5. The freedom *to transcend situations and to activate projects that makes possible all my creative work—notably my work in the arts.*

6. The beautiful, *which is the chief value of art. As the* in-itself-for-itself, *beauty is a golden impossibility, but art can come close to realizing it in* imagined objects, *because these extend elements of the real into the imaginary. The 'correspondences' between the objective and the subjective provide* symbols, *by means of which I can place the beauty of a work of art in a bracketed totality.*

SARTRE: Those ideas are not mine. I think that I would write my esthetics better than he. [*Laughter*]

GRUENHECK: *I think that is exactly what he would like to provoke.*

PUCCIANI: *Tenney goes on to say: It is sad that Sartre seems to be losing interest in esthetics.*

SARTRE: But I am not losing interest in it. That is the third thing he has decided on his own.

RYBALKA: *However, this article, like many others, is helpful inasmuch as it is characteristic of the things that are said about you and it functions as a catalogue of commonly accepted ideas. Since we are going on to Merleau-Ponty, I might interject that perhaps many of these authors are doing pseudo-Sartrism.*

SARTRE: That's right.

# Sartre Replies to Monika Langer

PUCCIANI: *Monika Langer's article on Sartre and Merleau-Ponty develops the following thesis: Merleau-Ponty, in attacking the philosophy of Sartre, actually turned it into a pseudo-Sartrism, as Simone de Beauvoir has shown. Yet, had he examined Sartre's philosophy in the light of his own and especially of the notion of 'interworld' (which he calls "flesh" and which is situated between pure transcendence and inert matter), Merleau-Ponty would have discovered a genuine Sartrism, in perfect conformity with his own philosophy, for, at least from Langer's point of view, there is a fundamental agreement between the two positions. The positive significance of the flesh for Sartre appears in his analyses of sexuality. There would thus be an in-itself, an interworld (that is, an intersubjectivity), and a for-itself. Can one consider that there is an interworld in your philosophy?*

SARTRE: I admit neither that I have the same philosophy as Merleau-Ponty nor that there is this element of interworld.

GRUENHECK: *Is it a question of a mere misunderstanding, or is there a fundamental incompatibility between your philosophy and that of Merleau-Ponty?*

SARTRE: I believe that there is a fundamental incompatibility, because behind his analyses Merleau-Ponty is always referring to a kind of being for which he invokes Heidegger and which I consider to be absolutely invalid. The entire ontology that emerges from the philosophy of Merleau-Ponty is distinct from mine. It is much more a continuum than mine. I am not much of a continuist; the in-itself, the for-itself, and the intermediary forms that we talked about a moment ago-that is enough for me. For Merleau-Ponty, there is a relation to being that is very different, a relation in the very depths of oneself. I spoke about that in my article 'Merleau-Ponty vivant'.

RYBALKA: *There are two versions of that article. Why did you abandon the first?*

SARTRE: Because it was neither well thought out nor well written. Simone de Beauvoir urged me to abandon it. So I said the same thing again, but a little better.

RYBALKA: *Was this difference between you and Merleau-Ponty obvious from the beginning of your relationship?*

SARTRE: I think we always felt it. We were starting from the same philosophy, namely, Husserl and Heidegger. But he did not draw the same conclusions from it that I did. It is impossible for me to get my bearings in the philosophy of perception. That is something completely different.

PUCCIANI: *Is not the major difference between the two of you that concern for ontology which we talked about last time?*

SARTRE: Yes. Merleau-Ponty does not do ontology, but his reflections lead to an obscure ontology, a little like that of Heidegger.

PUCCIANI: *I would like to come back to a question that has already been asked. How did you come to decide that the problem of ontology was fundamental, since that is rather unusual among twentieth-century thinkers?*

SARTRE: In spite of everything, I think it grew out of the few ideas on realism that I had in mind, although not very clearly, when I went to Berlin and read Husserl. I spent a year reading Husserl and wrote that article on the transcendence of the ego in which I indicated rather emphatically the necessity of an ontology. Yes, it started from the distinction between some vague, personal ideas—to which I have always remained faithful, as a matter of fact—and the thought of Husserl.

RYBALKA: *To come back to Monika Langer, she says that for you, "consciousness is engulfed in a body which is itself engulfed in a world."*
SARTRE: That is beautiful; but consciousness is not engulfed in a body nor is the body engulfed in the world.

RYBALKA: *She also says: "human being in the world and of the world . . ."*
SARTRE: Human being is of the world for the other but not for himself. He is in the world, yes, and he can also withdraw at a certain moment from his place, from his situation, although his only true thoughts are his thoughts in situation. That is baroque!

RYBALKA: *Langer specifically says that the separation of consciousness does not necessarily imply hostility.*
SARTRE: In any case, the separation exists, and I do not see any reason to speak of intersubjectivity once subjectivities are separated. Intersubjectivity assumes a communion that almost reaches a kind of identification, in any case a unity. It designates a subjectivity that is made up of all subjectivities and it thus assumes each subjectivity in relation to the others—at once separated in the same way and united in another. I see the separation but I do not see the union.

# Sartre Replies to Charles Scott

SARTRE: Obviously one can compare anyone to anyone. One can compare me to Heidegger, although I think that we are too far apart for a comparison to be made.
GRUENHECK: *Would you accept the definition of ontology proposed by Charles Scott? Ontology is a descriptive interpretation of things that enables us to see at a distance the conditions necessary for human fulfillment.*

SARTRE:  No, I would dissociate myself from all that. Ontology is the study of the various forms of being—nothing else.

GRUENHECK:  *Is it done for a particular purpose?*
SARTRE:  It is for the purpose of defining, of knowing what being is. It is obviously for the purpose of reconstituting the edifice of knowledge by basing it on the knowledge of being.

RYBALKA:  *The word* fulfillment *is not exactly part of your vocabulary.*
PUCCIANI:  *This author sees ontology as a kind of moral edification; ontology should give us a rule of life and help us to live better . . .*
RYBALKA:  *To overcome scarcity through ontology, that wouldn't be bad!*
SARTRE:  That is incredible. If ontology were able to show that man would be better off committing suicide, that would not be giving us a moral viewpoint: we would have to take a revolver and shoot ourselves in the head. Ontology is not done so that we can use it for a time and then move on to something else.

# Sartre Replies to Oreste Pucciani

RYBALKA:  *Inasmuch as time is running out, we should ask Oreste Pucciani to tell us about his own critical essay.*
SARTRE:  I was just about to ask him.
PUCCIANI:  *My thesis is that, from an early age, Flaubert represented for you the problem of art. . . .*
   *I myself floundered in the unreal for years and I was struck by the fact that, at a very young age and despite your neurosis, you grasped the problem of the real. From then on, there was a kind of inoculation by Flaubert that had a decided effect on your own acculturation . . .*
SARTRE:  It was not Flaubert that provided my acculturation, because at the time I read many things—Corneille, et cetera. Culture was not especially Flaubert, who, on the contrary, was an aborted attempt at reading, since ultimately I did not read him all the way through to the end. I stumbled onto a book that was too adult for me and I didn't understand it very well.

RYBALKA:  *In this connection, to what extent do the references to Flaubert you make in* Words *derive from your preoccupation with Flaubert during the 1950s and 1960s?*

SARTRE: Certainly I was writing the *Flaubert* at that time, but on the other hand, everything I said on the subject in *Words* is true. I had those memories for a long time, but perhaps I might not have talked about them if I had not written *Flaubert*. They were certainly connected. There certainly was a link between the two.

PUCCIANI: *I have talked about your grandfather in relation to Flaubert. You yourself have said that he had "socialized your pen" and that that pen had fallen from your hand. I saw in him a kind of bearer of the nineteenth-century culture that had affected you.*

SARTRE: It was certainly my grandfather who gave me my idea of culture. Not the idea that I have now, but the one I had for a long time, from the age of six onward.

RYBALKA: *You seem also to have reacted against the culture that he gave you, against visits to museums, speeches at awards ceremonies, and so on. Yet didn't he influence you regarding the image and the relation between the image and the word? He himself was one of the pioneers of the audiovisual method.*

SARTRE: No, that was over my head.

PUCCIANI: *In the course of your studies, there were two options: literary positivism and idealism. I took your former professor, Henri Delacroix, as an example of idealist immanentism and Gustave Lanson as an example of positivism.*

SARTRE: But Lanson was only the director of the Ecole Normale. I didn't take any courses from him.

PUCCIANI: *But hadn't everyone read his history of literature?*

SARTRE: Of course. [*The interview is interrupted here by the arrival of Simone de Beauvoir, who, however, leaves in a few moments.*]

PUCCIANI: *In the* Critique of Dialectical Reason *you define totalities and you say that, all the same, they require an imaginary status. Then you go on to practical totalities. Do these practical totalities also require an imaginary status?*

SARTRE: Not necessarily. For example, an object, a machine that represents a totalization of the product it makes or the action it performs, is not imaginary. It is a rational totalization.

PUCCIANI: *My understanding was that they both had the same status, required the same status in the social world. There are objects such as coffee mills that, with the passage of time, become esthetic objects, analoga of themselves. How can they do this if there is no imaginary status?*

SARTRE: They become imaginary at that moment, but they are then no longer practical totalities. If they have an esthetic quality from the start—for example, eighteenth-century ships had this quality—there may be a relation to the imaginary, but it exists above all for us.

PUCCIANI: *Is there not in your philosophy a constant crossfire between the realizing thesis and the irrealizing thesis?*

SARTRE: Yes, always. Our perception includes the imaginary.

PUCCIANI: *In* Psychology of the Imagination, *however, these two theses are mutually exclusive.*

SARTRE: Yes, but that was too radical. In the *Flaubert* I tried to point out that they are often combined, and I have there outlined another theory of the imaginary. In this sense, it is possible that certain practical totalities include imaginary elements. I have not reflected on that, but it is possible.

# Sartre on His Critics

GRUENHECK: *One problem that is raised several times in the critical articles we have been considering is that of self-knowledge. Do you have the impression that you know yourself?*

SARTRE: Yes and no. Yes, in the sense that, through consciousness, I can grasp a certain type of psyche or elements of the psyche that are in direct relation with myself. For example, I know my feelings. If I love or detest a person, I know it. If I love or detest many, I can draw a line: those I love, those I detest; I have such and such a type of affection, such and such a type of animosity. I can therefore describe myself from this point of view. I can truly know myself in my desires; I feel them immediately.

There is a whole psychology which is the relation to the Other. One's feelings and actions, the number of recurrences of an action or a feeling—it is the Other who knows them. I cannot grasp this psychology myself. Someone tells me 'You are like that', enabling me to realize that it may be true. But it is the Other who tells me. One can only have complete self-knowledge starting from that. If the Other does not tell you what you are for him, you cannot attain self-knowledge.

On the other hand, each person is made aware by others of such and such a relation to oneself or with others. He can thus learn from the world what he is, not in his consciousness or at least not through his consciousness, but through what others think. Thus there is a whole psychology pertaining to oneself that comes from the Other. I feel quite clearly what I feel myself and what I feel according to what others tell me, according to those who I thought were right. One would not know oneself without the Other. For example, anger, irascibility—these are things I can know only if someone describes them to me.

Through myself, I know that a number of times I have been angry at those who contradicted me, but that signifies nothing. I don't know if I am irascible or not. But someone says: 'You were really angry under certain circumstances, although the person's objections were facile and not malicious, and you were angry at other times under similar circumstances. Therefore you are irascible.' I discover that, I learn that through the Other. Perhaps I will be sorry about it. It is clearly part of myself, but part of myself in relation to others. Thus there are: 1. an easy psychology of oneself that one possesses as soon as one reflects a little on oneself; 2. another, deeper psychology possessed by people who think to the depths of themselves, because they are in circumstances such that the depths are revealed or because they think about themselves that far; and then 3. the psychology of relations to others, relations that one cannot define without what is given by the Other. As a matter of fact, these three kinds of self-knowledge are not completely in accordance with each other. One always remains a little ignorant of oneself concerning the knowledge that others give us. If someone says: 'You have an inquiring mind, you are ambitious, et cetera', one accepts that, if the examples are specific, but often one does not unravel it. This is the kind of knowledge that one would find if one were to read a book about oneself once one is dead. It is knowledge that one does not control and it does not correspond to the other two categories, the ordinary self-knowledge that everyone has and the deeper self-knowledge that some have.

RYBALKA: *These 'others' whom you allude to, are these not the critics, the people who write about you?*
SARTRE: No, they are not. [*Laughter*]

RYBALKA: *I think that in general—and today's example proves it—you learn rather little from others about your work.*

SARTRE: Thus far, rather little. When I was seventeen or eighteen I was always told that one learned a great deal from critics. So I approached them with positive ideas about criticism, with disciplined, sensible ideas. I read the critics, saying to myself, 'What are they going to teach me?' But they taught me nothing.

RYBALKA: *Even from the standpoint of you as 'Other'?*

SARTRE: Yes, because most of the time the critical articles about one's work in the course of a lifetime are not very carefully done.

RYBALKA: *Aren't there any critical works on you that you found notable?*

SARTRE: There are many that I have not read. From the ones I know, I never learned very much. However, sometimes, let us say in one one-hundredth of what I read, the critics contribute an idea.

RYBALKA: *And in those cases, what is it?*

SARTRE: It is a relation between two passages in a work, a comparison between two works that shows me something they have in common, and so on. It strikes me and I say, 'Well, that's true'. But that doesn't go very far.

RYBALKA: *Aren't there confrontations, other ideas that lead you to revise some of your own ideas?*

SARTRE: I have never been obliged to revise my ideas. I am perhaps an obstinate philosopher, but it has never happened. I read, I saw that indeed there were things to be said, and then I continued to do what I was doing.

RYBALKA: *Has your thought therefore developed relatively autonomously?*

SARTRE: In relation to the thought of critical writers, yes. If friends point out something to me, it may have more importance. Among the critics, the best I encountered were those who said what I meant.

RYBALKA: *Are you irritated at seeing your thought often simplified?*

SARTRE: No. Some people write those things, that's all.

RYBALKA: *You have said yourself that 'mediators' would be necessary for Flaubert. What do you foresee as a possible criticism of your work?*

SARTRE: To begin with, my work would have to be read. [*Laughter*] Many critics stop along the way.

RYBALKA: *Read the whole of your work?*

SARTRE: Indeed, yes. I do not ask that of the ordinary reader, but only of specialized critics: Let them take the time. Then, the work has to be presented in order to see if a single point of view extends over a whole lifetime or changes midway, to try to explain the developments, the breaks, to attempt to find my original choice, which is the most difficult part: What did I choose to be by writing such and such a work? Why did I choose to write?

RYBALKA: *The critic may not put himself in your place as much as you would like and thus would not completely do justice to you.*

SARTRE: In spite of all that, let him do something of what I did on Flaubert. I do not claim to have done justice to him entirely, but I hope to have found some directions, some themes.

RYBALKA: *You would like a work to be done on you like the one you did on Flaubert?*

SARTRE: Yes, that's right. That seems to me to be the meaning of criticism. Here are books; a man wrote them. What does that mean? What is that man? What are these books? I find the esthetic point of view so variable that it is this aspect that seems interesting to me.

RYBALKA: *Do you attach great importance to documentation?*

SARTRE: Yes. I can positively affirm that because I know what had to be done for *Flaubert.*

PUCCIANI: *However, there is relatively little documentation on you. If one compares what you have put in* Words *with what is known about the childhood of Flaubert, there is a huge difference.*

SARTRE: That's due to the time in which we live. Today fewer details are given about people, much less is known about them than in the preceding century, precisely because the problems of sexuality, the problems of life, become individual and disappear. For example, what is known about Solzhenitsyn are things that ultimately concern all of Russia. We know that he was exiled in a camp. Immediately when we reflect on the camps, we recall what they were, and so on. But, as for knowing whether he likes coffee or what is the nature of his sexuality—mystery. Perhaps certain elements can be defined on the basis of his books, but someone will have to do it.

Indeed, none of those things really is hidden. I think that my taste for coffee and my sexuality are in my books. They have only to be rediscovered and it is up to the critics to find them. In other words, the critics should, on the basis of the books and nothing but the books, together with the correspondence, establish what was the person who wrote these books, re-establish the trends, see the doctrines to which the author subscribed.

RYBALKA: *Will there be much correspondence in your case?*
SARTRE: There won't be any, or very little.

RYBALKA: *What you want, then, is a biography?*
SARTRE: Yes, a kind of biography that can be done only with documents. A literary biography, that is, the man with his tastes, his principles, his literary esthetics . . . rediscover all those things in him, from his books and in him. That, I believe, is the work criticism should do.

# Teaching Philosophy

RYBALKA: *Curiously enough, none of the articles we have before us mentions the teaching of philosophy, the way your philosophy could be taught. How did you teach philosophy?*
SARTRE: That was a long time ago.

RYBALKA: *The problem is especially acute today. What would you advise?*
SARTRE: That is a different question.

RYBALKA: *But what was your method?*
SARTRE: I had to cover the philosophers included in the program and I did not teach strictly contemporary philosophers. And if I had ideas of my own . . .

RYBALKA: *According to the French system, you were the only philosopher in your high school?*
SARTRE: Yes.

RYBALKA: *Therefore, there was no possibility for discussion with other philosophers?*
SARTRE: No. I gave professorial lectures, lectures *ex cathedra*, as they say. But I interrupted myself all the time to ask questions or to answer the questions I was asked. I thought that teaching consisted not in making an adult speak in front of young people but in having discussions with

them starting from concrete problems. When they said, 'This guy is an idiot: he says this, but I have experienced something else', I had to explain to them that one could conceive of the matter differently.

RYBALKA: *Did you succeed in establishing the beginnings of reciprocity, since it is never completely reciprocal?*

SARTRE: The reciprocity was rather strong. I should add that I was involved in other activities with my pupils, even boxing, and that helped. I also spent a lot of time drawing out the ideas they had in their heads.

RYBALKA: *Wasn't that method of teaching considered a little scandalous at the time?*

SARTRE: Yes. I got reactions from colleagues, from the censor, from all those people. Moreover, I allowed my pupils to smoke in class, which met with great disapproval.

RYBALKA: *What do you think of the teaching of philosophy today?*

SARTRE: As you know, in the proposed reform bill, philosophy is no longer required on the secondary school level.

RYBALKA: *Did you know that in the United States philosophy is not taught in secondary school but only in college?*

SARTRE: In my opinion, it should be the other way around. I think, as someone has suggested, that a little philosophy could be taught up to the junior year of high school, enough to allow an understanding of the authors: for example, three hours a week.

To me, philosophy is everything. It is the way one lives. One lives as a philosopher. I live as a philosopher. That does not mean that I live as a good philosopher, but that my perceptions are philosophical perceptions, even when I look at that lamp or when I look at you. Consequently, it is a way of living and I think it should be taught as soon as possible, in simple language.

RECORDED IN MONTPARNASSE, PARIS
12TH AND 19TH MAY, 1975

ALFRED JULES AYER (1910–1989) became a celebrity with his 1936 book, *Language, Truth, and Logic,* which explained the new Viennese ideas of logical positivism to the English-speaking world. He served in military intelligence during World War II, and after the war emerged as a public figure, an opponent of theistic religion, and a voice for progressive causes such as homosexual law reform. He continued to write philosophy books, distinguished by their persuasive clarity and reasonableness, and changed his mind on a number of philosophical issues. He continued in the news with his two deaths, in 1988 and 1989, the first of which he discusses below.

# A.J. AYER

## " That would indeed be a shock to common sense. "

I was born in London on 29th October, 1910, the only child of parents neither of whom was of English origin. My grandfather, on my father's side, was Rector of the Academy of Neuchatel in Switzerland, where he simultaneously occupied the chairs of French, Geography, and Economics. He was best known for his *Grammaire Comparée de la Langue Française,* which remained a standard work for many years. When he died in 1884, my father, in his seventeenth year, emigrated to England and eventually became a British citizen. After working in a bank and publishing a set of General and Comparative Tables of the World's Statistics, he secured a partnership in a firm of timber merchants, a business in which he took decreasing interest. He wrote one or two plays but did not succeed in getting them produced. He died in 1928.

My mother, whose maiden name was Reine Citroen, belonged to a Jewish family who had established themselves as jewellers in Amsterdam. A branch of the family migrated to France and a cousin of my grandfather's, calling himself André Citroën, founded the well-known firm of motor cars. After trading in fruit at Antwerp, where my mother was born in 1887, and prospecting for diamonds in South Africa, my grandfather, David Citroen, also became a pioneer in the motor car industry. The cars which he manufactured were Minervas, luxurious cars which enjoyed a high reputation in the first quarter of this century. With a partner in Belgium, he settled in England at around the turn of the century to promote the sale of Minervas there. In addition to his native Dutch, he spoke German, French, and English fluently and my mother and her siblings, two younger sisters, were brought up to speak English.

While his wife was Jewish, of Dutch extraction also but belonging to a family which had settled in England a generation earlier, and while he was in no manner ashamed of his Jewishness, my grandfather, an outspoken agnostic, was especially hostile to the Jewish religion. He believed that their obstinate adherence to this religion, which preserved them as a separate community, was a principal factor in causing the Jews to suffer persecution. He therefore made sure that all his daughters married gentiles. He had five grandchildren, three boys and two girls, of whom I was the eldest by over two years. While he was a man of wide reading, with a strong interest in history, he attached what might have been thought excessive importance to worldly success. This put pressure on his grandsons, especially myself. It probably stimulated a competitive strain in me, which was very strong in my youth, though it has weakened with the passage of years. He was proud of my early academic achievements, such as they were, though I think that he was disappointed when I embarked on an academic career. He had hoped that I would become a second Disraeli. I wished to please him and it is a grief to me that he died in 1935, only a few months before the publication and favourable reception of my first book.

My father also had high hopes of me. He used to encourage me and comfort himself by repeating, not quite accurately, that the younger Pitt had become Prime Minister at the age of twenty-two. He was a milder man than his father-in-law and though I was fond of him, he had less influence over me. His mother, who lived to be nearly eighty, and one of his sisters had both settled in London and it was thanks to them that I spoke some French with a good accent as a child. I still speak French with a good accent, though the gaps in my French vocabulary discredit the claim that I occasionally make to be bilingual.

# Early Reading

Though it is unlikely to have been the first book that I actually read, the first book that I remember reading is *Robinson Crusoe*. It caught my imagination less than the Uncle Remus stories of Joel Chandler Harris. I enjoyed books of adventure, most of which in those days had a strong jingoistic flavour and developed a precocious taste for the novels of Captain Marryat. From the age of about five I was an enthusiastic collector of postage stamps and cigarette cards. I fairly soon lost these interests though I started a new collection of cigarette cards when in my early twenties I myself became a serious smoker, a habit from which I was able to free myself only some six years ago. If I had preserved these early collections, I could sell them now at a high price, but in the matter of making money I belong rather to my father's than to my mother's side of my family.

Like other children, I was given a model railway set to play with and a series of Meccano sets, containing instructions which I conscientiously tried to implement, but usually failed. Apart from a fair ability to play games like lawn tennis, I have always been embarrassingly deficient in manual skills. To this day, for example, I have never learned how to drive a motor car.

After attending one or two local day-schools of which I have no recollection, I was sent at the age of seven in the summer of 1918 to a boarding school at Eastbourne, a holiday resort on the south coast of England, and the locus of a number of private preparatory schools. Presumably the climate was thought to be healthy. Ascham St. Vincent's, the school which I attended, was typical of its class and period. It contained about 70 boys of whom I was the youngest when I came there. The upper age was normally 13. The proprietor and headmaster was a clergyman who was reputed to have played Association Football for Cambridge University. There were four or five assistant masters and a matron. The school was housed in an ugly late Victorian building with a large playing field. The boys slept in dormitories and were adequately if plainly fed. Discipline was strict though the headmaster was not the sadist that many of his counterparts at other schools appear to have been. I was caned by him only once, though severely, for taking part in a dormitory rag. The worst feature of the school was the bullying of boys by one another, which the masters did hardly anything to check. It was more psychological than physical. For several terms I was the victim of xenophobia, surprisingly not because I was known to be partly Jewish but because I had confessed to being partly Swiss.

What parents expected as a return for the fees which they paid to such schools was that their boys be enabled to pass the entrance examinations into the private establishments which continue in England to be known as 'public schools'. The teaching was therefore adapted to what the requirements of these public schools were known to be. This still meant a heavy concentration on the classics, a good grounding in mathematics for those, unlike myself, who were able to take advantage of it, some temperate instruction in the Anglican religion, a modicum of history, some very elementary French and next to no science. In fact I cannot remember being taught any science at all at Ascham, though I started learning Latin as soon as I went there at seven years of age. There was none of the ill-advised contemporary mistrust of formal teaching. We learned our conjugations, declensions, and irregular verbs by rote.

# Surprisingly to Eton

It was a credit to the school, contributing to its growth and to the income of the proprietor, if its pupils obtained scholarships, especially to the major public schools. Boys who appeared capable of reaching this standard were given special coaching in ancient Greek, on which I was launched at the age of eleven. It had been arbitrarily decided that I should proceed to Charterhouse but in the summer of 1923 a boy, a year older than I, was thought good enough to try for a scholarship at Eton[1] and I was taken along with him to keep him company and for my own part to acquire some practice in undergoing examinations of this type. To everyone's surprise at Ascham, including my own, I came third on the list of admissible candidates and was offered a scholarship at Eton. My companion also made his way onto the list but was ranked too low down to obtain a place in a year when relatively few scholars were admitted.

I was not particularly elated by my success. On the contrary I thought of Eton as a snobbish school in which I should be out of place and even put some pressure on my parents to decline the scholarship. We were, however, persuaded by my grandfather that becoming an Etonian would be a source of future advantages which it would be stupid of me to forego. On the whole, I think that he was right.

---

1. Eton College is the best-known and most prestigious of English boys' public schools. A high proportion of British public figures are old Etonians.

I entered Eton in September 1923, just over a month before my thirteenth birthday, and remained there until the beginning of the Easter holidays of 1929. The King's scholars, the king in question being Henry VI who had founded the school in 1440, were known as Collegers and were housed together apart from the other boys. Their number was kept at seventy, out of a total number of boys, at that time, of about eleven hundred. There had been a tendency for the other boys, known as Oppidans, to despise Collegers as their social inferiors, but in the nineteen twenties this was already ceasing to be the case. Certainly, I was never made aware of it. Except that our schoolwork was expected to maintain a higher standard, so that we were obliged to take it more seriously, our way of life in College was not markedly different from that which prevailed in the Oppidan houses. We played organized games just as strenuously and were subject to the same forms of discipline, the task of keeping order being chiefly entrusted to the senior boys who had the right to cane their juniors, usually for quite trivial offences. I suffered this punishment several times but refused to inflict it when I was in a position to do so and indeed conducted an ineffective campaign against the whole practice, which I am glad to learn has now been discontinued at Eton and at other public schools.

I was not very happy at Eton mainly because I was unpopular with my seniors and contemporaries in college. I was not friendless but I had an unguarded tongue and a propensity for showing off which caused more offence than perhaps it merited, certainly more than I realized. Not that I had anything extraordinary to boast about. My schoolwork was competent but not outstanding. I enjoyed playing games but except possibly at tennis and in a specialized position at the Wall Game, a sport peculiar to Eton and even there not much played except by Collegers, my skills were not much above the average. In particular, the fantasy which I had nourished since my early childhood of excelling at cricket never came at all near to being transmuted into fact. This did not destroy my enthusiasm for the game which endures until this day. I should perhaps remark at this point that throughout my life, since I was nine or ten years old, I have taken a very lively interest in nearly all forms of sport. For example, I have supported the same professional soccer team for over 65 years and still watch as many of their home matches as I conveniently can. Many people have found this incongruous with my being a philosopher and in some cases treated it as an affectation. They are quite mistaken. It may be the case that not many philosophers, or indeed academic persons of any calling, take a strong interest in sport; but this in no way implies that the exceptions are not straightforwardly sincere.

# Arts and Politics

Traditionally, an Eton education was heavily biassed on the side of the classics, and this tradition was still maintained in my own time there. Not only did we painfully construe Virgil's *Georgics* and his *Aeneid* and the plays of Aeschylus, Sophocles, and Euripides, but we had to render pieces of English prose into Latin and Greek and very soon we were put on to verse. In our earliest days in college we were expected to master books of Homer's *Odyssey* in our spare time to a point where we knew them practically by heart. Mathematics was well taught to those who had a gift for it, which I was soon discovered to lack, and so was history, mainly English history, which I enjoyed. Modern languages were taught poorly and the sciences hardly at all.

The standard of music at Eton was high, but at that time my own taste did not rise above the musical comedies to which my parents took me in the holidays. I still have a vivid recollection of the popular tunes of the nineteen twenties and thirties. At the age of fifteen or so I toyed with the idea of going on the stage and went so far as to teach myself to tap-dance, but I was never very skilful at it, and though I had quite a pleasant light tenor voice, this was offset by a tendency to sing out of tune. My taste for musical comedies extended to the film musicals of the nineteen forties and fifties, though not to the popular music of the present time. I advanced to an enduring love of opera, especially the works of Mozart, Verdi, and Rossini, in my early twenties but on the whole I cannot claim that music has played a dominant part in my life.

I was slow also in taking an interest in the visual arts. It was not until my eighteenth year when I went with my mother, after my father's death, to stay with her relations in Holland that visits to the Rijksmuseum in Amsterdam and the Mauritshuis in The Hague caused me to take a pleasure in seventeenth-century Dutch painting which I have never lost. For many years Vermeer was my favourite painter. My newly-found interest in painting was further stimulated by the writings of Clive Bell, and I soon took a delight in the work of the French Impressionists, especially Renoir. In the course of years my taste in painting has constantly broadened, so that it easily encompasses such diverse artists as El Greco, Cranach, Mantegna, Stubbs, Bonnard, and Hopper. It has not, however, progressed beyond Surrealism.

In my early years at Eton I preserved my taste for stories of adventure, devouring the works of the older Dumas in translation and those of such

English writers as Sapper and John Buchan. I soon succumbed to P.G. Wodehouse, and gained a distorted view of life from the manly novels of Ian Hay and the short stories of Rudyard Kipling, in which I still see merit, as well as in his verse. Later on I acquired a strong appetite for humorous verse, especially the Bab Ballads of W.S. Gilbert and the fruit of A.P. Herbert's contributions to *Punch*. My taste in serious poetry was conventional, except perhaps for its including Andrew Marvell. Otherwise I chiefly admired Shelley, Tennyson, and Swinburne.

English literature was not much taught at Eton, but it was the custom at least in the junior divisions for books to be set as holiday tasks. Examinations were held on them when we returned to school and prizes awarded. The books were invariably selected from the plays of Shakespeare and the novels of Walter Scott, in alternate holidays. Though I read them conscientiously, I never gained much pleasure from any of Scott's novels, but I at once became a devotee of Shakespeare, winning the prize for the examination on the set play more than once. My favourites were *Twelfth Night*, *As You Like It*, and *Macbeth*. I think that I read nearly all the plays of Shakespeare before I saw one of them acted, though later I had the pleasure of seeing John Gielgud's *Hamlet* and Paul Robeson's *Othello*. At school my predilection for Shakespeare's plays extended to his sonnets, several of which I knew by heart.

As I grew older, I took to reading Bernard Shaw and H.G. Wells. I suppose that Shaw's *The Intelligent Woman's Guide to Socialism and Capitalism*, which I read when I was 17, was my introduction to political theory. If it did not immediately turn me into a Socialist, it set me on a radical course from which I have never deviated.

In my last years at school, my favourite authors were Aldous Huxley and Lytton Strachey. I still have a vivid recollection of Huxley's early novels, *Crome Yellow*, *Antic Hay*, *Those Barren Leaves*, and *Point Counter Point*, though it is a long time since I reread them, and still occasionally divert myself with the works of Lytton Strachey, especially his brilliant *Portraits in Miniature*.

# A Militant Young Atheist

I have said that I was instructed in the Anglican religion at my preparatory school. This did not go much further than attendance at the school chapel on Sundays. At Eton there was a daily morning service in the school chapel, fairly short on weekdays, and long on Sundays, evensong in the chapel on Sundays, and evening prayers every day in College and Oppidan houses. Participation in these ceremonies was compulsory except that Roman Catholics, for whom separate provision was made, were excused attendance at chapel. I cannot remember whether the same privilege was extended to nonconformists or orthodox Jews. They too, I think, would have been required, like the rest of us, to write an essay every Sunday in their own time on some set religious topic. These exercises, known as Sunday questions, were beneficial not only, or even primarily, as improving our understanding of the Christian religion, but as making us familiar with the Authorized Version of the English translation of the Old and New Testaments, a prerequisite to the understanding of much of English literature.

I had been baptised into the Church of England and at the age of fifteen underwent confirmation. I had never given much thought to religion, but yielded to the pressure put upon me by the master in college and to a lesser extent by my parents. Not that my parents were religious, though my mother, a nominal convert to Christianity, was at least a deist, but they wished me to conform to what they took to be a common practice. I took communion two or three times and then began to ask myself what the performance implied. It was not long before I decided that not only the theory of the Eucharist, but the doctrine of the Trinity, the assumption that Jesus had been divine, and indeed the hypothesis that the universe had been divinely created were all intellectually untenable. I became a militant atheist and annoyed my school fellows, who took little interest in the subject, by haranguing them about such things as the contradictions in the Book of Genesis and the inconsistencies in the Gospels. I did not disguise my views in my replies to Sunday questions, but this did not make trouble for me with the masters who read them, least of all with the headmaster Dr. C.A. Alington, who was himself a clergyman. He insisted on my continuing to attend chapel services as a matter of school discipline, but so far from attempting to put obstacles in the way of my disbelief drew my attention to books which would provide me with arguments to support it. But for him, I might never have discovered W.E.H. Lecky's *History of European Morals from Augustus to Charlemagne*, first published in 1869, and still as good an exposition as I know of the historical evils attendant on the early growth of Christianity.

I should add at this point that in the sixty years since I first became an atheist, I have never yet discovered any good reason to believe in the existence of a deity.

My lack of religious belief did not prevent me from gaining a mark of distinction for my paper on Divinity which was one of the subjects that I took in the examination for what was then called the School Certificate, for which I entered at the age of fifteen. I gained distinctions also in Latin, Greek, French, English, History, and Mathematics, failing only in Higher Mathematics. My incompetence in mathematics, once it ceases to be elementary has, I think, been a handicap to me as a philosopher.

General education came to a stop at Eton with the obtaining of one's School Certificate. After that one was obliged to specialize. The subject that most attracted me was history, but I needed to win a scholarship if I was to go on to Oxford or Cambridge, and I was advised that my chances would be better, mainly because there would be less competition, if I specialized in classics. Accordingly, for the next three years I concentrated almost exclusively on Latin and Greek, becoming well read in the literature of both ancient languages, and acquiring some mechanical skill in composing Greek and Latin prose and verse. My concern with the works I read was predominantly but not wholly philological. I read some plays of Euripides for pleasure, as well as the poems of Catullus and the Greek Anthology.

# First Interest in Philosophy

I was not an outstanding classical scholar, but I was well enough trained to be elected by Christ Church, Oxford to the first of its open classical scholarships in the winter of 1928–29. I was able to supplement the income which this brought me by a leaving scholarship from Eton which I had obtained in the previous summer in an examination open to specialists in all subjects. I came second to a modern linguist.

At that time members of the top classical form had the advantage of being taught not only by Dr. Alington but by two remarkable young masters: Jack McDougall, who remained with us only a short time before joining a firm of publishers, and Richard Martineau, who came straight back from Cambridge, having been Head Boy at Eton when I first went there. His leaving present to me, F.L. Lucas's short book on *Tragedy,* made a lasting impression on me.

One or other of them, most probably Jack McDougall, took us outside our classical syllabus by devoting a weekly period to the pre-Socratic philosophers. I found these lessons fascinating, though, as it happened, I never delved much further into this branch of philosophy, apart from a persistent interest in Zeno's paradoxes. I still think that if there is to be any teaching of philosophy in schools, it should be done in this way, not made a subject for examination, but allowing a master to communicate his own interest in some aspect of it, taking his pupils on a holiday from their curriculum.

My own interest in philosophy had already been awakened as an indirect consequence of my late development of some sensitivity to painting. As an introduction to aesthetics I bought and read Clive Bell's *Art*, first published in 1914 though I did not discover it until 1928. The book retains a historical interest through its championship of Clive Bell's and Roger Fry's concept of 'significant form', a concept that was never adequately defined, or even explained, but one that rendered service to its inventors in their rejection of a representational assessment of visual art. If I ever succumbed to their argument, I have long ceased to do so, but it was anyhow not on this account that the book was important to me. What made it so was Bell's inclusion of a chapter on Art and Ethics in which he asserted that 'good' is an indefinable quality and advised any of his readers who wanted a proof of this assertion to procure a copy of G.E. Moore's *Principia Ethica*. I took his advice and, like the members of the Bloomsbury circle when the book was first published in 1903, swallowed Moore whole. It was not until my second year at Oxford that I began to doubt whether 'good' was a simple indefinable non-natural quality or whether the rightness of an action entirely depended on the goodness of its consequences.

There is no reference to Bertrand Russell in Moore's *Principia Ethica* so that it must have been on my own initiative that I bought and read Russell's *Sceptical Essays*, when it was published in 1928. The opening sentence of this book has served me as a motto throughout my philosophical career. It runs:

> I wish to propose for the reader's favourable consideration a doctrine which may, I fear, appear wildly paradoxical and subversive. The doctrine in question is this: that it is undesirable to believe a proposition when there is no ground whatever for supposing it true.

I left Eton at the end of the Easter half in 1929 and passed most of the summer at Santander in Spain, taking lessons in Spanish from the householder with whose family I boarded and attending a summer school run by a professor of Liverpool University. In preparation for the work I knew that I should have to do at Oxford I took with me a copy, which I still possess, of Adam's edition of Plato's *Republic*. Judging by my annotations of the text, I appear to have got no further than a quarter of the way through it, but my detailed and disrespectful criticisms of the arguments of the first book still seem to me creditable for a beginner. It was at Santander that I attained my peak as a tennis player, reaching the semifinals of what was in fact a modest tournament but one that bore the grandiloquent title of the Championship of Northern Spain. In the following year, when I entered for the Freshmen's tournament at Oxford I was defeated in the first round. I found it very easy to acquire a smattering of Spanish but did not take the trouble to master the language thoroughly.

The classics course at Oxford normally took four years, the first five of the twelve terms being devoted to Honour Moderations, an intensification of the kind of work that one had done at school and the remaining seven to Literae Humaniores or Greats, devoted to Philosophy and Ancient History. I had tired of the classics and obtained leave from my college to reduce the four to three, taking a preliminary examination, requiring some acquaintance with the *Annals* of Tacitus and Aristotle's ethics, at the end of my first term, and gaining an extra term for reading Greats. The tutorial system was in force, perhaps to an even greater extent than it is now. From the beginning I was taught singly, and went for an hour's tutorial every week, once in philosophy, and once in ancient history, coming with a written essay on each occasion. Attendance at lectures was voluntary, as it still is, and I rarely attended them. An important exception was a preview of H.H. Price's book *Perception,* delivered in the form of lectures in 1932. This book has fallen out of fashion but it brought some Cambridge freshness into the stale philosophical climate of Oxford and I consider it a landmark in the development of its subject.

Philosophically, I owed a great debt to Gilbert Ryle. Indeed, it was his appreciation of the essays I wrote for him and of my resourcefulness in our discussions that first made me think that I might have an aptitude for philosophy. He was ten years older than I, just young enough to have escaped service in the First World War. He was one of the few Oxford philosophers of that time to take any positive interest in the work of contemporary philosophers outside Oxford. At the start of his career he had been captivated by the Austrian and German school of Phenomenologists, notably Brentano, Meinong, and Husserl. He had even ventured into Existentialism, writing a not unfriendly review in *Mind* of Heidegger's *Sein und Zeit.* By 1929, when I became his pupil, he had decided that he was being led into a blind alley and was turning his sights upon Cambridge, being most strongly impressed by Russell's distinction between logical and grammatical form, evinced in Russell's Theory of Descriptions and his Theory of Types. Ryle's article 'Systematically Misleading Expressions', which he published in the *Proceedings of the Aristotelian Society* for 1932, clearly showed the new direction which his thought was taking. A tutor whose merit lay less in dominating his pupils than in knowing how to guide them, he introduced me to Russell's books and also to the work of the Cambridge philosopher C.D. Broad. I remember writing essays for him on Broad's *Scientific Thought* and *The Mind and Its Place in Nature.*

I had less respect for Michael Foster, either personally or professionally. He was a shy, awkward man who found it difficult to communicate with his pupils. He was, however, a good historian of philosophy, within rather narrow limits, and I am indebted to him for such understanding as I achieved of the complexities of Kant's *Critique of Pure Reason.*

I joined the Poetry Society in my first term at Oxford and remember being vastly impressed by a speech delivered by Louis MacNeice, then in his final year. Of the group with which he has always been associated, Auden and Day Lewis had already left Oxford, but I overlapped with Stephen Spender, who remains my friend. Although I did not meet either of them until several years later it was at this time also that I acquired a taste for the poems of William Empson and the early poems of T.S. Eliot. My taste extended to French poetry of the nineteenth and early twentieth centuries. Verlaine was and still is my favourite, but I also admired Baudelaire, Mallarmé, and Valéry. In the field of classical French poetry I came greatly to enjoy Racine.

In general, I read at least as much French as English literature. I felt great enthusiasm for Stendhal, embracing his treatise *De l'Amour* as well as the famous novels, *Le Rouge et le Noir* and *La Chartreuse de Parme.* I read a great deal of Balzac, especially admiring *Le Père Goriot* and *La Cousine Bette.* Among contemporary writers I discovered Malraux and Céline as well as Proust.

My francophilia extended to films. Talking films had just come into fashion and René Clair was my favourite director. I still think *Sous les Tois de Paris, Le Million,* and *A Nous la Liberté* three of the best films ever made. I went on to admire the French films of the 1930s, with such directors as Marcel Carné and actors like Jean Gabin. In my undergraduate days at Oxford there was still a cinema that showed silent films and this enabled me to see and admire the work of the Russian directors Eisenstein and Pudovkin and that of the German expressionists, in which my favourite actor was the young Conrad Veidt. I was also entranced by the early German talking films, especially of course *The Blue Angel* with Emil Jannings and Marlene Dietrich, but also the comedies of the early nineteen thirties, usually featuring Lilian Harvey.

It was not long before I succumbed to Hollywood. My taste was very catholic. I enjoyed westerns, comedies, gangster films, and musicals throughout the next decade and still have a vivid recollection of many of them. My love of films outlasted the war and while it has diminished in more recent years I still regard it as an important factor in my life.

My addiction to the cinema reinforced, rather than replaced, my love of the theater, but it at no time revived my juvenile ambition to go on the stage. I joined the Oxford University Dramatic Society, but used its premises merely as a club. I never volunteered to take even the humblest part in any of its productions.

# Captivated by Wittgenstein

In common with most of my undergraduate contemporaries, I took little interest in politics. Nevertheless I joined the Oxford Union and spoke in several debates in the course of my first year. I was nervous, spoke much too fast, and after a conspicuous failure as one of the principal speakers at the end of my first summer term never again attempted to speak there. At that time I called myself a Liberal. This did not prevent me from being secretary of the Conservative Canning Club, but this was a purely social commitment, on a level with my membership of the White Rose Society, where one meeting to drink the health of the King over the Water did not imply any genuine allegiance to the Jacobite cause.

An office which I did take seriously was my secretaryship of the Jowett Society, the philosophical society for undergraduates. It was through this society that I met Isaiah Berlin, then an undergraduate at Corpus Christi College, and started a friendship that has lasted for close on sixty years. He was a year senior to me, but spent a year longer as an undergraduate, thereby securing a double first.

I think it probable that I read more than one paper to the Jowett Society, but the only one that I remember was a paper on the philosophy of Ludwig Wittgenstein, to which I had been introduced by Gilbert Ryle. Wittgenstein's famous book, *Tractatus Logic-Philosophicus,* had been published as long ago as 1922, but hardly any notice had been taken of it at Oxford and I believe that this meeting at which I gave an enthusiastic account of Wittgenstein's system, as I understood it, was the first occasion on which Oxford had been treated to any public discussion of his work.

My captivation by the *Tractatus* increased my appetite for philosophy. It had been intended that I should become a barrister and I had been enrolled in the Inner Temple and eaten my quota of Bar Dinners. I had read no law but it was then quite a common practice for prospective barristers to take their Oxford degree in Greats and then devote some time on their own to acquiring the modest amount of legal knowledge that would enable them to pass the Bar Examination. I was not averse from this course but thought that there would be no harm in my spending at least another year at Oxford and making some further progress in philosophy. I therefore applied for a Research Lectureship which Christ Church was offering. It happened, however, that Michael Foster had put in for a Professorship at the University College of Aberystwyth and the Governing Body of Christ Church took it for granted that he would obtain it. Accordingly, they appointed me, not to the position for which I had applied, but to a special lectureship with the intention that after the probationary year to which Christ Church subjected all its prospective Students, as it persists in calling those who would elsewhere be entitled Fellows, I should succeed Michael Foster. I had no hesitation in accepting this offer. Unfortunately, Michael Foster did not secure the Welsh professorship, so that Christ Church, having committed itself to employing me, awarded me a two-year lectureship with the possibility of an extension for one further year.

In these circumstances, it would have been an embarrassment to the college as well as myself if I had failed to obtain a first in Greats.[2] This very nearly happened, as two of my three philosophy examiners were hostile to my Cambridge orientation and the third, who was more sympathetic, intended to subject me to a searching viva. I was spared this ordeal, only because I had displayed an adequate knowledge of ancient history and Professor Wade-Gery, suspecting that the philosophers were treating me unfairly, gave me such high marks on my history papers that I emerged with a first, after only a formal viva on my performance in ancient history. This narrow escape was followed in the autumn by my failure to be elected to All Souls, Isaiah Berlin being one of those preferred to me.

---

2. A 'first', or first-class honors degree, is the British equivalent of the American *summa cum laude*. 'Greats' is a traditional course of study at Oxford, covering philosophy and ancient history.

# The Vienna Circle

With Michael Foster retaining his Studentship, Christ Church had no need of my services as a tutor and I was given two terms leave of absence. I proposed to spend them in Cambridge, learning from Wittgenstein, but Gilbert Ryle persuaded me to go to Vienna instead. He had met Moritz Schlick, the leader of the group of philosophers and scientists, mainly mathematicians, who entitled themselves the Vienna Circle, at some international congress a year or two previously and had been favourably impressed by him, and thought that it would be a good thing if I could discover what work was going forward under his auspices. For my part I had become engaged to be married and thought that Vienna would be a nice place in which to spend a honeymoon. I was married to Renée Lees on 25th November 1932 and we went almost immediately to Vienna.

As soon as we had found lodgings I called upon Schlick with a letter of introduction from Ryle and was invited by him not only to attend his lectures at the University but also to participate in the weekly meetings of the Circle. There was, indeed, the difficulty that I knew next to no German but I took private lessons and within a few weeks had learned enough German to follow the discussions that went on in the Circle, if not to make any positive contributions to them. In my private lessons I mainly studied the novels and plays of Arthur Schnitzler, of whose work I have always thought very highly.

Rudolf Carnap, perhaps the most famous member of the Circle, had left Vienna for the German University in Prague, but he continued to exert a strong influence through his writings, including the articles that he published in *Erkenntnis*, the Circle's official journal, which he edited jointly with Hans Reichenbach, the leader of a similar though smaller group in Berlin. I was impressed by Carnap's articles and still more by the book *The Logical Structure of the World*, which he had published in 1928. From the standpoint of what Carnap, somewhat disingenuously, called methodological solipsism, it consisted in a valiant attempt to use Russell's logic to develop a hierarchy of concepts, sufficient for the description of every aspect of reality, on the basis of the single empirical relation of remembered similarity between total states of the subject's consciousness. I now see that such an enterprise was bound to fail but I did not think so at the time.

Apart from Schlick, the chief participants in the meetings that I attended were the philosopher and sociologist, Otto Neurath, the philosopher Friedrich Waismann, and the mathematicians Karl Menger and Hans

Hahn. The logician Kurt Gödel, who had already published, at the age of twenty-five, his famous proof that even in elementary parts of arithmetic there exist propositions which cannot be proved or disproved within the system, was usually present but very seldom spoke. It is probable that he already dissented from the orthodox view of the Circle that the true propositions of logic and pure mathematics were tautologies, owing their necessity to linguistic conventions. Officially also, they were united in accepting the principle of verification as a criterion of empirical significance. Any nonformal utterance that could not be empirically verified was held to be literally nonsensical and this included most of what went under the name of metaphysics or theology. At that time the prevailing view was that empirical statements, other than those that were themselves directly observational, were reducible to the observational statements that would validate them. Later this requirement was relaxed to the point where nothing more was required of a scientific hypothesis than that observational statements be derivable from it. With regard to the criterion of significance and the character of explanation, no distinction was made between the natural and the social sciences. As for philosophy, apart from the exposure of metaphysical nonsense, its function was purely that of clarifying and analyzing the statements that were allowed to be literally meaningful.

The principal subject of debate, at the meetings which I attended over a period of three months, was the character of observation statements or *Protokollsätze* as they were called. One party led by Schlick held that they were statements referring to sense-data. His opponents, led by Neurath, refused to go below the level of references to physical objects. Neurath was soon to convert Carnap to the view that 'the physical language was the universal language of science'. On this issue I sided with Schlick.

A philosopher, a year or two older than myself, who also came to these meetings, was the American W.V. Quine, who went on to become perhaps the foremost philosopher of my generation. He had taken his doctorate in logic at Harvard, and was making a tour of Europe, in order to converse with mathematical logicians not only in Vienna but in Prague and Warsaw. He has a remarkable facility for languages, and I was deeply impressed by his delivering a lecture on logic to the Circle in fluent German.

It was in Vienna that I acquired a taste for opera which has never left me. One could get seats in the Upper Circle very cheaply, and Reneé and I went to many performances, mainly of works by Mozart and Verdi. I remember also a superb production of Hofmannsthal's and Strauss's *Der Rosenkavalier*.

Wagner was not in favor, but we saw a good production of *Lohengrin*. We also paid frequent visits to the Kunsthistorisches Museum with its splendid collection of Breughels, surpassed only in our favor by Tintoretto's *Susanna and the Elders*.

# Language, Truth, and Logic

When we returned to Oxford for the summer term of 1933 I gave a course of lectures on Wittgenstein and Carnap. They did not attract a large audience, but I had prepared them carefully and they were well received. Altogether I showed so much enthusiasm for what I had learned in Vienna that Isaiah Berlin advised me to put it all into a book. I accepted his advice but did not wish to undergo the labor of writing a book, without a guarantee that it would be published. At a dinner party given by Richard Crossman, who was still a Fellow of New College, I met a girl who worked in the office of the publisher Victor Gollancz and she made an appointment for me to see him. I outlined the plan of my book to him and came away with a contract. The result was *Language, Truth, and Logic*, which I started writing at Christmas and finished nineteen months later in July 1935 It was published by Gollancz in England in 1936 and later in the same year by the Oxford University Press in the United States. Its title was to some extent a plagiarism of Waismann's *Logik, Sprache, Philosophie*, advertised as the first of a series of books which the Vienna Circle was sponsoring, but never published, though a version of it appeared many years later after Waismann's death.

*Language, Truth, and Logic* was a short book, running to about 60,000 words. Its content was very much a summary of the views which I have attributed to the Vienna Circle, though my admiration for Russell and Moore led me to a stronger commitment to phenomenalism. I had also been influenced by C.I. Lewis's *Mind and the World Order*, and adopted his pragmatic view that all empirical statements, including those ostensibly about the past, were hypotheses the content of which was taken to be equated with what would count as the present or future evidence bearing upon them which was available to their interpreter. I also took what I later discovered to be the untenable position of adopting a mentalistic analysis of statements about one's own experiences and a behavioral analysis of statements about the experiences of other persons. A feature of the book, which became notorious, was its advocacy of the so-called emotive theory of ethics, according to which ethical judgements did not issue in true or false statements but only in expressions of moral approval or disapproval, which they encouraged others to share. I had in fact forgotten that a similar theory had been advanced as early as 1923 by C.K. Ogden and I.A. Richards in their book *The Meaning of Meaning*, though I was aware that the use of the word 'emotive' to embrace other than factual uses of language derived from them.

Mainly in England, *Language, Truth, and Logic* enjoyed an immediate *succès de scandale*. It was extensively reviewed and four impressions of the original Gollancz edition appeared before the war. Unhappily, this does not imply that a great many copies were sold. Victor Gollancz, when he received the manuscript, found it difficult to believe that many people would want to read a philosophical work of this kind and none of the impressions exceeded five hundred copies. It was only after the war when Gollancz consented to reprint the book on condition that I supplied it with a second introduction, which was in fact a misplaced appendix, that the book approached the status of a best-seller. A new impression of the second edition appeared almost annually for the next twenty-five years. It was translated into a dozen foreign languages—for some reason being especially well received in Japan, and it still maintains a steady sale in paperback, both in England and the United States.

# A Puzzling Best-Seller

I am not sure that I can wholly account for the book's popularity. I suppose that part of the reason lies in its simplicity and verve. I wrote it in the conviction that I had been led to discover the proper path for philosophy to follow, and this conviction, however ill-founded it may turn out to have been, does give the book an abiding force. There is also the factor that it created a disturbance in what, at any rate at Oxford before the war, had been a stodgy philosophical atmosphere. After the war it was seen as crystallizing several analytic tendencies that had been slowly coming to the fore and it also served as a springboard for the development of at least some variants of what came to be known as linguistic philosophy. All this made for its survival as a textbook, if nothing else.

The terms of my lectureship at Christ Church allowed me to function in a small way as a college tutor. I enjoyed this form of teaching and believe that I succeeded in arousing in at least some of my pupils quite a strong interest in philosophy. I also took an active part in the meetings of philosophical societies at all levels. Outside Oxford I found more sympathy for my views among the younger philosophers, mainly from Cambridge, whom I met at the annual Joint Sessions of the Mind Association and the Aristotelian Society. The first of these sessions that I attended took place at the University of Birmingham in 1933 and resulted in the founding of the journal *Analysis* which has continued publication to this day.

The sessions, consisting in four or five symposia, always took place over a week-end and one of their chief attractions was the presence of G.E. Moore who held an informal seminar on the Sunday afternoons. I was charmed by Moore as a person and much admired the wholehearted devotion to philosophical argument which he displayed in the discussions over which he presided.

A prominent disciple of Moore's and a senior member of the Editorial Board of *Analysis* was Professor L. Susan Stebbing who occupied the Chair of Philosophy at Bedford College, London. She had written *A Modern Introduction to Logic,* which I had read as an undergraduate and found very useful. It was through her that I first met Rudolf Carnap, whom she had invited to give a series of lectures at Bedford College in 1934. He had just published his *Logical Syntax of Language,* in which he drew his celebrated distinction between the material and formal modes of speech and made a forlorn attempt to treat all philosophical statements as syntactical. He was persuaded of the legitimacy of semantics by an abstract of Alfred Tarski's 'The Concept of Truth in Formalized Languages' delivered in German by Tarski at a large congress organized by the Vienna Circle in Paris in 1935. It was at this congress that I first set eyes on Bertrand Russell, then aged 63, who was deservedly lionized, so much so that I did not then venture to approach him. I did make friends with Karl Popper, whom I had not met in Vienna because he was not admitted to the Circle, though it sponsored the publication of his *Logic of Scientific Discovery,* which I had read and admired when it came out in 1934. He departed from the orthodoxy of the Circle to the extent that he put forward a principle of falsifiability not as a criterion of meaning but as a scientific shibboleth, a proposal which many scientists have welcomed as a faithful account of their procedure.

# Prejudice Against Logical Positivism

My enthusiastic advocacy of what had already come to be known as Logical Positivism had not endeared me to the senior philosophers in Oxford, so that it was clearly not going to be easy for me to secure a permanent position there. I had had some warning of this in the fact that when I competed for the John Locke Prize in Philosophy in 1933 the prize was not awarded. Nor was I the only victim of the examiners' prejudices. One of the other competitors was J.L. Austin, who had just been elected to All Souls.

My lectureship at Christ Church was extended for a third year but by 1935, since I was not inclined to take a junior post at another university, even if I could obtain one, it looked as if I should have to renounce any ambition of pursuing an academic career and address myself after all to the study of the law. I owed my salvation to the economist Roy Harrod who took a strong interest in philosophy and sympathized with my approach. *Language, Truth, and Logic* had not yet been published but I gave Harrod the typescript of two of the central chapters to send to Whitehead, then at Harvard, for his opinion. Whitehead had become an out and out metaphysician, so that he might have been expected to disapprove of my work, but in fact he gave me an enthusiastic testimonial, saying among other things that he could not imagine a greater blessing for English philosophical learning than the rise in Oxford of a vigorous young school of Logical Positivists. Harrod also asked Moore and Price for their opinion of my philosophical ability and obtained favourable answers in both cases. The result was that Christ Church elected me to a Research Studentship (a Fellowship), for a period of five years, thereby making me a member of the Governing Body of the College.

It was in the 1930s that like other members of my generation I began to take an active interest in politics. I gave a course of lectures on political theory and held a joint class with Frank Pakenham, later Lord Longford, who had been elected to a Studentship in Politics at Christ Church. Because of its contribution to the Republican cause in the Spanish Civil War, I briefly considered joining the Communist Party, but decided that I did not believe in Dialectical Materialism. There was an institution appropriately known as the Pink Lunch which served as a political forum for dons of at least a liberal persuasion and I regularly attended its meetings in Oxford. It was, however, in London, where we had taken a flat in 1935, that my political activity chiefly took place. I had joined the Labour Party and soon found myself Chairman of the Soho Branch of its Westminster Abbey division. It was a branch with few active supporters and the amount of canvassing and public speaking, especially at street corners, in which I felt obliged to engage was greater than I could have wished. In 1937 I stood for election in my local ward for the Westminster City Council, which was then composed entirely of Conservatives, and was narrowly defeated in a small poll. On that occasion I composed and published a shilling pamphlet entitled *Your Westminster*, of which I no longer possess a copy. I doubt if one is still in existence.

My absorption in philosophy and politics still left me leisure to read widely in other subjects. It had somehow come about that I had read hardly any of the novels of Dickens or Jane Austen in my adolescence and I made good this omission, acquiring a special affection for Dickens's *Bleak House* and Jane Austen's *Mansfield Park*. Among other nineteenth-century English novelists my favourite in addition to Peacock was Wilkie Collins and I frequently re-read them both. I also read a great many detective stories, a taste which I discovered that I shared with Bertrand Russell of whom I saw a certain amount when he came to deliver a series of lectures in Oxford in 1938. It was in the same year that on a scholarship from the English Speaking Union I paid my first visit to the United States, renewing my friendship with the poet e.e. cummings, whom I had already met in Oxford and making the acquaintance also in New York of the philosophers Sidney Hook and Ernest Nagel, and the polymath art-historian, Meyer Schapiro.

# The Foundations of Knowledge

The main fruit of my five years Research Studentship was my book *The Foundations of Empirical Knowledge* which appeared in March 1940, under the imprint of Macmillan, who became my regular publishers. The book was primarily a defense of a slightly weaker form of phenomenalism than I had embraced in *Language, Truth, and Logic*. Its fidelity to the theory of sense-data provided J.L. Austin with most of the ammunition for his onslaught on the theory, delivered in the lectures which were eventually published under the title of *Sense and Sensibilia*.

Besides writing the two books that I have mentioned, I wrote and published about a dozen philosophical articles in the nineteen thirties. The most important of them was 'Verification and Experience' which I contributed to the *Proceedings of the Aristotelian Society* for 1936–37. It contained what I still believe to be a decisive refutation of the manner in which Carnap and Neurath were then upholding a coherence theory of truth.

When *The Foundations of Empirical Knowledge* was published I was already a soldier. On the way to becoming an officer in the Welsh Guards I had first to spend some months as a Guardsman Recruit and an Officer

Cadet. In 1941 I was seconded to Military Intelligence, spending most of my time in offices in London, New York, and Algiers but having a roving commission in the South West of France after the Allied landing in 1944. I spent most of 1945 as an attaché at the British Embassy in Paris and was demobilized with the rank of Captain in November 1945.

I did next to no philosophical work during these years. It was not until 1945 that I found time to publish an article in *Mind* which was critical of Moore's treatment of sense-data. Moore replied to it in an appendix to the second edition of *The Philosophy of G.E. Moore* in the Library of Living Philosophers. In the same year I published a hostile review of Jean-Paul Sartre's *Being and Nothingness* and a mainly favorable appreciation of the work of Albert Camus, both in Cyril Connolly's journal *Horizon.*

A short-lived successor to *Horizon* was the journal *Polemic,* on the editorial board of which I served together with Bertrand Russell and George Orwell, with whom I had made friends when he came to Paris as a journalist. I published various articles in this journal including a survey of contemporary British philosophy, in which I unwittingly offended Wittgenstein, who had been well disposed towards me since Gilbert Ryle first took me to visit him in Cambridge in 1932.

The Fellow and Tutor in Philosophy at Wadham had retired through ill health during the war and I was elected, in absence, to replace him. My first marriage had been dissolved in 1942, and as soon as I was demobilized I moved into a set of rooms in Wadham, being immediately appointed Dean of the College, a disciplinary office which gave me no trouble, mainly owing to the maturity of the undergraduates, most of whom had served in the war. I resumed lecturing on Perception and being the only philosophical Fellow in the college undertook a full stint of tutorial teaching.

Though I was very well satisfied with my position at Wadham, I remained only a very short time there. An approach was made to me late in 1946 by the Provost of University College London, to become a candidate for the vacant Grote Professorship of the Philosophy of Mind and Logic in the University of London, tenable at University College. After some hesitation I applied for the position, was interviewed and elected. Wadham repaid my defection more generously than I deserved by making me an Honorary Fellow in 1957.

I had rashly accepted the appointment at University College London without inspecting its department of philosophy, and when I did inspect it found that it was moribund. My predecessor in the Chair had migrated to Scotland just before the war and had not been replaced. All that remained was one senior lecturer, an unqualified assistant, and at most half a dozen dispirited undergraduates. I put a great deal of energy into reviving the department and very much enjoyed doing so. I replaced the unqualified assistant with the highly qualified Stuart Hampshire, recruited the promising Richard Wollheim from Oxford and in the succeeding years promoted five of my London pupils, James Thomson, John Watling, Peter Long, Peter Downing, and Anthony Basson to lectureships. I recruited a great many more undergraduates, as well as graduates, revived the University College Philosophical Society which had ceased to function for the previous fifteen years, and made the department into a flourishing self-contained unit, installed in a house which it continues to occupy.

My inaugural lecture 'Thinking and Meaning' was published as a pamphlet in 1947. I still believe that it posed some of the right questions but doubt if it gave many of the right answers to them. When I repeated it before a small audience of philosophers in New York in 1948 Nelson Goodman raised objections to it which I could not meet. I had gone to New York to spend the autumn semester, lecturing at New York University, as well as at Bard in New York State. Apart from visiting Harvard and briefly attending a meeting of the Eastern Division of Philosophy at the University of Virginia, I met few American philosophers outside New York.

When I returned to London, I founded the Metalogical Society, remotely imitative of the nineteenth-century Metaphysical Society, though it contained no poets. There were about twenty members, mostly philosophers and biologists, as well as a physicist, a psychiatrist, and a Professor of History from University College, the Dutchman G.J. Renier, best known for his book *The English: Are They Human?* We met once a month in my flat, to discuss a paper which one or other of us had volunteered to read. A good account of these meetings is to be found in the book *Russell Remembered* by Rupert Crawshay-Williams, who was a friend and neighbor of Bertrand Russell's in Wales. Russell attended the meetings regularly and obviously enjoyed them. In the early 1950s he was living at Richmond and I quite often visited him there. I saw less of him when he returned to live in Wales and became increasingly absorbed in politics but our friendship lasted for the remainder of his life. I think that it was partly sustained by the fact that I upheld his approach to philosophy at a time when he had been given some reason to believe that his reputation had fallen below that of Wittgenstein and Moore. Current fashion has turned rather against Moore, but I fear that my preference for Russell over Wittgenstein is one that many of my younger colleagues do not share.

# My Abandonment of Phenomenalism

The book on the theory of knowledge was written by myself. It was entitled *The Problem of Knowledge* and published in 1956. Next to *Language, Truth, and Logic,* it has been my most successful book, and I myself consider it the better of the two. It represented the theory of knowledge as a set of attempts to rebut a characteristic pattern of skeptical argument. In a variety of instances such as the step from our acquaintance with sense-data to our belief in the existence of physical objects, the step from observation of other people's behavior and their physiological condition to the ascription to them of mental states, the transition from what appear to be present memories to the belief in the occurrence of past events, the skeptic argues that we make light of a gap which we are not justified in bridging. The theorist of knowledge responds sometimes by trying to bring the evidence up to the level of the conclusion, as when it is claimed that we are directly acquainted with the past, sometimes by trying to reduce the conclusion to the evidence, as in the phenomenalist analysis of statements about physical objects or the behaviourist's account of mental states, sometimes by treating the conclusion as the best explanation of the evidence, sometimes by simply disqualifying the skeptic for setting his standard of justification so high that it could not possibly be satisfied. For the most part in my book I followed the last of these courses, not without feeling that I was disposing of the problem rather too easily.

In 1950 it became my turn to be elected President of the Aristotelian Society. My presidential address was entitled 'Statements about the Past'. Its most controversial thesis was that events could be located in time simply by means of the relation of temporal priority, the terms of the relation being uniquely identified by description. There was, indeed, no logical guarantee that such a description would always be available but it was a safe empirical assumption. This was indeed one application of the general thesis that demonstrative expressions, including tenses, are not linguistically essential. They are eliminable by paraphrase, through the use of descriptions. This view, which I have put forward on various occasions, is one that has also been espoused by Quine and Goodman. Even so, I have come to doubt whether it is correct, partly because it allows only for indefinite reference. The chief argument on the other side is that if demonstratives are not eliminable, a large part of our use of language is incurably subjective.

I included 'Statements about the Past' in a collection of twelve essays ranging in date from 1943 to 1954 and published by Macmillan in 1954 under the title of *Philosophical Essays*. It included an essay 'On the Analysis of Moral Judgements', refining my emotive theory, as well as the reprint of a lecture entitled 'Phenomenalism' which I had delivered to the Aristotelian Society in the session of 1947–48. It marked my final abandonment of this doctrine, on the ground that the obstacles in the way of translating sentences about physical objects into sentences about sense-data were logically insurmountable. From that time onwards I have treated the common-sense conception of the physical world as a theory created on the basis of sense-data, or rather, since I think that there are advantages in starting with universals rather than particulars, on the basis of what, following the example of C.I. Lewis and Nelson Goodman in his *Structure of Appearance,* I refer to as sense-qualia, and I have made successive attempts in my later works to develop this view in detail.

Throughout the 1950s and 1960s I very frequently lectured abroad. In 1951 I was invited by the University of San Marcos in Lima, Peru, to take part in the celebration of the four hundredth anniversary of its foundation and I was then employed by the British Council to lecture in Chile and Uruguay, where I spoke in Spanish, and in Rio de Janeiro, where, in default of Portuguese, I spoke in French. I think that I was independently invited to lecture in Denmark and Sweden but it was on behalf of the British Council that I lectured at a series of Italian Universities, again speaking in French, and toured India and Pakistan in 1958, discovering that the philosophers in the Indian universities still taught versions of the Bradleyan idealism to which their predecessors had been converted by Scottish evangelists in the late nineteenth century. Despite its esthetic attractions, and the generous hospitality which I encountered especially in Delhi, I did not greatly care for India. What chiefly shocked me was the prevailing acquiescence in human misery. I much preferred China to which I had been invited as one of a small cultural delegation in 1954. Although the Communists had been in power for five years they had not yet ventured upon any violent reforms. Peking, which had been left untouched, appeared to me the most beautiful city that I had ever seen. The philosophers whom I met there had nearly all been trained in England, Germany, or the United States and they were much less interested in Marxism than in formal logic.

# A Public Figure in the 1950s

The decade of the 1950s was that in which I most frequently broadcast on philosophical topics, and also appeared on television. The BBC had devised a program called *The Brains Trust* which became very popular during the war when it was put out over the wireless, and was transferred to television after the war. When I first appeared on it, the program went out live on Sunday afternoons and lasted for three quarters of an hour. It took the form of a discussion between four persons under the control of a chairman, debating questions which had, at least in theory, been submitted by members of the public. From five to seven questions were commonly got through. They covered a wide range of subjects but chiefly concentrated on concrete and abstract moral issues. The membership of the panel changed from week to week but a few persons, notably Julian Huxley, Alan Bullock, and the versatile Jacob Bronowski, were invited sufficiently often to count as regulars. I myself made over forty appearances on the program before it was discarded by the BBC in 1961.

I played very little active part in politics after the war, but I was still sufficiently attached to the Labour Party to write occasional newspaper articles on its behalf and I appeared on a television programme in support of its unsuccessful campaign in the general election of 1959. By that time I had become quite a close friend of its leader Hugh Gaitskell and I still count his early death in 1963 as a factor in England's political decline.

My most effective involvement in public affairs consisted in my Chairmanship of the Society for Homosexual Law Reform. This society came into being as a result of the publication in 1957 of the Wolfenden Report which among other things recommended that the conduct of homosexual relations in private between consenting male adults should cease to be a criminal offense. We acted as a pressure group over nearly a decade and I think that we made some contribution to the change in the climate of public opinion which made it possible for a private bill, enacting the desired reform, to be introduced successfully by Lord Annan in the House of Lords and then to be accepted by the House of Commons.

In 1959 Henry Price retired from the Wykeham Professorship of Logic at Oxford and I decided to apply for it. Part of my motive was that the position carried greater prestige, part that I wanted to provide some local opposition to the form of linguistic philosophy which Austin had made fashionable, with what appeared to me its excessive concentration on the niceties of ordinary English usage. I had no particular wish to leave UCL, though I did feel that if I remained there I should be in some danger of resting on my laurels. Bertrand Russell and Isaiah Berlin consented to act as my referees and I was elected by a narrow majority. The professorship carried with it a fellowship at New College and I was allotted a very handsome set of rooms there. I was in danger of having to vacate them when I married the journalist Dee Wells in 1960, but since I arranged to spend the greater part of the week in Oxford during term, returning to our house in London only for long week-ends, I was allowed to keep them for the nineteen years that I continued to occupy the Chair.

My statutory duty was to give 36 lectures or classes in the course of an academic year. I slightly exceeded this quota by lecturing twice a week during two of the three eight-week terms and giving what was known as informal instruction once a week in every term. This was in fact a seminar attended by both graduates and undergraduates, about 25 in number. In its early days the seminar was devoted to a single topic such as 'causality' or 'time'. Later I tended to go through a volume of essays, preferably one that had been recently published. My method was to open the proceedings at the first meeting but afterwards to persuade members of the audience to volunteer to fulfil this role. Rather than indulge in lengthy expositions of my own views I tried to get the members of my audience to argue with me and with one another and in the main I was successful. A good many of these meetings were very lively and I believe that I was not alone in finding them intellectually profitable.

My lectures gave me less satisfaction. I prepared them carefully even to the extent on occasion of writing them out in full but I spoke too fast and tended to cover too many topics in a single lecture. As a rule they began by attracting quite large audiences, whose number steadily dwindled. Even so the few who remained faithful seemed to enjoy them.

One of the distinguishing features of post-war Oxford was the large increase in the number of graduates. This applied also to philosophy, mainly as the result of the introduction by Gilbert Ryle, who had succeeded Collingwood in the Chair of Metaphysics, of the new higher degree of B.Phil. combining a dissertation with a choice of several set papers. To reassure the college tutors whom he thought unlikely to welcome any increase in their load of teaching, Ryle had given the undertaking that the supervision of candidates for the B.Phil. degree should be entrusted solely to the three professors of philosophy, respectively holding the Chairs of Logic, Morals, and Metaphysics. The degree, however, soon became so popular that the professors, if they were to give their nominal pupils anything like an adequate measure of supervision, were not equal to the demand. When the number of graduates for whom I was officially responsible rose to 22, I suggested to Ryle that some of the better college tutors would be happy to take some graduate pupils, as a relief from the routine of teaching undergraduates. This turned out to be true and from then onwards I do not think that I ever had more than eight graduates to supervise. I saw them for an hour each once a fortnight and almost always enjoyed our arguments. Many of those whom I supervised became successful teachers of philosophy.

# Against Ordinary Language Philosophy

In the autumn of 1960, a year after my introduction into the Chair, I gave my inaugural lecture entitled 'Philosophy and Language'. Its main purpose was to show that philosophers like Ryle and Wittgenstein, though they might make verbal points, were not concerned in the same way as Austin and his disciples with the elucidation of ordinary linguistic usage. Their object was rather to induce their audience to take a different and clearer view of the facts which language was used to describe. In fairness to Austin, it should be said that he also claimed that the study of language illuminated the facts. In the end my opposition to his approach might have shown itself to be no more than a difference of emphasis. The question was never settled since he died before the end of the year and the interest shown by Oxford philosophers in ordinary usage as such virtually died with him.

One way in which Austin had maintained his philosophical power in Oxford had been his dominance of a class, meeting on Saturday mornings, attendance at which was confined to college tutors younger than himself. Conformably to my original intention of counteracting his influence, I founded a rival class of a very different character. It met on Tuesday evenings from five to seven o'clock from the second to the seventh week of term. A different member acted as host to the group each term and provided drinks which were served during the discussion of the paper devoted to a subject of the speaker's choosing. There was no question of my organizing the program or controlling the discussion. The original members of the group, besides myself, were Peter Strawson, David Pears, Michael Dummett, Brian McGuinness, Michael Woods, Patrick Gardiner, Tony Quinton, David Wiggins, and James Thomson. Later nearly a score of others were asked to join, including promising younger philosophers like Gareth Evans, John McDowell, Derek Parfit, and Christopher Peacocke, and when distinguished philosophers from the United States came to Oxford for a term or more they were also invited and often contributed papers. I do not believe that anyone ever refused an invitation to belong. In the course of time, three members have died, and several have ceased coming to meetings for one reason or another, but the group still meets regularly after 27 years. Though it is now eight years since Michael Dummett succeeded me in the Chair of Logic at Oxford, and I live in London, I still attend a fair number of its meetings.

In the autumn of 1961 I took a term's sabbatical leave from Oxford in order to spend a semester teaching at City College, New York. I gave an undergraduate and a graduate course and enjoyed them both very much. My audience of undergraduates was as responsive as any that I have ever had. I gave occasional lectures at a number of other universities, mostly in the eastern part of the United States and accepted a more exotic invitation to give a talk on the nature of philosophy at one of the seminars that President Kennedy was requiring the members of his family and his cabinet to attend in Washington. The President and his wife were absent on this occasion and the proceedings were conducted by his brother, Bobby, the Attorney-General. It being hardly possible to summarize the whole of philosophy in an hour, I contented myself with trying to show that the analytic conception of philosophy which I favored stood squarely in the Socratic tradition. On the whole the meeting went well, though some members of the Kennedy family were shocked by my patent disbelief in the existence of God.

From New York I went almost immediately to Moscow. I had visited Moscow over seven years before on my way to China but had not then made contact with any Russian philosophers. My current invitation to lecture in Moscow and Leningrad was the remote result of my making friends with members of the Russian delegation to the World Congress of Philosophy held in Venice in 1958 and the immediate result of my agreeing to contribute to the Soviet journal *Voprosi Filosofii* (Problems of Philosophy). My paper, to which Professor Kuznetsov wrote a reply, was entitled 'Philosophy and Science' and stressed the difference between them. This contradicted one of the basic principles of Dialectical Materialism,[3] but so far as our argument went I fancy that our disagreement was mainly verbal.

I gave four lectures in Moscow, one of which, a lecture on Truth, I repeated in Leningrad. I spoke in English and the fact that my lectures and the lengthy discussions which followed them had to be interpreted into and out of Russian extended the proceedings, on one occasion to as much as

---

3. Dialectical Materialism was the official philosophy of the Soviet state, based on the philosophical ideas of Marx, Engels, Lenin, and Stalin.

four hours. I was struck by the interest which the students took in what I had to say and surprised by the extent of their acquaintance with recent English philosophy. Dee had been invited to accompany me and my schedule of lectures allowed us some leisure for tourism. We were enchanted by Leningrad, which had been admirably restored after its destruction in the war. Unfortunately we were not given enough time to explore all the glories of the Hermitage gallery, though we did manage to discover its magnificent collection of Impressionist and post-Impressionist paintings.

One of my Moscow lectures 'The Concept of a Person' gave its title to a collection of twelve essays published in 1963. The lecture was provoked by Peter Strawson's thesis, expounded in his remarkable book *Individuals,* that the concept of a person is not susceptible to reductive analysis. Against this I argued that persons were identifiable by their bodies, and that the association of different sets of experiences with different bodies and so with different persons could be explained in causal terms. I have since come to doubt whether my causal explanation was satisfactory.

*The Concept of a Person* contained two essays in which I tried to clarify the notion of privacy and also took issue with Wittgenstein's so-called private language argument to which the majority of contemporary English and American philosophers appear to me to have assented far too readily. I contended that objects were intrinsically neither public nor private. A chair is a public object because we attach sense to saying that different persons perceive one and the same chair; headaches are private because we do not speak of different persons' feeling the same headache. But these locutions are adapted to empirical circumstances which might well have been otherwise. As for the ban on private language it results from Wittgenstein's requirement that there be criteria for deciding whether a word is being used correctly, that is, in accordance with a rule. The requirement is unobjectionable, but the belief that the criteria are satisfied must itself be grounded. In the end any descriptive use of language rests on what I call acts of primary recognition, and here it makes no difference what one is referring to.

I also included in the volume two notes on Probability. In the first of them, which I had previously published, I put forward what I still regard as a decisive argument against the interpretation, adopted by Keynes and Carnap among others, of statements of probability as assessing a logical relation between some conclusion and a given body of evidence. The argument is simply that by turning all correct statements of probability into logical truths, this procedure puts them all on an equal footing, so that so far as the estimate of probability goes there seem no rational motives for looking for further evidence. The second note showed that a somewhat similar difficulty arises for the frequency theory of probability, since any event will belong to a number of different classes in which the incidence of whatever property is in question occurs with a different frequency, so that one is faced with the problem how the choice of one reference class, in preference to the others, is to be justified.

Another of my Moscow lectures was entitled 'Pragmatism', a form of philosophy which had interested me ever since my last year as an undergraduate when I read F.P. Ramsey's praise of it in his posthumously published collection of papers *The Foundations of Mathematics*. I had dealt with it rather summarily in a series of lectures comparing contemporary or near-contemporary English and American philosophers, which I had delivered at UCL in 1957 and in the course of the 1960s I narrowed it down to a study of what I took to be the cardinal features of the work of Charles Sanders Peirce and William James. It was published under the title of *The Origins of Pragmatism* by Macmillan in England and by Freeman, Cooper in the United States. It was not a success in either country. The American devotees of Peirce found it insufficiently scholarly and other readers who might have been interested in some of my own ideas which it incorporated were put off by its title. I valued it chiefly for its critical treatment of Peirce's theory of induction and James's attempt to make good Hume's failure to analyze personal identity in terms of a series of experiences. I refined James's thesis in various ways and came quite near to validating it but in the end I encountered obstacles which I had to confess that I could not overcome.

# Defending Sense-Data

In 1967 I accepted an invitation to become a Visiting Professor at the University of Toronto. My lectures there were a preview of my book on Pragmatism. I lectured also in Toronto and Montreal. In Montreal I replied at long last to Austin's *Sense and Sensibilia*, a posthumously published book fashioned out of the notes of a series of lectures which he repeatedly gave in Oxford, attempting to demolish the whole theory of sense-data and singling out for especial ridicule the opening pages of my *Foundations of Empirical Knowledge*. I extracted 14 arguments from his book and rebutted all of them. I did not claim that my account of sense-data in that early book was faultless but I did and do claim that Austin's arguments did not refute it.

I included this piece, entitled 'Has Austin Refuted the Sense-Datum Theory?' in a collection of essays entitled *Metaphysics and Common Sense.* In the essay from which the book acquired its title I treated metaphysics more leniently than I had in *Language, Truth, and Logic,* arguing that G.E. Moore, in particular, had taken unfair advantage of the metaphysicians whom he criticized by assuming that they literally meant what they said. I remarked that while the conclusions which they advanced might be patently false or even nonsensical, the arguments by which they professed to reach them might well be of logical interest. My chief examples were McTaggart's denial of the reality of time and Zeno's denial of the reality of motion. In both cases the conclusion is absurd, but McTaggart raises acute questions about our concept of time and I am not at all sure that Zeno's paradoxes have yet been adequately solved.

In the 1960s I spent a couple of years serving on a Commission set up by the Department of Education and Science under the Chairmanship of Lady Plowden to enquire into the Conditions and Prospects of Primary Education in the British Isles. At that time the Department succumbed to the theory that so far as possible children should find things out for themselves, and accordingly displayed a pronounced hostility to formal methods of teaching. It appeared to me, as it turned out rightly, that this prejudice, which most of my colleagues unquestioningly shared, was being carried much too far, but I lacked the energy and confidence to write a dissenting report. I failed also to fulfil the hope, which I had entertained, of persuading the Commission to find some effective means of lessening the disparity in the academic standards of the private and state elementary schools. My only successes lay in obtaining a recommendation, by now very widely accepted, that corporal punishment be abolished in primary schools and in persuading a minority of my colleagues to join me in advocating the abandonment of compulsory religious instruction. The best part of our final report, on which some limited action was taken, consisted in its suggestions for paying special attention to the plight of schools in deprived areas, but this was not a subject to which I contributed anything of special importance.

In 1969, when Maurice Bowra was due to retire from the Wardenship of Wadham, one or two of the Fellows let me know that they would like me to succeed him. I was attracted by the idea and would have accepted the position had it been immediately offered to me. There was, however, a delay of some months, while the Governing Body of the College considered the choices open to them, and during this interval I came to doubt whether the administrative duties incumbent on the Warden were compatible with my dominant wish to pursue my philosophical career. As a result, though I went so far as to submit myself to an interview, I formally withdrew my candidature. In retrospect, I am inclined to think that this was a mistake.

Perhaps in an effort to prove my point, I got through a great deal of work in the following decade. In 1970 I spent a semester at Harvard, in response to an invitation to deliver the William James lectures. I lost no time in reproducing them as a book entitled *Russell and Moore: The Analytical Heritage*, published by the Harvard University Press in the United States and Macmillan in England. I think that my account, especially of Moore's work, was thorough and perceptive but that the book as a whole was somewhat pedestrian. So far as Russell goes, I rather prefer the book about him that I wrote shortly afterwards for the *Fontana Library of Modern Masters*. When some years later the Oxford University Press inaugurated a series on *Past Masters*, I wrote *Hume* for them. Since Hume and Russell are the philosophers for whom I feel the greatest intellectual sympathy, I found both books enjoyable to write.

From Boston I proceeded to New York to give the second series of John Dewey Lectures at Columbia University. The first series had been given by Quine and formed the substance of his book *Ontological Relativity*. Mine consisted of three lectures on probability, in which I expounded and in the main defended Hume's strictures on induction, and pointed out the fallacies involved in basing what I called judgments of credibility on the a priori calculus of chances. Conjoining with these lectures an essay on causality and a refutation of Roy Harrod's ingenious attempt in his book *Foundations of Inductive Logic* to justify induction on the basis of a logical theory of probability, I produced a book entitled *Probability and Evidence*, published by Macmillan again in England and by the Columbia Press in the United States. I think quite well of this book though I doubt if it gets to the root of the difficult problems with which it deals.

In 1972 I accepted an invitation to give the Gifford Lectures at the University of Saint Andrews. Since the intention of Lord Gifford, the nineteenth-century Scottish lawyer who bequeathed a sum of money sufficient for the regular provision of lectures at one or other of four Scottish universities was that they should examine the claims of natural theology, I felt bound to devote one lecture to this topic. Taking a less short way with theism than I had in *Language, Truth, and Logic*, I nevertheless argued that there was no ground for believing in the existence of a supernatural deity. Even if it were allowed to be intelligible as an explanatory hypothesis, it would still succumb to the charge of being vacuous, since in view of the fact that the course of nature as a whole exhibits no discernible purpose, it would be consistent with anything that happened.

My other seven lectures were, I think, such as to justify my calling the series, and the book which resulted from it, *The Central Questions of Philosophy.* The best chapters were the two in which I developed my thesis that the common-sense conception of the natural world should be treated as a theory created on a basis of sense-qualia. What was most original in them was my attempt to separate priority in the theory of knowledge from priority in existence. I suggested that the data on which the common-sense theory was based were taken over by the theory, being reinterpreted into it as states of the subclass of bodies which were represented in the theory as persons, and thereby assigned a minor existential role. In turn, I suggested that the entities which figured in the theories of physics could be regarded in much the same way as taking over the common-sense world which they were designed to explain. Borrowing the idea of Peirce, I argued that the person who emerged in the first theory as oneself was originally identified as the central body.

# The Ranking of Twentieth-Century Philosophers

Among my philosophical works, *Philosophy in the Twentieth Century* is probably the one which I found the most troublesome to write, partly because of the necessary presence of a chapter on Russell, where I was not happy simply to repeat what I had already written, partly because it was not clear to me what I could venture to include. The book was intended to be a sequel to Russell's *History of Western Philosophy* and it was eventually packaged in paperback by Allen and Unwin, who had published Russell's book. There is, however, no question but that it is a far less ambitious work. Understandably, in view of my own convictions, it devotes an amount of space to the ramifications of analytical philosophy that is out of proportion to its historical influence. Not that other avenues of philosophy are totally neglected. C.I. Lewis is selected as the representative of Pragmatism. A careful study of the work of Collingwood exemplifies Metaphysics. In choosing to expound and criticize Maurice Merleau-Ponty's *Phenomenology of Perception,* I believed that I was tackling the legacy of Husserl at its best. I did, indeed, ignore the later development of Marxism, but it was a subject on which Professor Kolokowski had published a detailed work of scholarship and I was content to refer my readers to his writings, rather than indulge in what would have been no more than plagiarism.

Both in my treatment of his work in *Philosophy in the Twentieth Century* and in the book which I devoted to him I was critical of most of the arguments that feature in the great bulk of Wittgenstein's posthumously published writings. My account of the *Tractatus*, though friendly, also failed to recapture the enthusiasm with which it originally overwhelmed me. In these circumstances it is surprising that I ended by marking him second only to Russell among twentieth-century philosophers. I think that I may have been swayed by my memory of his formidable personality and also, less justifiably, by the fervor of his admirers.

Professors at Oxford are obliged to retire at the end of the academic year in which they reach the age of 67 and this happened to me in 1978. This entailed that I was eligible only for an honorary fellowship at New College and forfeited my rooms there. It was some compensation that I was immediately elected to a five-year fellowship, entitling me to a set of rooms, at Wolfson. As it turned out, I made relatively little use of the facilities at Wolfson, but I was grateful for their being made available to me.

One of the colleges for graduates which had been founded at Oxford after the war, Wolfson had become, among other things, a center for the advancement of mathematical logic. Though I was titularly the professor of logic first in London and then in Oxford, I have never had anything more than a very slight command of logic, in the technical sense of the term, with the result that I entirely welcomed the appointment of a Professor of Mathematical Logic, assisted by two University Readers and a University Lecturer, to take charge of the new School of Philosophy and Mathematics which I was perhaps primarily responsible for bringing into being. I had previously tried to inaugurate the same combination at University College London but was frustrated by the opposition of the Professor of Mathematics. There was some opposition from the mathematicians at Oxford but just enough co-operation also to assist the logicians in making the venture a success. Unfortunately this was not true of the Joint School of Philosophy and Physics which was instituted at the same time, again chiefly at my instigation. It has not been a total failure but the physicists at Oxford have not so far shown enough enthusiasm for it to enable it to prosper to the same extent as the School of Philosophy and Mathematics. It has also suffered from the fact that of the seventy or more philosophers who hold teaching posts in Oxford the great majority resemble myself in having been trained in the humanities and not in science.

To mark my retirement from my Chair, Graham Macdonald, a lecturer at Bradford University who had obtained the B.Phil. degree at Oxford under my supervision, organized a symposium. The book was published in 1979, under the title of *Perception and Identity.* The contributors, to whose criticisms of my work I did my best to reply, were Michael Dummett, Peter Strawson, David Pears, David Armstrong, Charles Taylor, John Mackie, Peter Unger, Bernard Williams, Stephen Körner, David Wiggins, Richard Wollheim, and John Foster. A former pupil of mine who has been a Fellow of Brasenose, John Foster also published in 1985 a book about my philosophy, simply entitled *A.J. Ayer,* which had been commissioned by Ted Honderich for the series *The Arguments of The Philosophers* which he edits for Routledge and Kegan Paul. Foster paid a handsome tribute to my writing, while criticizing my theories in detail from the currently uncommon standpoint of subjective idealism.

In 1983 I accepted an invitation to deliver the Whidden Lectures at McMaster University, Ontario, with which I was already associated as one of its committee of advisers concerning the publication of items from its collection of Bertrand Russell's papers. The lectures, three in number, were devoted to moral philosophy and began with a fresh attack on the problem of free will. Many years earlier I had published in *Polemic* and reprinted in my *Philosophical Essays* an essay entitled 'Freedom and Necessity', in which I had argued that there was no inconsistency between free will and determinism as such but only an opposition between freedom of choice or action and the sub-class of causes which counted as constraint. In the interval, however, I had come to doubt whether this sub-class could be adequately identified. Accordingly, in the first of my Whidden lectures, I approached the problem from a different angle, endeavoring to pinpoint the conditions under which our choices were considered not to be free. My suggestion was that they were held not to be free to the extent that they were deducible from some accepted totality of singular and general propositions. Though it may appear paradoxical that an increase in what we take to be knowledge should in any way diminish freedom, I am still disposed to argue in favor of some such relativization of freedom to ignorance. Even so, I have no thought of claiming a final dissolution of the problem of free will.

My marriage to Dee Wells was dissolved in 1981 and I subsequently married Vanessa Lawson, only to suffer the great misfortune of her dying in August 1985. Just under three years previously we had spent a very happy period of two terms at Dartmouth College in New Hampshire, where I had enjoyed the honor of being appointed to a Montgomery Fellowship.

The year 1986 marked the fiftieth anniversary of the original appearance of *Language, Truth, and Logic*. The occasion gave rise to the publication of two sets of lectures about the book, one organized by Graham Macdonald and Crispin Wright, the Professor of Logic at the University of Saint Andrews, and the other by Dr. Barry Gower, a lecturer in philosophy at Durham University. I contributed a retrospective essay to the Durham volume and a short preface to the other.

In under two months' time I shall be spending a semester as a Visiting Professor at Bard in New York State, where my younger son will be entering on his third year as an undergraduate. I have agreed to give courses on the classical British empiricists and on *Language, Truth, and Logic*, thereby completing a circle in my philosophical career.

*A. J. Ayer*

LA MIGOUA, VAR
21ST JULY, 1986

# That Undiscovered Country

*In June 1988 Ayer underwent a "a somewhat agonising but very astonishing experience," a near-death experience which he described in an article in the* London Spectator *(16th July, 1988). One of the readers of the* Spectator *(Mr. Kenneth Carrdus) caught the spirit of Sir Alfred quite well in a limerick and letter to the editor in the issue of 16th July, 1988:*

*The rationalist, A.J. Ayer,*
*Has answered the atheist's prayer:*
*A Hell you can't verify*
*Surely can't terrify*
*Until you* confirm *that it's there.*

*Sir Alfred's account of his remarkable brush with death and his reflections on it appeared in the London Sunday Telegraph for 28th August, 1988, with the title 'What I Saw When I Was Dead . . .' and a follow-up piece appeared in the London Spectator for 15th October, 1988, under the heading 'Postscript to a Postmortem'. In the latter he tells us that the title he had given the former was the Shakespearian 'That Undiscovered Country'.*

My first attack of pneumonia occurred in the United States. I was in the hospital for ten days in New York, after which the doctors said that I was well enough to leave. A final X-ray, however, which I underwent on the last morning, revealed that one of my lungs was not yet free from infection. This caused the most sympathetic of my doctors to suggest that it would be good for me to spend a few more days in the hospital. I respected his opinion but since I was already dressed and psychologically disposed to put my illness behind me, I decided to take the risk. I spent the next few days in my stepdaughter's apartment, and then made arrangements to fly back to England.

When I arrived I believed myself to be cured and incontinently plunged into an even more hectic social round than that to which I had become habituated before I went to America. Retribution struck me on Sunday, May 30th. I had gone out to lunch, had a great deal to eat and drink, and chattered incessantly. That evening I had a relapse. I could eat almost none of the food which a friend had brought to cook in my house.

On the next day, which was a bank-holiday, I had a long-standing engagement to lunch at the Savoy with a friend who was very eager for me to meet her son. I would have put them off if I could, but my friend lives in Exeter and I had no idea how to reach her in London. So I took a taxi to the Savoy and just managed to stagger into the lobby. I could eat hardly any of the delicious grilled sole that I ordered but forced myself to keep up my end of the conversation. I left early and took a taxi home. That evening I felt still worse. Once more I could eat almost none of the dinner another friend had brought me. Indeed, she was so alarmed by my weakness that she stayed overnight. When I was no better the next morning, she telephoned to my general practitioner and to my elder son Julian.

The doctor did little more than promise to try to get in touch with the specialist, but Julian, who is unobtrusively very efficient, immediately rang for an ambulance. The ambulance came quickly with two strong attendants, and yet another friend, who had called opportunely to pick up a key, accompanied it and me to University College Hospital.

I remember very little of what happened from then on. I was taken to a room in the private wing, which had been reserved for me by the specialist, who had a consulting room on the same floor. After being x-rayed and subjected to a number of tests, which proved beyond question that I was suffering from pneumonia, I was moved into intensive care in the main wing of the hospital.

Fortunately for me, the young doctor who was primarily responsible for me had been an undergraduate at New College, Oxford, while I was a Fellow. This made him extremely anxious to see that I recovered; almost too much so, in fact, for he was so much in awe of me that he forbade me to be disturbed at night, even when the experienced sister[4] and nurse believed it to be necessary.

Under his care and theirs I made such good progress that I expected to be moved out of intensive care and back into the private wing within a week. My disappointment was my own fault. I did not attempt to eat the hospital food. My family and friends supplied all the food I needed. I am particularly fond of smoked salmon, and one evening I carelessly tossed a slice of it into my throat. It went down the wrong way and almost immediately the graph recording my heartbeats plummeted. The ward sister rushed to the rescue, but she was unable to prevent my heart from stopping. She and the doctor subsequently told me that I died in this sense for four minutes, and I have had no reason to disbelieve them.

The doctor alarmed my son Nicholas, who had flown from New York to be by my bedside, by saying that it was not probable that I should recover and, moreover, that if I did recover physically it was not probable that my mental powers would be restored. The nurses were more optimistic and Nicholas sensibly chose to believe them.

I have no recollection of anything that was done to me at that time. Friends have told me that I was festooned with tubes but I have never learned how many of them there were or, with one exception, what purposes they served. I do not remember having a tube inserted in my throat to bring up the quantity of phlegm which had lodged in my lungs. I was not even aware of my numerous visitors, so many of them, in fact, that the sister had to set a quota. I know that the doctors and nurses were surprised by the

---

4. In British hospitals, a nurse in charge of other nurses is often called by the title 'sister', while the head of nursing staff for the whole hospital is often called 'matron'.

speed of my recovery and that when I started speaking, the specialist expressed astonishment that anyone with so little oxygen in his lungs should be so lucid.

My first recorded utterance, which convinced those who heard it that I had not lost my wits, was the exclamation: "You are all mad." I am not sure how this should be interpreted. It is possible that I took my audience to be Christians and was telling them that I had not discovered anything 'on the other side'. It is also possible that I took them to be skeptics and was implying that I had discovered something. I think the former is more probable as in the latter case I should more properly have exclaimed 'We are all mad'. All the same, I cannot be sure.

The earliest remarks of which I have any cognisance, apart from my first exclamation, were made several hours after my return to life. They were addressed to a French woman with whom I had been friends for over 15 years. I woke to find her seated by my bedside and started talking to her in French as soon as I recognized her. My French is fluent and I spoke rapidly, approximately as follows: "Did you know that I was dead? The first time that I tried to cross the river I was frustrated, but my second attempt succeeded. It was most extraordinary. My thoughts became persons."

The content of those remarks suggests that I have not wholly put my classical education behind me. In Greek Mythology the souls of the dead, now only shadowly embodied, were obliged to cross the river Styx in order to reach Hades, after paying an odol to the ferryman, Charon.

I may also have been reminded of my favorite philosopher, David Hume, who, during his last illness, "a disorder of the bowels," imagined that Charon, growing impatient, was calling him "a lazy loitering rogue." With his usual politeness, Hume replied that he saw without regret his death approaching and that he was making no effort to postpone it. This is one of the rare occasions on which I have failed to follow Hume. Clearly I had made an effort to prolong my life.

The only memory that I have of an experience, closely encompassing my death, is very vivid. I was confronted by a red light, exceedingly bright, and also very painful even when I turned away from it. I was aware that this light was responsible for the government of the universe. Among its ministers were two creatures who had been put in charge of space. These ministers periodically inspected space and had recently carried out such an inspection. They had, however, failed to do their work properly, with the result that space, like a badly fitting jigsaw puzzle, was slightly out of joint.

A further consequence was that the laws of nature had ceased to function as they should. I felt that it was up to me to put things right. I also had the motive of finding a way to extinguish the painful light. I assumed that it was signalling that space was awry and that it would switch itself off when order was restored. Unfortunately, I had no idea where the guardians of space had gone and feared that even if I found them I should not be able to communicate with them.

It then occurred to me that whereas, until the present century, physicists accepted the Newtonian severance of space and time, it had become customary, since the vindication of Einstein's general theory of relativity, to treat space-time as a single whole. Accordingly, I thought that I could cure space by operating upon time. I was vaguely aware that the ministers who had been given charge of time were in my neighborhood and I proceeded to hail them. I was again frustrated. Either they did not hear me, or they chose to ignore me, or they did not understand me. I then hit upon the expedient of walking up and down, waving my watch, in the hope of drawing their attention not to my watch itself but to the time which it measured. This elicited no response. I became more and more desperate, until the experience suddenly came to an end.

This experience could well have been delusive. A slight indication that it might have been veridical has been supplied by my French friend, or rather by her mother, who also underwent a heart arrest many years ago. When her daughter asked her what it had been like, she replied that all that she remembered was that she must stay close to the red light.

On the face of it, these experiences, on the assumption that the last one was veridical, are rather strong evidence that death does not put an end to consciousness. Does it follow that there is a future life? Not necessarily. The trouble is that there are different criteria for being dead, which are indeed logically compatible but may not always be satisfied together.

In this instance, I am given to understand that the arrest of the heart does not entail, either logically or causally, the arrest of the brain. In view of the very strong evidence in favour of the dependence of thoughts upon the brain, the most probable hypothesis is that my brain continued to function although my heart had stopped.

If I had acquired good reason to believe in a future life, it would have applied not only to myself. Admittedly, the philosophical problem of justifying one's confident belief in the existence and contents of other minds has not yet been satisfactorily solved. Even so, with the possible exception of Fichte—who proclaimed that the world was his idea but may not have meant it literally—no philosopher has acquiesced in solipsism. No philosopher has seriously asserted that of all the objects in the universe, he alone was conscious.

Moreover it is commonly taken for granted, not only by philosophers, that the minds of others bear a sufficiently close analogy to one's own. Consequently, if I had been vouchsafed a reasonable expectation of a future life, other human beings could expect one too.

Let us grant, for the sake of argument, that we could have future lives. What form could they take?

The easiest answer is that they would consist in the prolongation of our experiences, without any physical attachment. This is the theory that should appeal to radical empiricists. It is, indeed, consistent with the concept of personal identity which was adopted both by Hume and by William James, according to which one's identity consists, not in the possession of an enduring soul but in the sequence of one's experiences, guaranteed by memory. They did not apply their theory to a future life, in which Hume at any rate disbelieved.

For those who are attracted by this theory, as I am, the main problem, which Hume admitted that he was unable to solve, is to discover the relation, or relations, which have to hold between experiences for them to belong to one and the same self.

William James thought that he had found the answers with his relations of the felt togetherness and continuity of our thoughts and sensations, coupled with memory, in order to unite experiences that are separated in time. But while memory is undoubtedly necessary, it can be shown that it is not wholly sufficient.

I myself carried out a thorough examination and development of the theory in my book *The Origins of Pragmatism*. I was reluctantly forced to conclude that I could not account for personal identity without falling back on the identity, through time, of one or more bodies that the person might successively occupy. Even then, I was unable to give a satisfactory account of the way in which a series of experiences is tied to a particular body at any given time.

The admission that personal identity through time requires the identity of a body is a surprising feature of Christianity. I call it surprising because it seems to me that Christians are apt to forget that the resurrection of the body is an element in their creed. The question of how bodily identity is sustained over intervals of time is not so difficult. The answer might consist in postulating a reunion of the same atoms, perhaps in there being no more than a strong physical resemblance, possibly fortified by a similarity of behavior.

A prevalent fallacy is the assumption that a proof of an afterlife would also be a proof of the existence of a deity. This is far from being the case. If, as I hold, there is no good reason to believe that a god either created or presides over this world, there is equally no good reason to believe that a god created or presides over the next world, on the unlikely supposition that such a thing exists.

It is conceivable that one's experiences in the next world, if there are any, will supply evidence of a god's existence, but we have no right to presume on such evidence, when we have not had the relevant experiences.

It is worth remarking, in this connection, that the two important Cambridge philosophers in this century, J.E. McTaggart and C.D. Broad, who have believed, in McTaggart's case that he would certainly survive his death, in Broad's that there was about a 50 percent probability that he would, were both of them atheists.

McTaggart derived his certainty from his metaphysics, which implied that what we confusedly perceive as material objects, in some cases housing minds, are really souls, eternally viewing one another with something of the order of love.

The less fanciful Broad was impressed by the findings of psychical research. He was certainly too intelligent to think that the superior performances of a few persons in the game of guessing unseen cards, which he painstakingly proved to be statistically significant, had any bearing upon the likelihood of a future life. He must therefore have been persuaded by the testimony of mediums. He was surely aware that most mediums have been shown to be frauds, but he was convinced that some have not been.

Not that this made him optimistic. He took the view that this world was very nasty and that there was a fair chance that the next world, if it existed, was even nastier. Consequently, he had no compelling desire to survive. He just thought that there was an even chance of his doing so. One of his epigrams was that if one went by the character of spiritualistic seances, life in the next world was like a pleasant Sunday afternoon at a nonconformist chapel, enlivened by occasional bump suppers.

If Broad was an atheist, my friend Dr. Alfred Ewing was not. Ewing, who considered Broad to be a better philosopher than Wittgenstein, was naïf; unworldly even by academic standards, intellectually shrewd, unswervingly honest and a devout Christian. Once, to tease him, I said: "Tell me, Alfred, what do you most look forward to in the next world?" He replied immediately: "God will tell me whether there are a priori propositions." It is a wry comment on the strange character of our subject, philosophy, that this answer should be so funny.

My excuse for repeating this story is that such philosophical problems as the question whether the propositions of logic and pure mathematics are deductively analytic or factually synthetic, and, if they are analytic, whether they are true by convention, are not to be solved by acquiring more information. What is needed is that we succeed in obtaining a clearer view of what the problems involve. One might hope to achieve this in a future life, but really we have no good reason to believe that our intellects will be any sharper in the next world, if there is one, than they are in this. A god, if one exists, might make them so, but this is not something that even the most enthusiastic deist can count on.

The only philosophical problem that our finding ourselves landed on a future life might clarify would be that of the relation between mind and body, if our future lives consisted, not in the resurrection of our bodies, but in the prolongation of the series of our present experiences. We should then be witnessing the triumph of dualism, though not the dualism which Descartes thought that he had established. If our lives consisted in an extended series of experiences, we should still have no good reason to regard ourselves as spiritual substances.

So there it is. My recent experiences have slightly weakened my conviction that my genuine death, which is due fairly soon, will be the end of me, though I continue to hope that it will be. They have not weakened my conviction that there is no god. I trust that my remaining an atheist will allay the anxieties of my fellow supporters of the Humanist Association, the Rationalist Press, and the South Place Ethical Society.

# Postscript to a Postmortem

My purpose in writing a postscript to the article about my 'death', which I contributed to the 28th August issue of the *Sunday Telegraph*, is not primarily to retract anything that I wrote or to express my regret that my Shakespearian title for the article, 'That Undiscovered Country', was not retained, but to correct a misunderstanding to which the article appears to have given rise.

I say "not primarily to retract" because one of my sentences was written so carelessly that it is literally false as it stands. In the final paragraph, I wrote: "My recent experiences have slightly weakened my conviction that my genuine death . . . will be the end of me." They have not and never did weaken that conviction. What I should have said and would have said, had I not been anxious to appear undogmatic, is that my experiences have weakened, not my belief that there is no life after death, but my inflexible attitude towards that belief. Previously my interest in the question was purely polemical. I wished to expose the defects in the positions of those who believed that they would survive. My experiences caused me to think that it was worth examining various possibilities of survival for their own sakes. I did not intend to imply that the result of my enquiry had been to increase the low probability of any one of them, even if it were granted that they had any probability at all.

My motive for writing the original article was twofold. I thought that my experiences had been sufficiently remarkable to be worth recording, and I wished to rebut the incoherent statement, which had been attributed to me, that I had discovered nothing 'on the other side'. Evidently, my having discovered something on the other side was a precondition of my having completed the journey. It follows that if I had discovered nothing, I had not been there; I had no right to imply that there was a 'there' to go to. Conversely, if there was evidence that I had had some strange experiences, nothing followed about there being 'another side'. In particular, it did not follow either that I had visited such a place, or that I had not.

I said in my article that the most probable explanation of my experiences was that my brain had not ceased to function during the four minutes of my heart arrest. I have since been told, rightly or wrongly, that it would not have functioned on its own for any longer period without being damaged. I thought it so obvious that the persistence of my brain was the most probable explanation that I did not bother to stress it. I stress it now. No other hypothesis comes anywhere near to superseding it.

Descartes has few contemporary disciples. Not many philosophers of whatever persuasion believe that we are spiritual substances. Those who so far depart from present fashion as not to take a materialistic view of our identities are most likely to equate persons with the series of their experiences. There is no reason in principle why such a series should not continue beyond the point where the experiences are associated with a particular body. Unfortunately, as I pointed out in my article, nobody has yet succeeded in specifying the relations which would have to hold between the members of such a series for them to constitute a person. There is a more serious objection. Whatever these relations were, they would be contingent;

they might not have obtained. But this allows for the possibility of there being experiences which do not belong to anybody; experiences which exist on their own. It is not obvious to me that this supposition is contradictory; but it might well be regarded as an irreparable defect in the theory.

If theories of this type are excluded, one might try to fall back on the Christian doctrine of the resurrection of the body. But, notoriously, this too encounters a mass of difficulties. I shall mention only one or two of them. For instance, one may ask in what form our bodies will be returned to us. As they were when we died, or when we were in our prime? Would they still be vulnerable to pain and disease? What are the prospects for infants, cripples, schizophrenics, and amnesiacs? In what manner will they survive?

"Oh, how glorious and resplendent, fragile body, shalt thou be!" This body? Why should one give unnecessary hostages to fortune? Let it be granted that I must reappear as an embodied person, if I am to reappear at all. It does not follow that the body which is going to be mine must be the same body as the one that is mine now; it need not be even a replica of my present body. The most that is required is that it be generically the same; that is, a human body of some sort, let us say a standard male model not especially strong or beautiful, not diseased, but still subject to the ills that flesh is heir to.   I am not sure whether one can allow oneself a choice with respect to age and sex. The preservation or renewal of one's personal identity will be secured, in this picture, by a continuity of one's mental states, with memory a necessary, but still not a sufficient, factor. I am assuming now that these mental states cannot exist on their own; hence, the need for a material body to sustain them.

I am far from claiming that such a scenario is plausible. Nevertheless it does have two merits. The first is that we are no longer required to make sense of the hypothesis that one's body will be reconstructed some time after it has perished. The second is that it does not force us to postulate the existence of a future world. One can live again in a future state of the world that one lives in now.

At this it becomes clear that the idea of the resurrection of the body had better be discarded. It is to be replaced by the idea of reincarnation. The two are not so very distinct. What gives the idea of reincarnation the advantage is that it clearly implies both that persons undergo a change of bodies and that they return to the same world that they inhabited before.

The idea of reincarnation is popular in the East. In the West it has been more generally ridiculed. Indeed, I myself have frequently made fun of it.

Even now, I am not suggesting that it is or ever will be a reality. Not even that it could be. Our concept of a person is such that it is actually contradictory to suppose that once-dead persons return to earth after what may be a considerable lapse of time.

But our concepts are not sacrosanct. They can be modified if they cease to be well adapted to our experience. In the present instance, the change which would supply us with a motive for altering our concept of a person in such a way as to admit the possibility of reincarnation would not be very great. All that would be required is that there be good evidence that many persons are able to furnish information about previous lives of such a character and such an abundance that it would seem they could not possess the information unless they themselves had lived the lives in question.

This condition is indispensable. There is no sense in someone's claiming to have been Antony, say, or Cleopatra, if he or she knows less about Antony or Cleopatra than a good Shakespearian scholar and much less than a competent ancient historian. Forgetfulness in this context is literally death.

I should remark that even if this condition were satisfied, our motive for changing our concept of a person would not be irresistible. Harmony could also be restored by our changing our concept of memory. We would introduce the ruling that it is possible to remember experiences that one never had; not just to remember them in the way that one remembers facts of one sort or another, but to remember these experiences in the way that one remembers one's own.

Which of these decisions would lead us to the truth? This is a senseless question. In a case of this kind, there is, as Professor Quine would put it, no fact of the matter which we can seek to discover. There would indeed be a fact to which we should be trying to adjust our language; the fact that people did exhibit this surprising capacity. But what adjustment we made, whether we modified our concept of a person, or our concept of memory, or followed some other course, would be a matter for choice. The most that could be claimed for the idea of reincarnation is that it would in these circumstances be an attractive option.

This time let me make my position fully clear. I am not saying that these ostensible feats of memory have ever yet been abundantly performed, or indeed performed at all, or that they ever will be performed. I am saying only that there would be nothing in logic to prevent their being performed in such abundance as to give us a motive for licensing reincarnation; and a motive for admitting it as a possibility would also be a motive for admitting it as a fact.

The consequence of such an admission would be fairly radical, though not so radical as the standbys of science fiction such as brain transplants and teleportation. Less radical too than the speculations of mathematical physicists. These speculations titillate rather than alarm the reading public. Professor Hawking's book *A Brief History of Time* is a best-seller. Perhaps the reading public has not clearly understood what his speculations imply. We are told, for example, that there may be a reversal in the direction of the arrow of time. This would provide for much stranger possibilities than that of a rebirth following one's death. It would entail that in any given life a person's death preceded his birth. That would indeed be a shock to common sense.

# About the
# Autobiographies

These original autobiographical statements by outstanding thinkers of the twentieth century appear here substantially as written (or, in the case of Sartre, spoken). In some cases sub-headings have been added; in others the original sub-headings have been retained or adapted. I have translated some foreign titles and expressions into English. Some of the original footnotes and a very few minor passages of little enduring interest have been deleted, and a few explanatory footnotes have been added.

All seven pieces first appeared as components of volumes in the Library of Living Philosophers (LLP). The Library of Living Philosophers is an ambitious project launched by Paul A. Schilpp in 1939. The early volumes were all conceived and edited by Schilpp, who was succeeded by Lewis Edwin Hahn, and he in turn by Randall E. Auxier, the Library's present Editor.

Each volume of the LLP includes twenty to thirty articles on the work of an outstanding living thinker, who contributes an intellectual autobiography and replies to each of the articles. Future LLP volumes are now in preparation on Arthur C. Danto, Michael Dummett, Jaakko Hintikka, Hilary Putnam, and Richard M. Rorty,

All the autobiographical essays, and all the original contents of all volumes in the LLP, are the sole property of the Library of Living Philosophers, Southern Illinois University, which commissioned them and caused them to be written and published.

The credit for conceiving the idea for the present volume goes to Jennifer Asmuth, then Marketing Manager for Open Court. Marc Aronson, Open Court's Publisher, selected the LLP autobiographies to include and determined the book's title.

Bertrand Russell's brief autobiography reproduced above appeared as 'My Mental Development' in *The Philosophy of Bertrand Russell*, Volume V of the

Library of Living Philosophers, edited by Paul Schilpp and first published in 1944.

Volume VII of the LLP, *Albert Einstein: Philosopher-Scientist,* also edited by the late Professor Schilpp, appeared in 1949. The above autobiography, which Einstein always referred to as his 'obituary', appears in that volume, under the title 'Autobiographical Notes', in both English and the original German. The English translation was made by Schilpp. It was later revised by Professor Peter Bergmann, formerly Einstein's scientific assistant, for the separate publication of *Autobiographical Notes* in 1979, the centennial of Einstein's birth.

The piece by Martin Buber first appeared in complete form as 'Autobiographical Fragments' in *The Philosophy of Martin Buber,* Volume XII of the LLP, edited by Paul Schilpp and Maurice Friedman, in 1967. A few of the sections were incorporated from earlier works by Buber. The 'Fragments' were later reprinted as a separate book entitled *Meetings.* The translation from the original German is by the leading expositor of Buber's thought and biographer of Buber, Maurice Friedman.

Volume VIII of the Library of Living Philosophers, *The Philosophy of Sarvepalli Radhakrishnan,* was edited by Schilpp and released in 1952. The 'autobiography' reproduced above was entitled 'The Religion of the Spirit and the World's Need: Fragments of a Confession'. Radhakrishnan had earlier published a brief autobiographical essay, *My Search for Truth,* which like this more detailed treatment, is reticent about personal events and concentrates on ideas.

The Gadamer autobiography reprinted here was entitled 'Reflections on My Philosophical Journey' when it appeared in 1997, in Volume XXIV of the LLP, *The Philosophy of Hans-Georg Gadamer,* edited by Dr. Lewis Edwin Hahn. It was translated from the original German by Richard E. Palmer. Many footnotes, mostly referring to specialized scholarly sources or to works in German, have been deleted for the present volume.

Shortly after Sartre made the commitment to participate in the Library of Living Philosophers, his eyesight began to fail. The deterioration progressed so rapidly that it soon became clear he would be unable either to read the articles or to compose an autobiographical statement. Sartre had long been used to editing as he wrote, and did not feel he could make effective use of a dictating machine. It was therefore decided to replace the autobiography and replies to critics with the transcript of a taped interview.

The interview spanned two afternoon sessions in Sartre's small apartment in Montparnasse. It is one of the longest interviews Sartre ever gave for publication, and it can be read together with the Sartre interview conducted shortly before by Michel Contat, 'Self-Portrait at Seventy', which is contained in *Life/Situations* (New York: Pantheon Books, 1977). The three interviewers were the well-known scholars of modern French thought, Michel Rybalka, Oreste F. Pucciani, and Susan Gruenheck. The interview was conducted in French, transcribed, then translated and edited. The critical articles to which Sartre responds in this interview can be found in *The Philosophy of Jean-Paul Sartre*, Volume XVI of the LLP, edited by Schilpp.

Volume XXI, *The Philosophy of A.J. Ayer*, edited by Lewis Edwin Hahn, came out in 1992. The Ayer autobiography reprinted above was there entitled 'My Mental Development'.

# Index

## DATE DUE

| | | | |
|---|---|---|---|
| | | | |
| | | | |
| | | | |
| | | | |
| | | | |
| | | | |
| | | | |
| | | | |
| | | | |
| | | | |
| | | | |
| | | | |